Eventful Cities: Cultural Management and Urban Revitalisation

Eventful Cities: Cultural Management and Urban Revitalisation

Greg Richards
Robert Palmer

AMSTERDAM ● BOSTON ● HEIDELBERG ● LONDON ● NEW YORK ● OXFORD
PARIS ● SAN DIEGO ● SAN FRANCISCO ● SINGAPORE ● SYDNEY ● TOKYO

Butterworth-Heinemann is an imprint of Elsevier.

Butterworth-Heinemann is an imprint of Elsevier.
The Boulevard, Langford Lane, Kidlington, Oxford, OX5 1GB, UK
30 Corporate Drive, Suite 400, Burlington, MA 01803, USA

Notice
No responsibility is assumed by the publisher for any injury and/or damage to persons or property as a matter of products liability, negligence, or otherwise, or from any use or operation of any methods, products, instructions, or ideas contained in the material herein.

British Library Cataloguing in Publication Data
A catalogue record for this book is available from the British Library.

Library of Congress Cataloging-in-Publication Data
A catalog record for this book is available from the Library of Congress.

ISBN: 978-0-7506-6987-0

For information on all Butterworth-Heinemann publications
visit our Web site at www.elsevierdirect.com

Printed and bound in Great Britain
10 11 12   10 9 8 7 6 5 4 3 2 1

Working together to grow
libraries in developing countries

www.elsevier.com | www.bookaid.org | www.sabre.org

ELSEVIER   BOOK AID
International   Sabre Foundation

Contents

v

Preface

The aim of this book is to analyse the ways in which events help cities become more dynamic and liveable places, and how cities can develop and manage eventfulness to achieve a wide range of cultural, economic and social objectives. This is not a book about event management, or the operational management of events, but about making cities eventful and utilising events to help 'make' places. It is not simply a book about *cities with events*; it is above all about the practice of *eventful cities*.

The structure of this volume follows the process of conceiving, developing, staging, managing, marketing and assessing events. Hopefully these analyses will provide a greater understanding of the relationship between events and their host cities – how events shape cities, and how cities shape events.

In order to illustrate these processes, this book draws on the experiences of cities as hosts for the European Capital of Culture (ECOC), an event held annually in different European cities since 1985. It is also based on the authors' experience of directing, advising and analysing different ECOCs, but also many other major events and festivals. Because ECOCs have been held in a range of different cities, and each city has interpreted the concept in different ways, the ECOC provides a fascinating comparative laboratory for studying the relationship between cities and events: a laboratory the authors have been following for many years. The unique insights into urban eventfulness provided by the ECOC and other examples from events around the globe provide an in-depth coverage of the major issues and opportunities facing eventful cities.

The decision to focus primarily on culture is based on a gap in current publications in this field. In doing so, we have decided on a wide conception of culture, of course encompassing the arts, but also focusing on other forms of cultural production and consumption. There are many studies of events, but these tend to focus on sport and popular entertainment, and particularly international sporting events such as the Olympic Games. This is not surprising, as major sports events tend to generate significant economic and media impact, which appear to make their role in specific host cities more noteworthy than most cultural events. However, relatively few cities will have the opportunity to host mega events of the scale of the Olympic Games, whereas every city has the ability to attract or create its own cultural events.

This volume begins a consideration of the reasons why cities might want to develop events. Chapter 2 considers the process of event creation, what 'events' are, how they are created and how cities choose which events to celebrate. For the eventful city, individual events are the building blocks used to construct a vision and create a cultural programme, which is the focus of Chapter 3. Programming the city also requires the collaboration and coordination of a wide network of stakeholders, an issue covered in Chapter 4. Drawing on theoretical perspectives from stakeholder theory and network theory, the chapter analyses issues of leadership, collaboration, partnership and coordination in bringing an event programme to fruition.

Chapter 5 considers the management and organisation of the eventful city, examining the relationship between strategic and tactical management issues, the methods of dealing with crisis management and the functioning of management and information systems. Chapter 6 considers the problems of raising money from different sources to fund event programmes, including public sector financing and sponsorship. Once the event has been created and finance secured, it needs to be marketed. Chapter 7 explores marketing, communications and the role of the media. The chapter considers the role of marketing and promotion, both as events in their own right, and their wider role in creating an image for a city or region.

The audiences and publics of the eventful city are the subject of Chapter 8. The profile of visitors to different events, their motivations and experiences are discussed. This information is vital when deciding how to reach the audience, and what kind of events to stage. Chapter 9 focuses on the outcomes and impacts of events. Events are increasingly designed to deliver a complex range of cultural, social and economic impacts. In most cases, the estimation of impacts prior to staging the event is an important consideration of whether or not to stage an event. Impact assessments are therefore being used as tools for advocacy, as well as for directing and evaluating policy. Chapter 10 considers different aspects of event programme sustainability, examining how the eventful city can be programmed and managed to ensure long-term success. The issues covered include environmental, cultural, social and economic sustainability, and the balance between these different aspects.

Additional critical reflections on the 'keys to success' for the eventful city follow in Chapter 11. Many people involved in conceiving, supporting and organising events, including political leaders, city officials, sponsors, event managers, urban planners and cultural policy makers, are interested in learning from experience in their own and other cities about how to make eventfulness work. The chapter outlines many of the key concepts that underpin successful events, drawing on the experience of the authors and others, and the analysis of specific events across the world. The concluding chapter looks at major key global trends and their implications for the development of eventful cities in the future. Key environmental, socio-economic, political and cultural trends are analysed, and some of the emerging event 'models', which are having a growing influence on the way cities think about their events are considered.

This volume intends to provide guidance for those involved in designing, running, funding, evaluating and studying cities and their events, for those who are interested in the board processes both of cultural management and urban revitalisation, as these relate to events in cities. Although we have tried as far as possible to cover a range of cities across the globe in terms of size and geography to illustrate different issues in eventful cities in an international context, prudence dictates that we concentrated largely to our experience and the availability of reliable and objective analysis. Although there is a particular focus on European cities, we have used many examples from different continents, when appropriate, to convey that most of the principles derived from the volume are applicable to a wide variety of cities in different geographical locations. Nevertheless, the way in which these principles are applied, are always acutely sensitive to the local context. What works for cities such as Barcelona or Glasgow or Montreal will not automatically work elsewhere in precisely the same manner. There is always a profound need to evaluate proposed action against the particularities of context and place.

We are grateful to a great many people for contributing to the knowledge contained in this book, and we apologise in advance for not being able to mention all of them. But a few people stand out in terms of their contribution to critical thinking about the ECOC and to our thinking about eventfulness in cities, including Carlos Fernandes, Robert Garcia, Luis Herrero, Erik Hitters, Dragan Klaic, Charles Margue, Mary Miller, Ilie Rotariu, Myriam Stoffen and many others. We are also grateful to Charles Margue (TNS ILRES), Leiden University, the European Festivals Research Project and Dieter Hardt-Stremayr (Graz Tourismus) for permission to use data, tables and figures for this volume, and to the European Commission that supported the Palmer-Rae study on European Capitals of Culture.

This book is dedicated to those whose commitment to the adventure of creating eventfulness is helping to make cities great places to live, for ourselves and the generations that follow, and this includes some special children – Eva, Megan, Melissa, Micole and Ryan, who are events in themselves inspiring the world with joy and spirit.

About the Authors

Robert Palmer is the Director of Culture and Cultural and Natural Heritage of the Council of Europe, based in Strasbourg, France. He has worked in the cultural sector for more than 30 years, directing festivals, managing cultural organisations and operating in key Director positions in local authorities and arts councils. He has been a consultant to various cities and national authorities, and has acted as an adviser to many European and international bodies in relation to cultural policy and strategy. In 2004, he directed the evaluation team which produced the Palmer Report on the ECOC for the European Commission. His experience as the Director of two ECOCs – Glasgow in 1990 and Brussels in 2000 – as well as his direct involvement as an adviser to more than 10 other Capitals of Culture in the conception, bidding and delivery phases of the event make him uniquely experienced. In Glasgow, he was appointed as the city's first Director of Performing Arts and Venues, with additional responsibility for managing a process of arts-led regeneration for the city over a 10-year period, of which Glasgow's designation as ECOC formed a part.

He is a member of the Boards of various arts institutions and international festivals, the Chair of European arts juries, and is asked regularly to be a speaker at international cultural conferences and workshops. Currently, he is also the Chair of Visiting Arts, UK. The main themes of his work concern creativity, cultural policy, cultural planning, cultural development in cities, intercultural projects, festivals and special events. He has undertaken projects throughout Europe, North America and South-East Asia. He has been given various awards in the UK, Belgium and France in recognition of his work.

Greg Richards is Professor of Leisure Studies at Tilburg University in the Netherlands. He has extensive experience in research and education, with previous posts at London Metropolitan University (UK); Universitat Rovira I Virgili, Tarragona (Spain); Fundaciò Interarts, Barcelona (Spain) and the University of the West of England, Bristol (UK). Greg is a founding Partner of Tourism Research and Marketing, an international consultancy in tourism and event development and marketing.

He has worked extensively on the analysis and development of cultural and creative tourism in cities such as Barcelona and Burgos (ES), London, Newcastle, Manchester and Edinburgh (UK), Amsterdam, Rotterdam and Den Bosch (NL), Sibiu (RO), Amman (Jordan) and Macau (China). His major publications include *Cultural Tourism in Europe* (1996); *Cultural Attractions and European Tourism* (2001); *Tourism and Gastronomy* (2002); *The Global Nomad: Backpacker Travel in Theory and Practice* (2004); *Cultural Tourism – Global and Local Perspectives* (2007) and *Tourism, Creativity and Development* (2007).

He was a member of the Palmer Report team evaluating the impact of the ECOC for the European Commission, an international jury member for the selection of the Hungarian Capital of Culture in 2010, a contributor to the European Travel Commission study of *City Tourism and Culture* and the author of the OECD report on *The Impact of Tourism on Culture* (2009). He has advised the Dutch city of Den Bosch on the development of multi-annual cultural events programme to celebrate the 500th anniversary of the painter Hieronymus Bosch. He has conducted evaluation research for many ECOCs, and has advised others on their bidding strategies.

List of Tables

List of Figures

CHAPTER 1

Why Cities Need to be Eventful

In recent years, culture has taken on a more instrumental meaning in cities. It now represents the ideas and practices, sites and symbols, of what has been called the 'symbolic economy', i.e., the process through which wealth is created from cultural activities, including art, music, dance, crafts, museums, exhibitions, sports and creative design in various fields. This new concept of culture increasingly shapes city strategies in the face of both global competition and local tensions.

(Zukin, 2004:3)

Festivals influence people's idea of a city. They provide many points of identification and contribute to the birth of non-mainstream urban identities. They consolidate subcultures and create togetherness among amateurs of a common field. At their best festivals culminate in a 'festival moment', creating a momentum born of dramaturgical excellence and high quality content, a powerful experience bringing together audience and festival performers and organisers.

(Silvanto & Hellman, 2005:6)

THE DESIRE FOR EVENTFULNESS

Cities of today face two choices. Either they develop to meet the challenges created by the pace of global change, or they resist the impulse for transformation and stagnate. At a time when economic systems are no longer predictable, in order to remain competitive, cities are turning to strategies that focus on their own innate resources – their histories, spaces, creative energy and talents. Pressures of globalisation and problems caused by economic restructuring, as well as the need to establish new civic identities, have prompted cities to utilise 'cultural' assets and resources in an attempt to become distinctive, to regenerate the urban fabric and to create economic, social and cultural prosperity. The creation and promotion of events such as festivals, shows, exhibitions, fairs and championships, have become a critical component of urban development strategy across the globe. No city believes it is too small or too complex to enter the market of planning and producing events.

Entire cities have transformed themselves into major stages for a continual stream of events, which can lead eventually to a 'festivalisation' of the city. With the growth of the 'symbolic economy' (Lash & Urry, 1994; Zukin, 1995) and the 'experience economy' (Pine & Gilmore, 1999), culture has become an increasingly important means of consuming the city (Ritzer, 1999). The growing prominence of events has led some cities to promote themselves as 'eventful cities'. Melbourne labels itself as 'the world's event city' (2008), and Seoul claims to be 'one of the most eventful cities of the world' (2006), while at the same time the Hong Kong Government (2006) has also been 'working to make Hong Kong one of the most eventful cities in the world'. Other cities make slightly less global claims, but focus on their competitive place in an increasingly crowded market for national events, such as Nevada's Reno-Tahoe Territory (2006) that profiles itself as the 'Most Eventful City in America'. Durban claims it is 'Africa's premier sporting and events destination' (Mlaba, 2009). Cities that have not yet become eventful are also making efforts to enter or reinforce their place in the urban events market, with initiatives such as the 'Singapore Roars! Roadshow' organised by the Singapore Tourist Board in 2003, which had a role in 'reinforcing the image of Singapore as a vibrant, sophisticated and eventful city that has something to offer to all Malaysians'. (Asia Travel Tips, 2006). Coventry (UK) has an 'Eventful City' programme which 'entertains visitors throughout the year in a way that reflects the enthusiasm of its community and the city's willingness to give a warm welcome to people from far and near' (City of Coventry, 2006). Other cities already calling themselves 'eventful', often through their promotion as 'festival cities', include Adelaide, Auckland, Bremen, Cardiff, Dubai, Edinburgh, Maastricht, Manchester, Muskogee, New Orleans, Puerto Vallarta, Regensburg, Reykjavik, Wellington and York.

The slogan 'festival city' or 'city of festivals' has become a popular choice as part of a city's brand image. Edmonton refers to itself as 'Canada's Festivals City', setting itself in competition with Montreal and Quebec City, which define themselves in similar terms. Milwaukee and Sacramento are two American cities, along with some 30 others, where being 'cities of festivals' has become a prime element of their destination marketing throughout the year. Guadalajara, Mexico's second largest city, similarly tries to gain national and international standing by communicating itself as a festival centre. The world status of Edinburgh is claimed on the official website of the Edinburgh Festivals: 'With the stunning Hogmanay celebrations heralding a brand new year and the start of Homecoming Scotland 2009, the World's Leading Festival City is gearing up for spring, and more of its exciting Festivals.'

Cultural events have become central to processes of urban development and revitalisation, as cultural production becomes a major element of the urban economy, and cultural consumption can dominate both the image of places and urban life in general. As Strom (2002:9) notes, today 'one would be hard-pressed to find an American city in which some sort of major cultural project was not the centrepiece of a downtown revitalisation effort'. Claiming distinction is no longer just a question of hiring signature architects and constructing grand museums; it also involves the creation of a lively atmosphere and a sense of place. Events are making cities fashionable and 'cool' places to be.

> *In a recent article in* Newsweek International, *Barcelona was dubbed 'the coolest city in Europe'. It is not hard to see why, as ever since its government pursued and won the right to host the summer Olympic Games in 1992, it has attracted attention as a place with vibrant cultural, architectural and planning attributes.*
>
> (Kirby, 2004:183)

What is an eventful city? What are the benefits of being eventful? How does an eventful city develop? Why do some cities seem more eventful than others? What is the relationship between city development and cultural events? How do cities create, shape, manage and market events, and how can those events in turn shape the city, its spaces and its image? This book attempts to address such questions. It argues that cities which successfully harness cultural events as an integral part of a broader development strategy will reap the benefits of generating wider cultural, social and economic benefits. Eventfulness should not be an aim in itself, but a means of improving the city and making it more attractive and liveable.

The book focuses on how to develop and manage an eventful city. The central issues are not event management and place marketing, but the strategies that need to be developed by cities to ensure that events reinforce and celebrate the identity or culture of the places in which they happen, and have the greatest impact on a city's economic and social prosperity.

CITIES AND EVENTS

As cities have developed physically through the centuries, the conceptions of what cities are and how they function have also changed. These ideas, or models of the city, are not just tools for describing and analysing, but they also affect the way in which we think and feel about the city.

How cities are envisioned has effects. Urban designers and planners have ideas about how cities should look, function and be lived, and these are translated into plans and built environments.... Ideas about cities are not simply formed at a conscious level; they are also a product of unconscious desires and imaginaries.

(Bridge & Watson, 2001:350)

The different representations of the city have spawned and been shaped by public events. Successive city rulers have sought to use events to cohere urban society around their own vision of civic life. In the pre-industrial city, the important role of ritual in everyday life meant that cities were designed around event spaces, such as the Greek agora or the Roman forum.

As cities developed further, public celebrations and events continued to have an important role in everyday life. The medieval city revolved around a festive calendar with a rich spectrum of feasts and saint's days, as well as major celebrations such as carnivals, which could last for weeks. Festivals were important in distracting people from the harsh reality of everyday life, and occasionally in upsetting the established social order. Rituals and cultural events became part of the weaponry deployed by religious leaders and royalty to support their own positions of power, placing themselves at the centre of an event.

Therborn (2002:29) illustrates this phenomenon in the context of European capital cities.

There was a ritual rhythm playing an important part in the life of royal capitals, of royal births, birthdays, marriages, coronations and funerals, with public ceremonies, and popular festivities, as well as court protocol and temporary monuments of arches and tribunes at coronations and marriages. There could also be military parades, and some cities, e.g. Berlin, Potsdam and St Petersburg, had centrally located parade grounds.

With the development of the industrial city, the festivals and fairs of the medieval city were located in more formalised spaces in the urban fabric – the market and the playhouse

(Evans, 2001). Recreation increasingly became 'rationalised' and controlled. The industrial revolution transformed the medieval festival into a break from work – a period of rest and relaxation.

Industrial capitalism brought new uses of the city that created more spaces for events, and events for spaces. The development of large cities brought a

> *layout of (a) major street(s), mainly for elegant commerce and promenading and traffic, but occasionally also for parades [and] a national capital had to have a set of institutions of national high culture, and their architectural materialisations were considered major tasks of capital city building. The function was national identity through a shared national heritage*
> (Therborn, 2002:35).

The growing civic culture of the industrial city not only gave birth to new cultural landmarks such as museums, opera houses and concert halls, but also new forms of cultural events themselves. The recognition of the growing working classes as a potential market caused wealthy manufacturers to sponsor culture in the form of museums, opera houses and elements of public festivities. Festivals became a showcase for goods and services, eventually reaching an international stage with the creation of the Great Exhibition of 1851 in the UK, the forerunner of subsequent World Fairs and Expos. Popular celebrations such as La Mercè in Barcelona were used as publicity vehicles in an early extension of commodification into public space (Crespi-Vallbona & Richards, 2007). Meanwhile, some influential citizens persuaded embryonic public administrations to relieve them of some of the burden of financing metropolitan culture (Hitters, 2000).

As the industrial city moved away from rural traditions, new traditions were invented to give meaning to urban life. Civic culture gradually replaced the church and royalty as the main creator of cultural events. Cities in particular began to create events that celebrated their own history and culture. For example, Nas and Roymans (1998) describe how the Third of October festivities developed in Leiden in The Netherlands, in commemoration of the lifting of the Spanish siege of the city in 1574. Every year since this momentous event, its citizens, and an increasing number of visitors, have celebrated *Leiden's Ontzet*, with foods connected to the lifting of the siege, such as herring and white bread and *hutspot*.

Many other popular celebrations were created in the seventeenth, eighteenth and nineteenth centuries. In the United States; the first St. Patrick's Day Parade was held in New York in 1762. Gotham (2002) describes how Mardi Gras emerged in New Orleans during the second half of the nineteenth century, and the first Labor Day Parade was held in 1882 in New York City.

As the popularity of civic rituals began to threaten the privileged position of religious and royal events, so the church and the monarchy also began to develop new events to communicate more effectively with the populace. In the Netherlands, for example, the first Princess's Day was held to celebrate Princess Wilhelmina's birthday on 31 August 1885. This was a deliberate attempt to shore up the waning popularity of the Dutch Royal Family. But it was so successful that it became an institution, later turning into Queen's Day and then moving to 30 April 1948 when Queen Juliana ascended the throne. When Queen Beatrix was crowned in 1980, she kept the April date, arguably in honour of her mother, but perhaps out of practical considerations – her birthday is in the middle of winter, a time less suited to public celebration.

As the cultural institutions of expanding cities began to mature, they too began to create their own cultural events, many aimed to counteract the impact of popular culture events. For example, the first Promenade Concerts (The Proms) took place in August 1895 at the newly built Queen's Hall in London. The aim was to reach a wider audience by offering more popular programmes, adopting a less formal setting and keeping ticket prices low. Robert Newman, the founder of the Queens Hall allegedly said 'I am going to run nightly concerts to train the public in easy stages. Popular at first, gradually raising the standard until I have created a public for classical and modern music' (Hewett, 2007). Both popular and high culture were brought into the open air by the use of public spaces such as parks and civic squares in an attempt to win new audiences, with the building of band stands, stages and amphitheatres. The Naumberg Orchestral concerts were started in New York's Central Park in 1905, and have been running ever since.

By providing a mass audience for culture, and generating a critical mass of cultural institutions and performers, cities began to create the conditions for the rapid growth of cultural events, in most cases ad hoc events, initiated by individual cultural intermediaries. As cities began to develop structures of public administration, so centralised support and management by public authorities for cultural events grew.

The managed city

The increasing public administration of cities necessitated by industrialisation had created a new vision of cities as systems, which needed to be managed. In the modernist vision of cities, which emerged in the nineteenth century, the city and its inhabitants could be managed rationally by an enlightened administration, which would plan for the economic, social and cultural needs of all. In this context, the public management of cultural festivals and events, especially in Europe, became an extension of the other cultural facilities provided by the public sector, such as museums, libraries and concert halls.

In the period immediately following the Second World War, the desire for international understanding and the growth of leisure time created a new impetus for the development of cultural festivals. Edinburgh is often seen as the prime example of the post-Second World War festival boom in the UK, but similar events were created in other cities across Europe, such as Avignon and Amsterdam. Established to fill the cultural vacuum partly caused by years of war, such festivals also became a means to cement international relations, a forerunner of what is now known as 'cultural diplomacy'. The growing number of arts festivals around the world also created alternative and less centrally managed spaces to present work that would challenge traditional programmes. 'Fringe' events were developed in reaction to the staid nature of many of the official programmes.

As the number and scale of festivals and cultural events grew, they also took on an increasing number of roles. City centres themselves became stages for events appealing to residents and visitors. In the 1960s, civic administrations in Europe and the United States began to take an interest in redeveloping their centres of cities around the wider notion of 'cultural capital', which encouraged historic preservation and offered opportunities for artists to present performances and exhibitions (Zukin, 2004). For example, the City of San Francisco began to fund its film festival in 1960, and in 1966 the Mayor of Buffalo made the first formal recognition of what would become the Allentown Art Festival. Festivals and events subsequently became part of the wider capital accumulation system of the modern city. Gerhard Schulze (1992) emphasises in his analysis of the *Erlebnisgesellschaft* (the experience society) that the economic motive for the development of culture is based on 'public experience production' and the creation of 'public experience amenities'.

The role of events has expanded significantly since the 1960s to the point where they have come to be considered as solutions to a wide range of urban problems. As the *Cape Town Major Events Marketing Strategy* (City of Cape Town, 2001:2) states:

> Events play a significant role in the context of destination planning, enhancing and linking tourism and commerce. Some aspects of this role include: events as image makers, economic impact generators, tourist attractions, overcoming seasonality, contributing to the development of local communities and businesses and supporting key industrial sectors.

This multifaceted role for events became all the more necessary as cities in many parts of the world were restructured after the oil shocks and economic turbulence of the 1970s.

The postmodern city

The economic environment for many cities worsened through the 1970s and 1980s, unemployment grew in many developed economies and culture began to assume roles linked to economic investment in the 'postmodern' or post-industrial city. Culture, tourism and leisure became vehicles for economic development and image enhancement. Miles

(2000) argued that 'cultural quarters' are one of the distinguishing signs of the post-industrial city. Events were created to develop competitive advantage relative to other cities. As 'time-based resources', events added dynamism to previously stagnant cities to help polish up jaded images in cities like Glasgow, Rotterdam, Turin and Dublin. The increasing importance of image, ephemera and spectacle have given a new impetus to events, and particularly cultural events, as creators and carriers of meaning and wealth in cities. The new centrality of events became marked by the creation of new administrative structures for creating or bidding for events and managing the festive calendar.

In the postmodern city, especially through the 1980s, economic restructuring often placed the cultural industries at the vanguard of the economy. Zukin (2004:7) demonstrates the close links between urban and cultural development:

> When central Governments became more involved in
> regional redevelopment during the economic crisis of
> the 1980s, they took to linking economic and cultural
> strategies. Indeed, the more socially devastated
> a region appeared, and the less likely to experience
> new industrial growth, the more public authorities
> turned to marketing cities as centres of culture, in
> order to create a new business climate. This seemed
> ever more important with the growth of computer
> software, media and consumer product industries,
> which gave priority to design innovation and access to
> the latest cultural trends.

The new centrality of culture in urban policy was linked to a series of externalities, such as the need to stimulate economic growth, the need to bolster social inclusion and the need to develop new identities appropriate to a rapidly changing urban landscape. In this situation, cultural events were no longer just a cultural matter, and events policy became part of a wider urban task of revitalisation. By moving creativity to the centre of the urban agenda, a new role was given to cultural events as the creators (rather than preservers) of meaning. This new vision also matches emerging models of the organisation of the postmodern or post-industrial city: the entrepreneurial city, the creative city and more recently, the intercultural city.

The entrepreneurial city

According to Harvey (1989), cities have tried to adjust themselves to complex new economic and social circumstances by shifting their policies from urban managerialism to urban entrepreneurialism. In North America this was prompted by the 'post federal' reduction of economic aid to major cities (Andranovich et al., 2001), in Western Europe by the collapse of the post-war social democratic consensus (Henry, 1996), in Central and Eastern Europe by the collapse of the Soviet regime, in Asia by the financial crisis of the 1990 and in Africa and Latin America by the demands of foreign debt and economic instability.

The new entrepreneurial approach clearly had an impact on the cultural sector. Cultural funding became more directly linked to the 'products' or 'outputs' of cultural institutions, now 'measured' by using a variety of 'performance indicators'. Although North American cultural institutions have always had significant private support, the new climate in Europe encouraged the cultural sector to seek private funding and increase earned income to supplement state subsidies. Major events became increasingly managed by specially created public-private partnerships or by private companies contracted by cities. One major example of this phenomenon is the ways in which large event strategies have been managed by cities that have been designated as European Capitals of Culture (ECOC), a programme of the European Union that began in 1985. The earlier designated cities such as Athens (1985) and Florence (1986) were managed directly by state and local authorities. Most of the later cities, however, such as Antwerp (1993), Copenhagen (1996), Helsinki (2000), Lille (2004), Luxembourg (2007), Stavanger (2008), Liverpool (2008) and Linz (2009), set up separate organisations charged with bidding for the event, and later created similar organisations to manage the event. Although the public bodies (city, region, state) usually remained the key stakeholders for the new organisations, they often included strong representation from the private sector and academic institutions.

The partnership between the public and private sectors has also become a main management model in developing city centres as consumption spaces, which include events to help make them attractive to consumers. Hannigan's (1998) 'fantasy city', Judd's (1999) study of 'tourist bubbles' and the emergence of the 'entertainment economy' have underlined the increasing focus on city centres for recreational and entertainment uses rather than residential uses (Andranovich et al., 2001). However, concurrent processes of gentrification are also bringing in new groups of residents who are attracted to the city centre by the proximity of such leisure and cultural services (Verhoeff, 1994).

Many cities now have specific organisations responsible for the management of city centres and important leisure zones, and in cities such as Rotterdam the functions of city centre management and leisure and cultural consumption and production have been united in departments responsible for the 'leisure economy'. As more cities adopt such leisure and culture based strategies, so competition grows and effectiveness must be increased. Verwijnen (2005:14–15) emphasises that the external pressures on cities need to be matched by internal changes:

> The increased competition between European cities has led to a new paradox: the more competition the cities confront from the outside, the smoother they must operate on the inside. Cities can no longer afford a freewheeling situation, but need to harness their internal resources. Urban policies become both the instrument itself and act as the showcase of this effort. A dynamic urban policy becomes part of the image of a city and acts as a catalyst for its symbolic economy.

Events are part of this process of transforming cities into smoother running cultural operations. Events may be considered ephemeral, and yet they generate that most precious of modern commodities – symbolic capital. The entrepreneurial city is not just considered entrepreneurial in terms of its development of strategies for image creation and event bidding, but increasingly in terms of its continuing renegotiation of relationships with its citizens and in its approach to cultural planning.

The creative city

The creative city idea emerged as a development of a concept that focused on the importance of design, cultural industries and cultural amenities as key resources for liveable cities. In the 1970s, the Council of Europe introduced such notions linked to cultural rights, and organisations such as Partners for Livable Communities (www.livable.com) were created to apply concepts to urban planning strategies in the United States. In the 1980s and 1990s, conceptions of cultural planning linked to creativity were introduced (Bianchini, 1990; Mercer, 1992). Following a first study on *Glasgow: the Creative City and its Cultural Economy* (1994), which emerged from the city's new strategies that had been developed in response to its designation as ECOC in 1990, and in work by Landry and Bianchini (1995), the creative city was subsequently publicised more widely in Landry's (2000) book entitled *The Creative City: A toolkit for urban innovators*. The creative city relates to a key strategy of urban development that emphasises the importance of the 'creative industries' (Smith, 1998), and more recently the attraction of the 'creative class' (Florida, 2002). Florida argues that economic development is driven in large measure by lifestyle factors, such as tolerance and diversity, urban infrastructure and entertainment, which can attract creative talent. In contrast to the entrepreneurial city, which treats culture as one element of the symbolic economy, the creative city model places culture and creativity at the forefront of inter-urban competition.

The advent of the twenty-first century has been 'a very marked convergence between the spheres of cultural and economic development', which is also 'one of the distinguishing characteristics of contemporary urbanisation processes in general' (Scott, 2000:2). Urban economies are increasingly concerned with the production of cultural goods, which by their very nature have intensely local characteristics. This close interrelationship between culture, economy and place has also been marked by a growing tension between place-bound culture and 'culture as a pattern of non-place globalised events and experiences' (Scott, 2000:3). Previous analyses of the cultural economy of cities were concerned largely with the commercialisation of heritage. Large-scale public sector-led urban renovation projects have now been overtaken by an expanding view of the intertwined nature of production, culture and place. As Scott (2000:4) shows, one of the results of this relationship is the tendency for cultural production to become concentrated in 'privileged localised clusters of firms and workers'. While Scott explains this from an economic perspective in terms of industrial agglomeration and clustering of producers, Florida and others have emphasised the clustering of individual members of the 'creative class' in particular cities. Although the logic of this process is in some respects circular (creative people are attracted to creative places, which are creative because they house creative people), there is a general acceptance that certain locations are more attractive than others in the global cultural and creative landscape.

The growing importance of the intangible qualities of cities has encouraged policy makers to think not just in terms of developing manufacturing and what are sometimes referred to 'real jobs' from a traditional Fordist perspective, but also jobs in the 'creative industries sector' and those that are linked to the 'symbolic economy'. In the past, cities competed to attract companies by offering ideal conditions of production: cheap land, cheap labour, cheap energy and good communications. Now cities compete to develop cultural and creative resources to attract the creative class on the basis of cultural production that helps supply the images and symbols that are vital to competitive success in the new economy.

Developing creativity implies not only that a city can place new products on global markets, but also that it can quickly respond to changing competition and demand. A creative city is one that has learnt how to use its cultural capital to attract innovative businesses and services as well as members of the mobile

*'creative class'. The flow of people and money that
pass through global cities continually replenish the
supply of potential creators. But to nurture creativity,
a city must have a generous and inclusive culture – it
must have what we may term 'an attitude'. It must
have nerve, it must value racial diversity and it must
have an impatient desire for new things, while valuing
the old.*

(Zukin, 2004:13)

Lee (2004) shows how Singapore's efforts to position itself
as a global 'Renaissance City' have led to privilege of creativity over culture. Following Florida's arguments, Singapore
has developed creative clusters, although it has had problems
in accepting the more 'bohemian' aspects of the recipe, such
as encouraging an active gay scene, which is part of the
formula that was identified by Florida (Ooi, 2007).

The drive to make places creative does not always
emanate from the leadership of a city (and perhaps should
not). There are many examples of grassroots creativity
movements, such as the 'Keep Austin Weird' campaign in
Austin, Texas. Red Wassenich, a librarian at the Austin
Community College, created the first blue-and-white 'Keep
Austin Weird' bumper stickers in 2000, and since then the
idea has mushroomed, embracing T-shirts, hats and
sporting events such as the 'Keep Austin Weird 5K' race.
The weirdness of the city, which arguably derives from
a combination of hippie and redneck culture, is now
maintained as an essential raw material for the 'creative
city', and the creative city strategy adopted by Austin.
According to the campaign's website (www.keepaustinweird.
com), this is the fruit of a 'collaborative fission of coordinated individualism'.

Creativity and innovation are both social phenomena
that emerge from specific geographic and productive
circumstances. Scott (2000) shows that in the creative
industries, agglomeration and clustering are important
determinants of economic success for cities. The idea that
certain locations gain competitive advantage by virtue of
agglomeration and clustering of the cultural and creative
industries is illustrated by Lai (2004) in the case of

'blockbuster' exhibitions. Increasingly, major museums lend one another works of art to enable them to stage major exhibitions, in return for other works of art, which will enable others to stage their own blockbuster events. This basic notion of reciprocity places major museums in large cities at a distinct advantage to smaller institutions elsewhere since they have large collections which can be offered to stimulate exchange of significant works and the international networks to initiate such exchanges. Lai (2004) demonstrates that the Metropolitan Museum in New York was not able to participate in such exchanges until it had obtained abundant financial and cultural assets in the 1970s. These exchanges are therefore also dependent on the local resources that can be tapped by each museum to secure works and to finance exhibitions, which will depend to a large extent on the agglomeration of the cultural industries themselves. This is one feature that helps to characterise and promote the creative city.

The intercultural city

The diversity of urban populations is a factor increasingly emphasised as a creative resource for cultural, social and economic development. The growing mobility of people, both long-term and short-term, is transforming the cultural landscape of most cities. As Zukin (2004) remarks:

> *Immigration is reducing the cultural boundaries between places, as the same cultural events are performed the world over. Immigrant communities are importing, adapting and developing their traditions.*

Some commentators have pointed to the emerging challenges and opportunities presented by the 'intercultural city'. Soja (2000:155) has used the term, the 'Fractal City', refers to cities that are:

> *Fragmented and polarised but also the scene of the creation of new hybridities and cultural politics aimed not just at reducing inequalities but also preserving differences and fostering flexible 'transversal' identities.*

Intercultural cities need to harness the vast reservoir of cultural and creative resources represented by the different cultural groups that inhabit them, and to use these resources and skills to develop a more cohesive and sustainable city. Lambooy (2005:54) argues that cities can use their internal cultural resources to adapt to new circumstances and to extend their 'competence base' beyond creativity and into the intercultural arena.

Cities are the settings for a growing number of intercultural events, which deliberately set out to cross and blur cultural boundaries as a means of promoting communication between cultures and increased appreciation for what may be termed 'diversity advantage' in cities. The intercultural approach moves beyond equal opportunities and respect for existing cultural differences ('multiculturalism') to the use of dialogue and exchange between people of different cultural backgrounds to facilitate the transformation of public space, civic culture and institutions. Different cultures engage proactively, with the conflict that may emerge seen as creative and growth promoting. All city policies, services and programmes need to be reviewed through the lens of interculturalism, which spans citizen participation in decision making, education and health care services, the management of public space and the practices of cultural institutions. The Council of Europe (Strasbourg) has developed a programme of 'Intercultural Cities' that is testing intercultural strategies and their practical implementation and delivery mechanisms. Eleven pilot cities have been selected, with the intention of extending the programme to other cities (Council of Europe, 2009).

Cultural events can provide focal points for intercultural engagement, one example being the practice of carnivals and parades that promote the mixing and celebration of different cultures:

> *Carnivals in Britain have become perhaps the most visible intercultural events of all, for example through the introduction of sound systems and floats on big lorries, which are specific British Jamaican*

*innovations on the Trinidadian tradition that originally
formed carnival in Britain. To this are now added
Brazilian and other Latin American themes, plus new
forms of music, such as garage and drum and bass,
which are unique British hybrids. However, the
intercultural character of British carnival is not
perceived or communicated as such. On the contrary,
the marketing of it often emphasises its 'ethnically
exotic' character, thus freezing it in time and taking it
back to its country of origin.*

(Wood, Landry & Bloomfield, 2006:36)

Interculturality includes issues of the openness of public
space and 'the extent to which people feel they have the
"freedom of the city", or whether there are spaces or whole
neighbourhoods that feel closed or even hostile to one or
more groups within the city'. Wood, Landry and Bloomfield
(2006:61) argue that this could be measured by:

*Evaluating the range of diverse cultural events/
festivals in the city's artistic programme and
whether they reflect the plurality of cultures in the
city.*

The intercultural city provides new challenges for the
management of culture and cultural events that have the
potential to promote intercultural dialogue and exchange.

WHY EVENTS ARE INCREASINGLY IMPORTANT

The 'entrepreneurial city', the 'creative city' and the 'intercultural city' encompass different forms of cultural practice
that offer sources of inspiration and engagement. Cultural
events have become one of the major avenues for harnessing
this creativity.

The events strategy for Edinburgh (Graham Devlin
Associates, 2001:4) argues that 'cities, governments and the
private sector have all invested in creating, sustaining and

developing a wide range of festivals in order to reap a number of benefits'. These include:

- improvements to the quality of life in the city;
- creative activity;
- the growth of audiences;
- the creation of partnerships;
- recreational and educational opportunities;
- economic and social benefits;
- national and international profile raising; and
- meeting civic objectives.

The widespread benefits of events have now come to challenge the previous dominance of the importance of built heritage in the cultural and economic development strategies of cities, often based on assumptions such as:

- Events are more flexible than certain types of fixed physical infrastructure.
- Events can help to differentiate physical environments threatened by 'serial reproduction'.
- Events have greater ability to offer 'spectacle' and 'atmosphere'.
- Events generally meet the need for co-presence and the feeling of 'being there'.
- Events can cost less and achieve greater impact in the short-term.

However, each of these assumptions can be challenged, and their accuracy is wholly dependent on the type of event being staged. There are many cases where poorly conceived and managed events do not offer spectacle or atmosphere, and may cost as much if not more than certain types of cultural physical infrastructure. The well publicised failure of the 'River of Fire' display in London as part of the Millennium celebrations is but one example of this.

However, the soaring cost of permanent high-quality physical landmarks in cities, often with significant future operational costs, coupled with a frequently lengthy development process, have pushed events to the forefront of inter-urban competition (Paddison, 1993). Events complement capital infrastructure by providing the means of adding flexibility to fixed structures, and offering a source of spectacle that can extend the image value of a landmark. As Ritzer (1999:38) argues, the new 'cathedrals of consumption' are 'designed artistically and scientifically to lure people into consumption'. A part of their attraction is the presence of large numbers of people, which gives 'atmosphere' to the setting. The new means of consumption create spectacles, not as ends in themselves, but in order to attract large numbers of people to buy more goods and services. 'A mall, a casino or a theme park that is half empty ... does not generate the same excitement as a full house' (ibid:107).

Events are sometimes used as a platform for creating physical landmarks, as in the case of the Festival of Britain in 1951, the 1998 Expo in Lisbon or the 2007 Universal Forum of Cultures in Monterrey, and as a means for cities to position themselves as distinct, urban places in contrast to their rural surroundings, as Prentice and Andersen (2003) have suggested in the case of Edinburgh in Scotland.

Cities are centres of 'cultural globalisation', that offer 'an acceleration in the exchange of cultural symbols among people around the world to such an extent that it leads to changes in local popular cultures and identities' (Nijman 1991:148). The exchange of symbols is supported by consumption and accelerated by mass communication. Consumption involves not just material commodities, but also ideas, values and information; in other words, culture. Events have become part of the cultural globalisation process in cities, as vehicles for the exchange of certain models of cultural, spatial and economic organisation. Because of their mobility and timeliness, cultural events, in particular, have the potential to serve as mediators of processes of cultural globalisation and localisation.

Localisation processes are important because smaller cities are aided in their competitive struggle against larger cities by the new-found importance of the local. Growing feelings of regionalism and attachment to locality have strengthened the efforts of smaller cities to create a distinct role for themselves. Events have also been utilised as an important tool in the growth of the 'city state'. For example, Barcelona used the Olympic Games in 1992 as a way of expressing its independence from the Spanish central government in Madrid (Hargreaves, 2000). The new city states need their surrounding regions and vice versa. Many are caught up in the resurgence of regional identities that has characterised post-Fordist reconstruction and postmodern identity flux. Cities have become the flag carriers for their regions in the same way as capital cities were for nation states in the nineteenth century. Current ECOC projects make this clear, as Marseilles positions itself as the centre of the region of Provence in France (2013) and Essen carries the flag for the entire surrounding Ruhr region of Germany (2010). Regions gain wider recognition as a result of harbouring dynamic cities, and cities utilise the hinterland of the region as a market and inspiration for its events. Cultural and sports events can become the symbols of distinct identities, such as the Eisteddfod in Wales, the Highland Games in Scotland or *castellers* performances in Catalunya.

At the base of certain urban event strategies, there is an underlying belief that events can be a new source of identity and help build social cohesion as they begin to redefine the way in which we look at cities and their communities.

EVENTS AS EXPERIENCES

Events add an intangible component to the physical culture of the city. One of the key features of the modern economy is the importance of 'experiences'. In their analysis of the 'experience economy', Pine and Gilmore (1999) argue that consumers are increasingly looking for experiences in addition to services. Services are characterised by easy reproducibility, whereas experiences are by definition unique. Experiences require an interaction of the consumer and the producer, in a process of 'pro-sumption' or 'co-creation'. However, taking Pine and Gilmore's argument one step further, events are excellent vehicles for experience production because they are limited in time and imply co-presence, not just between producers and consumers, but also the co-presence of fellow consumers. The shared experience of cultural events is often what makes them special, which is one important reason why people attend concerts rather than merely watch them on television. The practice of watching a film in a cinema enhances the experience and the impact of the film more than simply watching a downloaded version at home. Events in the modern 'fantasy city' create the sense of community and meet both an individual and societal need for kinship, which many people believe the modern city has lost.

Such feelings of togetherness may contribute to events becoming destinations in their own right, as Prentice and Andersen (2003:12) argue:

> *The recurrent importance of gregariousness may imply that the festival itself becomes a destination, rather than simply an attraction of place-based destinations. The experience of gregariousness may ultimately be independent of any specific place, and what makes festivals special has been found to centre on uniqueness and quality, as well as atmosphere.*

In looking for new forms of community, postmodern travellers seek 'intermittent moments of physical proximity to particular peoples, places or events and ...in significant ways this proximity is felt to be obligatory, appropriate or desirable' (Urry, 2001:5–6). Urry discusses the need for 'thick co-presence' or physical proximity which enables people to establish eye contact, and therefore intimacy and trust. People come together in 'tight social worlds to use each other and their shared understanding of "what's happening"' (ibid:9). Being there oneself is critical to the maintenance of such social networks. In spite of the growing availability of social networking sites, virtual travel, video conferencing and webcams, people continue to desire to engage in embodied, physical co-presence. The Glastonbury Festival becomes not just a location, but also a time and a shared experience, such as the in the special experience that has been termed 'year of the mud' (2009). This helps to create peculiarity in a world in which spatial distinction is becoming more problematic. 'Being there' emphasises the fact that the combination of space, time and people is what matters, and it is this combination that events are able to deliver.

Events provide a scenario in which human contacts are possible, however superficial, and there is the promise of *communitas* through the shared experience of 'being there'. In this sense, events have taken on a new meaning in post-modern societies, where they become not only an essential experience in themselves, but also an important underpin-ning of individual and group identity.

The North Sea Jazz Festival – Shared Intimacy for 70,000

'If you haven't been to the World's largest indoor Jazz festival you don't know what you've been missing. Chances are, after this year's 30th anniversary edition of North Sea Jazz you'll also be missing out on what made it such an unsurpassed event; intimacy on a scale of 70,000 people, sitting at a riffs' distance from past and future jazz legends, breathing in pure creativity and the smell of pancakes that a press photographer brought in, pressed for time to cover as many artists and not to miss out on the highlight of the festival. It's an elusive element if you hunt for it, but the highlight is where you make it, sharing the music you love with any of the other friendly faces who managed to make it to that show, at that stage, at that moment. Even if it's the full-to-the-brim Statenhal where Jamie Cullum has caused a temporary lockdown with his energetic jazz/pop gig, there's always something to give you that "I was there" feeling.'
(Riley, 2005)

CELEBRATING TIME AND SPACE

The production of events requires space in which people can come together in order to experience co-presence. Once spaces have been created, they often need to be animated. In some cases, this happens organically, as different groups colonise and use public space for their own ends. Public parks have historically been inhabited in this way, as different publics lay claim to their use at different times for football matches, picnics, skateboarding or music jamming and drumming. Increasingly, public space is being managed by municipalities, and animated in order to attract people and to ensure their safety. Otherwise, visitors and residents alike may withdraw from public space to the safety of more secure or better-managed locations, avoiding contact with others in a process that Goffman (1971) called 'defensive destimulation' – producing the opposite of a lively, eventful space.

The challenge is to create 'trusting spaces' (Richards and Delgado, 2002) in which, as Sennett suggests, 'human displacement is incorporated into everyday life as a positive force on human interaction. In this way, our sense of place is not that of a peaceful, untroubled sanctuary, but is also a scene in which people come alive, where they expose, acknowledge and address the discordant parts of themselves and one another (Sennett, 1994:354).

The interaction of people, events and spaces in cities produces a flow of activities, which gives life and rhythm to the city. Amin and Thrift (2002:17), borrowing from the work of Lefebvre, argue that the rhythms of the city 'are the coordinates through which inhabitants and visitors frame and order the urban experience', and that rhythm, in the sense of 'localised time' and 'temporalised place', registers the daily tempo of the city. It is also clear that events are registers of larger cycles of time. In the case of many traditional societies, events were used to mark the passing of the seasons, and echoes of this rhythm are still heard in modern cities today, for example, with cycles in many western cities that move from Christmas markets through springtime parades and running marathons, summer outdoor performances and street parties to the beginning of opera and orchestral seasons in September. With the development of 'special events', a new rhythm is established – not cyclical, but marking specific moments in the history of a city, and also marking the transition to modern and later postmodern rhythms of the city. By marking out a new beat within the urban rhythm, events have also established new ways of 'localising time' and 'temporalising space'.

The cultural life and rhythm of the city are intimately affected by human displacement through processes of globalisation and localisation. 'World cities' such as New York, London and Tokyo not only have large populations drawn from across the globe, but also attract a growing number of tourists, filmmakers and businesses keen to experience the atmosphere of these places. Smaller cities are becoming 'wannabe cities' (Short, 1999) that want to achieve a similar level of cultural vitality, economic activity and familiarity as their bigger cousins. Very often this leads to a process of event creation and competition for international events, which helps to stimulate visitation and focus media attention on the host city. Attracting and retaining mobile publics may require the eventful city to enliven and animate public space through the stimulation and production of events.

THE NEED FOR ANIMATION

Animation or 'vibrancy' is important to cities for a variety of reasons, including economic ones. A lively atmosphere makes people feel good about living in a place, and makes the city attractive to visit, which in turn drives inward investment. The relationship between atmosphere and attractiveness means that cities need to think carefully about the use of space. As Pep Subirós (undated) argues, space is more than a place where experiences occur: it also shapes and gives sense to that experience. Space adds value to experiences by facilitating the act of coming together, dialogue, exchange, tolerance, responsibility and sense of community, identity and collective memory.

The animation of space can be spontaneous, but it often needs to be managed. A space without a flow of events may feel empty and unattractive. On the other hand, if the flow of events becomes too fast, those who inhabit a space may experience stress. Scitovsky (1976) argues that individuals seek an optimal level of stimulation for a given situation.

Too little stimulation produces boredom and a search for a higher level of stimulation; too much stimulation produces stress and a search for reduced stimulation. An optimal level of stimulation may be comfortable, but it may not produce feelings of excitement or joy. Scitovsky argues that it is the change from one state of stimulation to another that produces excitement – we are exhilarated by the acceleration of a fast car, rather than a steady high speed.

A stimulating cultural place incorporates a flow of different stimuli, such as the visual display of a cosmopolitan crowd, which act as regular and irregular markers of time. Lefebvre observes that a space is also a time, whose passage is marked by the flow of everyday events. The flow of events becomes difference that can be consumed, an experience of 'atmosphere', produced in specific places at specific times.

In his study of the Joensuu Festival in Finland, van Elderen (1997) points out that the festival had an important role in turning the town into a 'town of the arts' in the 1980s. This was primarily achieved through the staging of processions that transformed the spatial relations of everyday life and imbued spaces with new meanings. The festival also transformed physical space in a permanent sense because a special venue was created for the musical performances held at the end of the procession. The participative nature of the procession created a dialogue between spectators and participants, underpinning a *festival communitas*.

The attraction, staging, management and marketing of events have become an important part of the urban planning process. Events imply an investment of resources, use of public space and commitment of political support. Cities increasingly are developing events strategies, which are designed to attract events to the city and ensure the maximum benefits accrue to the city itself. The cities of Auckland, Birmingham, Dubai, Edinburgh, Sydney and Toronto are only a few notable examples where strategies also include consideration of how the spaces in the city are used for events.

As the focus of cultural provision shifts from a preoccupation with a limited range of cultural facilities such as concert halls, theatres and museums, the notion of 'cultural planning,' has been introduced and significantly enlarged to encompass a very wide range of spaces and programmes. The practice of cultural programming in a city has expanded to include spaces and places that do not conform to the traditional or classical understanding of culture, which may include as waterfronts, civic squares, shopping precincts, gardens, sports stadia, train stations, stone quarries and non-cultural public and private buildings. Instead of cultural organisations running programmes across a limited range of traditional venues such as concert halls, theatres, galleries and arts centres a very large number of organisations, promoters, voluntary associations and businesses have become involved in staging events in many different spaces across the city, indoors and outdoors. The entire city becomes a stage across which a succession of events is paraded: a situation, which creates the sense of 'festivalisation' of the city.

FESTIVALISATION

There is a widespread feeling among certain policy makers that it is important to make cities eventful all year round, with a need to fill any gaps in the events calendar. This view was in evidence, for example in the rationale for the ECOC in Avignon in 2000 (Palmer-Rae, 2004: Part II:89).

> *There was a strong desire to increase cultural tourism and reinforce the reputation of Avignon, secured by the famous theatre Festival of Avignon, as an important cultural city. With their catchphrase 'Avignon – a permanent show' it was hoped that the cultural year would bring visitors all year round.*

Edinburgh as a Stage

Edinburgh is an example of the development of a city as a stage used throught the year. Edinburgh has one of the largest and longest running international arts festivals in the UK, and has used the International Festival as a springboard to develop other festivals, events and attractions. The increased popularity of the International Festival stems

Continued

from the wide range of additional events held and the historic city centre, which forms a backdrop to the festival activities. The previous 'high culture' image of the city as the cultural capital of Scotland has changed as more elements of popular culture have been introduced. Other phenomena such as impact of the film 'Trainspotting,' which captured an alternative view of the city. 'Trainspotting Tour' is included in the UNESCO-sponsored Edinburgh 'City of Literature' initiative. Some of the former 'villages' now incorporated into the city, such as Leith and Portobello, have been developed in terms of what Howie (2000) has called 'grey area' tourism, centred on the everyday life of the neighbourhoods and their inhabitants. The centre of the city has also been further developed as a stage for the annual Hogmanay festival on New Year's Eve, which was added to the existing offer of the international arts, fringe, book, film, jazz, children's and other festival events that take place annually in the city.

Edinburgh become a vast stage on which festivals and events are organised for the benefit of residents and visitors. The logical outcome of this process of event development is the city as a continuous festival, which some have described as the 'festivalisation' of the city (Hitters, 2007).

According to van Elderen (1997:126) festivalisation involves:

The (temporary) transformation of the town into a specific symbolic space in which the utilisation of the public domain… is under the spell of a particular cultural consumption pattern.

In this situation, events and event spaces come to dominate the public life of a city. Frank and Roth (2000) link this transformation with urban boosterism, usually based on a coalition of business leaders and civic authorities with a consensus on stimulating investment and economic growth while limiting the redistributional function of the state. In German urban sociology, boosterism is referred to as 'festivalisation' or 'politics through big events' (Häussermann & Siebel, 1993).

Hitters (2007) also links festivalisation to a crisis in the legitimation of the cultural policy model developed under the welfare state. He argues that rather than producing the intended democratisation of culture, consumption of 'high culture' remained largely the preserve of the higher socio-economic classes, and increased middle class consumption was driven not by public policy (such as subsidised cultural products) but through the type of status rivalry and distinction processes outlined by Bourdieu (1984).

> *Cultural policy then, was forced to shift its focus away from 'high art', towards a much more inclusive definition of (popular) culture. The policy arena thus widened its scope to pop-music, film, web-design, ethnic culture, entertainment, etc. And it searched for new means of distribution that were more accessible than the traditional theatres and museums.*
> *Consequently, festivals appeared to be the panacea.*
> (Hitters, 2007:283)

Lee (2004) broadens this argument by illustrating how cultural policy is moving away from a narrow focus on high culture towards more 'inclusive' concepts of culture as a whole way of life, which not only involves more of the population, but also widens the scope for intervention. He argues that this is an attempt to theme cities into commodifiable urban experiences to generate economic value. Lee points out that such developments are not new, but what is new is their general pervasiveness and the generalisation of knowledge about how spaces entertain people, knowledge that informs the notion of eventful city. However, eventful cities take theming to the next stage, where the themes themselves almost become irrelevant. What is important is the role of events as carriers of meaning: the event *is* the theme.

As festivalisation progresses, 'consumption and entertainment becoming increasingly indistinguishable', so that 'spaces compete with each other by promoting their performativity across a set of activities formerly set apart, such as shopping, dining, recreation and even education "hands-on" museums' (Amin and Thrift, 2002:124).

Festivalisation goes beyond the staging of formal festivals to embrace new forms of animation, including 'edu-tainment' and 'shop-a-tainment' concepts that combine the realms of education or shopping with features of entertainment. Cities such as Mumbai and Singapore have created 'shopping festivals', which are prime examples of the 'shop-a-tainment' phenomenon. The need for performative spaces has also led to the development of new spaces in the city which are interactive, theatrical, omni-sensory and adaptive to audience reaction. In such spaces, imagination and fantasy become an important part of the business model. This is effectively Pine and Gilmore's (1999) concept of the experience economy: 'a set of living, embodied geographies which provide a new source of value through their performative push' (Amin & Thrift, 2002:125).

These developments have resonance with the concept of the 'city as stage', which was evident in the 1970s urban literature. However, the difference seems to be that rather than simply functioning as a backdrop for a wide array of events, cities now actively seek to develop, manage and market events as a key part of their cultural life, social fabric and economic dynamism. Festivalisation has become used as a means of countering a wide range of cultural, social and economic problems. In turn, the justification for developing cultural festivals or sports events has focused increasingly on the economic or social potential of such events and enabling the city to compete more effectively in the global arena.

The notion of festivalisation reflects much more than an increase in the number of events being held in cities; it echoes a qualitative change intimately linked to the spatial and economic restructuring of cities. Cities need events to support the experience economy. Events have ceased to be a peripheral diversion from the everyday business of the city and become one of its prime concerns.

Pine and Gilmore (1999) argue that the search for greater added value and increasing competition has driven a progression of economic changes from the extractive industries to manufacturing, services and now to the production of experiences. A similar progression might be seen in the functionality of cities, from centres of production to service centres to backdrops for experiences.

As Amin and Thrift (2002:124) argue,

There is now a concerted attempt to re-engineer the experience of cities, one which is on a par with the construction of Haussmann's boulevards – but happening in many cities around the world – and one which is just as ambitious, but perhaps less known because it is the result of many different plans rather than one single master plan. (emphasis in the original)

This progressive transformation of urban space from productive functions to consumption and performative uses may be taken to the point where the city models itself on an event or series of events. At a physical level, the tendency for cities to model their spaces around events has already been analysed by Sabate i Bel et al. (2004). As noted earlier, many cities around the world have taken this a step further, and now identify themselves as 'eventful cities' or 'festival cities'. In some cities the events have become so important that they begin to define the city itself. In this sense, events have become a major tool in the process of 'placemaking'.

PLACEMAKING

Eventfulness is intimately linked to the process of place-making. For the last three decades there has been a convergence between the realms of cultural and economic development. In the resulting 'cultural economy,' ideas and artistic qualities contribute towards a new development paradigm. A wide range of activities are now concerned with the production and marketing of goods and services that are infused with symbolic cultural content. This phenomenon has shifted development approaches from a Fordist economic regime based on manufacturing to one that places high value on human creativity. In terms of the built environment, this paradigm shift to the commonly used concept of the 'creative economy' has in turn influenced the formulation of a new approach to the policy and practice of urban development, which includes urban design and destination marketing that focus on aesthetic value and the potential to reinforce the cultural importance of a place so that it attracts attention and invites participation.

Cities have long tried to promote themselves as attractive places to live, work, visit and invest. According to Skot-Hansen (1998), the provincial town of Holstebro in west Jutland 'invented' the use of culture for reimaging and development purposes as early as the 1960s (Bayliss, 2004). But the new climate of global intra-urban competition has been transforming the art of place making into an industry. Every city seems to be creating images to market themselves to residents and visitors.

Ashworth and Voogd (1990) argue that the primary aim of place marketing is to construct an image of a place in order to make it attractive to current and potential residents, investors and visitors. Such activities require the coordination of a large number of different functions within the public and private sectors. Ashworth and Voogd draw attention to the extent to which these functions are coordinated by the local authority and are part of its development strategy. As discussed further in Chapter 4, the role of local authority leadership in a city-wide events strategy is crucial to the success of the eventful city. The public sector needs to help engineer consensus amongst the residents of their localities (Kearns & Philo, 1993), for example through the creation of 'event-communities' (Frank and Roth, 1998) and in combining the overlapping but also divergent interests of public and private sectors.

Culture and Place Making in London

The Mayor of London's *London Plan* prioritises 20% of the city's wards for regeneration, and designates a further 42 locations for growth of housing and employment space. The plan argues that if the regeneration and growth of these areas is to result in successful places, they must incorporate culture.

- Cultural practitioners can engage residents and help identify what makes areas distinctive and should be protected in the regeneration process. There are many examples of artists collaborating with architects and developers to produce more creative and successful development schemes.

- Cultural facilities such as libraries and sports centres can be provided within larger development schemes. By doing so, development schemes can benefit from the improved profile and increased property value associated with cultural facilities.

■ New public spaces can be designed to support local festivals, art installations and sport. Development schemes can also build the creative workspace that is often in short supply. The regeneration and growth of London represents a major opportunity to deliver the full complement of local and sub-regional cultural infrastructure, which the city needs – particularly the less well-resourced parts of Outer London.

(Mayor of London, 2008)

Cultural events have emerged as a means of improving the image of cities, adding life to city streets and giving citizens renewed pride in their city. This enhancement of community pride and destination image following an event has been referred to as the 'halo effect' (Hall, 1992), the 'showcase effect' (Fredline & Faulkner, 1998) and the 'feel-good effect' (Allen, O'Toole & McDonnell, 2005). Zukin argues that 'culture is a euphemism for the city's new representation as a creative force in the emerging service economy...' and that '... culture is the sum of a city's amenities that enable it to compete for investment and jobs, its "comparative advantage"' (1995:268). Zukin's view of 'culture' as covering all the amenities of a city reflects the fact that the very notion of culture has expanded to take in not just 'traditional,' 'high' culture attractions such as museums, theatres and concert halls, but also includes elements of 'popular' culture, such as pop music, fashion, 'ethnoscapes' (Appadurai, 1990) and sport. Both high culture and popular culture have become important sources for the images that are used to underpin the 'brand image' of cities (Kearns & Philo, 1993). Event images are now so important that they 'are starting to dominate the natural or physical features in the identification of cities' (Burns, Hatch & Mules, 1986:5).

Competition between cities in a crowded field of images is one of the major factors stimulating cities to adopt branding strategies (Evans, 2003; Meurs & Verheijen, 2003) that seek to transform fixed cultural capital into competitive advantage through the staging of cultural events and the construction of cultural landmarks. City branding used to be associated with the flight from an industrial past (Holcomb, 1993; Bramwell & Rawding, 1996), but is now linked to enhancing the urban landscape with globally branded event and entertainment destinations, encapsulated in the 'fantasy city' (Hannigan, 1998). As Hannigan (2003) suggests, a successful brand should be instantly recognisable, play on the desire for comfort and certainty and provide a point of identification for consumers in a crowded marketplace (see Chapter 7).

Competing to be a Cultural Capital

In many countries, there is fierce rivalry between the capital and another major city for cultural supremacy. The 'second city' syndrome drives cities such as Glasgow, Rotterdam, Melbourne and Shanghai to develop cultural facilities to match or better those of the capital or largest city.

In China, the rivalry between Beijing and Shanghai increased as a result of Beijing's status as an Olympic City in 2008. Beijing planned to add at least 32 new museums by 2008, together with a €150 million expansion of the National Museum of China, the new National Grand Theatre, a €220 million performing arts complex with a 2400-seat opera hall and a 2000-seat concert hall and theatre. Establishing the theatre was a personal priority of President Jiang Zemin, who wished to see Beijing's deteriorating theatres replaced with new cultural landmarks before the 2008 Olympics.

Shanghai planned to open more than 100 new museums by 2010, a new €68 million Shanghai Art Museum, a new museum of antiquities, a €140 million science museum, the €100 million Shanghai Grand Theatre and renovations and expansions to practically every existing concert hall, theatre and arts centre in the city. As a cultural repost to the Beijing Olympics, Shanghai hosted the 2010 World Expo. The city already has a considerable programme of cultural events (including an extensive 'tourist festival'), which attracts five million visitors a year. Major international events include the Shanghai International TV Festival, the Shanghai International Art Fair and the Shanghai International Festival of Arts.

One of the major differences between the two cities is that 'most events in Beijing are organised by individuals, whereas in Shanghai the government has taken the lead' (Casale, 2004).

There is increasing competition by cities to host major cultural and sporting 'brand' events such as the Olympic Games, a World Expo or the European Capital of Culture. Cities are investing large sums of money just to bid for such events. In the race to win the nomination of the UK government for the European Cultural Capital in 2008 several of the 10 UK candidate cities were estimated to have spent more than 1 million (€1.5 million) each preparing their bids (Palmer–Rae, 2004). The very large investment, first on bidding for events and then to ensure their successful delivery, on events has become a common pattern as much in economically poor cities as wealthy ones as cities seek to secure the maximum economic and image benefits from their events (see Chapter 9).

A combination of factors is pushing cities to develop more events and, in many cases, to create bigger and better events than their competitors. All of these factors have collectively led to a growth in the level and scale of event activity worldwide.

THE GROWTH OF FESTIVALS AND EVENTS

As described at the beginning of this chapter, fairs, festivals and other cultural events have been part of the urban scene as long as there have been cities. What has arguably changed in the modern city is the level of professionalisation of the event organisation process and the instrumental use of events to achieve wider policy ends.

Prentice and Andersen (2003:8) state that:

The explosion in festival numbers is multifaceted in cause, ranging from supply factors (such as cultural planning, tourism development and civic repositioning) through to demand factors (such as

*serious leisure, lifestyle sampling, socialisation needs
and the desire for creative and 'authentic' experiences
by some market segments).*

This qualitative change also seems to have made festivals
and events a major growth market. Not only have the number
of mega-events mushroomed as cities try and exploit them
for economic ends, but local events have flourished too.
Quinn (2005:927) argues that 'the past 15 years or so have
seen a remarkable rise in the number of arts festivals in cities
throughout Europe and elsewhere. Their growth has been
such that it is now difficult to determine accurately the
number of festivals in existence.'

One of the reasons it is difficult to count the number of
festivals and cultural events is the problem of defining the
terms (see Chapter 2). However, even if robust definitions
were available, the sheer number and range of events make
enumeration a complex exercise. When evaluating events,
there is a lack of longitudinal data on the development of
events over time, and so the absence of accurate quantifiable
data on the growth of events necessitates the analysis of
evidence that is often circumstantial. (See Chapter 9)

There is evidence of increased importance and number of
local events in different countries. Referring to Spain, Pérez-
Díaz (2003:467–468) comments:

> *The importance of local fiestas has increased
> extraordinarily: the number of participants, the
> variety and range of activities, the amounts of money
> spent on them.... In the last two decades have seen
> a proliferation of carnivals and fiestas ... that have
> been widely disseminated from their original
> locations.*

In Singapore, National Arts Council (2008) statistics
indicate that the number of arts activities reached nearly
27,000 in 2007, or four times as many as in 1997. Attendance at ticketed performances doubled from 754,100
patrons in 1997 to close to 1.5 million in 2007. Since 1997,
the number of exhibition days has also multiplied five times
to exceed 19,000 days in 2007, while performances tripled to
a record high of 7450 in 2007. Much of the growth in

activities and performances is accounted for by the many festivals and cultural events organised in the city-state.

Another measure of cultural event 'proliferation' is provided by the growth of events dedicated to a particular discipline. In the case of film festivals, for example, the European Coordination of Film Festivals had to be created to remedy 'the disparity of practices and some dangerous excesses and trends of the continent's proliferating fests... (this body) listed 76 festivals when it began in 1995, a number that had more than doubled to 154 in 20 countries by 2000' (Turan, 2002). By 2009 membership of this group was up to over 180 festivals.

CONCLUSION

Cities around the world develop and utilise cultural events to achieve a range of objectives: economic, social and political and cultural. Cities have long been shaped by events, and the relationship between the city and its event programme has changed significantly over the centuries. The contemporary city is likely to have a large and varied event programme with a mixed economy of events run by the city itself as well as a large range of other stakeholders.

As events have become increasingly integrated into the daily life of cities, so the planning of events and their integration with civic goals have become even closer. The contemporary city is likely to see eventfulness as one more source of creativity that can be developed to stimulate the creative industries, enhance the attractiveness of the city and promote social cohesion. The growing diversity of cities also provides new opportunities for cities to harness the creative power of their citizens to develop events and to benefit even more from their effects.

The following chapters look in more detail at how eventfulness can be created and programmed, how event programmes and event stakeholders can be managed and how eventfulness can be marketed and monitored to enhance the impact on a city.

CHAPTER 2

Creating Events – From Concept into Practice

THE NATURE OF EVENTS

What constitutes an 'event'? Definitions of events most often relate to occurrences that are significant, interesting, exciting or unusual, but these remain rather generalised and ambiguous notions. The more specific term 'cultural event' creates an even greater definitional problem because of the absence of a commonly agreed understanding of what constitutes 'culture' (Richards, 2001), as well as 'event'. Many previous studies have concentrated on 'special events', which are more easily understood as unique occurrences, separate from everyday experience, and on specific categories of cultural events, such as arts festivals, sports competitions or traditional celebrations, which are clearly recognised.

According to Allen, O'Toole and McDonnell (2005:10) 'the term "special events" describes specific rituals, presentations, performances or celebrations that are consciously planned and created to mark special occasions or to achieve particular social, cultural or corporate goals and objectives.' Getz (1997:4) also argues that '[special] events are transient, and every event is a unique blending of its duration, setting, management and people.' He further suggests that a special event is best defined by its context. From the perspective of some organisers, 'a special event is a one-time or infrequently occurring event outside normal programs or activities of the sponsoring or organising body', and from the consumer's perspective, 'an opportunity for a leisure, social and cultural experience outside the normal range of choices or beyond everyday experience'. The idea of events as distinctive is echoed by Goldblatt (1990:2): 'a special event recognises a unique moment in time with ceremony and ritual to satisfy specific needs'.

When is a Festival Not a Festival?

The problems of definition equally relate to the notion of 'festivals', which span categories as diverse as beer festivals, Christmas festivals, fire festivals and festivals of film or contemporary dance.

Amsterdam has a strong calendar of cultural events and festivals, based on the presence of an appreciative audience and well-developed cultural infrastructure. But according to the festival policy document from the Amsterdam Cultural Department (Amsterdamse Kunstraad, 2003), there was increasing debate about whether the city had 'too many festivals'. Part of the problem was that the word 'festival' had become a marketing term, used for a wide range of events by public and private sector institutions to attract attention to their cultural products. Many of the theatres and other permanent cultural institutions had begun to use the 'festival' label to package many elements of their regular programme of arts events.

The policy advice called for a distinction to be made between events (such as Gay Pride/Canal Parade, the *Bloemencorso* and the arrival of *Sintaklaas* at Christmas), cultural events (such as the *Uitmarkt* and the Museum Night) and festivals. Festivals should further be divided into those organised by existing cultural institutions and those organised independently.

The advice called for festivals to be judged in terms of their 'added value' for the city, not just in terms of what they add to the normal cultural supply, but also their provision for specific target groups, attention for new or underdeveloped art forms and their ability to prolong the cultural season. Particular criticism was levelled at the current supply of large summer festivals, which are large-scale events, which arguably added little or nothing to the cultural supply of the city (Amsterdamse Kunstraad, 2003).

A report by Inkei (2005:6) also uncovered a variety of definitions used for arts festivals: for example, in New Zealand, 'Almost any event can be, and has been called an arts festival.' However, Creative New Zealand has tried to restrict the definition of an arts festival to events which 'have a primary focus on the arts, with an overall artistic vision that influences the programming and which is limited to a specific area and defined time period.' In Canada, a similar approach to defining arts festivals emerged, with a view that such arts events must be of a limited duration and cover a variety of arts disciplines to qualify for funding under the Arts Presentation Canada Programme. A different approach is taken by Festivals Australia, which sees a festival as 'a regular public celebration that is organised by members of the community and has clear and strong community support.'

In practice, there are variations in the understanding of the terms cultural events and festivals, with considerable difficulties in distinguishing between the two terms. The word 'festival' is often used as a primary marketing tool. Jan Moerman, Director of Rotterdam Festivals, recently remarked that if you call a cultural event a 'festival' it automatically attracts a larger audience, which is 'a miraculous phenomenon' (Rossie, 2003:9). In certain instances, the branding of almost any event that comprises more than one activity as a festival is purely a promotional technique.

Defining cultural events

Although precise definitions may prove difficult, it is possible to identify key aspects of cultural events: they comprise a series of activities, have limited duration, are generally recurrent and are usually celebratory. Cultural events commonly focus on artistic and community roots through their content.

A cultural event essentially has the following features:

■ Cultural content
A cultural event must by definition have a cultural focus, although it may contain other elements as well.
'Culture' in reference to 'cultural events' is taken to cover the cultural products of a specific society (such as artworks, music, literature, film, food, fashion) and its cultural processes (in other words, culture as 'a way of life' or tradition). In this sense, cultural events range from what are often termed 'high' culture events

programmed in formal venues to 'popular' culture events taking place in the public spaces of the city. All cultural events involve some form of programming (discussed further in Chapter 3). Whether an artist or artistic director a cultural association or individual citizens develop the event, programming is a crucial process that defines the shape and flavour of an event. It is also a vital means to achieve the aims of the event.

■ Timing and location
Events take place in specific locations at specific times. Although cities might be animated through 'festival marketplaces' and other facilities where there is permanent entertainment, cultural events have definite starting and ending points. In most cases, the programme will also link the spaces where different events take place, although in certain cases linkages are made more in the interests of marketing than to serve the programming coherence of a cultural programme.

■ Audience
A public audience, which is attracted to or invited to attend, must witness events. Audiences need to either be physically drawn to the event or, in the case of more recent digital events, engaged to participate virtually.

■ Stakeholders
In addition to those directly attending the events programme, cultural events have a wide range of stakeholders who are in some way affected by, or who can affect, those events. Stakeholders may be individuals and groups that have a direct interest, involvement or investment in the cultural, financial, political or other concerns relating to the event.

CREATING THE EVENTFUL CITY

There are many ways in which events can be created and linked to the culture, identity and physical space of the city. The mere staging of single events is insufficient for a city to move from being a city 'with events' to becoming an 'eventful city'. This shift requires the development of an integrated approach to the relationship between the city and its events, which maximises the benefits of the event programme as a whole. This means thinking about a number of key issues, including:

■ Developing an effective stakeholder network (see Chapter 4).

■ Creating a strategic vision (see Chapter 5).

■ Programming the eventful city (see Chapter 3).

■ Marketing events to publics and audiences (see Chapters 7 and 8).

■ Monitoring outcomes (see Chapter 9).

■ Ensuring sustainability (see Chapter 10).

Once the city has begun to think holistically about events and to organise and manage its event programme effectively, it can move from being a city with events to become an eventful city. Some of the key differences are summarised in Table 2.1.

Organising and managing such complex processes offer major challenges, even for those cities that already

Table 2.1   A city with events versus the eventful city

A city with events	The eventful city
Sectoral	Holistic
Tactical	Strategic
Reactive	Proactive
A container of events	A generator of events
Ad hoc	Coordinated
Competition	Cooperaton
Pandering to audiences	Provoking publics
Left brain thinking	Right brain thinking
Event policy	Events as a policy tool
Market led	Market leader
City marketing	City making
Spectacle	Involvement

have strong reputations for events. There are a number of clearly recognised stages that cities tend to move through as they develop their potential as eventful cities. One such stage is the recognition of the importance of the strategic coherence of events, which usually leads to the development of an event strategy and often to the creation of an organisational structure to help coordinate events programmes.

Marketing Manchester

In Manchester, responsibility for event strategy has been given to an organisation Marketing Manchester, a public-private partnership with more than 50 staff. Core funding is received from Manchester Airport PLC, the 10 Greater Manchester local authorities, the Greater Manchester Passenger Transport Authority and the Northwest Development Agency.

The remit of Marketing Manchester is to market Manchester as a place for tourism and culture. The strategy for developing eventfulness combines the pursuit of one-off mega events and a regular programme of 'pillar events' (see Chapter 9). Marketing Manchester was created to build on the successful organisation of the Commonwealth Games in the city in 2002 to attract more visitors to the city.

The Commonwealth Games provided Manchester with a unique experience as host to a world event. Manchester had invested in sports facilities of international standard and put in place partnerships with national bodies that link these facilities with sports development in schools and local areas. The city's theatres, concert venues, art galleries and museums produce and present events that tour internationally. The Spirit of Friendship Festival and Cultureshock in 2002 provided an opportunity both to develop links with Commonwealth countries and to celebrate the diversity of the city and region. Communities across the city produce a year-round programme of festivals – Chinese New Year, Irish Festival, Caribbean Carnival, Asian Mela. Manchester had the basis for a future events strategy to raise the profile of the city, attract visitors and offer new opportunities for residents.

The aims of the event programme were:

To promote Manchester as a 'cultural experience' where there are new and imaginative activities all year round, which are open to all and that are safe, attractive and welcoming to residents and visitors.

To coordinate the marketing of the city's cultural opportunities to key markets – residents, students, leisure and business visitors and inward investors – to ensure communication is consistent and to engage a greater and more diverse audience.

To develop a distinctive programme of quality events and festivals to build the city's image, encourage community participation and stimulate tourism.

To support initiatives from grass-roots: community celebrations, sporting events and exhibitions, which bring life to the city's streets and communities.

Manchester provides an example of how developing eventfulness has become part of the strategic activity of major cities, often by means of an integration with other 'marketing-related' policies, such as tourism, economic development and imaging. Increasing finance is being invested not only in specific events themselves, but also in the structures, or 'orgware', required to attract and run them. In the case of Manchester, events policy was developed in order to support a range of other civic objectives. In many cases, the 'orgware' that has been developed to support events in itself can also become a springboard for new initiatives and ways of working.

In the Belgian city of Antwerp, the ECOC (European Capital of Culture) in 1993 was the original catalyst for creating a longer term and permanent coordinating body to run major cultural events, called Antwerpen Open, which then later became the body responsible for coordinating all events for the city in 2005. Several of the key organisers and programmers of the ECOC of Antwerp 1993 were recruited to the board and management structure of the new organisation.

Every year Antwerp hosts around 120 major events, of which those that are supported and managed by the city are termed 'city events' (***stadsevenementen***). Antwerp views 'city events' not as ends in themselves, but as means of achieving the wider objectives of the city. The events director (***evenementenregisseur)*** is responsible for developing an overall vision for key events linked closely to the city's broader vision, and which are translated into general criteria for staging and evaluating events (Antwerpen Open, 2005:17). The activities of Antwerpen Open have been important in helping the city to establish the city's image (including its reputation as a world fashion capital) and for developing very practical coordinating mechanisms for events, such as a coordinated approach to ticketing for events and venues across the city as a whole.

The Role of the Public Sector in Events in Christchurch, New Zealand

The Christchurch events strategy states that: 'Festivals and events are an integral part of life in Christchurch. The City boasts a full and diverse calendar of events and festivals, including international sport and arts events, mass outdoor concerts and intimate local community celebrations.'

The events strategy was developed in 1998 in consultation with the 'festival and events industry'. The strategy states:

The Christchurch City Council is committed to a lively and dynamic city, which is enhanced by a range of events and festivals that:

- increase the well-being of residents;
- attract economic benefits through growth in the number and length of stay of visitors;
- promote the establishment of industry related business activity and employment opportunities for residents; and
- maintain Christchurch's position as a leader in events.

Achieving these aims involves the development of a number of objectives, including:

- establishing an advisory board;
- establishing transparent and consistent processes for bidding for events;
- establishing transparent and consistent processes for funding events;
- developing evaluation methods related to objectives; and
- increasing the ease of producing events in Christchurch.

The roles the Council will have in the events arena are as:

- provider: directly organising and funding festivals and events;
- funder: providing financial resources to external events providers;
- advocate: representing the interests of the local events industry;

- evaluation: measuring the success of Council funded events and festivals;
- monitoring: observing quality and delivery of Council funded events and festivals;
- resource facilitation and provision: providing an events advisory service and coordination of the events industry;
- promoter: generically promoting the Christchurch calendar of events and festivals; and
- encouraging: creativity, spontaneity, innovation and fun in events management.

The Christchurch example typifies the variety of roles taken on by city councils relative to events (see also Chapter 4). For some events, a local council will be the initiator, developer, organiser, promoter and funder, whereas for other events it will only offer support and leave the entire delivery to an independent body. Whichever approach is adopted, the eventful city needs to implicate citizens in the development, organisation and implementation of the event programme in order to maximise benefits.

THE SEARCH FOR INSPIRATION

Where do ideas for events come from? In some cities, there is already a rich tradition of events for a city to draw on. In Europe, for example, as outlined in Chapter 1, many events are based around traditional festivals, which date back hundreds of years, such as the Palio in Sienna, the Patum in Berga or St. Valentines Fair in Leeds (Harcup, 2000). However, in other cities events may need to be invented.

The European Capital of Culture event (ECOC) was entirely invented on the basis of an idea of a former Minister of Culture of Greece, Melina Mercouri, in 1985 as a means of demonstrating both the commonality of European cultures as well as their richness and diversity.

Many cultural events owe their genesis to individuals with inspirational ideas. Klaic et al. (2004:5) emphasise that many events are 'sparked by an idea or a single fan'. These festivals often focus on a specific topic and may encompass ideas which seem 'novel or perhaps even insane and are aimed at a relatively narrow audience'. Because such events are initiated and sustained by the enthusiasm of a limited number of aficionados, they may eventually need to expand their audience base or find new sources of support in order to survive. In many cases, a public authority, such as a city or a region, may be asked to adopt an individually inspired event as their own and to meet some of the cost.

Hansen et al. (2003) point out in their review of European festivals, that most events spring from two basic sources – either cities or regions trying to increase their popularity or economic advantage, or 'an idea or a single fan'. Events that emerge from the first motivation seem to be more sustainable, according to Hansen et al. (2003), because local communities and/or the public sector support them, whereas the second type may suffer problems of continuity if the originator moves on or loses interest. In many cases events combine a mixture of these two origins – often they are initiated by individuals and then supported by the public sector once they become successful. Some argue that the original entrepreneurial role of the inspired individual is being gradually taken over by the entrepreneurial city or region eager to capitalise on the festival 'boom'.

Differing interpretations of event origin can coexist. For example, Lyons (2004) discusses the origin of the numerous film festivals in the United States:

> *In many instances, regional film festivals emerge when local chambers of commerce finance them to promote economic development through cultural tourism. But some festival directors say their events are part of larger efforts to reclaim a film culture overrun by multiplexes and studio blockbusters. They say starting a film festival is a rebellious act and a sign of the growing democratisation of film.*

In their review of major summer festivals in the Netherlands, Ranshuysen and Jansen (2004) identify a number of festivals created 'from the street'. Many of these were the 'dreams' of particular individuals, who were often themselves embedded in creative networks. The choice of location for the event was usually dependent on these individuals or their networks. In other cases, initial ideas emerged from city councils themselves, as in the case of the Noorderzon Festival in Groningen and the Parkstad Limburg created by a group of seven municipalities. Certain festivals developed from the activities of other festivals, such as Holland's Festival of Fools initiative, which began as a mobile theatre concept in the 1970s and later helped to inspire the Oerol Festival and the Over het Ij Festival. The Festival a/ d Werf grew out of a student theatre festival held to celebrate the anniversary of Utrecht University.

The following sections examine catalysts and triggers for events in more detail.

Themes

The use of theming has become an important aspect of urban planning. Gottdiener (1997) explains that themes have become important in modern society because they provide a form of recognition and security for the consumer. By selecting a recognisable theme, an event can link itself to important potential markets of people who have an interest in that theme.

A Shakespeare Festival or an anniversary celebration devoted to Beethoven or Picasso will be immediately recognisable to a wide audience in terms of its content and likely activities. Other themes may be less immediately appealing to global audiences but popular with a local audience, such as the exhibition of works by the Dutch painter Piet Mondriaan in the Hague in 1995. This attracted only 185,000 of the 300,000 visitors who were expected, largely because of a disappointingly low number of foreign tourists. Mondriaan is a well-known name in his home country, but only recognised by those abroad with a good knowledge of contemporary art (Richards, 1996).

Themes for events may be used to link to the built environment of a city or to specific buildings or features within it. The City of Tarragona in Spain holds an annual Tarraco

Festival to celebrate the founding of the city by the Romans. Local residents are encouraged to don Roman dress, and emblematic features such as the Roman amphitheatre and forum are used as backdrops for the event.

Themes can be created from almost any cultural reference in a city. The Morecambe Punk Festival was held in a UK seaside resort where many punks used to congregate in the 1970s. However, in spite of the important orientation to Morecambe, the event later moved to Blackpool because it was less expensive to stage there, in spite of the extensive support provided by Morecambe Council (Long, 2004).

Many single events in a city may be grouped together around a theme, such as the Year of Architecture and Design awarded to Glasgow in the UK for 1999, or the Year of Antoni Gaudí created by Barcelona in 2002. The 2005 Alive event organised across the North East region of England was built around four distinct Festivals: the Festival of the Rivers and the Seas, the Festival of Sport, the Festival of Music and the Festival of Visual Arts, all of which took place around existing events such as the Great North Run and the British Art Show. By showcasing events in this way, the region was able to promote existing events as 'new', mainly to reinforce the image of a lively, dynamic region.

Celebrating events

International organisations, such as the United Nations, have declared many 'special days', which often provide the rationale for local, regional, national and international events. The world's events calendar has become filled with worthy causes, such as environmental, social, health and development issues. In May, for example, the United Nations recognises among other days, World Press Freedom Day (8 May), International Day of Families (15 May), World Day for Cultural Diversity for Dialogue and Development (21 May) and World No-Tobacco Day (31 May).

Europe has also witnessed a growth in the number of special events related to 'days' and 'years'. The European Union declared 2008 as the Year of Intercultural Dialogue, and 2009 as the Year of Creativity and Innovation, which stimulated many special events across member states of the EU. It is not uncommon for local authorities to organise events on birthdays of famous local residents. The Weimar ECOC in 1999 decided to celebrate a series of national and city anniversaries: Goethe's 250th birthday, Schiller's 240th birthday, 80 years since the foundation of the Weimar republic and the Bauhaus school, 50 years since the creation of the Federal Republic of Germany and 10 years after the fall of the Berlin Wall.

Rembrandt Year 2006

The Netherlands has a long tradition of using theme years as a means of generating tourism, especially using world famous artists, such as Van Gogh, Rembrandt, Vermeer and Hieronymus Bosch. For the 400th anniversary of the birth of Rembrandt in 2006, a comprehensive event strategy was developed. The event was seen as a good opportunity for Amsterdam, because he lived most of his life in the city.

The aims of the Rembrandt year were to generate extra tourism to Amsterdam and to strengthen its image as a cultural city. The event generated 1.2 million extra visits to Amsterdam, of which over 350,000 were made by foreign tourists. The development of the year was overseen by the Rembrandt 2004 Foundation, a private body whose board includes representatives of major museums. The Foundation worked closely with a committee set up to coordinate the celebrations at national level, which included representatives of the national government, the cities of Amsterdam and Leiden (Rembrandt's birthplace) and the Dutch National Tourist Board. The event included the participation of a number of partners, including sponsorship from Amsterdam Diamonds. A number of musical events were also developed, and means were found to link themes in Rembrandt's painting to culinary events as well.

(Rembrandt 400, 2006)

In Barcelona, the long history of event organisation has generated opportunities to celebrate the anniversaries of earlier events. In 2002, a concert was staged at the Olympic Stadium to celebrate the 10th anniversary of the 1992 Olympics and to launch the 2004 Universal Forum of Cultures. This latter event was itself linked to the 75th anniversary of the World Exhibition held in Barcelona in 1929.

In choosing which events to celebrate, cities need to consider fundamental issues of event concentration and dispersal. Events that are planned close together may help to boost interest and visitor numbers for a period in the year, as a number of cities have done in the run-up to the ECOC for a series of years. However, if every year or every month marks a celebration or follows a particular theme, visitor interest and willingness to travel may begin to wane; a constant stream of events may detract from the impact of each individual one.

Creating rituals

Certain cities have lost touch with older celebrations, the ritual rhythms that used to underpin a cyclical way of life, and many now try to recreate such rituals as a common focus, as a seasonal and social marker and as a means of animating the city. WaterFire (established in 1997) has become an established ritual in Providence, Rhode Island, and the Uitmarkt festival (founded in 1987) 'traditionally' marks the beginning of the new cultural season in Amsterdam. The Catalan 'tradition' of *correfoc* (literally 'fire running') was actually created for the La Merce festival at the end of the 1970s.

A deliberate attempt to create new 'traditions' is being mounted by the city of Rotterdam, as they celebrate the 500th anniversary of the publication of Erasmus' world famous book *In Praise of Folly* in 2011. For the event, the city developed a number of new 'Erasmus traditions', including:

- Night of Erasmus on 11 July (death of Erasmus);

- Day of Erasmus on 28 October (birth of Erasmus); and

- Day of *In Praise of Folly* (1 April).

The years leading to 2011 will be marked by themed years building the Erasmus traditions of the city, with the aim of establishing Erasmus as the 'unique selling proposition' for Rotterdam.

Following other cities

The source of ideas for events in one city may be derived from looking at other cities. In certain cases, events are copied including the names; in others, only some elements of an event are 'borrowed' and then reoriented. Cities which have already staged successful events or event programmes will have developed expertise from which other cities can learn. Edinburgh, with its various successful festivals, is an example of a city that has been a model to others. The approach to the new Manchester International Festival, despite its concentration on original work, was clearly influenced by the Edinburgh International Festival. Birmingham is planning a similar event. The fringe festivals in diverse cities such as Melbourne, Singapore and Vancouver have been modelled after the Edinburgh Fringe Festival.

EVENT DEVELOPMENT STRATEGIES

Event development is now far more structured and organised than it used to be. This is partly driven by necessity, because many events need the financial or logistical support that are offered by public authorities. In many cities, an increasingly crowded event calendar requires the city to coordinate events in order to avoid clashes between events, or to develop events into more powerful attractions for a city. So cities have created event objectives and development strategies, which on the one hand encourage a well-paced organic growth of events, and on the other help manage more effectively the creation of new events and to attract footloose events to a city. Whatever the strategy, it appears that some form of intervention by public bodies is increasingly required to ensure the growth and continuity of eventfulness that goes beyond the individual events in the city event programme.

There are several different strategies for developing events, many of which may be employed concurrently by the same city. These are summarised in Table 2.2.

Table 2.2	Event development strategies
Generic strategies	**Specific strategies**
Growing events	Organic growth
	Harnessing the creative 'life force' of a city
Creating events	Creating new events
	Commissioning artworks as events
Rejuvenation	Rejuvenating existing events
	Rejuvenating tradition
Bidding for events	Footloose recurrent events
	Enticing existing events from other cities
Emulation and copying	Franchising existing events
Meeting political objectives	Determined by political interests

Growing events

Organic growth

Many events start on a relatively small scale and then grow more or less organically. This is arguably the case with most arts festivals, including the Edinburgh International Festival which started after the Second World War as a relatively modest and rather traditional arts festival. Over the past 50 years, new elements have been added to the event, reflecting changing cultural and social circumstances. Only recently has the City of Edinburgh begun to take an active role in developing and marketing the event for economic, tourism and image impacts.

A local disc jockey started the Berlin Love Parade in 1989, after the fall of the Berlin wall. In 1990 it had 2000 participants, growing to 50,000 by 1992 and 300,000 by 1995. As the event grew, the parade route was changed to accommodate greater audiences and participants, which reached a peak of 1.4 million people and over 50 floats by 1999. The city became involved in organising a series of sponsored cultural events around the parade, including art shows, operas, clubs and films (Evans, 2007).

The Notting Hill Carnival in London is an example of a local celebration which first attracted 500 people in 1965, and which has grown to be 'the largest carnival in Europe and second in the world only to the Rio Carnival in Brazil' (Mayor of London, 2004), attracting over 1 million visitors at its peak.

Organic Event Growth in Toronto

The Toronto International Film Festival was founded in 1976, and has grown from a strictly local event organised by a group of Toronto businessmen into one of the primary stops on the international film festival circuit, the North American counterpart of Cannes, Berlin and Venice.

According to Piers Handling, Director since 1994, 'There was no one year when we incrementally grew. It was year-by-year, adding 10 films one year, 10 more the next. There have been no massive leaps, no huge shifts in terms of artistic direction. It's a festival that has valued its continuity and as a result has grown organically. It hasn't had to deal with outsiders. It was all insiders who were promoted into the key jobs, so there was nobody who came in and thought they had to change the whole thing.'

(http://tiffg.ca/)

Harnessing the creative 'life force' of a city

Paul Hoggett (1999) has analysed the way in the 'Bristol Sound' developed in the 1980s from grass-roots creative activity in the club scene to encompass record production and the organisation of international festivals. He links such developments to the creative drive of the voluntary sector, where the primary motivation in terms of music is 'pleasure-seeking'. He cites numerous examples of individual entrepreneurs starting small events from tiny premises and growing them into major international festivals. This growth is helped by the tight social networks connecting bands and performers with their audiences.

Cultural events themselves also provide a fertile breeding ground for creating new events, as Silvanto and Hellman (2005:7) explain in the case of Helsinki:

> *The festivals create a fertile ground for the birth and spread of new ideas, innovations and cross-cultural*

activities. Indeed, the main purpose of the numerous festivals is to provide a meeting forum for actors in their respective fields. And – to quote one of the festival arrangers – festivals tend to create new festivals.

Edinburgh – the Festival as Event Generator

The Edinburgh Festival originated in 1947, when Salzburg, Munich and other pre-war festival centres in Europe were in ruins. The Festival also capitalised on the post-war desire to extend high culture to everyone as a civilising force for good. However:

'It soon emerged that Edinburgh's festival space was a contested terrain, where cultural expression and representation would have to vie for a fragmenting and more youthful audience. The seriousness of the official festival culture was soon challenged by the young, playful and irreverent "Edinburgh Festival Fringe". ... Notorious for anarchic genre-flouting performances, the performers of the early Festival Fringe arrived in the city uninvited, hoping to appear somewhere in the festival's borrowed spaces. As a fringe to the International Festival, it operated unofficially until 1958 when the Festival Fringe Society acquired authorised status.'

(Jamieson, 2004:67)

A number of other festivals have grown up over the years around the International Festival. Most notably, in July and August the Edinburgh Festival Fringe, the Military Tattoo, and book, film, television, jazz and Mela festivals take place, but festival events have now been expanded into other times of the year with the Hogmanay Festival and the Science and Children's festivals.

Creating events

Creating new events

Many cities invent their own major events. The Universal Forum of Cultures was created by the City of Barcelona, as a response to not winning the World Expo or the ECOC title. Culture10 was created by Newcastle Gateshead as a reaction to losing out on the UK ECOC for 2008 (see Chapter 9).

Bloomfield and Bianchini (2003) describe how the Karnivale der Kulturen was created as a new intercultural event

Barcelona's Love Affair with Major Events

Barcelona is in love with the idea of reimaging through events. In fact, the very physiognomy of the city today owes much to the restructuring of whole districts under the auspices of major events. However, as Mayor of Barcelona Joan Clos pointed out in a speech in 2003, both the 1888 and 1929 World's Fairs also coincided with economic crises. A year before the inauguration of the 1888 Fair, the organisation responsible for managing it went into bankruptcy and the Barcelona City Council had to take charge to keep the Fair going. It was only after considerable struggle that the city began to see the wider benefits.

The 1888 Exhibition was used to reconceptualise the Ciutadella area as a high impact solution to serious economic crisis. The 1929 Exhibition was used to recuperate Montjüic area and to physically connect the various parts of the Barcelona metro system. A similar situation was replayed in 1992, when the Olympic Games also landed the city with a hefty bill, but the longer term development of the Olympic facilities and the boost the event gave to tourism helped to dull the memory of the financial cost and considerable physical disruption of the developments needed for the Games.

Joan Clos, Mayor of Barcelona, justified the staging of the Universal Forum of Cultures in 2004 in terms of the success of the Olympic Games. The influx of tourists generated after 1992 created more pressure not only on tourist facilities but also public space. The Forum was therefore partly designed to create more space in the city, both for local residents and visitors.

(Wilson, 2004)

in Berlin in 1993, with mixed results. The festival was held on the streets of Kreuzberg, a mixed area with a healthy network of cultural organisations. It became very popular, attracting an audience of 600,000 Berliners in 2000. However, the event was not fully 'intercultural' in terms of structure, as hybrid forms of music are presented on separate stages organised according to country of origin, and so does not fully capitalise on the unique intercultural nature of the city.

It appears that many cities launch festivals in this spirit of opportunism, and very often with motives linked directly to showcase a featured strength, and with an emphasis on identity building and increased consumption.

Fishing for Events

Catch, The Nova Scotia Seafood Festival, was initiated by the Nova Scotia Ministry of Fisheries and Aquaculture in 2009. Minister Ron Chisholm said 'This is an important new opportunity for our local fisheries to showcase the high quality and variety of seafood products offered in the province. The experience includes learning about seafood and cooking trends while creating a promotional opportunity for seafood companies, retailers and restaurants.'

Such events are now becoming commonplace as places try to link up their cultural and natural assets to support local identities and create new opportunities for economic development.

Commissioning artworks as events

The practice of commissioning artists to create an artwork, which becomes a public event in itself, is becoming more widespread. Commissioning art refers to a process where an artist or group of artists is asked to create an artwork (visual, performed, literary) for a particular situation, place, theme or event. A spectacular example of a commissioned work as an event is WaterFire, created by Barnaby Evans in Providence, Rhode Island. His fire sculpture installation has become a symbol of urban renaissance as a series of 100 bonfires are lit just above the surface of the river, illuminating public spaces from dusk to midnight. Evans has created similar installations for Houston, Tacoma, Columbus, Boston and Kansas.

Christo and Jeanne-Claude, a married couple and renowned artists who work often on large-scale commissions, are best known for their large works of environmental art using fabric to wrap existing structures, including the wrapping of the Reichstag in Berlin and the Pont-Neuf bridge in Paris, the 24-mile-long artwork called 'Running Fence' in Sonoma and Marin counties in California, and 'The Gates' in New York City's Central Park (see Chapter 9). These works are events in themselves, although the artists argue that their projects have a wider meaning beyond their immediate context. Their work is always temporary, and Christo has often stated that 'it takes much greater courage to create things to be gone than to create things that will remain.' Christo insists on total artistic freedom and maintaining control over the aesthetics of his installations.

A community-based example of art commissions, which become events in themselves, is provided by the *Festa Major* of the Gràcia district in Barcelona, where the residents of different streets are partially funded to decorate their streets. The decorations change theme every year, and the streets compete for prizes. The materials used are largely recycled and the production process is largely dependent on a high input of voluntary labour.

In Valencia, Las Fallas, the spectacular fire-based fiesta, is dominated by huge figures and tableau, which are ritually burned on the last night of the event. The figures are increasingly designed and produced by professional artisans who have now created a highly specialised 'creative cluster' on the outskirts of Valencia. The social and artistic history of Las Fallas is now presented in a museum located in the cluster.

Commissioned art generally has most impact as an event when the subject is deeply emotional and when it offers a powerful aesthetic experience. Work from all creative disciplines (visual arts, performed arts, film, etc.) can be commissioned. For certain events, a blueprint may exist from the outset in the form of a theme, and artists are pre-selected and asked to interpret it or submit ideas in reaction to a call for proposals. In other situations, event directors first respond to the original ideas of artists, and the programme then acts as a kind of post-curatorial, interpretative frame. There are some events such as the Venice and Istanbul Art Biennales or the Manchester International Festival that are largely composed of new commissions, and others that incorporate a small number or the occasional presentation of newly commissioned works.

Rejuvenation

Rejuvenating existing events

The inspiration for events can also be drawn from a rein-vention of local tradition (although it should be recognised that many 'traditional' events are themselves relatively recent inventions). In Barcelona, for example, Pablo (1998:33–38) argues that 'we invent tradition every day... only about 15% of the festivals are more than 25 years old. In Gracia and Sants over 70% are less than 15 years old. For Barcelona as a whole, 53.6% of festivals are less than 15 years old. Even so, many of these *festas* are based on traditional elements, which points to the reinvention of old traditions rather than the creation of new ones.' Magliocco (2001:167) has termed this 'festival reclamation'.

When the cultural climate of a city changes, or an existing event shows signs of fatigue, it may be time to rejuvenate or reinvent it. This has happened with many traditional cultural events in Catalunya, for example, where the climate of democracy in the post-Franco era allowed the new local administrations to rediscover Catalan traditions that had been repressed for decades. However, rather than just copying traditional events, contemporary culture was used as a source of inspiration to generate new cultural forms (Crespi-Vallbona & Richards, 2007).

Rejuvenating Traditional Events: Festes de la Mercè

La Mercè is effectively the *Festa Major* of Barcelona. The celebrations to honour Our Lady of Mercy (La Mercè) have their origins in 1868, when the Pope proclaimed La Mercè as the patron saint of Barcelona. The municipality of Barcelona organised the first Festes de la Mercè in 1871, and even at that time the event was dominated by spectacle, notably large-scale firework displays. In 1888 La Mercè was incorpo-rated into the World Exhibition staged in Barcelona.

In this early period of development, the event had a strong commercial element, exhibited through the competitions staged for shop window displays, the exhibitions of food and other commercial products. However, these elements, as well as the traditional and popular cultural content were reduced in the early years of the twentieth century leading up to the Spanish Civil War. In this period religious elements became more important.

During the Franco era La Mercè had a much more subdued tone. Religion continued to be emphasised, while symbols of Catalan identity and culture were either banned or restricted. The event was concentrated in the city centre, in order to increase the level of control that could be exercised over the crowds. The event was also used as a means of promoting tourism, and was declared a Fiesta of National Tourist Interest by the government in Madrid in 1965. There were also attempts to promote the event to foreign tourists, with promotional material being produced in English and French during the 1960s.

The post-Franco democratisation has seen an explosion of cultural expression in events such as La Mercè. Cultural events were used as a means of reclaiming public space and reproducing Catalan identity. In addition to the growth of representations of traditional and popular Catalan culture, contemporary cultural performers, such as Els Comediants, played an important role in the development of La Mercè. The modern festival arguably represents a balance between modernity and tradition, which is reflected in the main elements of the event. These include traditional Catalan cultural elements, fireworks and aerobatic displays; performances of traditional and popular music; activities aimed at children (games, creative activities), and exhibitions and demonstrations.

Today the festival has spread into new areas of the city, taking up an increasing amount of public space and staging a growing number of events. For example, in 1977 only three main spaces were used for the event, but by 2003 there were 24 different sites used in the city. The aim of this spatial dispersion is to reach different groups in the community, increasing access and stimulating cultural integration and social cohesion.

(Richards, 2004)

Another way to rejuvenate and extend the capabilities of events is transforming the events themselves into a focus for other activities. For example, the Luton Centre for Carnival Arts is an example of a space created for events by events. The event spawned the Luton Carnival Arts Development Trust, with 'the simple aim of getting more people involved in the International Luton Carnival' (LCADT, 2007). Over the years they have expanded their vision, raising funding for a dedicated centre for the promotion and development of carnival arts. The UK Centre for Carnival Arts opened in 2008.

> *Embracing the inclusive spirit of the Luton Carnival, the centre will become an expression of the living, breathing and evolving spirit of carnival arts. There will be a performance space, with seating for 250 people, where artists and musicians can showcase their talent. In the teaching and workshop spaces people from all walks of life, united by a love of carnival, will be able to meet and share knowledge and resources. Our staff will also be available to share their wealth of knowledge and encourage best practice in areas ranging from costume making, business skills and music development.*

> (LCADT, 2007)

The Centre for Carnival Arts provides a means of linking events to the city and linking those events in turn to the local community and economy.

Bidding for events

Footloose recurrent events

As mentioned earlier, cities are increasingly developing strategies to attract existing major events, which are 'footloose', circulating regularly between different cities. Well-known examples include the Olympic Games (and the associated Cultural Olympiad) and the ECOC. Recent years have seen the creation of new cultural events for cities to bid for. These include The Universal Forum of Cultures; Euro-Pride, the annual celebration of gay culture in Europe; WOMEX, the exhibition of world music; the UNESCO World Book Capital; the World Design Capital; and the Delphic Games. The advantage of this strategy is that 'winning' the right to stage the event brings with it considerable media attention and an almost guaranteed level of international participation. Even the process of bidding for the event can bring considerable benefits. However, these benefits need to be set against the costs involved in the bidding, the cost of staging such events, the demands made by the international bodies that run them, as well as cost of 'failure' in terms of a city's image if the bid is lost (see Chapter 11). In addition, bidding for different events at the same time can lead to conflicts about priority and financing. In Stockholm, for example, certain politicians were more concerned with the bid for the Olympic Games 2004 than the 1998 ECOC, right up until the decision in September 1997 was taken awarding the Olympics to Athens. The Stockholm ECOC team was disappointed that the event did not receive the same level of political support as the Olympic bid.

Enticing existing events from other cities

When events increase in visitor numbers, profile or importance, they begin to attract the attention of other cities that then decide to entice the organisers of the event to change locations. Events may also outgrow their existing host city or venue, so that the event itself starts seeking new locations. Rotterdam in the Netherlands captured the North Sea Jazz Festival from the Hague, where the event was held for 30 years up to 2005. The reorganisation of public space in the Hague to accommodate the new Europol headquarters and consolidate the 'Hague World Forum' grouping of international institutions led to demolition of the main venue for the event. Although the Hague tried desperately to keep the event by offering temporary solutions, North Sea Jazz eventually decided to move to the Ahoy Centre in Rotterdam. Jazz fans complained bitterly that the intimacy of the Hague venue would be lost in Rotterdam. However, the event moved to a city that had a clearly defined events strategy, and away from one that had prioritised the redesign of public space rather than extending public events. This defection may in itself have been one of the spurs for the Hague to review its own position as a 'festival city', and the creation of an events strategy.

Filling a 'Gap' in the Festival Calendar

Cologne suffered directly from event 'theft' when the Popkomm music fair, the second largest event of its kind in the world, moved to Berlin in 2004. The question for the city was, 'What does Cologne do after

Continued

Popkomm?' The city wanted to fill the gap left by Popkomm, but was unsure how the music clubs and record labels would react. The city didn't want a copy of Popkomm, but decided to develop a smaller event, c/o pop, dedicated to electronic music.

C/o pop Director Philipp Treudt admitted that the Sonar Festival in Barcelona had been an important influence in developing the new event. 'We all went to Barcelona and organised an event there (in the Sonar programme). Obviously, we were interested in learning from the experience of the organisers'. So much so that the organisers have been present at SONAR every year since (http://www.c-o-pop.de/). (González, 2004)

Emulation and copying

Imitation of an event in one city by another was discussed earlier in this chapter, and it can be extremely annoying to see the best event ideas being used by a competitor city. It is not possible to stop the process of other cities copying a successful event idea. One way of transforming emulation into a virtue is by emphasising the value of the 'original' (although most cities are likely to discover that their so-called 'original' events have to some extent also been copied from elsewhere), and using the various copies as a way of promoting the original event.

Copying Carnival?

The Brazilian musician Carlinhos Brown brought carnival to Barcelona for the 2004 Universal Forum of Cultures.

'I have to say that Barcelona will have Barcelona's carnival. Only people as charismatic, as beautiful, as happy as the people of Barcelona will have the miracles of happiness, and that's a feeling that will belong only to the people of Barcelona. We are not creating a Brazilian carnival: Brazil's carnival happens in Brazil. We're not creating a carnival for export; we're creating an encounter to bring different peoples together because, forgive me Barcelona but you're a global city, so there are going to be people from around the world.'

Copying event concepts from other cities sometimes has been encouraged through organising study visits to other cities, and cities setting themselves up as 'models'. Because very few cities or event organisers protect the intellectual property contained in their events, there is little they can do to stop other cities 'borrowing' their ideas. For example, the organisers of the Advanced Music Festival in Manchester openly admit that the inspiration is drawn from the Sonar Festival in Barcelona, although there is no link between these two events. Even when events are copied, the change of context when moving to another location often changes the event itself beyond recognition.

Cachet et al (2003) found that municipalities in the Netherlands increasingly look to each other for event ideas. For example, the Amsterdam Canal Festival was copied by nearby Leiden, which also has historic canals. Interestingly, the event was then also copied by the town of Thorn in Limburg, which has no canals, but which is located on the River Maas. A copy need not cover all aspects of an event, but very often consists of one part of the whole, such as the event concept or a single activity within a programme.

Cynics laughed and automobilists growled when Paris' newly elected Socialist mayor Bertrand Delanoë decided to close the Seine's riverbanks to traffic for six weeks in summer 2002 to set up a temporary *plage* (beach) complete with sand, parasols, lounge chairs, palm trees and grassy picnic spots. This event then became the surprise hit of the summer, as visitors and Parisians who could not get out of town for the annual August exodus enjoyed the laid-back seaside atmosphere. This event costs around €2 million a year to stage, and attracts about four million visits (admission is free). Gale (2009) argues that visitors become performers in this urban spectacle, helping to lure their fellow citizens to enjoy the beach. The success of Paris has been copied by more than 20 cities around the world, including Brussels, Berlin and Budapest. Paris has in turn tried to differentiate its beach by developing different themes such as 'Brazil' in 2005 and 'French Polynesia' in 2006, and by constantly adding new features, such as a floating swimming pool, concerts and a 3 km long picnic.

Copying Other Cities

The study of the different ECOCs clearly showed that there was a tendency for some cities to become the 'models' for others to follow. In particular Glasgow, which in 1990 was the first ECOC to explicitly pursue economic and image development aims through the event, in addition to strong cultural and social objectives, became an important reference point.

In some cases, there is a deliberate attempt to create models for others to follow. This offers advantages in image terms as the city becomes the focus of attention of other cities, and it also creates opportunities to 'sell' expertise on the model to other cities.

The effects of borrowing event ideas from other cities can be clearly seen in the large number of delegations from ECOC host cities that visit other ECOCs (see Chapter 7). It is also evident from the number of cities who cite Glasgow or another ECOC as a model and key source of inspiration. The idea to stage the 2001 ECOC in Rotterdam was developed by city officials on their way back from a visit to the Antwerp ECOC in 1993 (Richards & Wilson, 2004). Antwerp ECOC had in turn been influenced by the success and approach of Glasgow. Lille ECOC 2004 also cited Glasgow as a primary model, and although there was no clear acknowledgement as such, it is apparent that Liverpool ECOC 2008 adopted similar strategies to Glasgow 1990.

For some cities, the creation of event copies may be viewed as a form of promotion for the originating city. A group from Pamplona exported the famous bull-running festival of San Fermin to Shanghai in 2005. This event was supported by San Miguel beer, who were using the global image of San Fermin to sell their beer worldwide – for example by organising a bull-running event in New York for a TV commercial. The Shanghai event was supported by the 250-strong Spanish expat community there.

The Valencian tradition of burning Fallas was recreated in the city of Nottingham in the UK. A group of artists from the city visited the festival in Valencia in order to learn about the construction and eventual cremation of the giant effigies for their own Lumos festival in the winter of 2005–2006. Fallas were also a centrepiece of the Lille 3000 event held in 2006, where the concept was applied to the Indian Diwali Festival (Festival of Lights) to create a spectacular intercultural experience.

Franchising existing events

Event organisers themselves have franchised new editions of existing events, which may simply be in the form of a repetition of an existing event in another location. This might even happen when the name of the festival is closely linked to the event, as in the case of the Hay Literary Festival. In 2006 the Spanish city of Segovia was host to an edition of this festival, which has its home in Hay on Wye in the UK, an example of a town that has built a strong reputation through the branding of a single event, propagating that event and then marketing the city in which it occurs through franchising.

Other events, such as the BREAD & butter fashion show originally based in Berlin, have themselves developed copies in other cities. In 2005 Barcelona hosted a version of the event, which was designed to spread its appeal into Southern European markets. There were arguably benefits for both parties in such an arrangement. The host city could capitalise on the brand value of an existing event:

> BREAD & butter is a strong, internationally acknowledged trademark that expands its activities with a clear goal in mind. This makes BREAD & butter a strong pan-European partner, who caters to and meets the diversified needs and requirements of his (sic) clients.

In turn, the event can build new markets:

> BREAD & butter responds to the diversity of both cultures and markets and thereby respects the differentiation of these markets. While Barcelona targets the Southern European market, Berlin's focus is on Northern Europe.
>
> (BREAD & butter, 2007)

However, this does not always work as planned. The Barcelona edition of BREAD & butter proved so successful that it detracted from the Berlin show. Eventually the organisers decided to move the show back to Berlin in its entirety. Barcelona then created a new event, The Brandery, to fill the resulting gap in the city's fashion event calendar. This underlines the increasing global mobility of events and event concepts between major cities.

Copies, although taking a similar event name, may not have a clear relationship to the originators. For example, the American Capital of Culture event is a copy of the title European ECOC, but is awarded by an organisation that calls itself the 'International Bureau of Cultural Capitals'. The American Capital of Culture title is based on a very different set of principles and processes than the European model. This organisation 'awards' the title in return for an investment by the host city of around $450,000 (€329,000) for marketing costs. The organisation has tried to create something of a growth industry of Capitals of Culture, since it has also established the Brazilian Capital of Culture (www.capitalbrasileiradacultura.org) and the Catalan Capital of Culture (www.ccc.cat).

With so many strategies for creating, rejuvenating or attracting events, the development and initiation of events can become a self-justifying system. A city may be under pressure to support existing events, and at the same time it needs to attract and develop new events to serve new markets and interests. The cultural events sector in particular is subject to the same competitive pressures as is often the case for museums, orchestras and other civic cultural institutions. In one report on festivals in Amsterdam, it was argued that festivals had become just another cultural institution in the city (Amsterdamse Kunstraad, 2003).

Meeting political objectives

Some events are motivated by a political rationale or interest. French Presidents have personally supported *Grands Projets*, and many politicians wish convenient to be associated with cultural or sporting events. In Catalunya, Pascual Maragall enhanced his image as Mayor of Barcelona by facilitating the staging of the 1992 Olympic Games, and in Romania, Klaus Johannis consolidated his political position as Mayor of

Sibiu through the ECOC in 2007 (Chapter 3 provides more examples).

Politicians find events useful for a number of reasons. Most importantly, the relatively short lead times needed to organise certain events means that an administration may be able to commission an event as well as have a reasonable chance of still being in office when the event is held. Events may provide photo opportunities and positive media coverage and attract crowds of people that political figures can impress. Events themselves also attract celebrities, either as performers or as VIPs in the audience, and this in turn may help build the image of a city and its administration.

Events have a range of externalities, which can help to achieve the political goals of a local, regional or national government, including stimulating economic growth, improving place image and developing social cohesion (see Chapter 9). This is an important advantage if events are successful, but if they fail to meet their objectives (or are perceived to fail), they can also become a political liability.

The failure of cities to secure certain events may offer incentives to chase others, or to invent new events themselves. Manchester twice failed in its bid to stage the Olympic Games (in 1996 and 2000), which led to the city hosting the arguably very successful Commonwealth Games in 2002. Berlin also failed to secure the Olympic Games in 2000 and this gave an impetus to the Open City event in Berlin. It is valuable for cities to learn from unsuccessful bids and problematic events, rather than simply forget them.

EVENT SPACES IN THE CITY

As a city creates and stages more events, it needs to develop additional mechanisms for dealing with them and spaces in which to stage them. As events develop, they often expand to fill more space within the city than had originally been conceived. Gotham (2002:313) demonstrates how Mardi Gras has taken up an increasing amount of physical space in New Orleans:

> From 1857 to the late 1930s, there were
> approximately 4–6 krewes that paraded each Mardi

Gras season in New Orleans. The number of parades doubled from 5 in 1930 to 10 in 1940, increased to 15 annual parades in the late 1940s, reached 21 by 1960 and 25 by 1970. Since the 1970s, the number of parades has increased dramatically, reaching 55 in 1986, and peaking at 62 in 2004.

Although events may appear to create their own spaces in the city, the event space is frequently the result of interplay between the production and consumption components of the event and factors relating to the management of public space. As Jamieson (2004) remarks in the case of the Edinburgh festivals:

Although spaces appear as though spontaneously formed by the company of strangers and the collective experience of performances, the city en fête is also the result of painstaking planning by a city administration that seeks to control the ways in which public spaces change. The city is nonetheless redefined by the altered energy and velocity of strategically planned festivalised spaces.

Because events take place in public space, their legitimacy in using that space may be subject to the views of different groups. Since events are generally ephemeral, the argument for the use of space must be made repeatedly. Although a festival may build up such a sense of tradition that it is regarded as a permanent institution in its own right, most events continue to be challenged on the conditions under which they should exist, their financing and their organisation as this relates to the use of space, security and access. The continual discussion surrounding the staging of the Notting Hill Carnival in London is one example. The nature and form of this annual event is questioned every year, usually a few weeks before it is due to take place. Changes are made to the carnival route in order to solve problems of congestion and to reduce crime. Discussions rage about responsibility and payment for activities in the pubic spaces used by the Carnival, usually a four-cornered argument between the local council, the Greater London Authority, the Police and the Carnival organisers.

A further dimension of the argument about the occupation of event space concerns the nature of the cultural content of the event. Certain cultural events, such as particular types of refined arts festivals, may rely on support from committed elites of enthusiasts, usually from within the cultural sector, and outsiders are often unable to understand the justification for public support for an event that appeals to minority interests. In other cases, traditional events that focus primarily on popular culture may not be supported strongly by cultural elites whose interests focus primarily on modern or contemporary culture.

There is increasing recognition of the legitimate use of cultural space by events. For example, the recent designation of selected 'cultural spaces' as components of intangible heritage by UNESCO (2007) states:

> In proclaiming masterpieces of the oral and intangible
> heritage of humanity, UNESCO seeks to draw
> attention to cultural spaces or traditional and popular
> forms of cultural expression. We have to be quite clear
> about the difference between a cultural space and
> a site. From the standpoint of the cultural heritage,
> a site is a place at which physical remains created by
> human genius (monuments or ruins) are to be found.
> A 'cultural space' is an anthropological concept that
> refers to a place or a series of places at which a form of
> traditional or popular cultural expression occurs on
> a regular basis.

The concept of a cultural space can be applied to locations that regularly host events and which might be considered part of the intangible heritage of a city. A number of cities are now trying to obtain intangible cultural heritage designations by UNESCO for their events, and the number of submissions for events grew from 32 in 2001 to 100 in 2009. By 2009, about 90 'masterpieces' had been inscribed in the UNESCO list of intangible heritage. Successful designations include the 600 year-old Patum in Berga (Catalunya), the traditional procession of giants and dragons in Belgian towns (Ath, Brussels, Dendermonde, Mechelen and Mons) and French towns (Cassel, Douai, Pézenas and Tarascon), and the Gangneung Danoje Festival in Korea.

The physical development and investment in public space has become a major element of the event infrastructure of a city, most notably in cities designated as ECOC. During the ECOC in Thessaloniki in 1997, 23% of the total budget was allocated to the development of public spaces. Liverpool's developments for the 2008 ECOC included the Paradise Street Project, a retail-led quarter which includes a two-hectare park, at a cost of £920 million (€1066 million).

The cultural spaces created by and for events are generally influenced by urban planning strategies, particularly in relation to the built environment. Gospodini (2001) argues that as modern structures have become increasingly globalised and standardised, what cities need is the development of 'counter structures' to 'placeless' development. Liveliness is dependent on the expansion of simultaneous development of space and 'low syntactic depth'. Events are an ideal vehicle for this, as their open structure encourages a more playful relationship between people, places and meaning.

To create such a positive relationship, spaces need to be animated or programmed, and the style of animation needs to be defined by the spaces in which it occurs. Space is not just a bare stage on which any events happen, but also provide the rationale for events happening in that space at a particular time.

THE DIALECTIC OF CITIES AND EVENT SPACES

Events can be defined by the spaces in which they take place, but can in turn come to redefine those spaces. This relationship has been studied in some detail by a research team from the Massachusetts Institute of Technology (MIT) and the Polytechnic University of Catalunya (UPC) (Sabaté i Bel et al., 2004).

The Palio in Sienna is one of the world's great traditional events, first staged in 1310. The event is held in the centre of the medieval city of Sienna in the Piazza del Campo. The square has a radiating paving pattern constructed to symbolise the power of the city's medieval rulers. In spite of more modern fashions for the construction of fountains or the placing of monuments, the Palio horse race has ensured that the Piazza remains bare and local people and tourists alike sit and lie down as if the Piazza really were a field. Cities make events; some cities are made by events. In the past, this was basically an organic process, but in modern cities it is often the result of planning.

Bernard Tschumi (1994, 2001) demonstrates how architecture and urban planning can help develop events, which then redefine urban realities. The architectural forms of public spaces, venues and arenas can either accelerate or interfere with the development of the notion of cities as event spaces.

Cities are natural locations for special events, where large numbers of people are in close proximity and where accessible transport, accommodation for visitors, linkages with communication systems and the media are readily available. Cities include public spaces where people can come together to share in events, and those spaces are in turn shaped by the live experiences of the public who gather there.

In cities with long traditions of cultural production and consumption, there are well-developed 'consumers' of culture. In cities without such histories, new publics may have to be developed, such as case of the ECOC in Porto, Portugal:

> *Although Porto has always had an active cultural life as a bourgeois, commercial city, people have not been so interested in the arts. In general, Porto was a place where cultural components from other countries were displayed, and the city never developed a real culture core. The city had an image of being hard working, and people had little time to dedicate themselves to culture.*
>
> *Perhaps because of this, the city has always found it difficult to create spaces for cultural events or to develop audiences. One of the main aims of Porto ECOC 2001 was therefore to create new audiences and to attract people to the city. In this way, cultural*

events could become a natural part of the city, and not ephemeral events.
(Antonio Alves da Silva, pers. comm., 2002)

Not surprisingly, space has become one of the major issues in event development. Without appropriate event spaces in the city, it is difficult to stage large-scale events. As Sharon Zukin (1995) has noted, the creation of more spaces for cultural display and performance has been an important issue in cities in recent decades, as cities have sought to capitalise on the 'real cultural capital' of the built environment.

Over the past 20 years, the building and design of new spaces for the consumption of cultural experiences have become the basis of many urban regeneration programmes in cities. As urban areas increasingly lose their status as centres of production, regeneration programmes that offer opportunities for new forms of consumption based economic activity are perceived to be a relatively simple, quick and uncomplicated solution to emerging problems.

According to the Project for Public Spaces (2007), 'what makes a successful place' is accessibility, comfort, sociability and activities. In terms of activities, 'having something to do gives people a reason to come to a place – and return. When there is nothing to do, a space will be empty and that generally means that something is wrong. The more activities there are, the better the mix of people (in terms of gender, age, singles and groups), the more those activities are spread throughout the day, the better.'

Cities are increasingly trying to plan for the development of 'successful places' that act as homes to events. For example, Montreal's Quartier des Spectacles is an attempt to create a new 'cultural heart' for the city, 'where residents, artists, students, business people and festival goers coexist in harmony to create a hub of artistic creation, innovation, production, exhibition and broadcast.' It has 25 event venues of varying sizes designed to host local, national and international events (Quartier des Spectacles, 2007). The Quartier des Spectacles is viewed and managed as a coordinated space, with a partnership between 25 stakeholders, including representatives of the culture, real estate, education, and business sectors, local residents, the Borough of Ville-Marie, the City of Montreal and the Government of Quebec.

The area is also viewed as developing cultural vibrancy for the city:

> *Visitors first experience the Quartier des Spectacles by exploring its vibrant streets. With their ground-level storefronts, predominantly cultural establishments, each street is a window to the varied worlds of culture.*

And it provides:

> *A coherent and complete neighbourhood, connected to its neighbors. Streets of the Quartier des Spectacles keep a special rhythm that makes it easy to follow a lively route from one place to the next.*
>
> (Quartier des Spectacles, 2007)

There are many cities that clearly have major shortcomings as event locations, including lack of space, problems of security and troubles with traffic congestion, and the absence of convenient public transportation. Event spaces need to be managed to attract, animate and entertain people, but also to ensure safety, not disrupt mobility, promote accessibility and avoid conflict. These issues are dealt with in more detail in Chapter 5.

The development of the eventful city takes on logic of its own as the city develops and redevelops its spaces. However, events are not solely created to fill spaces, but most often as part of wider processes of city making.

URBAN REDEVELOPMENT

Events are increasingly being linked to the spatial development of the city; they provide an incentive for physical regeneration of areas of the city and regeneration itself in turn provides an inspiration for events.

Events make a very direct contribution to redevelopment through the upgrading and rehabilitation of spaces in the city. This was a major reason for the creation of 'garden festivals' in Germany after the Second World War. The festivals inhabited areas affected by bombing and helped to create green spaces in the place of dereliction. There was also an important cultural component to the festivals, designed to recreate the sense of community, which had also suffered during the war.

The original philosophy of garden festivals was changed when the British took up the idea in the 1980s:

> *It has been suggested that Garden Festivals were constructed more as political and ideological devices, rather than cultural celebrations. With their emphasis on regeneration and revitalisation of deindustrialised landscapes, they served to encourage these areas into a new, entrepreneurial way of thinking and acting, while presenting the archetypal image of a 'united, green and pleasant land'.*
>
> (Davies & Russell, 2001)

Rotterdam – Post-war Cultural Development

In its long trajectory of post-war development, Rotterdam adopted an event-based strategy to tourism generation, but unlike Barcelona it does not have the physical advantages of climate or an attractive coastal environment. Events have therefore arguably been even more important in generating tourism.

The city positioned cultural policy at the forefront of urban development and invested heavily in cultural facilities. However, the city also reduced its operational budget for culture at the same time in order to promote private sector involvement. Culture and the arts were essential contributors to a new urban élan aimed at improving the urban quality of life. Rotterdam's cultural policy in the 1990s had four basic priorities.

Firstly, stimulating the international character of the city; secondly, developing a wide ranging and high quality package of urban cultural facilities; thirdly, providing opportunities for renewal and experiment and fourthly, diminishing the dependence on public financing, encouraging greater independence for institutions and increasing audience support. For Rotterdam, cultural events and festivals were ideal to meet the four objectives of the new cultural policy. Their programming is typically international: they improve the cultural infrastructure, they provide opportunities for artistic renewal and experiment and they do not depend solely on public financing since they draw a large audience and business sponsors (Hitters, 2000).

The city therefore embarked on a policy of developing arts festivals and leisure events in the 1990s, which made use of the new creative spaces in the city. Such developments were marked by an entrepreneurial approach to the arts and leisure, which included the establishment of a 'leisure industries' department of the city government and the staging of privately managed publicly funded events. This strategy was arguably very successful in attracting visitors to the city, which saw a threefold increase in event visitation between 1993 and 1998 and a further doubling between 1998 and 2005.

The overall aim was to replace the image of a harbour city with that of an active cultural and leisure city. By making the city more attractive to residents, visitors and investors, it was hoped to generate economic activity and employment and to improve the quality of life in the city. It was realised that Rotterdam would need to develop both physical and intangible aspects of its image – physical development and events were both important aspects.

An interesting example of the use of regeneration projects to develop events is found in Berlin, where the *Schaustelle Berlin* (Showplace Berlin) event was launched by the public-private partnership Partner für Berlin. After the fall of the Berlin Wall in 1989, the centre of the city became 'the largest building site in Europe'. Schaustelle Berlin was launched in 1996 to give the public a glimpse behind the scenes, turning the daily nuisance of construction into a visitor attraction. The event was an instant success, and ran for 10 years before closing its last edition in 2005 with 140,000 visitors over 10 days (www.schaustelle.de). The project taught Berliners how to understand better their new city and appreciate the visual art of a skyline filled with cranes (lit at night during the event) (Häussermann & Colomb, 2003).

CONCLUSION

Cities are creating a growing number of events to help them achieve a wide range of cultural, social and economic aims. Events are created and developed in many different ways. They may be the ideas of individuals with a particular cultural interest or obsession, but if successful these events can end up dominating the cultural life of a city.

Cities provide the space for events and in turn become shaped by those events. Successful eventful cities tend to be those that have used their events not only to create physical space, but also fill those spaces with vibrant social and cultural interaction.

Many cities are undergoing pressure to create, house and support events of all types. This is leading to an increasing range of strategies to develop new events or to rejuvenate existing ones. Cities are not only looking at their own cultural heritage as a source of events (for example in the celebration of significant anniversaries), but also they are increasingly competing with other cities for the chance to stage 'footloose' events and copying event concepts from other places. There is a proliferation of music festivals, film festivals, carnivals, melas and other event models around the world, as well as extensive rejuvenation of traditional events. The most successful cities are those that use these events as a bridge between local and globalised culture and between traditional and contemporary culture.

However, creating successful events and ensuring that these contribute to the wider vision of the city also requires organisation and direction, and so an increasing number of cities have specialised events units to lead and manage their eventfulness (see Chapter 5).

CHAPTER 3

Event Vision and Programming

Events can be viewed as repetitive structures. An international arts festival, a cultural Olympiad, a parade or world music weekends often follow similar patterns. The events industry has created its standard formats, which may compete with each other in terms of marketing reach and impact. That competition is often based on famous names, event 'brands' or the scale of the event. This means that the distinction between one event and another and between cities that host and manage events often rests on the choice and content of the event programme. Programming refers to the approach to the selection of various projects, activities or elements that make up an event and to the reasoning behind the choices that are made.

The programme is important because this is what the public sees and experiences. The programme offers evidence of the realisation of an event's vision and mission, and the effectiveness of its strategic approach. The programme is the vehicle that promotes public participation, on which the financial forecasts are based and which offers incentives to those who finance or support the event. Most of those involved in the ECOC (European Capital of Culture) believed that the programme was crucial to the success of the whole exercise (Palmer-Rae, 2004), and similar views are likely to be expressed for most events. The programme of an event needs to capture the imagination of the public, professionals and the media. An event that fails to engage its publics or to generate sufficient attendance is likely to meet financial problems that can transform into disaster (Palmer-Rae, 2004). On the other hand, events should not automatically aim to provide 'something for everybody' in the programme, a tactic that sometimes runs the risk of lowering quality and diluting the impact of an event. In programming events for the city as a whole, however, there is often a need for a multi-layered approach to ensure that there is a focus for the different target groups the city wants to serve (see Chapter 8).

The choice of programme matters both for single events and for the whole series of events held in a city. Some cities integrate events into their cultural planning, knowing that the combined impact of event programmes can contribute to building a consistent brand image. The growth of the experience economy and city competitiveness has also led to a heightened awareness of the role of the city as a stage or backdrop for events. As Chapter 2 noted, many cities have enhanced their roles as promoters of events by not only supporting events financially, but also by coordinating events on a citywide basis. The notion of 'city programming' in the eventful city reflects the management or coordination of activities and experiences across the city as a whole. City programming as an approach is not centralised planning, which can stifle spontaneity and dynamism; nor does it advocate homogenisation and control of creative development, which by its very nature may be anarchic and unpredictable. City programming emphasises an approach that encourages coordination, synchronisation, the avoidance of duplication, and synergies between stakeholders and partners.

Practitioners are increasingly applying the term 'curation' to the function of programme development. Programming, though its association with writing computer language may have overtones that reflect a kind of mechanical act. Curation (adapted from the world of exhibitions and galleries) conveys a more subtle development of interrelationships between activities, people and concepts. Some directors talk about 'curating a festival' and discussions among urban cultural policy makers can refer to 'curating the eventful city'.

Curating the City

The curation approach to city programming is exemplified in the project 'Curating the City: Wilshire Boulevard', which aims to illustrate the cultural heritage of Los Angeles (L.A.) through a series of events and attractions linked by this famous thoroughfare. The project was launched in October 2005 with an architectural tour of six historic sites on the boulevard linked with a series of other events: youth workshops; the TarFest: Festival of Film, Music and Art and a self-guided architectural tour available in English, Spanish and Korean. The events continued in 2006 with *L.A. Koreatown: A Celebration of Continuity and Change*, an exhibition tracing the history of the Korean community in L.A. from its beginnings on Bunker Hill to the creation of 'Koreatown'. (http://www.curatingthecity.org/).

Although there are common approaches and structures, there is no science of event programming or curation in the context of an eventful city. The first step is to ensure that there is a clear vision for the eventful city. Without this, it is difficult to even start the programming process, and events that do not have clarity of vision are the ones that appear most often to fail in terms of public engagement.

CREATING A PROGRAMME VISION

The event programme itself provides the tangible evidence of a vision. A programme vision is a statement of the central idea behind the programme of activities for an event. For example, Gerard Mortier, when appointed Director of the established Salzburg Festspiele in 1991, executed a new programming vision based around a central idea of challenging renowned artists and producers. He used the provocation of his programme choices to give the festival a second life – a tactic that seemed to work, given the increase in spectators at the event during his tenure.

Gerard Mortier made it his task to overcome the stagnation that had become evident especially in the last years of the Karajan era. 'The New Salzburg' that he proclaimed followed a policy of opening up the festival to a broader and modern repertoire to unfamiliar, and occasionally also provocative views as regards aesthetics to different and younger generations of audiences (Salzburg Festival, 2007).

But Salzburg went back to its roots when Mortier moved on to direct the Ruhr Triennale, staging events against the backdrop of old industrial buildings in the region that is ECOC in 2010 (Loney, 2001). During the Mortier period, the new programming vision for Salzburg seemed to have worked, at least in terms of visitor numbers. Attendances rose from 204,700 in 2005 to 244,000 in 2006, with seat occupancy of over 95%. Tourist numbers (and particularly foreign tourists) have also increased in the city since 2001. This seems to indicate that it is not only the content of the vision that matters, but also its clarity and its effective transmission to the target audience.

A programme vision is created for its own time and under the conditions that are right to achieve it. When the conditions change, the vision may no longer be successful as a force behind the programme, and the vision and the programme may need to change. This is a vital aspect of the sustainability not just for individual events, but also for the whole event programme of a city (see Chapter 10).

For example, the Directors of two successive festivals in Los Angeles each managed one version of very different programming visions for the same festival. Robert Fitzpatrick's programme vision for the LA Festival in 1984 (with the impetus of the Summer Olympics behind it) was to bring together the best of the known creators of European theatre to be in the same place at the same time. This was only possible with the funding and sponsorship opportunities that the Olympics offered; the experience could not be repeated again. In 1990 and 1993, Peter Sellars, as Director of the next version of the LA Festival, brought a distinctly different programme vision by focusing only on work from the Pacific Rim, and restaged art, which might otherwise have been treated as ethnographic, varying from Japanese court dances to gospel choirs; 50 cultures were represented. Sellar's vision aimed to show inhabitants of LA their own city, with people being seduced into visiting neighbourhoods of the city that they had never visited. Many have tried to duplicate the vision of Peter Sellars in L.A.; all have failed. At best, copying offers a pale and uninspired version of the original and deprives the event or a city of the opportunity to create something special that relates uniquely to its own time, space, history and identity (see Chapter 2).

The Rotterdam ECOC in 2001 had more success with the development of arts programmes related to different neighbourhoods, linking with the theme 'Rotterdam is many cities.' The programme emphasised small-scale, creative activities such as Preaching in Another Man's Parish, which involved ministers of different faiths preaching in each other's churches (Richards and Wilson, 2004). Similarly, Frei Leysen founded the Kunstenfestivaldesarts in Brussels in 1994 with a programming vision of a bipolar festival for all inhabitants of Brussels. The central idea of establishing an event for all communities challenged cultural policies in a city of the two main linguistic communities, French and Flemish. The vision was one of 'a cosmopolitan city festival', based on the assumption that cities like Brussels are increasingly becoming part of a complex network of communities that cross and redefine national, linguistic and cultural borders. 'The city is the environment par excellence in which this cosmopolitan society can be seen' (Kunstenfestivaldesarts, 2008). In spite of continuing linguistic tensions and problems of persuading governments to allocate subsidies to an intercultural approach, the public responded well to this vision and the festival continues to survive.

The small Oerol Festival on the small island of Terschelling in the northern Netherlands was created with a vision that focused on the presentation of site-specific outdoor performance, not only for local inhabitants but also to help develop the tourist industry. The programme concept combined an exciting artistic experience with a sense of fun (adding a different kind of colour to the natural landscape). Because of its success, an evergrowing number of families schedule their annual camping holiday in Terschelling during the festival. In 2007 there were 50,000 festivalgoers on the island during the 10-day event who bought 95,000 tickets. The pressure of tourism on the artistic programme means that the Oerol Festival has to constantly seek new programming ideas to maintain its creative edge. In 2008 the festival theme of time and space was underpinned by a unique temporal experience: the clocks on the island were turned back 2 h to Greenwich Mean Time, which had been used on the island at the beginning of the nineteenth century.

Festivals in Eastern Europe were once known for their unique qualities because of the intensity of the local experience offered to inhabitants suffering under communist regimes. The programmes offered platforms for new ideas and visions of hope. Many of these festivals have been transformed with aspirations to be world famous and attract large numbers of visitors, and in doing so are becoming similar to festivals everywhere (Puczkó and Rátz, 2001). Examples are the Exit Festival in Novi Sad, Serbia and the Hradhouse Festival in Boskovice, Moravia. A new breed of young Directors have emerged with new concepts and fresh ideas, but are finding it hard to establish themselves in a climate in which festivals are introducing more competitive and sometimes expensive international programming.

Programming International Festivals – the Budapest Case

The Budapest Spring Festival (BSF) was first staged in March 1981, aimed at attracting international audiences to generate much-needed foreign currency. The programme of the Festival was based on three major elements as follows:

- The BSF would become the first international cultural event in the European festival season.

- The Hungarian organising team created an eclectic programme including different arts, sport and gastronomic events and congresses, but with classical music as the central theme.

- Bringing Hungarian culture (mainly music) into the limelight.

The budget of the BSF was rather limited, so the organisers decided to invite world famous Hungarian artists living abroad to participate. In the first year, Béla Bartók was chosen as the theme, as that year was the 100th anniversary of Béla Bartók's birth; this timing made a favourable contribution to the marketing activities. The name of Bartók led to better international recognition of the BSF.

The Festival was initially successful, leading to full hotels and restaurants in Budapest. Unfortunately after the political changes in 1989–1990, changes in the organisational structure of the festival led to programming and financial problems. The festival was relaunched in 1997 with new aims as follows:

- introducing many facets of the Hungarian cultural life, create interest towards domestic tourist sites and quality artistic events both in Hungary and abroad;
- stimulating new performances and products/works;
- increasing awareness about Hungarian artists;
- increasing the hotel occupancy rates before the main season;
- generating more foreign exchange by selling tourist services and cultural programmes; and
- enhancing the cultural touristic image of Hungary.

In recent years the cultural aims of the festival have become more explicit in its programme vision, which is now based on a two-way flow of culture between Hungary and the rest of the world. The hope of Festival Director Zsófia Zimányi is not just that the Sao Paulo Symphony Orchestra will perform Bartók in Budapest during the festival, but that they will take his work back to Brazil.

A programme vision therefore is a form of mission statement for an eventful city. Although the vision of each event may be unique and will depend on a range of contextual factors, there are a number of key questions that should be asked in order to arrive at an effective vision statement for each event and for an eventful city as a whole. Some of the key questions that need to be addressed are as follows:

1. What is our core business? (Who are our stakeholders?)

2. What is our special competence? (What can we do better than other cities?)

3. What is our unique position? (Who are our competitors?)

4. What are the needs of our stakeholders? (How will we serve them?)

5. What do we want to achieve in the future? (Where will our eventfulness come from?)

Although the vision and the resulting events programme should link together the interests of the city, its events and their stakeholders, the programme vision also needs to consider the concept of artistic risk.

Artistic risks

In a globalising world with greater competition for audience attention and resources, it is perhaps not surprising that many cities are accused of 'safe' programming that is generally risk free or risk averse. London has seen a rising tide of musicals aimed at a mass audience and particularly at tourists who may find musicals more accessible. The Edinburgh International Festival and many other large-scale arts festivals have at various points of their histories focused their programmes on more popular 'tribute' shows, with re-creations of works by famous performers. Such productions arguably increase the accessibility of culture by using recognisable cultural icons and instant recognition with the audience, and so reduce the risk of failure.

Certain strategies may appeal to directors and organisers of events, but the public evaluates what they see, and not the process that leads to create or produce the work. Many artistic directors understand the importance of processes that encourage artistic innovation. Risk taking is one element of a process for certain events. The artistic director of this kind of event takes risks, but also understands the concept behind the awaited end-result, and tries to minimise the risk by building strong relationships with the artists and between artists and audiences. This means that by being involved in the production process, identifying and locating the resources that are required to produce the work and taking decisions that balance the artistic needs with other factors such as public expectation and financial realities, the risks can be reduced. Unexpected results along the way require action, varying from postponing or cancelling performances that are not yet ready to present to the public, or where artistic ambitions do not match with financial realities, to rethinking the strategies for marketing to enable the production to succeed. The objective is frequently to safeguard the event so that those creative risks can continue to be taken in future without raising the spectre of past failure.

Brett Sheehy, Director of the Adelaide Bank Festival remarked that:

> *It's partly instinct in curating a program but much of it is in the lap of the gods – the gods being the artists themselves. I have said frequently that I am not keen on theming festivals and imposing that kind of straitjacket on the visions of individual artists and companies. I'd much rather let it grow organically and be as surprised as the audience with what ends up.*
> (Adelaide Review, 2006)

The London International Festival of Theatre (LIFT), which was created in 1980 by Rose Fenton and Lucy Neal as a biennale festival to bring challenging international contemporary productions to local communities in London, was a risky journey not only in artistic terms, but also for the faithful LIFT audience. In the event, the gamble paid off, and the productions received a warm welcome in 'tough' neighbourhoods (Klaic et al., 2004). In many such festivals this means creating room for more avant garde style productions, such as a 'play' performed to an 'audience' of two people in a pub, or to an audience of six people in a hotel room. Without events that push artistic boundaries, it is difficult to develop contemporary events and create new 'products', which eventually may also appeal to wider audiences. When speaking to directors and organisers, especially of risk-taking events of an artistic nature, the notion of breaking with tradition is often central. In other events, especially those where artistic development is not a central objective, the reverse sentiment is frequently very strong: to take few risks, to focus only on public demand and to adopt an entirely market-led approach. There are significant differences between events that aim to be 'market leaders' and those that aim to meet the interests of a predetermined stable market. Invariably, each group of events or festival organisers is sometimes critical of the other, and the 'leader' versus 'led' approach can become the core of the debate between event directors and their funders or between event organisers and their audiences and critics. The strategy of an eventful city needs to address and reconcile diverse approaches.

Sydney: An Artless Festival?

A critique of the 2008 Sydney Festival observed that 'the word "arts" is nowhere to be found in its title, so no reason for us to expect a collection of high-minded fare. In this heat and humidity it's hardly the season for it anyhow. But is the Sydney Festival doing its job? The event is certainly putting lots of bums on seats – and dollars in the coffers. And crowds were wowed by "the three Bs": Bjork, Brian Wilson and Black Watch. But beyond that, some sober souls question whether there isn't room for something more enduring (Hallet and Lawson, 2008). These critics went on to ask whether 'Sydney Festival sees itself simply as a "grab-bag of ideas from Edinburgh crossed with a version of Womad?"'

Another critic observed that 'We expect hits and misses at any festival but all except one of (the events reviewed) by Hallett and Lawson as the event's greatest successes had already proven their worth elsewhere. *Black Watch* wowed audiences and critics alike at the Edinburgh Festival, with The Guardian's Michael Billington calling it "a landmark in modern Scottish theatre". Both Brian Wilson and Bjork have toured before and easily managed to fill houses under their own steam. La Clique was a repeat outing after its sell-out success at the festival last year. And Sydney has become almost an annual stopover on the rightly acclaimed James Thierree's calendar.

Or what? If a big, profitable festival like ours can't afford to take a risk any more, who can?' (Dobney, 2008).

DEVELOPING THE CITY EVENT PROGRAMME

Although many event directors believe that programme planning is more alchemy than science, patterns emerge; there clearly are significant overlaps in the approaches and programmes of events in different cities. The headline acts for rock festivals are virtually the same the world over, and even the pyrotechnic displays that open and close many major events are developed by a small number of international specialist companies. For example, the Valencian company that produced the firework display to close the Barcelona Universal Forum of Cultures in 2004 also closed the same event in Monterrey in Mexico in 2007. There is always room for individual directors to assert their personal tastes and special relationships with particular artists, but this takes boldness. Easy choices can be made making connections to increasingly well-organised global event markets that focus on the buying and selling of event programmes; several events are now programmed entirely in this way. Cannes not only has the long-established film festival, but also the MIDEM exhibition, a professional event that attracts 10,000 music professionals to the city to do business. Essentially a trade show, it also includes many live performances featuring established stars as well as showcases for new talent promoted by agents actively selling the same programmes to event organisers from different cities.

Often there is a degree of convergence in programmes and programming styles because organisers the world over are subject to many of the same factors that influence their programming decisions. These include the following:

- mission and objectives of the event programme;

- the main programme concept;

- target publics to be served and their expectations, including special publics (children, minority groups, people with disabilities, particular tastes and interests, foreign tourists, domestic tourists, etc.);

- role of the event organisation in developing the programme;

- relationship to existing local cultural provision (ideally to enhance or supplement but not duplicate the local offer);

- balance sought between local, national and international works;

- balance sought between different categories of production: traditional/experimental, existing/new, star names/emerging talent, own productions/co-productions/received productions;

- ability to market and communicate effectively (including factors such as reputation of artists and likely media response);

- timing and dates of the events;

- availability and quality of work on offer;

- facilities and event spaces to be used for presentation;

- financial resources, expectations and conditions of bodies providing the finance;

- ability to recoup or amortise costs through cost-sharing, co-production or touring and pricing/price resistance;

- technical resources and meeting special conditions;

- opportunities to extend the impact of the programme (through educational activity, touring, residencies, contribution to local policies such as social inclusion);

- other special factors (relationship to a theme or anniversary, special relationships, historical connections, etc.); and

- balancing risks with safe choices.

This is quite a formidable list of factors to consider, and unfortunately no easy formulas or computer programs exist to guide decision making. The weight given to different factors will depend on circumstances and the particular interests of organisers and sponsors in each city. The complexity of the task is echoed in comments from organisers themselves:

We sometimes make lists of the criteria we use to help guide the selection. This is a kind of aide memoire *and offers a guide to the entire team of why we take the decisions we do. Our Board and the city council like to see the rationale behind each choice. But in the end, after all the balancing, just 'feeling right' about doing something becomes a key factor – the jargon calls it* the truth of the right side of the brain.

(Unpublished interview with festival organiser,
Palmer, 2004)

Programming dimensions and styles

So, the approach to event programme planning is kaleidoscopic; there are many different possibilities and many choices to consider. Event organisers make choices of programme based on the many factors identified earlier. What follows is a categorisation of some of the more common dimensions or factors that are taken into account when defining a programme, and that help distinguish one event programme from another.

Programme defined as producing or receiving

There are events that mainly *produce*, such as when an event director commissions (often in collaboration with partners) artistic work. The Salzburg Festival, the Avignon Festival and the Adelaide Festival invite artists (producers, directors, choreographers, designers, writers, composers) to create original theatre, opera and dance productions of new or existing work and cover all or a proportion of the cost. In exchange, they often insist on an element of exclusivity (for example, the first run of performances) and sometimes a share of income derived from the production for a certain period of time in the future. The same is true for the visual arts (such as the Venice Biennale and Documenta). The level and scale on which events originate work by commissioning or producing are determined by an event's objectives, the public it serves and its financing. The Manchester International Festival, staged for the first time in 2007, positioned itself as the first major UK festival that comprises solely commissioned work. In this case, the high level of originality is used as a means of distinguishing itself from its competitors, notably the Edinburgh International Festival.

Other events mainly *receive* work; the event invites artists and companies with ready-made performances, exhibitions and activities, and presents them as part of its event programme. There is no investment by the organisers in the origination costs of the production; a financial fee or guarantee is offered to the producers, organisers, artists or companies themselves directly or through agents or distributors. Popular music events and film and literature festivals regularly follow such patterns. Often the agents of most popular artists organise appearances one after the other in the form of a tour to events that *receive*, leading to event programmes that are almost identical.

An adaptation of the receiving role occurs when event directors or organisers leave the choices of the programme entirely to the owners or managers of facilities and spaces where work is presented, or artists and companies themselves who rent spaces at entirely their own risk to perform or exhibit. The event director may provide assistance in locating appropriate spaces or companies, and sometimes helps with financing, marketing and ticketing, or logistics and technical requirements. The event organisers, however, do not decide what is finally presented and seen by the public, and take no financial risk. The programme, in a sense, becomes self-selecting. The event organisers may set criteria for the inclusion of activities in an omnibus catalogue or brochure, and thereby shape the resulting programme to a certain degree, but they do not actively select components of the programme. The Edinburgh Fringe Festival, the Toronto First Night Festival and the Bumbershoot Festival in Seattle are examples of such events. This kind of 'wrap around' programming for festivals is becoming more common; taking everything that is happening anyway in a city and packaging it in some way. Rotterdam does this with its Summer Festivals, bringing together the main events in the city, such as the Summer Carnival, the Dunya Festival and World Harbour Day. Other events may link together single performances with no coherent theme or concept and package them in marketing terms as a single festival (such as the Alive 2005 festival in the North East of England, which collected many existing festivals into a regional programme).

Programme defined by roles of organisers

In developing an event programme, organisers adopt different relational roles to others with whom they work. For simplicity, these might be categorised as follows:

- As *architects*: The director, other specialists or committees take responsibility for the concept, designing the programme and selecting its components. The image and shape of the event are determined internally, and all key decisions are centralised. Darmawan et al. (2005) indicate that many of the major festivals staged in East Asia are programmed in this way.

- As *facilitators*: The event organiser works closely with others on a collaborative basis to develop the concept and design the programme. Resources are shared between the partners and the programme is developed as a joint venture.

- As *engineers*: The programme is originated, developed and financed by others outside the organisation, and the event organisers take the responsibility to deliver the programme in terms of technical and financial resources.

- As *contractors*: The programme and other elements of delivery are subcontracted entirely to other groups, organisations or individuals who are expected to follow a brief or set of guidelines provided by the event organisers. For example, the Rotterdam Summer Festivals are run by Ducos, a cultural events and production company (www.ducos.com).

Combining Roles

Many individual event programmes combine these different roles, and the programme for the eventful city will certainly include examples of each model. This combination of programming styles is evident when examining the programmes of the ECOC events. Although all the cities produced projects themselves, some were much more involved than others as architects of production. In the year 2000 in Helsinki, the staff of the Capital of Culture Foundation were given the specific role of acting

Continued

as facilitators and developers of ideas coming from the outside and were not themselves generators of ideas. Bergen and Reykjavik ECOC both followed the Helsinki approach. In Bologna ECOC, a decision made to support local producers meant that the organisation initiated only 27 projects (and produced 20 of these themselves) out of a total of approximately 550 projects. In Krakow the Cultural Capital bureau produced 10% of the programme's projects, and in Brussels ECOC ideas from the artistic director were combined with those from other organisations (Palmer-Rae, 2004). For the ECOC in Luxemburg in 2007, venues directly managed by the ECOC organisation housed events dedicated to young audiences, an important target group for the event.

A recent benchmarking exercise in the UK identified several different models of local authority event programming as follows:

- programme of recurring annual events;

- one major council-led event every other year; up to four partnership smaller events each year;

- small number of events plus occasional one-off events;

- town centre programme only;

- no programme – promote the events of other organisations only ('What's On'); and

- tie-in with national or regional programmes only – e.g., Black History Month, Hampshire Food Festival.

(Basingstoke City Council, 2008).

This indicates that the organisational role of the city may differ considerably, not just by type of event, but also by event location, event size and event theme.

Programme defined by content and discipline

Generic types can categorise event programmes. At their simplest, events that focus mainly on one type or discipline of activity may be termed *subject specific*, referring to a main concentration or preoccupation with one form of presentation – contemporary music, site-specific installation art, rock bands, poetry, clowning, film, etc.

Programmes that encompass a range of different types of activity genres are termed *interdisciplinary*. Interdisciplinary, or cross-disciplinary, events combine different forms of cultural expression. For example, the Dutch Electronic Art Festival (DEAF) is an interdisciplinary festival in Rotterdam, which features crossovers between art, technology and society. In a series of exhibitions, performances, seminars and workshops, DEAF attempts to generate a synergy of thought among different disciplines about media technology (DEAF, 2008). Similarly the House of World Cultures in Berlin stages the interdisciplinary performance festival IN TRANSIT, which brings together performers, artists and theorists to think about the nature of performance art. In 2006 this event included the 'Cultural World Cup' sponsored by the Brazilian government, which showcased Brazilian culture in seven German cities during the football World Cup.

There are refined nuances beyond such broad categorisations. The Bath International Music Festival (subject specific) presents a very large variation of types of music, and sometimes combines with other art forms. The programme of the Edinburgh Book Festival (subject specific) also ventures into music, film and other activities.

Darmawan et al. (2005) analysed a number of festival events in East Asia using a broad categorisation of programme types. Their analysis indicates that there are two basic types of festival: broad-based interdisciplinary events and those that concentrate on a narrow range of disciplines (Table 3.1).

The trend towards the blurring of boundaries between different styles and genres make the contemporary/classical divide between events less easy to discern; music or theatre as distinct forms of presentation are no longer easy to define; visual art often integrates with performance; food can be art; dance is sometimes viewed as sport; new technologies and media are being used across all frontiers and are cutting across most lines of demarcation; sumo wrestling and ice skating can be conceived as 'art forms'. The World of Wearable Art in Nelson, New Zealand organised a series of art events in which clothes were turned into artworks, and the show eventually became a national success, transferring to the capital city, Wellington.

Table 3.1 Programming Elements in East Asian Festivals (Darmawan et al., 2005).

Contents	Classical/popular music dance theatre	Contemporary music dance theatre	Live arts	Fine arts*	Others**	Approach
Shanghai	●●			●	●	Interdisciplinary
Hong Kong	●	●			●	
Tokyo	●	●			●	
Macao	●●				●	
JakArt	●	●	●	●	●	
New Vision (Hong Kong)	●	●●			●	Specific type
Seoul		●				
DaDao			●			

Notes:

●: Programme emphasis

●●: Stronger emphasis within its own programme

*: Including exhibition and expo

**: Including films and multimedia

The Palmer-Rae (2004) study showed that all ECOC used an interdisciplinary programme approach, although there were variations in the balance of sectors. Programmes generally included a mix of classical/traditional and contemporary/modern, across the sectors of theatre, dance, opera, visual arts, film and audio-visual media, literature, architecture, design, fashion and crafts. Music was presented in many different forms (including classical/traditional, contemporary/modern, pop/rock, jazz, folk, world, electronic), and projects were developed that focused on heritage/history, archives/libraries and digital art/new media/IT. Special television projects, street parades/festivals/open-air/sports events and interdisciplinary projects were also staged.

The following sectors were cited most frequently as being most prominent within ECOC programmes (in order of importance):

- theatre;
- visual arts;
- music;
- street parades or open-air events;

■ heritage and history; and

■ architecture.

When examining the programmes in more detail, however, it is clear that 'contemporary' art forms dominated the ECOC programmes. Classical music is the only 'traditional' form that has a heavy presence. It also seems clear that the more performance-orientated artistic disciplines were more likely to be programmed than others.

When speaking more generally about analysing programme selection within a large range of different cultural events, some studies have used programming strands to help define similarities and differences in event programmes. In conventional arts festivals, typical strands include categories such as 'foreign productions', 'home productions', 'experimental events', 'promotion of new talent' and 'new productions'. Ranshuysen and Jansen (2004) used programme strands as a basis for their study of Dutch summer festivals. From interviews and policy documents, Ranshuysen and Jansen discerned six key variable strands of programming: Foreign productions, Experimental productions, Quality productions, Young/New talent, Coproduction and New productions.

Too Much of a Good Thing?

Deffner and Labrianidis (2005: 249) in their analysis of the Thessaloniki 1997 ECOC programme show some of the dangers in adopting more risky forms of programming. There were lots of events in the ECOC, but there was poor planning. The local audience was not large enough to support the wealth of events, which were organised due to the large budget made available by the Greek state and the city of Thessaloniki, particularly as the events were concentrated in the tourist season. 'The large number of performances (10,257) meant that people had the choice of an average of 27.8 events per day'. On top of the flood of culture, there was also a conscious effort to educate new audiences. There was a significant element of 'new types' of cultural activities including the following:

a. Workshops: schools of cultural production for young persons.

b. Lounges: areas offering immigrants the opportunity to amuse themselves, to be engaged in creative activities, or to attend language courses and lectures.

Continued

c. From Far Beyond: it presented the Greek element of Diaspora as a synthetic historical factor of globalisation.

d. Special Actions: concerning people with special needs.

In developing the programme, the ECOC organisation became a 'cultural impresario' that produced and received work, without due consideration being given to the overall programme strategy. Many of the performances with paid admission were poorly attended: 37.6% of events had attendances below 34% of capacity, while only 21.6% had over 75%. The relatively low attendance rates were attributed by Deffner and Labrianidis (2005:250) to: the excessive supply of events in 1997, the concentration of events during the summer tourist season in Greece, and the very large number of similar events aimed at the same audience.

International vs. local orientation

The growing international dimension of cultural production and distribution, coupled with increased ease and low cost of travel, makes the option of international presentation feasible for most event organisers. In the period following the Second World War, some saw the international dimension of an event as proof of prestige. While this is still true in certain countries on the fringes of the global cultural marketplace, most productions and exhibitions are now made for an international market and will tour anywhere if the price and conditions are right. With an expanding series of networks that promote artistic mobility, the international component of events programming is a matter of choice and cost. The presentation of international work, however, does have risks other than financial. Moving a production, exhibition or project from one cultural context to another requires experience and sensitivity that takes into account different traditions, habits of receptivity to new experiences, and language; it is a task of mediating cultural difference from one context to another.

Montreal World Film Festival – an International Event

The Montreal World Film Festival, founded in 1976, was one of the events created at the time of the Montreal Olympic Games, as part of a strategy to encourage smaller scale events. The focus of programming was to attract a prestigious international audience and put

Montreal on the film industry map. The Festival now ranks among the most prestigious festivals in the world and has become the largest publicly attended film festival in the western world. It is the only competitive film festival in North America recognised by the International Federation of Film Producers Associations. Every year, films from more than 60 countries, including well-known and first-time filmmakers alike, are selected. 'The goal of the Montreal World Film Festival is to encourage cultural diversity and understanding among nations, to foster the cinema of all continents by stimulating the development of quality cinema, to promote filmmakers and innovative works, to discover and encourage new talents, and to promote meetings between cinema professionals from around the world.'

'To support the festival atmosphere, all the theatres of the Festival are within walking distance, an exceptional situation in North America. This contributes to the pleasant and easy-going atmosphere, while allowing participants to further contacts. Each year, the event draws numerous professionals from the film industry as well as some 700,000 visits from film buffs, 40% of which come from outside Montreal, thus generating valuable economic spin-offs for the region. Considering that, yearly, roughly 70 countries take part in this Festival and that over 500 media representatives from five continents are instrumental in promoting the event here and abroad, the World Film Festival plays an important role in building our image as a "City of Festivals."'

(www.ffm-montreal.org/en/).

At international events, beyond the products sold by international agents, producers and impresarios, there is work that has not reached the level of fame needed to have 'market value'. The work of emerging artists, for example, is unknown, and so programmes do not relate to market demand. There are some artists who refuse for ethical or artistic reasons to be included in market-led transactions. For such artists, fees are only part of a package of incentives, which might also include appearing in particular locations to gain inspiration, and testing their work away from the familiarity of their own local circumstances.

Mieskuoro Huutajat (Shouting Men's Choir) was formed in 1987 in Oulu, Finland 'by a group of young men who confess they had nothing better to do' (BBC News, 2004).

The choir consists of 20 men dressed in black, shouting famous Finnish songs. The group gained popularity and is in wide demand across Europe, the US and Japan. The composition of the group changes regularly as older members find the touring incompatible with family life. The main motive for the singers in touring from one location to another is not the fee, but their own personal and collective enjoyment from singing and travelling to new cultures.

For certain events the cost of presenting international work can be lower than that produced in the host country, due to local employment conditions or lower production costs. Some countries offer public subsidies and financial incentives as part of a state-supported programme of public diplomacy or image enhancement, which offers inducements to include particular artists or companies in an events programme. The choice of country-based themes may be motivated partly or largely by the availability of finance directly from these countries, or channelled through cultural institutes, national embassies or the artists and companies themselves. In Germany, for example, the Foreign Office funds cultural exchange, sending German artists abroad and hosting foreign artists in Germany. For them:

> Promoting art and exhibitions, music, theatre, dance, literature and film has traditionally been a key feature of foreign cultural and education policy. It gives the rest of the world an idea of the high quality and great diversity of artistic activity in Germany and projects an image of this country as a highly innovative and creative civilised nation. Such work is an ideal way of encouraging intercultural exchange and encounter beyond the realm of political discourse, thus facilitating and strengthening mutual understanding and communication.
>
> (Federal Foreign Office, 2008)

Many other countries have similar motives to support international cultural exchange, usually organised through national cultural institutes such as the British Council (UK), the Cervantes Institute (Spain) and the Italian Cultural Institute.

The programming of international work in local events can sometimes provoke jealousies by local groups who may be deprived of resources to continue their own work, as event organisers sometimes use subsidies to help cover large expenditures on one-off presentations of foreign work.

Many events therefore seek to build a relationship between the foreign and local elements of the programme, consciously selecting programmes that will offer inspiration to those operating in the more localised cultural context. Additional activities are frequently added to international programmes, and include special workshops, residencies, debates and other activities that help bridge the foreign–local divide and create synergies and contacts between visitors and locals that can be long lasting. In the Los Angeles Festival of 1993 foreign work was presented in communities across the city and local groups were involved in either hosting or performing alongside international groups. The Brouhaha International Street Festival in Liverpool is an example of an event that offers a platform for international work, which is presented along-side local work. This event welcomed 220 artists from over 24 countries in 2005, and ever since has developed an approach that integrates resident and foreign performance. Giles Agis, Executive Director of Brouhaha explained that: 'The festival creates platforms for international performance projects, local community tours and cultural collaborations that bring people together, foster mutual respect and encourage a greater degree of understanding and insight into our cities multicultural landscape' (BBC Liverpool, 2005).

Cape Town Jazzathon

The Cape Town Jazzathon was created in 1996 with the distinct goal of showcasing purely local talent. The event's founders recognised that the African music market was being flooded with products from America and Europe: 'Africa, a continent rich in cultural diversity, and rich in natural mineral wealth, was a perfect target for the American and European music and film Industry. They moved into Africa with their own music and films and offered Africans a reflection of what they believed was a perfect way of life; they even tried to show Africans what African music should sound like.'

Continued

To begin with, the festival invited international artists in order to raise the profile of the event, but insisted that the international stars be backed by local musicians. After the first 3 years, international performances were phased out. The event also began touring to different regions to give local musicians and audiences access to the festival.

Jazzathon Objectives

- To provide a platform for local musicians to showcase their talents.
- To provide an opportunity for emerging musicians especially those from previously disadvantaged sectors of the community.
- To facilitate the interaction of local and international artists.
- To provide opportunities for local charity organisations to use the event as a vehicle for awareness.
- To promote reconciliation, unity and a common nationhood.
- To pay tribute to those who used their musical talents to shape our cultural, intellectual, moral values and traditions in pursuit of Human Rights and Democracy.
- To contribute to the growth of tourism in South Africa.
- To educate and develop the cultural heritage of South Africa.

(www.jazzathon.co.za).

Bilateral cooperation between countries or cities may be an important aspect of the international dimension of event programmes. In 2007, for example, there was a considerable amount of collaborative work between the two ECOCs that had been selected for the year, Luxemburg and Sibiu. Over 90 events with a Romanian theme were organised in Luxemburg, and Sibiu also hosted events linked with Luxemburg. This collaboration was strengthened by the cultural ties between the two regions, as Sibiu (or Hermanstadt in German) was originally founded by German migrants from the Luxemburg region. The collaboration should continue well beyond the ECOC, thanks to the signing of cultural collaboration agreements between the two cities, which included the establishment of a Luxemburg Cultural Centre in Sibiu.

The international orientation of a cultural events programme can have a significant positive or negative impact on visitor numbers depending on the choice of programme. According to Morris (2007) London had an apparent 'dip' in visitors to blockbuster exhibitions in 2006, largely because of the content.

In 2005, there were five London exhibitions in the top 50 blockbuster exhibitions. In 2006, there was only one, 'Kandinsky' at Tate Modern at number 45. The reasons for the drop in visitors are nearly all to do with exhibition content: in 2005 Tate Britain put on London's top show 'Turner, Whistler, Monet' with a daily average of 4024 visitors. Although critically acclaimed, the follow-up in 2006 'Degas, Sickert and Toulouse-Lautrec' was less overtly popular, attracting an average of 2008 visitors a day.

By programming internationally renowned artists such as Turner and Monet, an event can guarantee a large international audience. The more 'local' the artist, the more local the audience tends to be.

Programme defined by quality

Quality is largely a subjective concept, and therefore difficult to define or measure. Quality may be judged in different ways by different potential markets or by different event stakeholders. When event directors consider the quality of their programmes, the final judgment usually combines the views of different constituencies, which may include some or all of the following:

- the view of the director or organisers of the event themselves and their teams;

- the view of the public, discerned by their behaviour at events, informal comments or more formally organised surveys and focus groups;

- the view of the media, journalists and critics;

- the view of the Board;

- the view of indirect stakeholders;

- the view of funding bodies, such as city councils, arts councils and committees who are mandated to make such evaluations;

- the view of the experienced peer group of organisers and directors who plan similar events elsewhere; and

- academics and researchers whose judgments are based on an independent review of evidence.

Events normally do not have the capability, resources, time or inclination to undertake rigorous quality reviews of their programmes. Most events, however, have some process of reviewing the quality of the programme, even if the review is dominated by the views of the organisers themselves, which they then need to defend against those of other constituencies.

For example, the Scottish Arts Council's (2007) assessment of music events has a section for 'artistic quality', which includes the following elements:

- Quality of production – was the event successful overall in relation to any stated aims (e.g., in the programme or other printed material)?

- Vision and imagination.

- Performers – where performers are not trained, reflect this in your comments.

- Quality of Presentation – was the event professionally presented from a technical point of view?

- Audience – assess the appropriateness of the production for the audience, estimate the size and reaction.

- Educational value.

Most of these judgments are subjective, and the outcome will depend on the experience and outlook of those chosen to evaluate or assess a particular event. Some events now engage professional consultants that specialise in evaluation, often based on surveys and focus groups.

Programme defined by external vs. internal drivers

Events can be categorised in terms of the main impulse of their programme, which might either be *externally driven* or *internally driven*. The drivers are defined by the business components of festivals: the target audiences and the sources of resources. Externally driven events depend on income generated from ticket sales, public bodies and sponsors. If the prime drivers or influencers of the programme are outside of the organisation and have greater impact on the programme than those on the inside, then the event can be considered to be primarily externally driven.

The Venice Biennale: a Multifunctional Event

The Venice Biennale has an illustrious history, the first event having been staged in 1895. Today it is considered one of the leading contemporary art shows. The event has undergone a number of programming shifts in its history, reflecting the pressure of both internal and external drivers. In the early years of the twentieth century, many countries established national pavilions designed to showcase their artistic talent. In 1930 control of the event passed to the newly elected fascist government of the city, who added many new elements, including music and film. External political events continued to leave their mark on the programme down the years, such as the 1974 edition being dedicated to Chile in protest at the toppling of the Allende government.

Between 1942 and 1968, art was also openly sold at the Biennale. 'The Italian dealer Ettore Gian Ferrari had the official job of selling works by any willing artist, earning 15% for the Biennale and 2% for himself' (Cocks, 2007). The political climate in the 1960s favoured an end to this 'commercialism', but the sale of artworks is now back on the Biennale agenda. There is a new art fair, Cornice, which coincided with the opening of the Biennale in 2007 that included 60 dealers.

There has been strong opposition to this move from galleries exhibiting in the main event. This is because, despite the global proliferation of biennials and triennials, the Venice Biennale remains the best-attended international exhibition and offers dealers a unique opportunity to promote their artists. They lobby hard to get their artists into it and often subsidise the production, transport and installation of works.

For events whose mission is focused primarily on the individual interests of the event organisation itself, its directors, artists or Board members, the programme is considered to be internally driven. Audience response and the

Table 3.2	Features of Internally and Externally Driven Programming	
Element	**Internally driven**	**Externally driven**
Resources	Own resources, volunteers	Sponsorship, grants, ticket sales
Audience	Local residents	Visitors
Mission	Determined by director, staff	Determined by funders or sponsors
Organisation	Autocratic, fanatic	Accountable, democratic

need to generate earned income from ticket sales might be factors, but are not the primary drivers of decisions concerning the programme. Successful internally driven events may have at their centre an individual or core group that is obsessed and have the internal experience and knowledge to realise an event idea through their programme. Religious events such as the Holy Years declared by the Catholic Church or the Hajj in Mecca are examples of internally driven programmes.

Most events have components of external and internal forces; events can place themselves at some point along this continuum. Table 3.2 illustrates some of the major differences between these two positions.

In a study by Darmawan et al. (2005) of selected festivals in East Asia, the main external and internal drivers of each festival were analysed. The primary sources of drivers were defined as resources, systems of activity and product offer (Table 3.3).

In East Asian festivals, sponsors and audiences exerted a dominant influence as external drivers. The sponsor-oriented organisation was usually independent, which may secure some support from the government, but which still needed additional resources to mount event programmes. In East Asian events directly managed by governments, the organisers were invariably public servants attached to a government office. In Macau, government officers developed interdisciplinary programmes where about a quarter of the productions combined popular entertainments, such as pop singers and films and more than half of the productions included local productions featuring local performers, Portuguese or Cantonese, or traditional Chinese operas. Conversely, the government offices managing New Vision in

Table 3.3	Programming Based on Festival Target Group (Darmawan et al., 2005)						
		Resources		**Activity System**		**Product Offering**	
Stakeholders	**Festivals**	**Artists**	**Expertise**	**Organiser**	**State**	**Sponsor**	**Audience**
Independent organisations	Shanghai				●	● ●	●
	Hong Kong			●			● ●
	Tokyo			●		●	●
Government divisions	Macao			●	●		●
	New Vision (Hong Kong)			● ●	●		●
	Seoul	●		● ●	●		●
No legal status	JakArt	●					●
	DaDao	●					
Perspectives		**Internal**		← →			**External**

● : *Stakeholder target groups*
● ● : *Stronger emphasis comparing among its own stakeholders for each festival*

Hong Kong focused on the encouragement and development of contemporary work. However, both examples were "internally driven' events, with government policies and priorities as the key driving forces, and using bureaucratic mechanisms to determine the event programmes.

Darmawan et al. (2005) argued that events that were more externally driven tended to adopt an interdisciplinary and contemporary approach to programming. Events that had a more internally driven perspective were more likely to focus on specific types of traditional programming. However, in the final analysis, it was the event's artistic director (government official or independent) who exerted the greatest influence on the programme decisions. The artistic director's role was to ensure that the programmes were aligned to the purpose of the event, to maintain and develop the event's image and reputation and to ensure that the programmes attracted the agreed set of target audiences. The artistic director, however, did not act alone and usually created a committee or team to help him/her in daily activities. In the primarily externally driven events, the committee usually comprised not only experts and artists, but also representation of some of the key external stakeholders, including governments.

Programmes defined by themes

Many events develop approaches to thematic programming. Themes may help make the event readable and recognisable by tying different programme elements together. The initial programme for the ECOC in Istanbul in 2010 was built around the theme of the four elements 'which have a special meaning to Istanbul: "Earth" referring to tradition and transformation; "Air - heaven sent" brings local and foreign musicians together. "Water - the city and the sea" focuses on a multitude of activities on the Bosphorus and "Fire - forging the future" focuses on modern arts and events for large parts of its population' (Istanbul 2010, 2008). It is not only specific events that may choose to base their programmes around themes, but also cities have begun to engage in 'themed years', as citywide events (a phenomenon discussed in Chapter 2). Liverpool in the lead up to being ECOC in 2008 declared a citywide events theme for each year from 2003, as follows:

2003: Celebrating Learning.

2004: Faith in One City.

2005: Sea Liverpool.

2006: Liverpool Performs.

2007: Liverpool's 800th.

2008: European Capital of Culture.

2009: Year of Environment.

2010: Year of Innovation.

Following the success of Glasgow's year as European Capital of Culture in 1990, the Arts Council based in London created a UK cities competition for themed years from 1992 to the year 2000, such as the Year of Music and Opera, the Year of Literature and the Year of Architecture and Design. The year 2000 was dedicated to Artists. The competition extended beyond cities to city-regions and wider regions that competed for the special designations. As detailed in Chapter 2, many cities have embarked on an approach to self-declared programmed themed years. Barcelona used this strategy to good effect in following up the success of the 1992 Olympic Games in the cultural sphere. The 'Barcelona is Culture' programme ran for 5 years from 2000, and culminated in the 2004 Universal Forum of Cultures, a UNESCO-sponsored event. The Gaudí Year held in 2002 was particularly successful, attracting more than 600,000 visitors and generating more than €47 million in additional tourist income. Visitor numbers to the main Gaudí attractions were 20% to 50% higher than in 2001.

The range of themes used in the ECOC programmes shows some of the possibilities for the theming of large-scale events. Over one-third of the Capitals of Culture had at least one central unifying theme for its programme as developed. The following are a few examples:

- *Art and Creativity* (Avignon, 2000).

- *The Journey* (Genoa, 2004).

- *Bridges to the Future* (Porto, 2001).

- *Culture and Nature* (Reykiavik, 2000).

- *City of all Culture*s (Luxembourg, 1995).

In almost half of the ECOC cities studied, themes were developed that related to the subject of *the city*. Two examples are:

- Brussels (2000) had the overall theme of *the City* with six thematic axes including *Celebrating the City* and *Re-imag(in)ing the City*.

- Prague (2000) had three major themes: *the Story of the City*, *City of Open Gates* and *a City to Live In*.

A few ECOC chose seasonal themes to structure the year.

- Bergen (2000) used spring: *dreams*, summer: *wandering*, autumn: *spaces*.

- Copenhagen (1996) used several themes per season: the spring season included *the Historic City* and *the Twentieth century*, summer included *the Green City*, and autumn *the Future* and *the new Europe*.

Some ECOC structured their programme around key words or principles as well as or instead of themes.

- Cracow (2000) focused *on thought, spirituality and creativity.*

- Bologna (2000) on *communication.*

- Helsinki (2000) on *innovation, internationalisation, inhabitants and investment.*

- Stockholm (1998) on *cross-fertilisation, participation and boundary breaking.*

Although all ECOC programmes had themes, the visibility of and adherence to these during the year varied. In Rotterdam and Brussels, for example, the themes were found to be clearly visible, whereas the public in Avignon and Prague commented on the lack of thematic cohesion making it more difficult to understand the unity of the programme. In some cases the theme is used as a serious programming device, while in others the theme is simply an attempt to package a highly disparate range of unconnected activities.

Programme defined by density of activity

As mentioned in Chapter 2, an event might be characterised as a space. The intensity with which that space is used is vital in determining the atmosphere and festive 'feel' of a city.

Programme density refers to the average number of performances or number of events over a defined period and is useful when comparing a specific event to another event with similar aims. It is far more complex to compare all the events of one city to another (or the overall 'eventfulness' of a city), although the City of Edinburgh commissioned a study that benchmarked Edinburgh as a festivals destination against other international cities (AEA Consulting, 2006). Different criteria were established for comparative purposes; one basis of comparison was the calculation of 'festival days' per year. This rough measure evaluates densities of events in different cities, but not their reach or quality.

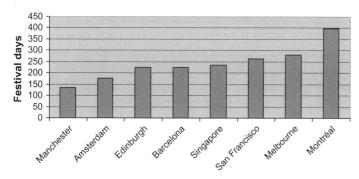

FIGURE 3.1 *Festival days per year for selected cities (AEA Consulting, 2006). Only major events are included.*

Figure 3.1 shows that in terms of festival days, Edinburgh's programme is far larger than UK rival Manchester, but smaller than most of its European or global competitors. The total number of festival days does not tell the whole story, however. The number of events per day also needs to be taken into account to measure the true intensity of festive activity. When compared to other international arts festivals, the Edinburgh International Festival's performance per day ratio is mid-way between Singapore (largest) and the Holland Festival (smallest). In particular it is the Edinburgh Fringe that delivers a high intensity of events. Among the jazz festivals, it is Montreal that is ahead of the others in terms of its performance ratio. These variations can be used to support a number of cities' claim to the title 'festival capital of the world'.

Programme defined by space

The locations where events take place offer another dimension of programme definition. The event organiser begins with a grid of spaces into which suitable programmes and projects fit in technical, operational and financial terms. Spaces may include both indoor and outdoor venues, varying from theatres, concert halls, sports arenas and conference halls to public squares, parks, historic buildings, rivers, streets and bridges. Disused industrial buildings, railway stations, stone quarries, ship yards, factories, river banks, market places, ice rinks and swimming pools have all been adapted to stage performances, exhibitions and for other event uses. There is an increasing trend for certain events to use unusual and unexpected spaces as venues; new spaces often inspire new programmes, attract publics that normally do not go to the traditional venues used for events and can generate substantial media attention. Some events such as the Documenta in Kassel and the Oerol Festival in Terschelling are almost entirely site specific and concentrate on programmes of performance or visual arts in unexpected locations. The notion that an event should take place only in buildings that are specifically constructed for events is considered a limiting factor for many event organisers.

There is nothing new in using festivals and events as a stimulus to identify alternatives to standard venues. In 1920, five artists including the composer Richard Strauss and the director Max Reinhardt staged the first performances of the Salzburg Festspiele on the steps of the Cathedral in Salzburg, and then later in the baroque Summer Riding school. In founding the Festival d'Avignon in 1947, Jean Vilar created the outdoor performing space in the Court d'Honneur. In the 1950s the Dubrovnik Summer Festival used fortresses, chapels, palaces and beaches for performances. The outdoor *Théâtre de l'Archevêché* is the centrepiece of the annual summer Aix-en-Provence Festival of opera. Summer festivals usually focus on outdoor performances with the moon and stars as part of the stage set. France alone boasts over 100 such outdoor summer festivals, which take place during the months of July and August. Most ECOC have created impressive alternative event spaces to supplement the traditional infrastructure of cultural facilities, many of which continued to host events after the cultural year had finished: including the Tramway (a former tram workshop and museum) in Glasgow, the Tripostal and the Maisons Folies around Lille, the Island in the River Mur in Graz and the Rotundas (former railway workshops) in Luxemburg.

Events may also make use of transient spaces. For example, the Spiegeltent is a travelling Belgian 'mirror tent' and entertainment venue. Originally built in the 1920s, the Spiegeltent travels around the world as a feature attraction at various international arts festivals, including the Edinburgh

Fringe, the Melbourne International Arts Festival, the Adelaide Festival of Arts, the Brighton Festival Fringe, the Belfast Festival at Queen's and Just for Laughs in Montreal, Canada.

When defining an event programme by space, event programming takes into account the best use of each space, both in terms of what is presented, and which audiences (new or existing) are likely to be drawn. The programming of an orchestral concert in a purpose-built indoor concert hall and the same concert in an outdoor amphitheatre will attract two different audiences. Whatever space is selected, it must have the conditions that are required for a high-quality experience in its own terms. One common problem is poor acoustics in venues that are not designed for performances. Many festivals make use of unusual venues, which may add to the experience in other ways, but solutions need to be found to provide a reasonable quality of sound and sight. Open-air venues also present problems with the weather, a trend that is likely to continue as more festivals make use of dramatic outdoor settings and as climate change makes the weather even less predictable in many areas (see Chapter 12).

When events programmes that take place at the same time overlap, the spaces used by each event might be linked together to create a sense of spectacle that any single event programme would find difficult to achieve. Edinburgh in the month of August and Avignon in July are examples of this phenomenon. As Prentice and Andersen (2003:10) note in the case of Edinburgh:

> (T)his essentially historical [city] is transformed in
> August. The castle esplanade carries a temporary
> stadium for the Tattoo; part of the Royal Mile is closed
> to vehicles and becomes an open air and largely
> informal performance space; and many buildings
> become venues for formal performances. Museums
> and galleries have special temporary exhibitions.
> Within the historic setting of the city, the overt tourism
> product becomes temporarily dramatic and
> carnivalesque. During the festival, the Royal Mile offers
> carnival and drama freely to excite the appetite of
> tourists, and to mark a 'boundary' between the normal
> historic city and the festival. It becomes a special space.

Increasingly the pressure to be spectacular creates a need for event organisers to spread their programmes across different city spaces to facilitate visual consumption and generate increasingly concentrated moments of co-presence. The selection of certain spaces for events may have symbolic and social significance. Particular spaces in some cities are associated with and sometimes even appropriated by particular groups; other spaces are neutral and visibly belong to everyone. Placing events in different spaces has overtones and may attract or deter particular publics, thereby creating either tensions or new harmonies in the way in which a city conceives such spaces. Peter Sellar's decision in the 1993 L.A. Festival to use many different neighbourhoods in the city for the programme was a deliberate act of reconsidering and redefining public space and was one of the programmes main objectives. Yardimci (2001) shows how different groups contest the different spaces of Istanbul, as groups from different religious and ethnic backgrounds compete for the use of public space. This competition can manifest itself in the form of 'hot violence', where public space must be policed, or through 'cold violence', where certain groups are excluded from certain spaces or their presence is ignored by others.

Programme defined by star names

Certain events are circumscribed by and focused on the appearance of star performers or artists; the programme is dominated by their presence or identity, and names are used as the main marketing tool. In the themed years celebrating the work of Vincent van Gogh (Amsterdam, 1990), Gaudí (Barcelona, 2002) or Amadeus Mozart (Salzburg and Vienna, 2006), the main lines of the programme were dominated by their work or influence. The association of name and place for historical and other reasons offers a powerful and memorable hook on which to combine an event, a personality and a city. The Mathew Street Festival in Liverpool, for example, centres on the Beatles and the Cavern Club, located in that street. The festival attracts 350,000 visitors, and it is estimated that 'Beatles tourism' as a whole is worth some £32 million (€46 million) to Liverpool each year. Surviving Beatles Paul McCartney and Ringo Star were also used to lend cachet to the

Liverpool ECOC in 2008 through their live performances in the city (although Ringo was not thanked for an interview after the opening night in which he indicated he would not like to live in his native city any more).

Star attractions appearing in festivals attract substantial media and public attention and, deliberately or not, they can define event programmes. In terms of mass popular events, determining the line-up of well-known stars is part of an acknowledged formula of successful programming in ECOC. The Hieronymus Bosch exhibition in Rotterdam (2001) attracted 220,000 visits, or 10% of the total audience for the year. In Thessaloniki, the Treasures of Mount Athos exhibition (1997) generated 700,000 visits, and concerts by Oasis and Van Morrison in Salamanca in 2002 were a major draw for the ECOC.

Particularly where 'star names' are used as a centrepiece of programming to attract larger audiences, there is a danger that these 'stars' begin to overshadow the event. In the case of the Over het IJ Festival in Amsterdam, for example, the festival became too closely linked to the performance group Dogtroep. This meant that many people attending actually thought they were going to a Dogtroep event rather than one performance at a larger festival.

A more extreme and less common version of this problem is when an event becomes bigger than the city it is located in. This may be a problem for smaller cities that host very high-profile events, such as the Spoleto Festival in Charleston, South Carolina, or the Edinburgh Festivals (where the power of the festivals is compounded when they act as a concerted pressure group).

Programme defined by political dimension

Events can be motivated by political or religious causes with the objective of conveying messages, passing information and stimulating increased interest and belief. As events, such programmes are conceived to pass information about and generate public interest in a cause or political issue. The phenomena of global televised concerts such as Live Aid and LIVE 8 are good examples of this; the Holy Year declared to mark the Millennium in Rome is another and was estimated to have attracted 26 million visitors.

After the rejection of the proposed European Constitution in a referendum in France in May 2005, the French government and other supporters of the constitution decided to use Europe Day, which takes place on 9 May each year, to restore a positive European outlook. With deep divisions on the future of Europe within the government and French political parties, as well as in the European Union, Europe Day in May 2005 used the slogan *fête l'Europe*. Events in Paris included the Eiffel Tower illuminated in blue, evoking the European flag with its 12 stars, a large party for students who had benefited from the EU's Erasmus programmes and numerous debates about Europe's future and events taking place in and around embassies of European governments and cultural institutes. Europe Day 2006 was conceived to be a 'true celebration, a time for meetings and debates, a day when we affirm our pride to make Europe live' (statement by the government of France, 2006). The programme was influenced entirely by a clear political objective (see Chapter 2).

Festivals organised to promote a country, often combining cultural and economic activity, is a further example of politically motivated events. The programmes may be of high quality, and the political messaging may be discreet, but the primary force and usually the source of finance is a country that wishes to reinforce or change its image or reposition itself on a national or international stage. In 2006, France sponsored a cultural season called *Printemps francais* that took place across Turkey, featuring exhibitions concentrating on the work of the photographer Bresson and sculptor Rodin, and a spectacular outdoor performance by a company called *Zingaro*, with 40 horses flown by plane from Paris to Istanbul and 20 large trucks filled with equipment travelling by road. The Russian Federation is focusing events on France in 2010, declaring this 'Russian Year in France'. In 2009 the Dutch Government paid most of the €1.2 million cost of staging the New Island Festival on Governor's Island in New York as part of the celebrations for the 400th anniversary of Henry Hudson's voyage to what was then 'New Amsterdam'.

Events might also be organised as a direct support for political programmes, as in the case of the Greater London Authority's (GLA) Cultural Programme. This gives support to a limited range of cultural events across London, and aims to promote and enhance London's cultural and creative diversity. Although the programme does not grant-aid events, it seeks:

> *To add value to existing events and initiatives, and to commission new activities, which meet the Mayor's policy priorities. In many cases, the activities promoted will act as demonstration projects, promoting the ways in which culture can make a difference to people's lives and inspiring others to action. The GLA Cultural projects programme will be pursued by:*

> ■ *directly running a small number of events;*

> ■ *lending political and financial support to and helping to promote a number of others; and*

> ■ *encouraging and developing a wide range of other events, which reflect the Mayor's policy priorities.*

GLA (2001:1)

The Singapore Arts Festival is operated by the National Arts Council, which ensures that the festival reflects the political approach to culture that is prevalent in this small island state (Ooi, 2007). Although the Festival Director has a strong influence, there is collective and committee decision making within the council along with input from local artists and arts experts. These 'external drivers' ensure that the festival matches Singapore's overall tourist vision and positioning as a global city, a process similar to other examples of Asian festivals mentioned earlier.

The Hong Kong Harbour Festival held from 17 October to 11 November 2003, was part of a HK$1 billion (US$129 million; €96 million) programme to revive the economy of Hong Kong following the effects of SARS (severe acute respiratory syndrome). It was a government underwritten event organised by InvestHK, under the auspices of the Economic Relaunch Working Group, in collaboration with the American Chamber of Commerce.

The event was billed as 'a dazzling series of live shows catering to all tastes and ages, encompassing rock n' roll, family entertainment, blues

Continued

and jazz, classical, theatrical performances and a Vegas Night'. Its organisation, which resulted in massive cost overruns, was heavily criticised and a criminal investigation was launched into the handling of the event. Of the HK$155 million (US$20 million; €15 million) spent on the event, over HK$75 million was spent on artists fees for performers such as the Rolling Stones and Prince. It was hoped that the event would generate substantial global media coverage, but the US audience for the televised performances was only 314,000 (Legislative Council Panel on Financial Affairs, 2004).

Programme defined by stakeholder dimension

Governments are not the only stakeholders who exert an important influence on programming. Tourism authorities will want to attract tourists at particular times of the year and to particular places, and economic development agencies will seek job creation benefits. Certain stakeholders, especially if they are the main financial supporters, may believe that they have the right to influence decisions about programmes, or may undertake the programming functions themselves. This happens regularly in corporate events organised by companies to launch products, increase sales or reinforce their brand image. Companies from Spain may opt for Spanish artists, and insist on performers who already have an association with the company or who have endorsed the company's products. Commercial stakeholders may be subtler in their influence on programmes managed by independent organisations or public authorities and are unlikely to insist on the obvious connection between the programme and their products; this sometimes depends on the scale of finance that is involved (see Chapter 4).

If the local community is itself a prime stakeholder, local associations and artists might characterise the programme. A Gay Pride event will usually promote gay artists; the Finnish Institute may insist on a Finnish programme and an anti-war host organisation is likely to develop a programme with themes and activities associated with its message.

The 'host stakeholder' may exert programming influence in a manner and with consistency to the point that an entire events programme can be named after or be defined by the stakeholder. This is the case with the ROBECO summer concerts in the Amsterdam Concertgebouw, for example. The concert series was started as a means of filling empty space during the summer months, but grew into a tradition, with inexpensive tickets financed by the sponsorship from the investment bank. In return, the concert series took on their name and the bank received 10% of the tickets for entertaining clients and staff.

Competition as programme strategy

A number of cultural events include an element of competition. This is the historic rationale behind some traditional festivals, such as the Welsh Eisteddfod. It is also an essential aspect of many film festivals and a large number of music festivals that present prizes and awards.

The original model for competitive cultural festivals is arguably the Delphic Games, founded in Greece in 582 B.C. The Delphic Games, just as their sporting counterpart the Olympic Games, have now been resurrected. The first modern Delphic Games were held in Moscow in 2000. The principle is similar to the Olympic Games, with individual competitors representing each country:

> The distinctive feature of these competitions is the fact that besides the individual performance, every participant being the member of the official delegation defends the honor of his (sic) city, region, country and shows the cultural potential and the contemporary level of art development of his (sic) territory.
> (International Delphic Committee, 2009)

In New Zealand, Richards and Ryan (2004) describe how stakeholders rejected the idea of removing the competitive element from a cultural event although participants were convinced that competition helped to maintain high standards and improve the quality of performances.

PROGRAMMING THE EVENTFUL CITY: MORE THAN THE SUM OF ITS PARTS?

A wide range of factors influence events programmes. However, when programming for the eventful city as a whole, the organisation and coordination of many events need to be brought sharply into focus. What is the difference between programming individual events and programming the eventful city? What does city programming add to the eventful city?

Edinburgh, as discussed earlier, clearly shows the advantages of citywide programming. By concentrating a series of cultural events in the main summer season, Edinburgh can stake its claim to be one of the leading festival cities in the world. The density of programming helps to add liveliness and atmosphere at a time when many cities are relatively quiet. The concentration of these events in a relatively small area of the city centre helps to add to the feeling of festivity. Alongside the summer 'blockbuster' season, Edinburgh has also developed a series of events to fill the historically low tourist period in the winter season, such as Edinburgh's special Christmas and Hogmanay celebrations.

Helsinki offers another model in which a disparate range of events is stimulated and supported by the city, but with no overall direction or control (Silvanto and Hellman, 2005). This looser model presents some challenges for Helsinki:

> *With the proliferation of festivals, public authorities, and especially municipalities are confronted with a dilemma as to which festivals to support and with how much subsidy, to what extend to pool them together for the sake of some presumed efficiency, or rather leave them apart, respecting their autonomy and conceptual specificity. Inevitably, festival proliferation forces public authorities to define their objectives and expectations and in fact profile a local festival policy that will include monitoring, assessment and evaluation of individual festivals that seek public support.*
>
> (Klaic, 2007:2003)

Careful planning of the events programme can help a city to achieve its cultural and other goals. The plans for the Hague to establish itself as a 'festival city' indicate some salient points (Gemeente Den Haag, 2005);

Recommendations for Festival City Policy

- The festival offer should be broad, appealing to all residents and spread overall disciplines while avoiding duplicating events.

- Risk financing should be found for new plans and initiatives.

- Success depends not only on mega events – there is also room for smaller festivals.

- Coordination is needed, for example, through collective marketing and the development of an umbrella website.

- There should be a one-stop-shop for event organisers to obtain licenses and other services and the council should also reduce the costs of such regulation where possible.

The indications are that effective programming of the eventful city can offer a number of advantages in terms of coordination, stimulating ambiance and cultural vitality, social inclusion, organisational capacity, innovation, marketing and positioning.

City Programming in European Capitals of Culture

One consistent set of programming models is the ECOC. The ECOCs face issues relating to how their programmes fit into the ongoing cultural life of a city, similar to how any special event or a new event that adds to the existing cultural supply might fit in. While some ECOCs attempted to weave special projects carefully through the existing cultural fabric of a city, others simply added projects and events on top of existing cultural programmes. Although the former is a more complex way of working, it has generally proved to be a more successful programming strategy, reducing the negative consequences of competitive positioning between different events, over-supply and media and public fatigue. Integrated programming fostered a greater sense of genuine partnership and reinforced strategic alliances and networking between the entities that provide the year-round cultural offer. In the period 1987–1997 the city of Glasgow initiated such an approach, which has been instituted in most of the subsequent ECOCs.

Continued

Most ECOC programmes encompassed a very large number of unconnected initiatives, often grouped under themes or titles. In most cultural cities the means of understanding the extent of the programme was by looking at the promotional material that divided the programme in terms of discipline or theme. Coherence was usually viewed more as a communications or marketing issue than one of programme. This fragmentation of disparate elements of a cultural programme may be one of the reasons for the lack of overall impact and understanding of the programme in many ECOCs.

All ECOCs sought advice during the project selection process. They all consulted cultural organisations and artists, and almost half also consulted government officials and politicians. Less than half consulted local residents and community organisations and very few capitals of culture sought advice from the business community or the tourism sector. As well as undertaking consultation, all ECOCs used specific criteria to select projects for their programmes. The most common criteria used by almost all cities were:

- the quality of the project; and
- the cost of the project.

Following these, the most often cited criteria were:

- the relevance of the project to the programme's aims;
- the experience of the organisers; and
- the long-term impact or sustainability of the project.

Other less common criteria used by cities were the educational potential of the project, the originality of the project, the attractiveness of the project to audiences and the opportunity offered to local producers.

PROGRAMMING CHALLENGES

The city that takes charge of developing its events programme finds itself trying to cater to the needs of all stakeholders, and rapidly discovers that it may not be possible to meet all demands and priorities; choices will need to be made. The key issue for the eventful city is therefore how to strike the programming balance in order to maximise the outcomes for the city as a whole.

The Programming Dilemma

Christian Radu, Director of the Sibiu ECOC in 2007, summarised the dilemmas involved in striking such a balance as follows:

- Strategic dilemmas
  - Culture as art or culture as a way of life?
  - Cultural democracy or democratisation of culture?
  - Culture as quality of life or culture as development?
- Implementation dilemmas
  - Consultation or active participation in decision making?
  - Prestige or practical?
  - National or international allure?
- Social dilemmas
  - The community or communities?
  - Cultural diversity or monoculture?
- Economic dilemmas
  - Subsidy or incentives for cultural operators?
- Management dilemmas
  - Centralisation or decentralisation?
  - Direct provision or contracting out?

(Radu, 2007).

Clearly the problem of balance in the cultural programme of a city is a complex multi-dimensional issue to which there is no perfect answer. At every turn, difficult decisions need to be made and it is best to prepare for the negative as well as the positive consequences of such decisions.

Managing disappointment

The process of selecting programme elements is, in most cases, a necessary quality control, but the selection process also creates a need to manage the inevitable disappointment caused by rejection. In the 1998 ECOC in Stockholm, approximately 5000 project submissions and ideas were received but the operational team was unable to process them quickly (not many decisions could be made before 1997 as the budget was not fixed). The organisers eventually turned down almost 4000 projects, leaving 1218 projects in the programme, but only 532 of these could be supported financially from the budget of the ECOC. The selection process therefore generated a high level of disappointment among those who were not selected or funded. Cities need to be aware of this problem, which is particularly acute where an open call for project proposals is used as a tool to increase involvement in the cultural programming process between the organisers and local residents.

One potential solution to the problem of disappointment is being tested in the development of the ECOC candidacy for Aarhus in Denmark (2017). Rather than launching an open call for project proposals, the idea is to invite actors from the cultural sector to join the project as participants. Those individuals and organisations who contribute to the development of the event will then be eligible to receive support from the ECOC. This principle of reciprocity has the intention of reducing the arguments about funding later on, since those who are willing to invest in the development of the whole event might benefit in return later on.

FROM CULTURAL POLICY TO CULTURAL PROGRAMMING

Supporting eventful programming requires cities to change the way they think about events. This is also part of a broader shift in the strategic approach that cities take to culture, which Hitters (2007) identifies as a change from making 'cultural policy' towards a 'cultural programming' approach.

City cultural programming not only places the emphasis on the role of the city as stage or backdrop for a series of events, but also changes the role of the public sector from the supplier of events into that of programme coordinator. In order to communicate the new complexity of cultural programming to potential audiences, cultural and event managers increasingly need to think in terms of themes which will help to increase the 'readability' of the programme as well as increasing identification of the different audiences with the programme.

The forms of culture that are programmed combine high culture, popular culture and 'everyday' culture (Richards, 2007a). These forms need to be programmed in such a way that they articulate with the more 'traditional' cultural supply, producing a distinctive cultural programme for the city that situates it in time and space. As the Strategic Plan for the Cultural Sector of Barcelona emphasises, there is a need to link past, present and future:

> *The cultural legacy of the city is expressed in tangible elements – collections, museums, buildings, urban design, etc. – and in intangible elements: lifestyles, the use of the streets, festivals, traditions, etc. The city must be capable of valuing this heritage as the best guarantee of expressing singularity within an increasingly global context.*
>
> (Ajuntament de Barcelona, 1999:135)

Melbourne illustrates the wide variety of events now being programmed either actively or passively by cities. Table 3.4 shows the events issued with a permit for use of public space in 2006/2007. This table illustrates that a large proportion of the total 'programming' that a city may deal with is made up of small-scale community- or business-related events.

The growing range and scale of events now dealt with by the eventful city means that more thought has to be given to

Table 3.4	Events in the City of Melbourne by Type, 2006/2007	
Activity		**Number**
Hallmark events		3
International one-off events		3
Major events		78
Community and corporate events		305
Filming		58
Weddings		178
Community sport		52
Total		677

how programmes will be conceived and developed. Care has to be taken to avoid clashes of major events, which may generate problems of congestion or security. Connections can be made between different events to achieve coherence and impact. There is a need to develop partnerships and synergies between all those people in a city who organise and promote events. The leadership offered by public authorities to facilitate strong working relationships across a city is one of the prerequisites of the realisation of the eventful city. What is required is strategic planning for eventfulness as well as effective programming of individual events and event programmes. In this way, individual events and entire event programmes can be integrated into the wider processes of cultural planning and urban planning, helping the city to achieve its strategic goals.

CONCLUSION

Programming is a process that is subject to a wide range of pressures, both internal and external. The programme for the eventful city should be a product of the vision for the city: a means of reaching and engaging with its stakeholders and publics as well as positioning itself relative to other cities. The vision of the eventful city should provide a basis for making programming decisions and ensuring that the right balance of different programme elements is achieved.

In terms of developing eventfulness, event programmes should be conceived in a strategic, holistic way. Inevitably there are a range of objectives that need to be achieved by the event programme, and there is a tendency for cities to try and provide 'something for everyone' in their programming. However, such scattergun approaches to programming run the risk of producing safe and potentially boring programmes at the cost of creativity and innovation. Achieving balance should not be equated with the middle way or taking the path of least resistance. In many cases, the city will have to defend its vision and deal with the conflict that programme decisions may create.

Programming requires an effective working relationship to be developed between the city and all event stakeholders because, although the city may set the general vision of what it wants to achieve, most of the actual work of programming is done by others. The role of stakeholders and their relationship with the eventful city is the subject of the following chapter.

CHAPTER 4

Leadership, Governance and Stakeholders

In an increasingly complex global environment, staging an event invariably involves a wide network of stakeholders and actors. A city that wishes to be perceived as eventful needs to link stakeholders together and provide the leadership which will ensure that the event programme can meet the broader goals of the city and meeting the needs of individual events and their stakeholders. Leadership of the eventful city needs to be set within an overall framework of governance that ensures that the interests of stakeholders are represented and that events are accountable to the community.

Drawing on theoretical perspectives from stakeholder theory and network theory, this chapter analyses issues of collaboration, partnership and coordination in bringing an event programme to fruition. The importance of winning and maintaining political support, managing stakeholders and raising finance are examined through examples from the ECOC (European Capital of Culture) and other events. The role of the public, private and voluntary sectors, and the need to balance the interests of these different stakeholders are also considered.

LEADERSHIP

There has been much research on leadership, but what makes people leaders, or what leadership precisely is, remains largely unclear. 'Never have so many laboured so long to say so little' (Bennis and Nanus, 1985:4). Almost everybody who studies leadership defines it differently.

In recent years, many analysts have begun to emphasise the difference between managers and leaders. Not all managers are good leaders, and not every leader is a strong manager. The basic distinction lies in how leaders organise themselves and react to external challenges. 'Leaders conquer the context – the volatile, turbulent, ambiguous surroundings that sometimes seem to conspire against us and will surely suffocate us if we let them – while managers surrender to it' (Bennis, 1989:7). Conquering the context is clearly important in the eventful city, where a complex programme of events and different event stakeholders have to be coordinated in the face of major internal and external challenges.

In the eventful city, the leadership of the event programme also needs to be set in the wider context of the leadership of the city or region as a whole. Overall 'place leadership' involves political issues, economic and financial issues, as well as social, educational, business and environmental concerns. Place leadership supposes that places need vision and effective leadership of different kinds in order to achieve their objectives. The leaders of places – mayors and other elected officials – have a key role in helping to improve place prosperity and attractiveness. Leadership styles and substance can have an impact on the image of places and the extent to which people will visit or choose to live and work there. Although leadership can be spread across different parts of a city's ecology, with different roles assigned to different lead individuals or organisations, there is often the need for a strong symbolic unifying leader, who acts as the 'champion' and whose overall strength and power of communication can unite or fragment a place and significantly influence its external image. For example, Nelson Mandela not only helped to unite South Africa in the post-Apartheid era, but also had a significant role in improving the country's international image. Conversely, it has been argued that the policies and style of US President George Bush played a role in the decline of the image of the US abroad in recent years (Greenwald, 2007). The same can be said for cities, where the strength or weakness of a mayor can be a determining factor of success or failure. The fortunes of many cities have been tied to the leadership provided by the mayor, as with Ken Livingstone in London, Mayor Daley in Chicago, Rudolph Giuliani in New York or Pascual Maragall in Barcelona.

The tendency for places to be identified with their leaders means that the character of the leader may come to resemble the character of the place they lead. It is therefore important that synergy is achieved between the two. As Allen (2005:5) notes, for example: 'Authentic places deserve authentic leadership ... that is true to the purpose of the place and true to the values and beliefs of those who are its leaders.'

Place leadership depends on the ability of the leader to inspire and empower other leaders and to communicate a clear vision that can inspire the city's main stakeholders. Allen (2005:14) argues that this process,

> ... is different. It is not like leading an organisation with its own board of directors or governance committee. It is about sharing the lead of an organisation with many masters who have agreed to work together as equals for a common purpose that could not otherwise be achieved.

However, not all political leaders are as good at sharing the lead with stakeholders as might be desired. As this relates to the eventful city, political leadership is one key component of a successful strategy, but equally important is that stake-holders have a forum in which their views can be heard, and also feel that they have some influence over the event programme of the city. The collective strength of skilled event stakeholders can often overcome the weaknesses or insta-bility of the city's political leadership at any given time. The city of Edinburgh is one example of such a situation. That is why the understanding of city governance, or more specifi-cally event governance, is such a crucial issue; it embodies the essence of leadership, but the concept is wider and of critical importance to eventful cities.

Leadership can also be exercised in different ways. Caust (2004) maintains that the leadership style that has most relevance to the arts and to arts events is the charismatic leadership style. She argues that charismatic leaders create an inspirational and transformational 'aura' that persuades others to believe in a new reality. Many cultural events owe their very existence to charismatic individuals, as evidenced by the examples in Chapter 2 (Salzburg, the Proms, the Oreol Festival). Evidence that contemporary event organisers are seeing the value of charismatic leaders is provided by the High Line Festival in New York, which asked David Bowie to curate its 2007 edition, and the Brighton Festival, which invited Anish Kapoor as guest curator in 2009. As well as providing a fresh vision, such names serve to generate substantial media interest and persuade other celebrities to involve themselves with the event.

Charismatic leadership is also arguably needed in a sector where a major challenge exists in managing creativity and creative people. A lack of charisma can be problematic, because even when people have all the other tools for the job, a leader must convince the rest to follow. A specific form of leadership required in the cultural sector is referred to as 'cultural leadership', and when applied to the arts sector, specifically 'artistic leadership'.

Leadership is often summed up in terms of a series of qualities that a good leader might be expected to possess. Peter Hewitt, Chief Executive, Arts Council England (2006:10) argues that a good leader in the arts sector needs:

- to display clarity of vision;

- to have a steely determination to deliver;

- to resist the temptation to get caught up in detail;

- to concentrate on the issues that really matter;

- to identify with the success of their organisations in an entirely personal way;

- the ability to empathise and engage with people; and

- the emotional detachment – ability to take difficult decisions.

Similarly, Bushell-Mingo asks: 'What makes a great cultural leader? Vision, respect, a sense of humanity, an unshakeable faith in the rights of people to a creative life, the power of the arts to change the world and the continued striving for the ownership of the arts by people, no matter where it is' (Arts Council England, 2006:16).

The Scottish Arts Council (2007:5) identifies the following elements as being important in the artistic leadership of arts organisations:

- The organisation has a clear artistic vision that is communicated clearly to all stakeholders (funders, audiences/participants, artists and staff).

- Create and/or present a programme of work of high artistic quality.

- The views of the stakeholders are formally evaluated and inform programme planning.

- Partnership within and/or beyond Scotland is present within the programme.

- The organisation participates in recognised national and/or international forums.

- The organisation aims to develop and promote equality of opportunities and to ensure inclusion and accessibility to all services, employment and the artistic programme.

Similar qualities are argued to be important in the leadership of an events programme. For example, the review of events in Edinburgh (AEA Consulting, 2006:10) notes that:

Visionary artistic and managerial leadership are essential, and conditions for recruitment, selection, retention and succession need to be carefully considered to attract the best talent and to support the creativity that such leadership inspires. The Festivals are in a globally competitive market for administrative and programming talent. The quality of their curatorial and administrative leadership, together with the resourcing of that leadership, is perhaps the most important factor in retaining pre-eminence. As leadership changes take place, the Festivals' boards and their stakeholders should ensure that every step is taken to attract and retain executive leadership of internationally competitive calibre.

This analysis suggests that good cultural leaders, apart from having charisma, need a range of other qualities, which include vision, the ability to empathise and communicate and the capacity to make difficult decisions.

Artistic Leadership or Place Leadership?

When a city stages major cultural events, a debate inevitably arises about what type of leadership is required. For a cultural event, one might assume that artistic leadership is critical. The majority of ECOCs, for example, have appointed artistic directors whose primary job is to oversee the cultural programme. Perhaps not surprisingly, when a leader is appointed whose job is to focus solely on artistic questions, rather than on political concerns and relations with multiple stake-holders, conflicts often emerge between the artistic leader and others, such as the Board, the cultural organisations in the city or the public authorities.

This problem was addressed directly by Robert Garcia, Coordinator General of the Luxembourg ECOC in 2007, when he reflected on his experience of leading the event (Luxembourg and Greater Region, 2008). He points out that many artistic leaders, usually appointed from outside the place they are supposed to be leading, 'land like a Zeppelin on the cultural field and ... some ... actors will see them as a tempo-rary invader rather than a friendly guest' (p. 110). This seemed to be the view of some when an Australian, Robyn Archer, was appointed as artistic director of the 2008 ECOC in Liverpool. Although her early departure from the post in 2006 was attributed by the Liverpool Culture Company to personal reasons, it was clear that not everybody was happy with her commitment to Liverpool, as she only spent a quarter of her working time in the city. Andrew Pearce, chairman of the Liverpool Heritage Forum, was quoted as saying 'A lot of people are glad to see the back of her. We want this to be led by people here in the city. This is not just a great gig for anybody to swoop in on, this is about the city that we are so proud of' (Indymedia Liverpool, 2006). With only 18 months to go before the start of the event, a leadership crisis was averted by appointing Phil Redmond as Deputy Chair (with responsibility for Creative Direction), relying on his local roots and affinity with the local cultural scene to pull the event together.

Appointing artistic or cultural leaders from outside the city itself has worked well, however, in other ECOCs, and local appointments have not been successful either in some cities. The key issue is not the nationality or place from which a leader is appointed, but rather one of the skills, experience and competence that are matched to the job at hand. Because most ECOCs have had cultural, political, social and economic objectives, there has been the need for leadership with multiple skills, either found in a unique individual or spread across a leadership team.

When cities consider appointing leaders for complex events and event programmes, there is often confusion over the primary skill that may be required. Robert Garcia points out that political support is perhaps the most important precondition for a successful major event, and unless a leader is able to draw on this, they are likely to be in a much weaker position (Luxembourg and Greater Region, 2008). However, an individual who has political support but not the other essential skills that are required in terms of cultural sensitivity, decision making, coordination, communication and team building will likely not be a successful leader.

GOVERNANCE

Governance is the act or process of governing. This includes the structures used to govern, as well as the processes these structures exercise. In the publication *Governance and Risk Management Self-Assessment Program*, the Auditor General of Queensland (2000:1) defines corporate governance as:

> ... *the way in which an organisation is controlled and governed in order to achieve its objectives. The control environment makes an organisation reliable in achieving these objectives within an acceptable degree of risk.*

In cities, as indcated earlier, governance is partly exercised by the leaders of the public administration, such as the Mayor, but not only by political structures. The difference between 'city government' and 'city governance' is crucial in that city governance always involves a range of key city stakeholders and the relationships between them. Savitch and Vogel (2000) argue that 'government' is characterised by formal institutions using coercive power in a more centralised way, whereas 'governance' is more likely to involve existing institutions, using incentives to engage stakeholders and emphasizing decentralisation. In many cities the perceived need to change and dynamise existing institutions of government has created a trend towards 'strong mayors', leaders with significant powers to make decisions and mobilise resources. The role of the new strong leaders, it is argued, should be to use their powers to achieve the goals of the city rather than exercising power over the city. In the new and emerging forms of governance, emphasis is placed on collaboration across boundaries and sectors, encouraging stakeholders to share decision making.

In the context of the city as a whole, different models of governance can be identified, ranging broadly from highly centralised to decentralised systems. The way in which power is exercised in the city can also vary, with different forms of political power, types of power structures and modes of decision making (Table 4.1).

In the context of events, governance may be exercised partly by the public sector through one of its departments (usually the Mayor's Office, Cultural or Events Department), through an arms-length quango or by voluntary sector organisations, but it invariably involves other players, which may include event organisers and organisations, the private sector and other civic and community leaders.

Governance is therefore a collective term that applies to the combination of different layers of promoting. presenting

Table 4.1 Types of Power in the City		
Type of power	**Urban power structure**	**Mode of decision making**
Dominating	Rival factions	Conflict
Bargaining	Coalitions	Contingent cooperation
Pre-emptive	Regimes	Enduring cooperation

After Digaetano and Klemanski (1999)

and developing events in cities. Events which are organised directly by the public sector may be supervised directly by an elected political committee of the local authority, or increasingly have a Board or Committee with representatives of major stakeholders and those who have appropriate supervisory experience (for example in legal, financial or cultural matters). Independent event organisations are structured in similar ways with a Board of Directors that has legal and financial accountability for the event. Distinctions need to be drawn between for-profit and not-for profit organisations. In the broader events marketplace in cities, there is a place for both structures and both can be considered as event stakeholders. The Board may then appoint a Chief Executive or a Director who executes the strategies of the Board, and who remains responsible to a Board that generally represents the major stakeholders in the event or to the shareholders as investors in for-profit companies. In this sense, cultural events generally function in the same way as other cultural organisations such as museums and theatres. The roles and interaction between the Board and the appointed Director are crucial to the success of individual events, and so to the successful development of eventfulness in a city.

The Role of the Board: A Scottish View

In the cultural field, management boards often have fairly standard roles. For example, the Scottish Arts Council expects management boards to have:

- access to professional financial advice;
- demonstrable evidence of probity (approval limits, risk register, financial scrutiny, etc.);
- active involvement in planning; and
- policies on reserves, pensions, equalities, etc.

Core requirements of the board include:

- All members of the board and the senior management team are responsible for Artistic, Audience, and where possible, Marketing and Education development, and are actively engaged in strategic planning and organisational review.

Continued

- The board composition comprises an appropriate mix of skills and abilities to support the business of the organisation.
- The board plans and reviews financial performance regularly.
- The organisation is committed to increasing income from non-public sources, including trading.
- Staff competence levels are maintained.
- Support to individual artists.
- Support to staff, board, volunteers, etc.
- Staffing budgets are specified within the overall budget and reviewed regularly.
- Remuneration packages and pension provisions are regularly reviewed within the context of staff experience and industry standards agreements.

In addition to the individual leader of an event or event programme, the Board is often a crucial tool of governance. Arts Manager (www.artsmanager.org) suggests that:

The Board of Directors (or Trustees) of an arts organisation is meant to be a leadership and support group that cares deeply for the institution and works diligently to find the resources required to achieve its mission.

In principle, the Board gives strategic direction, while the professional managers carry out the day-to-day operations (see Chapter 5). As stated above, the Board is accountable to the stakeholders of the organisation and the management is responsible to the Board. However, such a division of roles is sometimes not clear or overlapping, which then creates potential for conflict between the Board and the staff in charge of managing and running the event. A clearly worked out and agreed set of principles, and a carefully conceived list of relative responsibilities, authorities and decision making levels are required between the Chief Executive Officer of an organisation and the Board.

Similarly, where Boards appoint two or more key executives, such as an Artistic Director and a General Manager, the authorities for decision making between each of the parties and the others require complete clarity and transparency. This is one of the prerequisites of good governance.

Taking into account the high frequency of clashes within Boards managing events and disputes between the Board, the appointed Directors, and often the public authority as a major financial stakeholder, there needs to be clear responsibility for the effective running of the organisation in order to maintain a balance between board accountability and interference. The relationship between the Board and event managers is a dynamic one that responds to external and external forces. In many organisations there is an identifiable 'governance lifecycle'. As the organisation matures, the demands placed on the Board and management change as well. Typically, operating functions become more the province of professional staff, thereby reducing the need for Board involvement in management. As the scale of financial requirements grow, Board members may also be called upon to play more active roles in fundraising. This means that Board members who had initially been involved in the early stages of event development, where creative and practical skills are at a premium, may no longer be required to deal with professional decision making, but rather only with broader long-term strategy. In such cases, membership of the Board may need to change to reflect a new set of responsibilities and skills. The principle of undertaking a 'board skills' audit every few years is a recommended action to ensure alignment with the developing needs of the organisation. Although often delicate, a similar 'skills audit' may be required for the appointed Director and Chief Executive, with an appropriate and fair appraisal system in place for performance.

For the eventful city, there may also be a change in the relationship between the city and its programme of events over time. In the early stages, the city may be faced with an eclectic programme of independent events that evolved in an ad hoc way long before the civic administration took an interest in events. As the city attempts to engage these events in the achievement of civic objectives, it will have to negotiate with pre-existing event governance structures and vested interests. Over time, some of these events may align themselves more closely with civic policies in response to incentives, while others may continue to develop independently. A collection of core events in the city programme may emerge (as in the case of Manchester's 'pillar events' – see Chapter 9), perhaps with the addition of new events stimulated more directly by the public sector in order to address specific needs.

Governance of the City Event Programme

The Edinburgh Festivals review (AEA Consulting, 2006) identified many problems surrounding event governance in the city:

In terms of governance, many festivals studied have articulated problems: large and unwieldy boards, political interference, difficulties in recruiting skilled artistic directors and unclear divisions of responsibility. In most festivals, the Artistic Director remains the key figure within the organisation, although the styles of direction vary enormously. Friction between Directors and their Boards, or Boards and their public funders are often concentrated on poor performance at the box office or negotiations over levels of public subsidy in the governance of cultural events.

In spite of these common problems, the Edinburgh study noted that few cities have developed overarching governance structures for events and that there is little evidence of collaboration between individual festivals within the same cities. Therefore the ability of different events within a city to share experiences, learn from each other or adopt common solutions to common problems is a major weakness. The recommendation made to Edinburgh was that the city should match the political will to support the festivals with strong leadership and political independence.

In order to achieve this, the report suggested that:

- Members of governing bodies should have an appropriate expertise and an appropriate balance of skills, interests and contacts to support a festival's objectives.

- The programme should not be influenced by political interests and the operational structures should be autonomous, characterised by strong governance.

- Political and operational alliances must work towards commonly agreed goals.
- The Festivals' boards should be strengthened in composition, vigour of oversight and organisational articulation to overcome any impediment to long term organisational development. (AEA Consulting, 2006:13)

Governing an event programme is far from easy. More than half of the ECOCs have experienced major problems in governance. Bearing in mind the rate of failure, the Palmer Report (Palmer-Rae, 2004:48) identified different ways of organising the governance of the ECOC:

- an autonomous structure with legal status as a not-for-profit company, trust or foundation;

- direct administration within an existing local government structure (municipality, mayor's office, etc.); and

- a mixed model comprising both the above.

Centralised Decision Making – A Potential Source of Problems?

The Spoleto Festival, USA was plagued for years by clashes between Gian Carlo Menotti, the artistic director and the founder of the festival, and Nigel Redden, the general manager. Although the dispute ostensibly revolved around programming, it was actually a power struggle for control of the event. Nigel Redden had balanced the festival's books and introduced avant-garde programming. But he also openly debated programming with Menotti. In 1992 things came to a head. The Board backed Nigel Redden, but Menotti announced that either he or Redden had to go. The Mayor of Charleston also told the Board that the festival would not be welcome in Charleston if it forced Menotti out, and the Board backed down (Kozinn, 1992).

Avoiding such problems means that responsibilities need to be clearly set out in the strategic plan of the organisation and backed up with clear task descriptions for all involved.

Smaller ECOC Boards tended to have fewer problems in relation to their functioning. However, the priority of many Boards was not operational effectiveness but political balance and representation. In Bergen, the Board doubled in size from what had been originally planned, mainly to represent the range of political interests. Membership of the governing structure also varied in representation, although most frequently it was a mix of politicians from city and regional authorities, representatives from national authorities, cultural institutions, universities and foundations.

The most frequently cited responsibilities of the Board were:

- To take financial decisions and have overall financial control.

- To develop policies and strategies.

- To take decisions about cultural projects.

- To raise funds and sponsorship.

The autonomous structure was most frequently cited as having the most advantages in developing partnerships and focusing on delivering the event.

The Palmer-Rae (2004) report also identified a number of common problems with ECOC Boards:

- Being dominated by political interests.

- Difficulties with relationships between Board members and the operational management team.

- Having a Board which did not fully represent cultural interests.

- Having a large, unwieldy Board.

The precise role of the ECOC Board was not clearly worked out in the majority of cities, creating overlaps and confusions with the responsibilities of the operational management structures. There can be significant conflict if roles and responsibilities are not clarified.

The most frequent recommendations for improving ECOC governing structures were:

- Develop a small independent structure with a clear role and common direction.

- Ensure strong leadership.

- Appoint members who have appropriate expertise and have good relationships with the public.

The Palmer Report concludes that:

> *The importance of strong Board leadership of ECOC cannot be underestimated. Whether this is the Mayor, a business leader, an academic or a cultural expert, the key qualities of leadership: inspiring and motivating Board members and staff, managing conflicts and being a strong spokesperson identified with the ECOC are essential.*
>
> (Palmer-Rae, 2004:49)

ORGANISATIONAL STRUCTURES

The way in which event programmes are organised varies widely, even in the same city or region. In the UK, for example, Long and Owen (2006:79) identify four main organisational categories for arts festivals:

- a local authority, other public body or venue with no separate legal status for the festival;

- a private enterprise or partnership;

- a limited company or registered charity with company, board directors or trustees, or both; and

- a voluntary club, society or unincorporated association.

Each of these different types of organisational structures may be associated with a different style of management, different strategic priorities and different resource constraints. The eventful city usually incorporates many different management structures within its event programmes, and therefore should understand the differences and be able to handle the differing management styles and motivations associated with them.

A common means of dealing with such diversity is to devolve responsibility for the management of events to bodies outside the city administration. Events can be run on behalf of the city by individual event organisers (often commercial companies), or else by a specific body set up by the city to manage its portfolio of events.

For example, Promotion & The Arts is an independent subsidiary of the Baltimore Development Corporation, and is the official arts and events agency for the city. Founded in 2002, the non-profit organisation was formed through a fusion of the Office of Promotion with the Mayor's Advisory Committee on Art & Culture. Its mission is:

To make Baltimore a more vibrant and creative city in which to live, work and play by:

- Producing high-quality special events, festivals and arts programming that stimulate communities economically, artistically and culturally.

- Inspiring and promoting literary, performing and visual arts and artists.

- Celebrating Baltimore's rich, diverse heritage while enhancing the quality of life and sense of community for all residents.

- Forging partnerships that make Baltimore a premiere visitor destination.

- Managing cultural and historic attractions.

- Generating positive local, national and international publicity about Baltimore.

The organisation has 40 full-time and 15 part-time staff, aided by more than 100 volunteers. The organisation has a budget of almost $5 million (€3.6 million) and produces hundreds of events each year. It is overseen by a Board of Directors drawn from Baltimore Promotion & the Arts and Baltimore's Festival of the Arts.

'Ottawa Festivals' is a non-profit membership organisation that was established in 1996 in response to festival organisers, politicians and the tourism industry recognising the need for Ottawa's events to be carefully scheduled, properly planned and effectively promoted. At present, there are over 40 not-for-profit festivals, special events, and fairs that are members of Ottawa Festivals. As a cohesive body, Ottawa Festivals is able to advocate on issues affecting events and assist festivals, fairs and special events of varying sizes attain their goals. Ottawa Festivals is dedicated to providing support, presenting a united voice and creating an effective networking environment. (www.ottawafestivals.ca)

However valuable such coordinated approaches to management are, there remains a strong need to ensure the effective management of every individual event. A key issue that is often raised relates to the level of political involvement in the management of events.

Office of Citywide Event Coordination, New York

New York City is a frequent backdrop for special events, cultural activities, marketing opportunities and film shoots. To ensure that the City maximises its ability to properly accommodate these uses, it is imperative that City agencies coordinate their policies, procedures and permitting operations that pertain to the management of events in public spaces.

Founded in 2007, the Office of Citywide Event Coordination and Management (CECM) has oversight of all event permitting activity in New York City. CECM gathers and disseminates information about upcoming and ongoing public events, including gatherings in City parks, processions, parades, street fairs, block parties, commercial and promotional events, street events, displays and filming of motion pictures and television. The aim is to ensure informed decision making by the various permitting agencies, as well as compliance by permit applicants. CECM works to enhance communication among various agencies involved in the issuance of permits. This ensures that affected agencies are provided with timely information for proper advance planning to avoid vehicular and pedestrian traffic disruptions, as well as excessive noise in surrounding neighbourhoods.

www.ci.nyc.ny.us/html/cecm/html/about/about.shtml

As has been mentioned earlier, the differing roles played by the city with respect to event organisation require the development of adequate management structures. As discussed, this has been a clear issue in ECOCs, which are often expected to manage complex event programmes over many months or years and across the entire city, and sometimes its neighbouring regions. For this reason, it is valuable to study the organisational structures used by ECOCs, most of which have created 'independent' management structures (e.g. Luxembourg, 2007, Liverpool, 2008), although a few have been managed directly by a public body (e.g. Santiago de Compostella, 2000).

The organisational structure for Turku 2011 displays a functional approach to the management of the ECOC. Strategy is determined by the Board and a Steering Committee which includes Government Ministers, the Mayor of Turku and representatives from the cultural sector, the media, education and the private sector. The strategy is then made operational by an executive management team comprising a Managing Director and functional managers for finance, communication and programme. Long-term projects are treated as a separate issue, because they run beyond the time limits of the 2011 programme itself.

This division of strategic and governing roles, and the differing executive management roles are common in the management of most event programmes. In the ECOC in Luxembourg in 2007, the management of events was devolved to an arms-length body known as the General Coordination. This organisation made a distinction in the management of the programme between events that it directly funded and managed, and the other events in the programme, which were organised by external project managers. Although the General Coordination (39 staff) worked very well in running its own projects, there were a number of problems with the coordination of projects run by other bodies. This illustrates the tension between keeping tight control of events (which limits the number of manageable projects) and devolving control to third parties (which increases capacity but may introduce problems of coordination).

Helsinki 2000 Organisational Model

The Helsinki 2000 ECOC was governed by a Foundation which included representatives of National, Regional and City authorities, as well as the private sector and universities. The Foundation devolved operational issues to the Helsinki 2000 office, which was responsible for initiation and development of projects; coordination of the cultural programme; communication; promotion and marketing; fundraising and sponsorship; and finance and budget.

The production of almost all projects was decentralized and external to the Helsinki 2000 organisation, which signed cooperation agreements with the producers when projects had been approved. The Helsinki 2000 staff were not generators of ideas but facilitators and developers of ideas coming from outside. The cooperation agreement contained a project plan, marketing plan and budget and it defined responsibilities, obligations and rights of both parties. Financial payments were based on interim reports describing the progress of the project. Helsinki 2000 only directly produced a few projects, including Kide (Crystal), a public artwork consisting of nine glass cubes, which were originally erected in the nine European Cities of Culture in 2000 and which were permanently erected in Helsinki in 2002.

This model was new to Finland and necessitated an increased competence on the side of the producers who had to find partners and develop and implement strict budgets. The Foundation hoped that this model would act as an important training and learning experience for producers, who over the long term would help to develop the skills of the cultural profession and the creative industries of Finland.

The major benefits of this model were seen to be the creation of new partnerships and new operators in the field and new ways of working and networking across disciplines. Some producers criticised this model and saw the Foundation as an institutionalised funding organisation with heavy administrative demands.

ANALYSING STAKEHOLDER NETWORKS

As suggested above, implementing effective governance and providing strong and effective leadership require an understanding of the different event stakeholders in the city and their motives and needs. Mapping and analysing stakeholder networks allow a city to identify key players, areas of potential development and the policies and actions that might be needed to utilise stakeholder networks to their full potential. A number of theoretical approaches have been used to analyse the networks of stakeholders involved in the organisation of events. The most important of these are stakeholder analysis and network analysis.

Stakeholder analysis

Stakeholder theory provides a number of concepts that can be useful in analysing the construction, development and impact of events on the various groups involved in creating them. According to Schmeer (1999:4):

> *Stakeholder analysis is a process of systematically gathering and analyzing qualitative information to determine whose interests should be taken into account when developing and/or implementing a policy or program.*

Stakeholder analysis begins by looking at the groups and individuals who can affect an organisation or event. A stakeholder is defined by Freeman (1984:46) as 'any group or individual who can affect or is affected by the achievement of the organisation's objectives'. Different stakeholders have differing 'stakes' and degrees of influence. They can generally be seen as 'voluntary' (or primary) stakeholders who have made some form of investment in the event, and without whom the event would not exist, or 'involuntary' (or secondary) stakeholders who stand to be affected by the activities or outcomes of the event.

Direct or primary stakeholders include employees, volunteers, sponsors, suppliers, spectators, attendees and participants in an event, people without whom the event would not exist. Secondary stakeholders include government, host community, emergency services, general business, media and tourism organisations who have an interest in an event programme, but who are not indispensable for event production (Reid and Arcodia, 2002). Differing stakeholder roles also imply different degrees of power. Those funding the event, providing the cultural content or the audience will likely have most power.

> ## Event Stakeholder Groups
> In her study of the Malmo Music Festival, Larson (2004) identified both primary and secondary stakeholder groups:
>
> ### Primary stakeholders
>
> - The visitors
> - The music and artist industry (music/arts performers/bands and their contractors, production companies)
> - Public authorities (the local municipality and public organisations)
> - Sponsors (companies using the festival as a marketing tool)
> - Volunteers
> - Associations and clubs (members of various clubs working for the festival to earn money for their organisation/clubs participating in the festival performing different activities)
>
> ### Secondary stakeholders
>
> - Restaurants, hotels
> - The local trade and industry (suppliers of products and services constructing the festival product)
> - The media industry (journalists representing television and radio stations, newspapers and magazines)

According to Mitchell, Agle and Wood (1997) stakeholders therefore vary in terms of their possession of one or more of three relationship attributes:

- power;
- legitimacy; and
- urgency.

Those stakeholders with most power can usually impose their will on an events programme, but in order to effectively exercise power, stakeholders also need to be seen to have a legitimate claim (Larson and Wikström, 2001).

Urgency reflects the extent to which stakeholders can make a claim on immediate attention. Each stakeholder in a given situation will have differing degrees of these three attributes, and the most important will tend to have high levels of all the three. In the context of city event programmes, for example, established arts festivals dealing with international high culture often tend to have high levels of legitimacy, based on their links to art forms which are closely related to established cultural institutions and funding bodies. In the realm of popular and traditional culture, however, legitimacy and power often have to be gained via other means, such as high levels of civic participation; their attractiveness to visitors; and their potential for earning substantial revenue through ticket sales, merchandising, business hospitality, sponsorship and other means. In Barcelona, the established Grec arts festival is able to claim more legitimacy than newer events such as Sonar, which has to fight for its position based largely on audience numbers and economic impact (see Chapter 8).

The legitimacy of local government, as the representative of the local population and the authority responsible for regulating events in public space, is rarely questioned as a key stakeholder. However, many other groups will also try to identify ways of establishing legitimate claims over the staging or management of an event. The cultural sector is usually able to stake a legitimate claim to influence, on the basis that culture is 'good' for the community (Crespi-Vallbona and Richards, 2007).

Stakeholder theory emphasises that each group of stakeholders has differing levels of investment and influence in and expectations of events. Studying the role of stakeholders is essential from the perspective of developing and monitoring policy, and consequently on the role of events, as the ability of policies to mobilise stakeholders will have a large influence on the success of the event.

Event organisers must ensure that all stakeholder groups are given a voice and therefore that they are all consulted. This enables stakeholder groups that are not as strong as some others to be heard (Sautter and Leisen, 1999). Freeman (1984:46) further states 'to be an effective strategist you must deal with those groups that can affect you, while to be responsive (and effective in the long run) you must deal with those groups that you can affect'.

Network analysis

Network analysis is built on the idea that it is impossible to understand the behaviour of stakeholders without analysing the complex social relationships that link them or the context in which they operate. A network is formed by the actors (stakeholders), their activities and resources. The different actors in a network control different resources and create the potential for action by combining resources, which usually implies cooperation with other actors.

> *While stakeholder theory focuses on stakeholders and their potential for cooperation or threat from a focal firm's perspective, network theory views a phenomenon, such as a festival, from the perspective of the whole network, focusing on network structure and relationship processes. .... Whereas stakeholder theory is a somewhat static theory, network theory takes into consideration the dynamic processes going on between actors, which change the structure of the network.*
>
> (Larson, 2004:3)

Network analysis therefore adds a further dimension to stakeholder theory, allowing us to analyse the connections and power relationships between stakeholders. In Australia, an analysis of networks surrounding events policy (Stokes, 2006) explored the relationships within strategy networks; the relationships between actors/participants and their network positions; and network structures, membership and processes.

This research indicated a clear linkage between government motives for events investment, the policy environment and the institutional arrangements used to shape events. However, with the policy agenda often dominated by economic concerns, it was clear that community involvement often posed major challenges.

Events tourism strategies were emergent, rather than deliberate, which prompted the formation of loose, cooperative networks with changing leadership and irregular communication. Tight, formalised and collaborative networks consisting of multiple stakeholders were not evident in … these agencies. Network participants were mostly drawn from the government and corporate sectors, with limited recognition of the role of the community at the decision 'table' (p. 691).

Because the stakeholder networks around the event studied were not planned, but rather emerged from existing structures, they tended to be dominated by the public sector and provided limited opportunities for wider community involvement. This underlines the point that stakeholder involvement in an event is not just a question of including different groups related to the event on a board or management committee, but of ensuring that there is a broad network of stakeholder relationships, and that the position of different stakeholders is clearly represented within them.

Network theory emphasises that all stakeholders in the eventful city should be understood by knowing the precise context in which they operate and the interactions between the different stakeholders.

EVENT STAKEHOLDER GROUPS

It is clear from this analysis that although many different stakeholders can be identified for any given event or for a collectivity of events in a city, in general they can be classified into several main groups, including public authorities (local, regional, national), event organisers, staff and performers, the tourism sector, the private sector (local businesses), other donors (foundations, trusts, patrons), the media and local residents.

The public sector comprises a wide range of stakeholders at all levels of government, as well as many quasi-governmental organisations set up to deal with specific policy issues. In terms of the eventful city, the key stakeholders are frequently local governments, but national and regional bodies also tend to play an important role in funding events or backing bids to win events. Supranational governmental bodies, such as the European Union, are also increasingly becoming involved in the creation and support of certain types of events of international significance.

From the point of view of the public sector stakeholders, events are usually viewed as a means of generating various externalities, such as economic, tourism and social impacts, which support the wider policy agenda of government. No city stages events just to be eventful – the development of eventfulness is a deliberate attempt to improve the city, by making it more liveable, more equitable or more creative, or to improve the positioning and image of the city.

As the development of eventfulness responds to policy agendas, it is no surprise that there are often conflicts between different areas of the public sector about the aims and outcomes of events. There may be tensions between national and local governments in the development of events. For example, the identification of one city to host an event may run counter to policies for culture as a regional development tool. In Sweden, the organisation of the ECOC in 1998 was affected by the fact that the national government and the municipal government had different aims for the event. The national government wanted to reflect the social democratic ideal of inclusion by turning the year into a national event. However, the city of Stockholm, not surprisingly, wanted the spotlight to remain firmly on the capital, and the idea to have the cultural year in the whole country was seen by many as being too ambitious. The national government eventually created a separate organisation for 'culture in the whole country' during 1998 and there was lack of cooperation between the two projects. In many ECOC's, there has been a drive to ensure that the impact of the event is wider than its host city. In 2007 the ECOC was expanded to include Luxembourg and its Greater Region (which also included parts of France, Germany and Belgium); the 2010 ECOC covers the city of Essen and the whole of the Ruhr Region of Germany.

National government

National governments play a leading role in attracting and supporting major events, particularly in the sports sector. Hosting major competitions such as the Olympic Games, the Commonwealth Games, the World Cup or a World Championship is sometimes not feasible without the political support and funding provided by central government. This is also the case for certain events in the cultural field. The national government is most frequently a major funder for the ECOC and also has the responsibility of either nominating or managing the competition for the title.

As well as attracting and supporting major events, national government can also play a role in coordinating the organisation and collaboration of events across the national territory. In 1992, for example, Spain played host to the World Expo in Seville, the European Capital of Culture in Madrid and the Olympic Games in Barcelona. Robertson and Guerrier (1998) argued that the national government used these events as a means of building the national image of Spain. For the cities concerned, this meant that the events had to be 'sold' to the government as national projects, as well as satisfying the needs of the local stakeholders essential to stage the event. National support became important not just in terms of funding, but also in political terms, which was an essential element in winning the bidding process. They concluded that the national-city partnership is a delicate balance that is usually more beneficial to the individual city than the nation.

Winning the approval of national government for large-scale events of national or international significance is becoming increasingly important as the cost of events rise and government backing becomes a crucial component when competing for major events for a city, some of which are collaborations between different national governments. Joint hosting is becoming one way for smaller countries to compete for major events against bigger rivals, as the recent shared European Football Championships in Belgium and the Netherlands (2000), and Austria and Switzerland (2008) demonstrate. For cultural events, cooperation between national governments is being stimulated in the ECOC by the pairing of cities from different countries, as well as the increasing tendency for the event to spread across national borders.

Several national, regional and local governments have established organisations whose job is to attract major events to the country. One example in the UK is the Northern Ireland Events Company, which has supported almost 200 events since 1997 that have contributed an estimated £31 million (€46 million) to the economy.

A National Events Body for Scotland

In 2002 the Scottish Executive created a new agency, EventScotland, with an initial 3-year operational budget of £10 million (€16 million), designed to position Scotland as a world-class events destination. In 2005–2006, EventScotland supported 71 events with a total budget of £5 million (€7.5 million). These included not only major sporting events, such as the Heineken Cup Final and the Edinburgh Marathon, but also a large number of cultural events. These included international events such as the Edinburgh Festivals and the Glasgow International Festival of Contemporary Visual Art, as well as a raft of regional events, such as South Ayrshire's annual Burns Festival, the University of Aberdeen Writers Festival, the Mull of Kintyre Music & Arts Festival, the Fort William Mountain Film Festival and the Loch Lomond Food and Drink Festival. Although it is a national body, many of the events supported by EventScotland clearly have an important role for the eventful city. In 2006 EventScotland funded Edinburgh's Night Afore International event that led up to the annual Hogmanay celebration in the city (EventScotland, 2007).

The criteria used by EventScotland to select which events to fund clearly underline the economic rationale for national government intervention in this area. The questions that EventScotland poses to event organisers to see if their event is eligible for international event funding are:

- Will your event bring a significant number of spectators/ participants to Scotland?

- Will your event provide significant international media coverage of Scotland?

- Will your event provide an economic return on investment through additional visitor spending?

- Will your event leave a sustainable legacy for Scotland? (EventScotland 2007:2)

In the Middle East a number of Gulf countries (UAE, Bahrain and Qatar) have committed significant funding towards attracting major events, with event tourism seen as a fundamental component of their drive to capture more tourism expenditure. In Asia, Singapore has committed SG$500 million (€240 million) to its 'Sports Hub', with SG$6 million a year currently being invested in major sports events. Hong Kong styled itself the 'Events Capital of Asia', and introduced a major sports events programme that contributed to its later hosting of the equestrian competition at the 2008 Olympic Games in Beijing.

Local authorities

Because of the place specificity of most events, regional and local authorities usually have a central role in eventfulness. As the Coventry Cultural and Events Strategies Consultation (Creative Cultures and Associates, 2007:7) notes:

> As far as events are concerned, the Council holds most of the cards. Not only as the landowner do they have the absolute power to stop any event application in its tracks, but they are also the primary source for funding. Funding of events, and in particular its vulnerability, is a key issue, particularly when competing against other local authority priorities, which the Council has a statutory duty to fulfil.

Because of this responsibility of local authorities, there has been a widespread development of regional and local organisations dedicated to the attraction and management of events in recent years (see also Chapter 5).

One of the major issues for any local authority is the decision to finance events that generate significant costs for the public sector without generating much direct financial return. The escalating cost of events has exacerbated this problem. As Cruces (1998) notes in the case of Madrid, the cost of staging festivals more than doubled in the years immediately following the death of Franco and the return of democracy, as more grass roots celebrations were organised:

> In the 1980s there was growing friction between the local authority and local associations. The

administration of fiestas was therefore split into two parts – one dealing with citywide events and the other with local celebrations.

The local authority may play multiple roles as an event stakeholder. In some cases the public sector will be responsible for the conception, development, management and marketing of an event. The role of the local authority as event initiator emerged in many countries in the 1980s, as events were identified as a source of local economic development. More recently, this proactive role has declined as more cities have taken the role of event 'enabler' and either support independent organisations, or have created public private partnership organisations to develop and manage the events. There are certain events where the local authority creates the vision. Cattacin (1994) compares such an urban vision to the notion of a constitution for a nation, and argues that it represents a basic local consensus, which provides the framework for urban politics and collective action. Within this general framework, a cultural event may play a role in developing personal potential, education, social cohesion and economic benefits.

Many cities delegate event policy to an independent body that oversees the event programming on behalf of the local authority. One example is Rotterdam, where the Rotterdam Festivals Foundation coordinates event policy and undertakes initiatives to increase cultural participation in the city. Rotterdam Festivals Foundations was itself a positive spin-off from the events organised to celebrate the 650th anniversary of the city in 1990. Rotterdam Festivals Foundation has helped to attract major international events to the city, and has created a very successful programme of events year round.

The main activities and programmes coordinated and supported by Rotterdam Festivals Foundation are:

- Rotterdam Summer Festivals;

- Rotterdam Winter Festivals;

- September in Rotterdam;

- other activities; and

- thematic years and random projects.

The aim is to position Rotterdam as the main festival city of the Netherlands. In 2006 the city was given the accolade of Festival City of the Netherlands for the third time in the National Event Awards. Rotterdam Festivals Foundation has an annual programming budget of more than €2 million and has funding from the City of Rotterdam, the Rotterdam Development Corporation and the Port of Rotterdam.

As well as funding events, local authorities also set the policy context for events and develop visions of the role of events in city life (see also Chapter 3). In Barcelona, for example, Miralles (1998) argues that

The city of Barcelona has a history of a progressive festival policy. This policy tries to integrate things that are sometimes difficult to reconcile: orchestrating innovation and tradition, combining creativity and research, making the social and cultural dimensions of the fiesta compatible, decentralising elements of major events to the districts and elevating elements of local fiestas to major events.

Although local and regional authorities are usually the biggest supporters of events, they can also hinder event development. Because public events often have to be licensed by the local authority, any problems that an event might be perceived to cause, such as public order problems, noise or environmental damage, may create resistance by cities to the organising of events in some areas. For example the Beltane Fire Festival in Edinburgh was established in 1988, and received regular financial support from the City Council. However, in 1997 the council withdrew this support, and in 2003 the event was cancelled after the Council expressed concerns about safety, local residents complained about the noise and fire risk and the organisers complained about the escalating cost of the event. The festival was restarted in 2004, with visitors being charged entry to cover the cleaning bill for the Council. (http://www.beltane.org)

EVENT ORGANISERS, STAFF AND PERFORMERS

The importance of cultural producers and workers as a factor in the production of cultural events has not been studied extensively. This is probably related to the relatively small size of most festival organisations. Yet there is evidence to suggest that groups of cultural workers are responsible for a high proportion of cultural event startups. Event staff also has a vested interest in the continuation of events, or the creation of new ones. As noted above, cultural organisations such as events tend to have a 'life-cycle' (Maughan and Bianchini, 2003). In their early years, certain events subsist largely on the enthusiasm of a few dedicated individuals, and then as the events grow, they are forced to create more formal structures in order to survive.

The professionalisation of the events 'industry' has also created a new stakeholder group – the event organising company. It should be noted that the events industry as a whole encompasses services to a wide variety of areas including product launches; press conferences; corporate meetings and conferences; marketing programmes; special corporate hospitality events like concerts, award ceremonies, film premieres and fashion shows; and private events such as weddings and parties. A small and specialised branch of this larger industry deals more specifically with cultural events, often in cities. For example, DUCOS Productions in Rotterdam was originally founded in 1986, and now has 13 staff. DUCOS organises events such as the Rotterdam Summer Carnival, the Dunya Festival, Parkpop and the Terra Festival. The events organised by DUCOS reach an audience of around two million people a year. DUCOS operates behind the scenes on behalf of organisations such as Rotterdam Festivals Foundations (see above). In order to grow the business, DUCOS needs to generate new events and event-related products, which means it is a strong advocate for the eventful city. As Director Guus Dutrieux remarked recently after one major event: 'What we are doing now is looking for follow up. The purpose is create a national network in

Holland (that involves) programmes, venues, festivals, record labels, radio stations and television.'

The performers and artists at cultural events are also a principal stakeholder group. In some cases this group can assert their power, as in the 2005 strike of festival workers in France, which severely affected major events such as the Avignon Festival. Performers are important not just because they are central to the cultural product, but also because of their sheer numbers. For example at the Brighton Festival, which attracts 400,000 visitors, there are a total of over 6500 artists and performers involved in 1200 events. At the Edinburgh Festival, which includes several festivals, over 20,000 performers are involved in over 2000 different performances. Clearly, as key stakeholders their interests need careful attention.

CULTURAL AND COMMUNITY ASSOCIATIONS

Cultural associations are civil society organisations that often have a direct role in cultural festivals and events, where they provide a large proportion of the content of events, as organisers, helping to produce artworks or performing or working as volunteers. As Putnam (2000) notes, such organisations fulfil a vital role in undertaking social and cultural tasks that the public sector cannot or is unwilling to undertake.

There seems to have been an increase in cultural associations in a number of countries in recent years. In Croatia, for example, the number of cultural associations grew from 2174 in 2001 to 5032 in 2008, representing an increase in the share of the total number of associations from 11.2% to 13.8% (Compendium of Cultural Policies, 2009). Parramon (1997) shows that the number of ethnic (non Catalan) associations in the Baix Llobregat district of Barcelona Province grew substantially in the post-Franco era. The concentration of immigrants in major cities tends to form a major stimulus to the creation of cultural associations, and also to the staging of cultural events.

In Catalunya, much volunteering is related to cultural festivals and events (Pascual et al., 2001). A survey by the

Department of Culture of the Generalitat in 1996 found that almost 21% of respondents had taken part in neighbourhood cultural events, almost all of whom had also been involved in organising. Pascual et al. (2001) estimated that about 8% of the total Catalan population, or about 400,000 people, were involved in organising events of this kind. Cultural associations are frequently direct stakeholders in cultural events because of their concern with the content of such events. In Barcelona, over 30% of local fiestas are organised by cultural associations, and another 25% by neighbourhood committees. The high level of civic involvement creates a much more 'socialised' model of event creation and management (Richards, 2007b).

The Feria de Abril

The Feria de Abril in Barcelona is a smaller clone of the original event staged in Seville. The Barcelona version is held later in April so that Andalucians living in Barcelona can attend both events.

In the case of the Feria de Abril, García (1999) shows that the staging and running of the festival is an intensely political process, involving tensions between the organisers, politicians and suppliers. The event is aimed at almost 850,000 Andalucian migrants in Catalunya. The Feria is organised by the Federacíon de Entidades Culturales Andaluzas de Catalunya (FECAC), which aims to promote Andalucian culture in Catalunya, defend the rights of its member associations and to protect diversity in cultural values, identity and heritage.

However, as García points out, the FECAC is hardly representative of the whole Andalucian population, as it includes only about half the Andalucian associations in Catalunya. In fact, a new association, the Federacíon Andaluza de Communidades (FAC) was formed in 1999, including many groups who left FECAC. This development reflects the political power struggles that have raged over the Feria, as the organisers and politicians try to turn the event to their own ends. For example, the President of FECAC, Francisco García Prieto, is a businessman who has exclusive contracts to supply services to the Feria. There is a strong political and public financial support for the event, in spite of it's doubtful 'cultural' value. In 2007, local and regional

Continued

government contributed over one third of the total budget of €800,000. Politicians are keen to be associated with an event so closely linked to an important social group in Catalunya, and with a claimed three million visits a year.

In some cities, local authorities are attempting to devolve more control over events to local cultural and community groups. The basic argument for this is to give the local community more control over 'their' events, although some cynics may detect cost saving motives as well. In Luton, for example:

The local authority plans to hand over control of the carnival to the Luton Carnival Arts Development Trust, incrementally, over a period of 5 to 6 years. At present, the Trust acts as a steering group, with the council setting out clear milestones and acting as mentors. This is the process they followed with the Luton Mela, though the first attempt at handover in 2002 ended in conflict between community groups fighting over control. The council resumed control, but slowly brought in 'cultural activists' from the South Asian population. Last year an ad hoc Mela group was formed, and this year there was a fully fledged independent organisation, with a constitution, etc., to take the event forward.

(City University, 2006:5–6)

COMMERCIAL ORGANISATIONS

Commercial organisations are vital to events as suppliers of services to events and their visitors and increasingly as sponsors of events. Sponsorship is an increasingly important source of income for many events (see Chapter 6).

Commercial suppliers are responsible for many of the basic inputs to an events programme, including the provision of venues, light and sound equipment, catering, security, ticketing, marketing and a host of other services. As the professionalism of the events industry increases, so the degree to which services are contracted out to specialist suppliers will tend to increase. This means that more attention needs to be paid to contractual relationships with suppliers (see Chapter 6). For event programmes it may be possible to organise supply arrangements centrally to some extent, raising the bargaining power of individual events and cutting costs.

Commercial organisations are also important as suppliers of the cultural experiences provided by festivals, or as entrepreneurs involved in the production of festivals. Major performers are also getting directly involved in event development:

> *Coldplay is taking a cut of the revenue at the new Pemberton Festival. The band's manager is a major investor in the festival and helped select the location in British Columbia. At Stagecoach, a country-music festival in its second year in California, the Eagles were promised a percentage of the festival's ticket sales and merchandise in addition to the group's performance fee.*
>
> (Jurgenson, 2008)

Increasingly, however, there are also indications that business sponsors may try and influence the content of the event. Research among sponsors in New Zealand (Ministry for Culture and Heritage, 2008:5) indicated:

> *A trend towards businesses expecting to have a greater involvement in the content of sponsored events or activities continued in the 2007 results. More than 63% expected to have some influence on content and 10% always wanted a say.*

The amount of sponsor influence depends to a large extent on the event. In Hong Kong, the Arts Festival arguably limits the influence of the sponsor successfully and focuses more on the audiences. Although the Hong Kong Arts Festival has famous sponsors such as the Jockey Club and IBM, the sponsorships are linked to the Board of the festival, not the programmers. The DaDao Festival based in Beijing also sees itself as a 'sanctified place for artistry in the programming process that is never compromised'. The organisers use the event as a place for artists, and attracting a paying audience is not of major concern. There are individual and corporate sponsors, but they do not demand much and do not influence the event in any way.

THE MEDIA

The media is an important indirect stakeholder in events because it has the power to shape perceptions of an event's success or failure and to project its image locally and internationally. Most events therefore try and maximise their coverage in the media in order to increase the number of visitors and to raise the profile of the event and the city.

Effective partnerships with the media are vital to the success of events. The media provides publicity for the event, an outlet for reviews, an advertising medium and a potential source of sponsorship. Recognising the synergies, some major festivals have built very close working relationships with the media. For example, the BBC broadcasts live from festivals, such as Edinburgh and Glastonbury, and Sky Television provides a platform for the Hay-on-Wye book festival through its 'Hay-on-Sky' programming.

In other cases, the media can also become an adversary of an event or of the events programme in a city. For example, it is believed by some that the negative press campaign left an overall myth of Stockholm 1998 having been not very successful, thereby unintentionally legitimising a weak position for culture in subsequent municipal politics. In the city of Porto, many people have memories of the ECOC in Porto in 2001 as being besieged by road works and mud. Many of the infrastructural projects were not finished in time for the opening of the year and accessibility to cultural venues was hindered. The problems faced by Porto 2001 received considerable negative media coverage. Stories of mismanagement, misspent money and poor planning fuelled the frustrations of the local population. The Casa da Musica was originally planned to be opened in 2001 but, following a series of problems, finally opened in 2005. The building exceeded its original budget by three times and continues to be scrutinised by the press.

Frank and Roth (2000) analysed the way in which the media shaped the discourse among different actors about Weimar ECOC in 1999. They illustrated that the media does not act as a concerted block of stakeholders, but may vary in attitude according to their relationship with the city. In the case of Weimar, the national and local media took different views of the event. The national media still debated the feasibility of the event, while the local media had moved on to discuss who should provide the necessary resources. Paradoxically, by raising the issue of feasibility at the national level, the national media helped local organisers to make a case for providing funding for staging the event.

THE LOCAL COMMUNITY

The 'community' is often seen as one of the key stakeholders of an events programme, even though the concept of the 'community' is difficult to define. What is often meant by the community is a combination of individual local residents and others who inhabit, work in and otherwise have a commitment to the local area.

The local residents of the area in which an event programme takes place are important not only as a possible core audience, but also as event initiators and as a vital source of sustainability for most events. However, residents can also use their power as stakeholders to curtail or remove events that cause problems for segments of the local community, such as noise pollution, increased traffic and overcrowded parking. Local communities are not just passive observers of the process of festivalisation in the city, but active participants in shaping the festivalisation process.

Clearly, it is important to ensure the support of local residents for an events programme. In many cases, this support is built partly by ensuring that events are relevant to and have direct advantages for the local community. For this reason, the issue of access to events becomes an important component of social and cultural policy. The Council of Europe (1997:110) points out that the support of the local community may also be given in exchange for strengthening of local identity and pride – by giving local people ownership of the event. This local ownership has to be carefully managed, because inclusion of one group often implies the exclusion of others:

> *Exclusion is not simply an objective consequence of poverty or cultural difference; it can also be a political and social project to promote a group's sense of its identity. That is to say, it is a component, often a crucial one, of the politics of* inclusion. *The social cohesion of a club rests in good part on the reassuring knowledge that there are many people outside it who are not, and never could be, members.*

Willems-Braun (1994) similarly argues that festivals, like other forms of cultural capital, are consumed as part of the means of distinguishing self and others, and that participation is often limited to specific groups. This is a phenomenon that many event programmes are designed to overcome, by increasing access and reaching out to particular groups within the community that do not usually participate in culture (see Chapter 8).

The ECOC in Liverpool in 2008 aimed to stimulate participation across the population as a whole. The event's website claimed:

> *No other European Capital of Culture has attempted such ambitious levels of participation; the scale and reach of the programme make it unique. At the core of Creative Communities is a simple aim – to harness the creativity of Liverpool's people by making creativity an integral component of everyday life.*
> (http://www.liverpool08.com/participate/
> CreativeCommunities/index.asp)

Although such a superlative claim is debatable if one studies local participation in other ECOCs (Palmer-Rae, 2004), Liverpool 2008 did include a broad programme of events and activities aimed at celebrating diversity, increasing social cohesion and stimulating participation among young people. Around £11 million (€14 million) was invested in this programme, although the impacts of this may be difficult to assess.

Stakeholders in the Brugge 2003 ECOC

For Brugge (Bruges) 2003, an extensive study of stakeholder attitudes was conducted after the event (WES, 2003). Personal interviews were held with 30 stakeholders drawn from the cultural sector, event organisers, the tourism sector and policy makers.

The results of this research indicated that all stakeholders were pleased with the infrastructure developments that had taken place in advance of the ECOC, and particularly with the fact that €50 million in subsidies had been released by the government for this. Most stakeholders were also happy with the content and balance of the programme. Some emphasised the weakness of the programme with respect to contemporary art and events for younger audiences. These weaknesses were directly related to the nature of the city – Brugge is primarily a heritage city, and this was also reflected in the balance of the programme. It also lacks a significant student population to support youth culture events.

Stakeholders were also generally happy with the organisation and communication aspects of the event, and there was a general feeling that collaboration between cultural actors in the city had been improved.

Although there was general satisfaction with the social impact of the event, some stakeholders felt that the content of many arts events 'went over the heads' of local people. There was also a feeling that too many events were concentrated in the city centre, with little attention being paid to other parts of the city.

The stakeholders felt in general that the collaboration between different stakeholder groups was positive and professional. However, some forms of collaboration worked better than others. There was friction between the Brugge 2002 organisation and tourism promotion organisations, such as Toerisme Vlaanderen and Toerisme Brugge. The latter, in particular, was criticised by Brugge 2002 for a lack of proactivity and a lack of clarity over the division of tasks. In the end, a number of tasks were taken over by the ECOC itself.

There was general satisfaction over the marketing and promotion of the event and the impact it had on the image of the city. However,

Continued

some stakeholders were concerned about the ability of the city to maintain the mix of old and new that had been created for the event. This was also linked to concerns about the dissipation of the knowledge and expertise built up by the ECOC organisation during the event organisation process. Many suggested that the city should adopt a similar strategy to Antwerp, which created the Antwerpen Open organisation to carry on innovative projects (see Chapter 2).

However, in another independent study (Boyko, 2008b:174), a different picture emerges. He found that considerable differences existed between the local residents and events organisers: 'Many residents believed that their needs were not met throughout the tourist hallmark event lifecycle. Goals for the hallmark event often differed between what residents wanted and what organisers desired. Such disparities suggest that organisers may have been less interested in seeking local input for the hallmark event than they implied. Limiting the extent of public expression for the sake of creating a successful tourist hallmark event indicates that host communities are sometimes overlooked in favour of outside ideas and more autocratic leaders. As a result, some residents may have become disillusioned with Brugge 2002 and experienced resentment due to the non-local focus of organisers'.

This research underlines the fact that it is almost impossible to please all of the stakeholders all of the time. It is therefore important to use stakeholder network analysis to identify the groups that are most crucial for the achievement of the aims of the event, and to ensure that their support for the event is maintained. Any stakeholder evaluation needs to be conducted independently and objectively so that criticism and negative attitudes are not subsumed by positive views that hide or distort the reality of diverse points of view.

STAKEHOLDER CONFLICTS

With so many different stakeholder groups involved in event programmes, it is inevitable that from time to time conflicts will occur. For cultural events, some of the major conflicts often relate to programming. For example, not all stakeholders or stakeholder groups may agree with the programming strategy of the artistic director or coordinating body.

This has been most clearly demonstrated in the ECOC when selection procedures have been put in place to select projects to be funded as part of the programme. In Luxembourg in 2007, the decision not to fund a number of major projects proposed by museums led to conflicts between the museum directors and the ECOC coordination. The museum directors felt that, as part of the long-term cultural fabric of the country, they should have been given priority in terms of funding. The coordination of the ECOC argued that in order to stimulate innovation, new creative projects and younger organisations should be given preference. This type of conflict can sometimes become very public, as was the case in the Cork (2005) and Stavanger (2008) ECOCs. In Cork, opposition by some segments of the local cultural sector led to the formation of the organisation 'Where's me culture'? which organised alternative cultural events during the ECOC. A similar approach was taken by the organisation Ka Då Ittepå (What About Afterwards) in Stavanger.

National Arts Festival, South Africa – Stakeholder Conflicts

The National Arts Festival (NAF) in Grahamstown is one of the major events in the South African arts calendar. However, in charting the history of the event, Grundy (1994) illustrates how power struggles between the state, the black population and the largely white artistic establishments shaped its development.

Artists were keen to assert their freedom to express themselves, which 'put them in natural opposition to the mechanisms of state control' (p. 388). They were also opposed to avant garde art forms, which they did not always comprehend and 'mobilisation models of cultural governance (which) threatened entrenched arrangements' (p. 389). However, in the historic and political context of South Africa, this desire for artistic freedom cannot be divorced from the power structures created by apartheid. The Foundation running the event was originally an all-white affair, whose council appointed the chairman for the festival committee, who in turn selected members of the committee. 'Ostensibly these appointments are made to bring onto the committee professionals representing each of the key artistic disciplines involved in the NAF (p. 390).'

In the early years the committee reflected 'audiences at Grahamstown (who) were largely financially well-off English-speakers who

Continued

wanted to see and hear the classics, the "names". For them, contemporary theatre and music were threatening' (p. 392).

On the other hand, the Standard Bank, who was sponsoring the event, wanted to avoid controversy and negative associations with the white settler past. The Bank secured greater representation on the board in order to distance the festival from the foundation. During the 1980s it also programmed more artists who were in tune with liberal white South Africa, including works by Athol Fugard and Pieter-Dirk Uys. This also brought the festival more into line with the political climate in the later years of the apartheid regime, when dissent was more openly expressed.

CONCLUSION

The importance of stakeholders in event programmes has long been recognised, but attention is also increasingly being focused on the positions of different actors in relation to events and each other. Cities need to be aware of the positions and needs of their different stakeholder groups, and how stakeholder networks will impact on the development, organisation and success of the event programme.

Because there is a wide range of direct and indirect stakeholders in any event programme, stakeholder networks are likely to be extremely complex in most cities. Clear communication with stakeholders is therefore crucial to ensure that these diverse groups feel included in the process of event development.

The city itself needs to examine its own position as a key stakeholder in most event networks. The public sector will often function as a gatekeeper for other stakeholders, regulating flows of funding and the controlling organisation of events. In this position, public sector bodies also need to avoid excluding other stakeholders through adopting too dominant a role. They also need to recognise that their role relative to different elements of the event programme can change, with governments sometimes operating as gatekeepers for some events and as a primary stakeholder for others.

At the same time, the stakeholders of the eventful city also need to be effectively 'managed' to reduce friction between potentially conflicting interests and to maximise stakeholder support for the aims of the city and its event programme.

CHAPTER 5

Managing and Organising the Eventful City

Given the complexity of the external environment in which event programmes operate, effective management and organisation of eventfulness in cities are essential. Not only do the expectations and activities of event stakeholder networks need to be managed (as outlined in the previous chapter), but cities also need to marshal the resources required to support events, manage those resources effectively and generate the desired outcomes and impacts from the event programme.

As Long and Owen (2006:78) point out, a professional approach to management and organisation is increasingly demanded from cultural events in general:

> *A professional approach to management in arts festivals is necessary due to the complex legal and regulatory frameworks within which they operate; budgets that typically include a combination of public funding, earned income and private sector sponsorship; and the consequent need to demonstrate accountability and returns on investment.*

Cities and events organisers need to work together not only to ensure that separate events are effective but also to ensure that the resulting event programmes create additional benefits beyond those of each individual event. If individual events simply follow their own agendas rather than contributing towards the strategic aims of the places that host them, any support offered to them may be considered questionable.

This chapter concentrates on the strategic management of the eventful city rather than the management of individual events, which has been exhaustively covered in other studies. This chapter also links with issues of governance and as discussed in Chapter 4 (Leadership, Governance and Stakeholders), and financial management, dealt with in Chapter 6 (Finance and Funding for Event Programmes).

THE MANAGEMENT OF EVENTS

There is a considerable body of literature on the management of events, which is increasingly seen as specific area of management, requiring a specific set of skills and knowledge (Bowdin and et al., 2006; Getz, 2005). As Silvers (2004:1) summarises:

> *Event management is the process by which an event is planned, prepared and produced. As with any other form of management, it encompasses the assessment, definition, acquisition, allocation, direction, control, and analysis of time, finances, personnel, products, services and other resources to achieve objectives.*

However, the management of the eventful city is different from event management per se. In effect, it involves the management of resources and stakeholders to achieve the objectives of a city or region as a whole, not just a single event.

Managing the eventful city therefore concentrates on a series of processes which utilise events as resources to achieve a wider set of strategic objectives. These processes include the following:

- Coordinating a programme of events.

- Dealing with a wide range of event stakeholders, both direct and indirect.

■ Creating structures for accountability.

■ Increasing the accessibility of events.

■ Ensuring equitability in event organisation and participation.

■ Ensuring event sustainability.

■ Ensuring compatibility between the objectives of individual events and the objectives of the city.

Managing all of these processes is a complex business that requires the application of diverse management skills, including strategic management, human resource management (HRM), financial management and visitor management.

One of the key strategic decisions that a city needs to make is the level of involvement it will have in events. Will it be directly involved in the production of events or will it stand aside and let others organise them?

The roles taken by cities in relation to events might be seen as a spectrum that stretches from almost 'laissez-faire' (light or limited influence, with few conditions) to 'controlling' (heavy involvement, with major conditions). Indeed, some cities adopt a model of 'direct provision', where the city administration itself or another body that is controlled by it manages events directly; others prefer 'indirect provision' by supporting other independent organisations or companies to manage. Once again, cities may use both models, depending on the nature, scale and cost of the event programme (see also Chapter 3 in relation to programming).

The Roles of City Authorities in Relation to Event Programmes

In the City of Auckland, New Zealand, the council identifies the following range of roles it may have in events:

Leader – The council champions, coordinates, advocates, plans and provides an events focus for the city. It is a catalyst for partnerships and cooperative arrangements for events.

Continued

Provider – The council provides for the organisation of events it funds directly. It also provides event venues.

Sponsor – The council invests in events organised by others.

Communicator and promoter – The council generates enthusiasm and energy for events it or others put on by enhancing communication and promotion, undertaking public relations and leveraging the council's profile.

Facilitator – The council assists events by taking a coordinating, regulatory and advisory role through relationship management.

(Auckland City Council, 10 Year Plan, 2009–2019)
http://search.aucklandcity.govt.nz/cgi-bin/MsmGo.exe?grab_
id=0&page_id=5163&query=10%20Year%20Plan&SCOPE=WWW

Therefore, management of the eventful city can be exercised directly or indirectly, or in combination. In the case of Liverpool, for example, the approach to organising the ECOC (European Capital of Culture) in 2008 was to facilitate event production largely by guiding others in the organisation and management of events. The Liverpool Culture Company produced an event planning guide, as well as individual guides for different types of events, available to prospective event organisers on their website:

As an event organiser you are responsible for the planning, organisation and operation of the event. The Liverpool Culture Company, together with other organisations, has produced an Event Planning Guide to enable you to plan your event safely and legally. There are also a series of accompanying brochures containing helpful hints and tips for specific types of events.
http://www.liverpool08.com/Images/Event%20Guide_
tcm146-126272.pdf

In contrast, some cities have adopted more centralised organisational models for their ECOC programmes. In some cities, such as Athens (1985), Florence (1987) and Bologna (2000), the local authority took a much more central role in organising the event:

Although an independent organisation, Bologna 2000 had close links with the municipality. Besides the

prominent role of the counsellor for culture, the
General Director was an employee of the municipality
and had been the head of cabinet for the Mayor. The
Mayor was also a strong supporter of the project.
Respondents held very different views on the links
between the two organisations. Some thought that
close political links were necessary to drive the project
forward; others thought that the project was too
dependent on one administration, and was vulnerable
when the government changed in 1999.

(Palmer-Rae, 2004:116)

When looking at the contemporary eventful city there is
a general tendency for public authorities to adopt a more
'arm's length' approach to offering support to events in the
same way that most authorities offer support to arts or sports
organisations. There may be no strong case for treating
events in a different manner.

The City of Ottawa has an excellent arms-length
policy for determining levels of funding. A jury of
experts in the field reviews all grant applications and
assesses them on excellence in programming, quality
of management, contribution to the community,
support of local artists, economic impact and impact
on tourism. All festivals that receive ongoing city
funding are required to submit highly-detailed reports
including annual audited statements. People who run
successful festivals are among the best managers you
will ever find.

(Armour, 2006)

However, there is also evidence of some cities taking
a more 'controlling' approach with some events. For example
in Melbourne:

Chinese New Year 2007 was the first major event
conducted by Events Melbourne under the
'Community Events Model'. Under this event
management model, in addition to the City of
Melbourne contributing sponsorship funds for the
event via the Event Partnership Program, Events

Melbourne also assumed the role of event organiser, in association with the event owner, coordinating and delivering all logistical components of this major event.

(Report to Marketing and Events Committee, Melbourne City Council, 8 May 2007)

Another example is the Caribana Festival in Toronto:

As an indication of how serious local officials are about festivals, the City of Toronto this year intervened directly to replace the Caribbean Cultural Committee, which has been running Caribana for 38 years, with the Festival Management Committee. It says it made the move after an audit of Caribana's financial statements. But it was also done to ensure the beleaguered festival – renamed the Toronto Caribbean Festival – survives and continues to pump dollars into the local economy.

(Prashad, 2006)

These examples of management models indicate a number of common patterns, one of which is a division of managerial responsibilities between different bodies. In many cases, the bodies responsible for a higher-level city-wide event strategy are different to those with responsibilities for the delivery of the operational aspects of event programmes. In general, the strategic function tends to be closer to the city administration to ensure that the aims of the event programme are aligned to political goals and the operational aspects are usually more devolved, either to an events unit with the city administration or to independent event organisations and other forms of event management structures.

In the following sections, first the issue of strategic vision and management is analysed, and then the more operational areas of management, including HRM, risk management and performance and quality management, are outlined and their implications for the eventful city are discussed.

VISION AND STRATEGY FOR THE EVENTFUL CITY

Strategic management involves marshalling resources in order to ensure the long-term future of an organisation (Dobson and Starkey, 2004:3). In the eventful city context, effective strategic management involves analysing the external and internal environments of the city, making decisions about the direction of the events and taking action to achieve its goals.

The first step in strategic management is an analysis of strategic goals – setting a vision, mission and strategic objectives. The vision should include the following:

- a purpose: some explanation of why events are important;

- a strategy: defining relevant product markets and the positioning in them, bearing in mind the wider strategic context within which events are developed;

- a set of values: the beliefs that underpin the management style and its ethics; and

- standards and behaviours: a summary of some of the most important standards to which the city and its event programme need to adhere.

The vision of EventScotland, set out in *Scotland's Major Events Strategy 2003–2015: Competing on an International Stage*, is 'To become one of the world's foremost events destinations by 2015'. This sets out the basic purpose of the organisation and also the market within which it will operate. Its mission is then:

To deliver a viable portfolio of major events to attract visitors to Scotland, to enhance Scotland's international profile, to strengthen our sporting and cultural infrastructure and to maximise the economic, social and environmental benefits of events to all parts of the country.

(Scottish Government, 2002)

This mission statement clarifies purpose and strategy, while the values, standards and behaviours of EventScotland are explained in more detail elsewhere in its strategy. The values of the organisation are implicit in some of its key priorities, including the desire to attract 'events which stimulate a sense of pride in the local population' and 'events which are sustainable and which are accessible to a wide range of communities and groups'.

The strategic vision for EventScotland illustrates some of the key elements which should be contained in the vision for public bodies:

■ the public value their activities seek to generate;

■ the sources of legitimacy and support they can rely on to produce that value; and

■ the operational capacity they require to achieve their goals.

In the case of EventScotland, the public value is clearly expressed in the mission through the development of infrastructure and the creation of economic, social and environmental benefits. Legitimacy for the strategy is based on the involvement of major national bodies in its formulation. The strategy was drawn up by a 'steering group involving representatives of the key public sector bodies already involved in events in Scotland, including SportScotland, VisitScotland, the Scottish Arts Council, Scottish and Highlands and Islands Enterprise, the Convention of Scottish Local Authorities (CoSLA) and the city councils of Edinburgh and Glasgow' (p. 2). By gathering such key stakeholders behind the strategy and implicating them in the formulation of the mission, the resources necessary to undertake the strategy can also be mobilised. The organisational context was also clearly set out in the strategy:

EventScotland will be a joint venture between the (Scottish) Executive and VisitScotland. Although it will receive its funds through VisitScotland, it will account for these funds separately and EventScotland will operate independently of VisitScotland in its day-to-day activity. It will be governed by a Supervisory Board chaired by the Minister for Tourism Culture and Sport with representatives of Sportscotland, VisitScotland, the Scottish Arts Council, Scottish and Highlands and Islands Enterprise, CoSLA and the cities of Edinburgh and Glasgow. The Minister will also invite key private sector organisations to be represented on the Supervisory Board (p. 6).

In the City of Auckland in New Zealand, a high level of involvement and control of the event programme is evident.

City of Auckland

In Auckland, New Zealand, the city council itself develops and implements the events strategy. This strategy allows Auckland City to be more proactive, collaborative and supportive of events that enliven the city.

It seeks to:

- support Auckland's unique identity and Pacific flavour;
- acknowledge the importance of events as a major economic driver for Auckland city;
- support a flourishing economy;
- contribute to a strong sense of place through arts, culture and recreation; and
- increase Auckland city's profile, nationally and internationally.

The strategy is complemented by the Central Business District (CBD) public activity strategy that focuses more specifically on enlivening the CBD through events and other activities.

When putting resources into events and activities the council wants to achieve:

- a vibrant event-friendly city with lots happening that contributes to Auckland's sense of place; and
- a place that celebrates its identity, has a flourishing economy and engages its communities.

The strategy has three goals, each with a number of strategies:

- goal 1 focuses on developing the council as a more event-friendly organisation;

Continued

- goal 2 includes strategies and guiding principles for a calendar of events, which apply citywide, although the signature events are largely located in the CBD; and

- goal 3 is about developing venues and outdoor spaces for large events.

http://www.aucklandcity.govt.nz/council/documents/events/default.asp.

Some cities have recognised the benefits of a more decentralised approach to event strategy-making by devolving the management of events across several different public bodies, rather than concentrating functions in a single organisation.

The Management of Major Events in London

In London, the management of major events is effectively split between three different bodies. The Mayor of London deals with event management, administration and event delivery. Visit London (the city's tourist board) is responsible for business planning, research, bid development, branding and marketing. Finally, the London Development Agency deals with event funding, performance management and event evaluation. The activities of these different organisations are coordinated by the Events for London Board, which over the period 2004–2009 was allocated a total budget of £11.8 million (€14.5 million) for the major events programme (London Development Agency, 2007). The remit of Events for London is to:

- Provide a 'one-stop-shop' leadership.

- Own and manage the major events programme.

- Market London as a destination for major events.

- Be a key channel for major events' funding.

- Develop strategic and collaborative relationships with partners/ stakeholders to bid for and win major events for London.

- Be the 'voice' of London's major events sector.

In terms of event delivery, there are a myriad of event organisations in London, some financed primarily by public sector bodies (the Mayor of London, different London Borough Councils, the Arts Council, Visit London, London Development Agency), and others through private sources (businesses, foundations, different forms of revenue-generation).

The strategic role of the city with regard to the event programme can also change over time, depending on how the programme is developed and organised. In many cities, for example, there is now an emphasis on bidding for and attracting events (see Chapter 2). In these cases, the process of securing an event will require those responsible for the event programme to exercise different skills at different stages of the process.

For example, Frank and Roth (2000) in their analysis of the discourse surrounding the Weimar ECOC in 1999 identified a number of key stages in event development, which can usefully be extended using the experience of other ECOCs.

Application phase

The application phase involves gathering support from stakeholders for the event and the preparation of an event bid or application. In the Weimar ECOC application stage, various issues were mentioned in both local and national newspapers: the costs and benefits of the event for the city, the image and identity of Weimar and the understanding of the event. Getting major stakeholders behind the bid is crucial in influencing arguments at this stage.

Nomination phase

In the case of Weimar 1999, the nomination stage was the shortest phase, lasting only one week: the days before and after 5 November 1993, the day the nomination was announced in the media. For events where there is considerable competition to stage an event, this phase may be much longer. For example, during the process of selecting the ECOC for Hungary for 2010 the nomination phase lasted 8 months. The selection process for designating the ECOC in the UK in 2008 took more than 2 years.

For many events, no competition exists, but the process of gathering support remains important, since the stakeholders are essential for staging the event even if no right to stage it has to be 'won'.

Preparation phase

While feasibility, costs and benefits still remain important issues during the preparation stage, responsibility and participation are equally important. The question of who should be responsible for what and who should participate in what aspects of staging the event often dominates the public debate, including the responsibilities for finance, organisation, programming and marketing.

Once the funding is in place and an organisational framework has been devised, the attention of the organisers invariably shifts towards programming and the selection of projects. For the ECOC this generally involved consultation with a wide range of stakeholders although ultimately, difficult decisions about which projects to fund have to be taken by the organisation. This often created a need to manage the disappointment of the projects which were not selected. As the Palmer-Rae (2004:49) report notes:

> Organisations managing programmes of the cultural year in about half the cities studied indicated that issues surrounding 'political interference' created substantial problems. Such 'interference' from the points of view of the organisers included incidents where politicians insisted on the inclusion of projects that were of particular interest to them or which took place in the neighbourhoods which elected them, the allocation of funds from the ECOC budget to support particular initiatives with which they were associated, personal priorities for infrastructure improvements, the selection of images for media campaigns, or even the 'censorship' of controversial projects.

If this process is not handled effectively, it can have far-reaching consequences. In some ECOCs there were fierce arguments about the vision of the event and its programming between different stakeholder groups. In the case of Liverpool 2008, for example, such discussions eventually led to the original 25 member governing body being reduced to six members and Phil Redmond being appointed as a new Deputy Chairman of the Liverpool Culture Company just weeks before the official opening. There are many examples of resignations and new appointments in the run up to ECOC as a direct result of differences of view that arise in relation to funding, priorities and programme selection.

Implementation phase

Once the event actually starts, the marketing and public relations strategy often focuses a great deal of attention on the opening and the early events in the programme.

Once the programme is underway, the organisation then concentrates on administering the programme and on marketing activities. Many recent ECOCs have shifted towards a seasonal model of programming (see Chapter 3) as this provides a number of themes during the year, which can be used to regenerate media and public interest in the event.

Evaluation phase

For non-recurrent events, once the event is over, those responsible for organising may move on to new jobs, and there may not be a serious attempt at evaluation. Although all events should go through the final evaluation stage, if the organising team is moving on to another event, they may not be so concerned about evaluating the impacts of the last. This is a familiar story with many of the ECOCs. As Silke Roth (pers. commun. 22 January 2007) noted: 'we applied for grants to evaluate the effects of Weimar 1999, but did not get funding. Since all those involved in carrying out the project were on fixed term contracts, we looked for work elsewhere'. This underlines the importance of establishing an organisation in the city, which has responsibility for monitoring major events. Without this, the city may not evaluate the success of the event and as a consequence will not learn anything from the experience.

The ECOC experience indicates that different managerial and organisational skills are required at different points in the programme life cycle. Issues of vision and strategic management will be more important in the early phases of implementation, and gradually operational issues, such as HRM, performance management, financial management (Chapter 6) and marketing (Chapter 7), will be given more attention.

HUMAN RESOURCE MANAGEMENT

Staging events in any city requires a substantial collective input of labour, and finding and managing staff is a major issue for the eventful city. The central team of full-time paid staff involved in coordinating a city-wide, region-wide or even nation-wide programme of events may be very small. However, there also may be a mass of performers, contractors and volunteers engaged in producing events, which may add complexity to the human resource issues of an event programme. In spite of this, many events do not have a specific HRM strategy (van der Wagen, 2007). For individual events, considerable attention has to be paid to issues such as recruitment and selection, training, retention and volunteer management. For the eventful city, however, the human resource issues are somewhat more restricted when the city is more occupied with strategic than operational management issues. In terms of implementing the strategy, the key issues are often the recruitment and retention of event leaders and other key event staff, and the recruitment and management of volunteers.

As discussed in Chapter 4, leadership is crucial to event programmes. Finding, managing and retaining good leaders are therefore key issues in HRM for the eventful city. When leaders for individual events are being appointed, the city will often have a direct or indirect influence on the selection process. As a major stakeholder in the event programme, the presence of city representatives on the board of major events will often give them a direct say. Indirectly, the city may also influence decision making as a factor in relocation decisions by key staff.

Often the search for leaders for major events is international, involving the use of headhunting firms as well as seeking personal recommendations from those in the cultural sector. Major events can also hope to attract leaders who bring experience and charisma with them. The Australian Director Brett Sheehy was in charge of four Sydney Festivals and two Adelaide Festivals before taking over the Melbourne Festival in 2009.

The possibility that event leaders will move from one city to another to develop their own career throws light on the importance of retaining talent. Although the appointment of a new leader can be an opportunity to inject fresh vision and energy into a programme, the departure of key staff may also mean that some of the organisational capital relating to events is lost. Some cities seem to suffer particular problems in this regard, as the ECOC experience indicates:

> *The operational team for Thessaloniki 97 experienced major changes in personnel over the course of preparations: three different Managing Directors in turn; four different Artistic Directors; three different managers of the Press office; and numerous other resignations. One factor seems to have been the lack of clear responsibilities within the organisation, especially between the Board, its many sub-committees and the operational team. Besides the operational directors, influential figures included the Minister of Culture at the time, the Vice-President of the Board of Directors and the Secretary of the Board (also Director of the Administrative department).*
>   (Palmer-Rae, 2004, vol. 2:47)

Just as in more permanent organisations, event programmes need to be able to offer staff clear guidance and stable working conditions at all levels of the organisation if they want to prevent high rates of turnover. The experience of the Stavanger ECOC in 2008 illustrated that a lot of work was needed to avoid potential conflicts between 'permanent' and more ephemeral staff in the organisation (Miller, 2009).

Managing volunteers

Volunteers are increasingly an important part of major events, but are also vital for smaller scale events. An eventful city needs to consider how volunteers are recruited and retained, and how all events that are staged in a city might benefit from a volunteer pool. Culture and sport are important areas of volunteering in society as a whole, so volunteers become an important element of the human resource pool for cultural events. Cities are also increasingly developing semi-permanent pools of volunteers, who can be called upon as and when the need arises.

Arguably, people will be more willing to volunteer for events, as they are limited in time. People have more pressure on their leisure time now than they did in the past, and it appears that volunteers may be more interested in '...finite project-based, team-based activity rather than a year- or decade-long commitment' (Hollway, 2002:58). Slaughter (2002) also argued that there was a growing trend towards higher levels of volunteerism in community events in Australia.

The experience of the Olympic Games underlines the growth in volunteer labour. As Karlis (2003) notes, the concept of 'Olympic volunteer' is fairly young. It was not until the Olympic glossary of the Official Report of the Barcelona Games that the concept was first defined. However, the number of volunteers for the Summer Olympics has increased from 28,000 at the Los Angeles Games (1984) to 100,000 for the Beijing Games (2008). Managing such a large number of voluntary staff poses enormous challenges, not least because the many motivational tools applied to paid staff (such as remuneration levels or the threat of dismissal) cannot be equally applied to volunteers. Ensuring that volunteers are motivated, happy and satisfied can be a vital part of creating the right atmosphere for events.

The Barcelona Olympic Games in 1992 generated 102,000 responses to its call for volunteers. Of these, 35,000 were eventually selected to work for the Olympics and the Paralympics. Each volunteer went through a training course on-site and off-site, and management structures were put in place to coordinate the activities and evaluation of volunteers before and during the event. A manual was produced and given to each volunteer, as a means of creating a common culture among the volunteers themselves as well as informing them of procedures.

The keys to success of the Barcelona 1992 programme according to Clapés (2002) were the following:

- The development of a detailed training plan which was flexible enough to allow the training to be carried out at the times and in the forms most appropriate to the organisation and the volunteers.

■ A motivational plan to link the training to the actual experience of the volunteers during the Games.

■ A selection process to choose volunteers and match them to specific tasks.

■ Giving the volunteers a thorough knowledge of the installations in advance of the Games.

■ Clearly defined rights and duties for the volunteers.

■ A volunteer management manual, giving clear guidance on the supervision and management of volunteers and groups of volunteers.

■ A Volunteers Champion to look after the interests of the volunteers and to solve their problems during the event.

As Clapés (2002) points out, it is easy for an event organiser to recruit too many volunteers, without considering the cost that this generates in terms of recruitment, training, supervision and use of materials. Recruiting and training volunteers can be an expensive exercise; for example, the average cost per volunteer at the Olympic Games in Sydney in 2000 was AUS\$700 (€400) per head (Hollway, 2002:59).

In the case of the Sydney Olympics in 2000, Brettell (2001) explained that:

The volunteers were, as we always believed they would be, absolutely fundamental to the success of the games. They were an extraordinary, powerful force in creating an atmosphere which left so many visitors and even some hard-nosed Australians with such special feelings about our city, about our country and above all about ourselves.

According to Brettell, the keys to volunteer success in Sydney included the following:

■ recognition of the importance of volunteers to us;

■ the uniqueness of our product;

■ community support;

■ positioning our volunteers as part of the team; and

■ our Pioneer volunteers.

The organisation had a team of 500 volunteers who were involved for a number of years before the Games, and who became known as the 'Pioneers'.

For major events, managerial structures need to be created in order to manage such large numbers of people. The appointment of volunteer supervisors to oversee a team of volunteers is a method often used at large events. Human resource planning has to be undertaken in order to assess the resource needs for individual events, and in the context of the eventful city, for the whole programme of events. For example, the Australian Sport Commission (2000:14) argues that:

A well-defined job description for event volunteers should contain the following:

■ an appropriate job title;

■ an outline of the benefits of the job to event volunteers;

■ a brief description of the aims of an event;

■ the purpose of the job;

■ the tasks to be performed;

■ the name of the event volunteer's immediate supervisor;

■ the time the job requires, including the amount of time the job requires per day during the planning and staging of an event;

■ the qualifications, attributes and/or skills that may be necessary to effectively carry out tasks associated with the job; and

■ any information that helps event volunteers decide whether to take the position, including special conditions such as a matters of confidentiality, special training or attendance at meetings, and security checks.

Once recruited, event volunteers also need to be given an orientation, which might include the following:

- history and aims of the event, when and why the event began and for whom the event is conducted;

- how the event is funded and managed;

- staffing of the event, such as how many people there are and what they do;

- structure of the event organisation, including where event volunteers fit within it; and

- details about volunteer management policies.

(ibid:20).

In order to manage a large team of volunteers, supervisory volunteers (or 'pioneers') need to be recruited early in the event planning process, as they will usually take over more complex tasks (including training other volunteers).

Brettell (2001) recommends a two-phase volunteer recruitment process to coincide with the planning and coordination of an event and actual event delivery. Supervisory volunteers should be recruited early in the event planning and coordination process, whereas operational level volunteers may not be required until the date of an event draws closer. Supervisory level volunteers are usually required to carry out more complex and time-consuming tasks and have higher levels of responsibility than operational volunteers. Clear and concise volunteer policies are important to the fair and consistent management of event volunteers. Recognition activities, both informally at a post-event celebration, and more formally, are important components of successful event volunteer HRM programmes.

This underlines the fact that volunteers are not 'free' – they require considerable investment in planning and management time if they are to be used effectively.

Some of the European Capitals of Culture developed extensive 'ambassadors' programmes, using volunteers to act as a relay for information and assist the operational team. In Lille (2004), for example, the main tasks of the ambassadors were to spread the message about the event and to help behind the scenes with logistics and welcoming artists and tourists. The ambassadors were kept informed about events with regular newsletters, the first of which was produced in December 2002. The vast majority of ambassadors were local residents, but about 10% came from abroad. By the time the programme opened in January 2004, the ambassadors' newsletter was also being produced in English, as well as in French. This system worked so well that it was repeated for the 'Lille 3000' event, which was designed as part of the follow-up to Lille 2004. The Lille 3000 events held in 2007 were supported by 33,000 ambassadors, almost twice the 2004 number.

Attempts to use volunteers in the absence of a culture of volunteering or without purpose-built management structures can create problems. When Sheffield in the United Kingdom made its bid for the 1991 World Student Games, for example, they drew up a budget on the basis of using 5000 volunteers. They were relying on the experience of previous editions of the event, where thousands of volunteers (mainly students) had worked at the Games. They overlooked the fact that all previous editions of the games had been staged in socialist countries where 'volunteering' for such events was an expected duty for young people. When it came to recruiting volunteers in the free market, post-industrial environment of Sheffield, volunteers were much harder to find.

There is also a need to ensure that a volunteer programme does not reduce employment opportunities for local people. In Brugge (WES, 2002) there were complaints that the volunteers were extensively used to fill relatively low-level functions that could also have been done by locally recruited labour, reducing the economic and social impacts of the event.

ACCOUNTABILITY IN THE EVENTFUL CITY

One of the basic management tasks for the eventful city is ensuring the accountability of the events programme. Performance needs to be measured in various ways to see if the programme is delivering the desired outcomes established in the events policy of the city. This in turn helps the event programme to be effectively steered, and it allows the event producers and others involved in the events process to be held accountable for their activities. This ensures that the development of eventfulness is subject to democratic control and gives stakeholders the opportunity to exercise some influence over the process.

In the Australian city of Melbourne, the staging of events is overseen by a Marketing and Events Committee, which screens events that require an investment of over AU$50,000 (€30,000). The Committee meets every 2 months and members include the Lord Mayor and Deputy Lord Mayor, seven councillors and a legal adviser. The Manager of Events Melbourne also presents regular reports to the Committee.

The need to manage events effectively is clearly set out in the events strategy:

> The strategic focus of the City of Melbourne is to ensure that events contribute to the objectives of Council by maximising their benefits through the effective management, marketing and facilitation of the Melbourne events calendar. This ensures the safe and effective management of events as well as the building and maintenance of relationships with all event organisers and tourism industry stakeholders.

Events are evaluated in terms of their fit with the policy framework of the city, the context of the event, its contribution to the city and the legal implications. For example, one of the most important considerations is the extent to which an event contributes towards the strategic objectives of the city, which includes as Strategic Objective 3:

Inclusive and engaging city

- *Attract, facilitate and maximise the benefits of major city events and festivals.*
- *Attract, support, partner and create a range of key events that reflect the diverse needs of the*

Melbourne community and visitors to the city and ensure a balance between major international events and local events.

■ *Promote the city and 'city experience' as the focus of the Melbourne major events and festivals Programme.*

Performance and quality management

It is very important for a city to ensure that the events in its programme are well run and provide a certain quality of service and experience for participants. Achieving this requires the design and implementation of effective performance and quality management systems.

Designing effective performance measures means that a number of indicators need to be developed, which are related to the aims of the eventful city. If some of the main objectives of the eventful city are characterised by the ECOC, for example, we can begin to identify some of the potential indicators which can be used (Table 5.1).

It is clear that different types of indicators are needed in order to gauge the success of an eventful city. In general, we can identify three types of potential indicators:

■ Input indicators – the amount of effort invested in the event programme in terms of time, money, etc.

■ Output indicators – what was achieved as a result of staging the event programme.

■ Impact indicators – what effects the event programme had.

The basic input indicators will relate to the resources mobilised for the events programme, such as human resources, sponsorship or number of licences granted. The number and scale of events organised or performances staged and the size of the audience will usually be the key output indicators, but other outputs such as the number of website hits or the number of partners involved in the events programme can also be relatively easily measured. The impact that these outputs have on the wider community is often more difficult

Table 5.1	Potential Performance Indicators for Aspects of an Events Programme
Objective	**Potential indicators**
Raising the international profile of the city/region	International media coverage
Running a programme of activities and events	Number of events and activities organised
Long-term cultural development of the city/region	Growth in cultural production
Attracting domestic and international visitors	Visitor numbers, overnight stays, proportion of foreign tourists
Enhancing feelings of pride and self-confidence	Surveys of local attitudes
Growing and expanding the local audience for culture	Attendances
Creating a festive atmosphere	Audience surveys, image of city as a festival destination

to measure, but could include media coverage, visitor spending or the 'leverage' obtained for the public funds invested (see Chapter 7).

For example, the city of Wellington in New Zealand has developed a number of performance indicators related to its strategic goals. In terms of the goal to attract and retain major events, the measures used include a calculation of the number of events and their estimated economic contribution, the production and implementation of a targeted national events marketing and promotion strategy, and the development of evaluation and performance measurement for events supported by Wellington City Council.

It is also important to think about the indicators that need to be developed for different target groups of the eventful city (see Chapter 8). For example, even when high-quality cultural products are offered, for the consumers it is the quality of experience that is most important. For this reason, much research on the quality of events has concentrated on this issue (Lee and et al., 2004; Cole & Illum, 2006; Lee and et al., 2008).

In essence, the only way to monitor the quality of experience of event participants is to ask them directly. Many cities carry out research at major events, but rarely in a structured manner. Surveys are often designed ad hoc for individual events, and it becomes very difficult to compare one event with another or to identify trends in audience reaction, motivation or behaviour. These problems are compounded where the intention is to measure reactions to a programme of events as a whole, rather than single events within the programme. For the ECOC, for example, visitor surveys carried out in Rotterdam and Porto (2001), Salamanca (2002) and Sibiu (2007) indicated that the visitors were more likely to rate the quality of the specific event they were attending higher than the programme of the ECOC overall. A large proportion of visitors in all cities were unable to rate the ECOC programme, which indicates that the cities had problems in communicating the programme to their audience. The rating of the ECOC programme was higher for those visitors who had attended a number of different events in the programme, however.

Research carried out during the Luxembourg ECOC in 2007 indicates one of the reasons for this; it is not always clear to visitors if the events they are attending form part of a larger programme. Just over 50% of visitors to different events in Luxembourg in 2007 said that it was clear to them all of the time or most of the time that the event was part of the ECOC. But almost 20% indicated that it was not usually clear or never clear (Luxembourg and Greater Region, 2008). The Luxembourg research also underlines the importance of measuring visitor participation and experience at different points in the programme. For example, levels of visitor satisfaction were highest in the middle of the ECOC year, and then declined again towards the end of the programme. Awareness of the ECOC event in Luxembourg also grew steadily over time, from less than 50% of the population knowing that Luxembourg and Greater Region were jointly hosting the event in early 2005, to 80% by the end of the programme.

It is important for the eventful city to measure the performance of events at a city programme level, and not just at the level of individual events. Developing standardised indicators and research instruments which allow events and their outcomes to be compared is therefore desirable (see also Chapter 9).

RISK MANAGEMENT IN EVENT PROGRAMMES

Substantial risks are often associated with the staging of certain events. Even when the city has a well-managed events programme, there are external risk factors that are outside the control of event managers, such as the weather, or terrorist activity, but much of the risk involved in a pro- gramme of events is foreseeable, if not totally predictable, and therefore can be planned for.

Risk management is effectively 'the process of evaluating alternative regulatory and non-regulatory responses to risk and selecting among them. The selection process necessarily requires the consideration of legal, economic and social factors' (United Nations, 1997).

The risks that relate to an eventful city strategy may include the following:

- Not being able to control or influence the events programme sufficiently to achieve your aims.

- The financial risk posed by unsustainable event programming.

- The operational risks of the programme, such as the capability of event organisers, or lack of audience enthusiasm.

- Event fatigue caused by too many events being organised.

- The operational and maintenance costs of facilities built for events.

- Post-event depression.

- Competition from other cities striving to create their own event programmes.

- Withdrawal of funding, leading to event cancellation and programme changes.

- Negative image impacts from poor delivery of the event programme.

There are clearly many potential areas of risk, and an eventful city may have to face several of these simultaneously in different elements of the programme. Some of these risks relate to the individual events rather than the event programme as a whole. However, there are clearly some risks which relate directly to the level of eventfulness in the city. 'Event fatigue' is clearly one of these, because the more events that are held in the city the more likely it is that some residents will complain about negative impacts (see also Chapter 9).

In Edinburgh, a report showed that 'Some consultees also believed too many festivals take place in the summer, and that the city would benefit from spreading these out to become a year-round "Festival City"' (City of Edinburgh Economic Development Department, 2008:33).

Withdrawal of funding, often at short notice, seems to be a common hazard for events. This might put event programmes at risk. The election of Boris Johnson as Mayor of London in 2008 was presaged by a television appearance in which he proclaimed 'If we are to have a Polish festival, I was saying I would encourage a Polish vodka company to sponsor it, that's all.' He later softened these remarks by promising to 'put on some festivals' for London but only if 'he can sponsor them with private cash rather than public funds' (Radio Orla, 2008). Johnson later implemented this policy shift, removing funding from a number of events supported by the previous administration, including the anti-racism event RISE and Soho Pride, cancelling the annual Africa Day festival in Trafalgar Square, and reducing the budgets for festivals such as St Patrick's Day (see also Chapter 6).

Successful development of eventfulness can increase the risk of competition. As soon as other cities see one of their rivals has developed a successful formula, they may be tempted to follow. New competing events may draw away audiences, performers and key staff, undermining the strength of the original event. The fear of such competition was instrumental in the review of events undertaken by Edinburgh in 2006 (AEA Consulting, 2006).

Too Much Success?

In some cases, too much success may also pose risks. The Stokefest event in the Stoke Newington neighbourhood in London became so popular that it was closed by the organisers themselves.

'It is with great sadness and a lump in our collective throats that we announce there are no current plans for Stokefest to continue.

Stokefest 08's programme was as strong as ever and Hackney's artists, DJs, workshop leaders, bands, tent owners, sound systems, local businesses and, of course, festival lovers came out in force to play, dance, party, paint, sing and generally have fun in the sun.

Due to the growing success and appeal of Stokefest, more and more people have been turning up on the day and we know there were many who were unable to get into the park this year.

Clissold Park has a premises licence permitting events with a maximum capacity of 15,000 people in one portion of the park. For years we've had to stick to extremely limited print marketing runs and media-feature blackouts in order to get permission from Hackney Council to run the event; this has made it extremely difficult for our producing partners to solicit sponsorship to pay for their areas.

Additionally, Hackney Council's Parks and Licensing Departments, alongside Hackney Police Licensing Department, has developed an outdoor events policy stating that any event over 3000 capacity must be completely fenced in. This is not an altogether unreasonable policy in itself, and is only there in principle to negate any potential risks of having lots of us all having a great laugh in one place at the same time. Unfortunately we, as the organisers of Stokefest, cannot bring ourselves to organise a free community festival inside a great big steel box! It just doesn't feel right. We feel sure that the atmosphere will change, the essence of what we all collectively had would be diluted and our memories of the fun we had would be tainted by the security systems, ridiculous entry conditions and a general lack of freedom.'

One way of dealing with risk is to share it among event stakeholders. In many cases there are a number of partners in an event programme who, to some extent, all share the potential risk. In the case of the Edinburgh Fringe, much of the financial risk as well as the artistic risk is taken by the performers themselves:

> *If you want to bring a show to Edinburgh, you need to find a venue, pay a small fee and you're in. You take the risk along with everyone else in trying to find an audience for your show: you may end the festival by being a star and hosting your own TV series, you may end it poverty stricken, never wanting to set foot on a stage again. It's an event on a huge scale – 28,000 performances of 1900 shows in 230 venues, and last year we sold 1.5 million tickets.*
>
> (City University, 2007:1)

Cultural Perception of Risk

The perception of risk also depends on the cultural context. In many traditional cultural events, risk is part of the event itself. This is particularly visible in Spain where events such as the running of the bulls in Pamplona centre around deliberate risk taking by large numbers of participants. Every year people are injured; very often these are tourists, many of whom had been drinking the night before. In Pamplona, the spectators are well protected from the bulls, but in other cases little distinction can be made between 'participants' and 'spectators'. In the Fiesta Major in Elche, for example, the throwing of fireworks in the 'battle of the streets' is a central event. Many injuries are caused every year by stray fireworks, not only to the young people who usually throw the fireworks, but also to bystanders. The debate about safety is particularly intense at traditional events, where safety measures are often perceived as interfering with tradition or reducing skill by removing danger. One can contrast this approach to risk with recent developments in the UK, where a number of firework events have been cancelled on health and safety grounds. For example, the 2008 Barrio Fiesta, a celebration of Filipino culture that was expected to attract 60,000 people to Hounslow's Lampton Park, was cancelled because of health and safety problems. Organisers failed to get backing from the police and fire brigade for the event amid fears about traffic congestion, and this caused the local authority to refuse the event a licence.

There are always potential risks attached to the organisation of events, and it is important to recognise that problems encountered in one event may reflect on the whole city event programme. For example, in Rotterdam in 2009, a dance festival organised on the beach was broken up by hooligans who attacked police. One festival-goer was shot by police and six others were injured. This incident led to the Mayor of Rotterdam being questioned about the events policy of the city, and doubts were cast on the overall public safety of the events programme.

Risk assessment

The purpose of risk assessment is to identify threats, hazards or potential problems that might create difficulties for event programmes, so that plans can be made for suitable measures to eliminate, or control, the risks. Event organisers have a responsibility to the public to ensure that the event programme is run in a safe and appropriate manner, to time, within budget and to the agreed standard of quality. A risk assessment ensures that organisers have thought through the implications and taken all possible steps to reduce risks, where appropriate. A risk assessment does not guarantee that nothing will go wrong, but acting on its findings will significantly reduce the chance of problems occurring. If anything does go wrong, a risk assessment should show that the organisers have done their best to predict and remove any risks.

Many cities undertake risk assessment analyses for major events. The Events for London Programme, for example, identifies a number of major risk areas, including security risks, reputational risks and overspending (Table 5.2).

As indicated earlier, one of the major areas of risk for events in general is the uncertainty of funding. Because most public bodies only make decisions about funding events one year in advance, many events organisers are forced to spend a considerable amount of their time lobbying for funds, and may be thrown into turmoil if the funds are not forthcoming. One of the potential ways of reducing this risk for events is to move towards a longer cycle of funding. In Melbourne, for example, the council has moved towards a 3-year funding

Table 5.2	Greater London Authority – Risk Implications of Events for London Programme		
Risk	**Level of risk (low, medium, high)**	**Area**	**Action plan (P – proactive, R – reactive)**
Event programme is perceived to be politically driven.	M	Reputational	P – Publish the guiding criteria and strategic objectives of the programme on eventsforlondon. org website. P – Engage with all community groups.
If an event is not deemed a success or LDA funding is considered inappropriate, then it is reputational risk.	M	Reputational	P– LDA commissioned the London Major Events Strategy which recommended transferring delivery of events to the GLA. R – LDA communications unit to develop appropriate messages in response to any adverse commentary.
Representation from equality groups not receiving any funding.	M	Strategic	R – GLA Events for London have reviewed and assessed which events to support and are confident that the allocation of funding is justifiable.
Major terrorist attack or incident at any of the major events.	M	Operational	P – GLA Events for London team have strong links to Met Police and inherently monitor and manage this risk for each of the events they manage and develop contingency plans accordingly.
Project outputs/ deliverables not accurately defined/ strongly agreed resulting in funding being used elsewhere/ outcomes not being realised and £ wasted.	L	Behavioural	P – LDA Project Manager to ensure clear understanding by GLA of the deliverables required for this funding prior to release of grant.

Table 5.2	Greater London Authority – Risk Implications of Events for London Programme—*Cont'd*		
Risk	**Level of risk (low, medium, high)**	**Area**	**Action plan (P – proactive, R – reactive)**
Events going over budget and organisers looking for additional funding from GLA/LDA. GLA making additional funding requests to LDA.	M	Financial	P – Regular liaison between GLA Events Team and events organisers to ensure team is alerted to early warning indicators. Regular liaison between LDA Project Manager and GLA.
Procurement for event production not compliant with LDA procurement code.	L	Contractual	P – The GLA has robust procurement systems. Furthermore, the GLA requires (as part of contracts) event organisers to be equally robust in their procurement practices. This is therefore considered to be a low risk.
Health and safety not appropriately managed at events resulting in accident or incident.	L	Operational	P – Include requirement for proper Health & Safety risk analysis and measures within third party funding agreements GLA.

GLA = Greater London Authority.
LDA = London Development Agency.

model. Triennial sponsorship provides a level of certainty to allow the organisers of these events to embark on long-term growth strategies. Financial sponsorship of events in the Cultural Events category on a triennial basis is recommended in Melbourne by a panel comprising the Director of Commerce & Marketing, the Manager of Events Melbourne and three industry representatives appointed by Council.

The risk associated with economic uncertainty is illustrated by the global downturn in 2008, which had an impact on the budgets of major festivals (see Chapter 12). As arts funding organisations looked at how they could cut their spending as available funds dried up, so cultural events such as the Edinburgh International Festival had to be aware of the increased economic risk. Jonathan Mills, director of the Festival said, 'There's no way of knowing whether our funding will be affected. I'm afraid it will come down to who is winning a particular argument at the bank when funding decisions are made. It's as fragile as that' (Grauman, 2008).

CONCLUSION

The development and running of event programmes requires the eventful city to encompass a wide range of management skills, or to be able to coordinate the managerial efforts of others. The need for these managerial skills is also increasing as cities strive to become more transparent and accountable in their dealings with stakeholders. This places growing pressure on the management capacities of the city, which may only have a small team of people to deal with the events programme. This means that cities rely increasingly on collaboration with external partners to deliver and manage elements of their programme. In externalising management tasks, however, cities must work harder to monitor performance and manage contractual arrangements.

The managerial tasks for the eventful city are potentially becoming more complex as fewer cities take a direct interventionist stance in relation to event organisation and management. The trend towards decentralisation also allows cities to take a more strategic role vis-à-vis their event programmes and take informed decisions about which events to organise and manage directly, which events to fund, and which events to enable in less direct ways. This mixed model of funding for event programmes is dealt with in more detail in the next chapter.

CHAPTER 6

Finance and Funding for Event Programmes

Financial management is an essential process for the eventful city. As the cost of organising events rises and claims on public funds from the cultural sector grow, it becomes increasingly important to manage available resources effectively and to seek funding from a variety of sources, such as private sector sponsorship, merchandising and television sales, as well as public sector subsidies and ticket income.

As indicated in the previous chapter, the raising of funding for events is a time-consuming business, with event managers and entrepreneurs spending much of their time and energy looking for and securing resources:

> *It's unbearable. Three months before the Elephant was due, my budget was £500,000 (€735,000) adrift. The money is the hard part – the other stuff is what we love. There's an adrenaline rush in problem solving, but that stuff about artists making their best stuff when they're starving is rubbish. The view that this adds to the artistic buzz is held by people who have salaries.*
>
> (Helen Marriage, Artichoke Productions, talking about The Sultan's Elephant project. City University, 2006:4)

One of the tasks of the eventful city must be to remove some of the uncertainty and financial risk surrounding the

203

creation and staging of programmes. Unless it can do this, it may lose events to its competitors, or see them disappear altogether as a result of insolvency and debt. For both public sector bodies and private sector sponsors, decisions about which events to fund and maintain must be made in a strategic way that helps ensure their financial stability and at the same time contributes to the overall quality and impact of the programme.

THE COST OF CULTURAL EVENTS

One of the key questions in the staging of events is 'how much will they cost'? Unless there is a clear picture of the likely financial implications of a programme of events, it is impossible to decide which events should be supported and how available resources should be distributed.

Utilising events in a strategic way to animate and market a city can bring additional costs as well. Staging events is generally cheaper than constructing iconic buildings (Richards and Wilson, 2006); but they may also imply one-off and recurring costs which need to be considered. The nature of staging events is such that costs inevitably rise year after year beyond the rate of inflation due to many factors outside the control of event organisers and public authorities. In addition to price rises in industries that serve events (transportation, equipment hire, hotel accommodation), the programme cost itself does not conform to traditional market trends. This has a particular impact on cultural events that feature performing arts, such as theatre and music.

In the performing arts, there has been considerable study of the issue of rising costs. In 1966, William Baumol and William Bowen published *Performing Arts: The Economic Dilemma*. Their book was extraordinarily influential and it is generally agreed that analysis of the economics of the arts had its origin in that work. The economic dilemma Baumol and Bowen referred to was the problem of financing the performing arts in the face of rising unit costs. These, they argued, are the result of 'productivity lag'. The resulting cost pressure has come to be known as 'Baumol's cost disease'. Productivity is defined by economists as physical output per work hour, and increases in productivity have often come from improved technology. But because live cultural productions depend primarily on labour inputs that cannot be replaced by technology, the productivity of culture is difficult to increase, and as wages rise in the economy in general, over time, cultural events will become more expensive to run, even if they maintain the same format and programming (Baumol and Bowen, 1966).

The same principles will apply to most cultural event programmes, because there is usually a heavy dependence on live performance. The following section considers some of the factors influencing the costs associated with the ECOC (European Capital of Culture) since 1985.

Trends in ECOC budgets

Looking back over the history of the ECOC since 1985, it is clear that the economic scale of the early ECOCs was relatively modest (Table 6.1). This was due to the shorter time-scale of many events, and the fact that the early capitals focused primarily on cultural rather than economic goals. This effectively changed in 1990 with the designation of Glasgow, which had a clear economic development and image improvement agenda. The achievement of these objectives required an operating budget twice as high as any previous ECOC and the strategy included substantial investment in marketing. This makes the point that budgets for events need to be clearly related to the objectives that the city wants to achieve. High ambitions often carry a heavy price tag, and a failure to invest sufficient resources in the programme may lead to a failure to achieve ambitions. The increasing scale of ambition embodied in the ECOC as the programme developed in different cities over the years is therefore also linked with growing financial investment in the event.

Effectively, the budgetary development of the ECOC can be divided into three periods:

1985–1989: Expensive Festival
The early development phase of the event, in which most cultural capitals were seen as extended cultural festivals. The majority of the host cities were capital cities that already had considerable cultural infrastructure.

1990–2004: Investment in Cultural Regeneration
The consolidation of the ECOC as a major force for cultural and economic development in the host city. The majority of cities were 'second cities' that saw the event as an opportunity to develop their cultural facilities and international profile. Much more attention was paid to the infrastructure projects and the attraction of tourists than in the earlier cities, although some cities also had strong cultural and social objectives that complemented the economic development focus.

2005 Onwards: Investment in Infrastructure
The trend towards greater infrastructure spending seems to be strengthening and in most cases capital budgets far outweigh operational spend. Although the cities in Western Europe generally have had larger operating budgets for the event, the cities from the new member states of the European Union have been able to call on the newly available structural funds from the EU to boost the capital budget of the ECOC in order to renew their cultural infrastructure.

Although these figures relate mainly to expenditure on capital projects, there has been a similar trend in operational budgets, although these show considerable variations. The total costs have been influenced by many factors, including the scale of ambition, the relative 'wealth' of a city and its surrounding region, the availability and magnitude of finance from public bodies (local, regional and national authorities) and the potential for private sector sponsorship. The interpretation of the comparative cost of one ECOC as against another needs to be viewed in the light of such factors.

Exceptionally high operating expenditure is noted in Liverpool ECOC 2008, which stands out when compared to most ECOC budgets. Liverpool spent almost twice as much on the cultural programme as the city with the next highest expenditure, which was Lille. Liverpool's €142 million operating budget is almost four times as high as the long-term average for all the ECOCs. Even discounting Liverpool's very high cost, it seems that the trend in operating budgets for ECOC continues upwards, with certain exceptions mainly in smaller cities and cities in Eastern Europe (Figure 6.1).

Table 6.1	Operating and Capital Budgets of the ECOC, 1985–2014		
		Operating budget million €	Capital budget million € (where known)
1985	Athens	7.7	
1986	Florence	24.4	
1987	Amsterdam	3.3	
1988	Berlin	27.0	
1989	Paris	0.6	
1990	Glasgow	60.0	51.1
1991	Dublin	8.6	
1992	Madrid	22.6	
1993	Antwerp	40.8	
1994	Lisbon	23.6	400.0
1995	Luxembourg	24.4	16.4
1996	Copenhagen	86.2	219.0
1997	Thessaloniki	67.0	232.0
1998	Stockholm	54.4	
1999	Weimar	28.1	220.0
2000	Helsinki	33.0	
	Prague	10.4	
	Brussels	32.0	82.0
	Reykjavik	8.5	
	Avignon	21.0	8.0
	Cracow	12.8	
	Bolonga	33.8	7.7
	Bergen	12.8	
	Santiago	22.8	
2001	Rotterdam	34.1	
	Porto	58.5	168.5
2002	Brugge	27.2	68.0
	Salamanca	39.2	46.5
2003	Graz	60.0	56.0
2004	Lille	73.0	70.0
	Genoa	30.0	200.0
2005	Cork	13.5	
2006	Patras	36.0	100.0
2007	Sibiu	16.0	40.0
	Luxembourg Region	56.0	
2008	Liverpool	142.0	984.0
	Stavanger	37.0	293.0
2009	Linz	65.0	300.0
	Vilnius	25.0	442.0

Table 6.1	Operating and Capital Budgets of the ECOC, 1985–2014—*Cont'd*		
		Operating budget million €	Capital budget million € (where known)
2010	Pécs	37.0	141.0
	Essen	48.0	30.0
	Istanbul	64.9	
2011	Turku	55.0	145.0
	Tallin	38.0	
2012	Maribor	57.0	143.0
	Guimarães	41.0	70.0
2013	Marseilles-Provence	98.0	
2014	Umeå	40.5	690.0

Source: Richards and Palmer (2009)

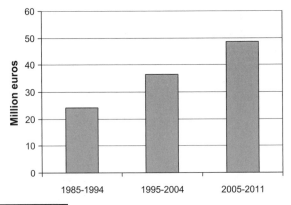

FIGURE 6.1 *Average ECOC operating budgets by decade.*

Total capital spending for ECOC in particular has increased dramatically over the past 10 years (Figure 6.2).

These figures indicate how the transformation of events from purely cultural celebrations into tools for economic, social and image change can place a much larger financial burden on the eventful city.

Annual festival programmes

Even if a city does not stage a major international event such as the ECOC, the costs of running an events programme can still be

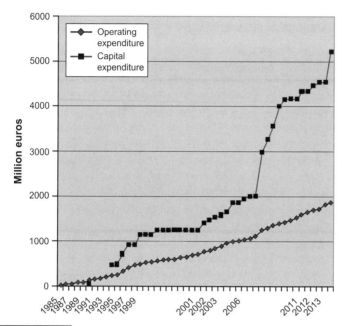

FIGURE 6.2 *Cumulative capital and operating expenditure of the ECOCs, 1985–2013.*

considerable. Table 6.2 indicates that many large UK cities invest large amounts of money in their events programmes. Big spenders in recent years include Edinburgh, which needs to uphold its reputation as a 'festival city' and Liverpool (see above). For other cities, however, events spending may not seem excessive, particularly when expressed in terms of euros per inhabitant.

We can also express levels of spending in terms of cost per visit, since many cities will also attract many visits from non-residents. The City of Manchester invests €1.5 million in seven 'pillar events' every year, generating 550,000 visits at an average cost of €2.72 per visit (Table 6.3). The cost per visit is much higher for smaller cities (such as Chester in the UK, which spent over €34 per visit in 2004). In general, costs will increase with the complexity and extent of the programme, particularly as administration costs tend to rise as a proportion of the total budget. As mentioned earlier, a city that wants to attract and/or organise many events may decide to create an additional body to bid for and coordinate events, which in itself adds to the indirect total cost of the events programme.

Table 6.2		Event Programme Budgets for Major Cities in the UK		
City	Number of events	Budget (euro million)	Visitors	Spend per inhabitant (euro)
Liverpool	17+	53.7	633.000+	122.0
Birmingham	6	6.3	110.000+	6.4
Newcastle Gateshead	91	11.9	-	23.8
Glasgow	8	-	128.000+	-
Edinburgh	17	39.8	3.200.000	88.8
Manchester (Pillar Events)	7	1.6	551.000	4.0

Data for 2005–2007 from city reports.

Table 6.3	Visits and Costs of Major Event Programmes		
Programme/event	Visits	Total cost €	Cost per visit €
Liverpool ECOC 2008	15,000,000	142,000,000	9.46
Lille ECOC 2004	9,000,000	70,000,000	7.78
Luxembourg ECOC 2007	3,300,000	45,000,000	13.60
Graz ECOC 2003	2,700,000	60,000,000	22.22
Rotterdam ECOC 2001	2,300,000	34,100,000	14.83
Salamanca ECOC 2002	1,900,000	39,200,000	20.63
Brugge ECOC 2002	1,600,000	27,200,000	17.00
Avignon ECOC 2000	1,500,000	21,000,000	14.00
Porto ECOC 2001	1,200,000	58,500,000	48.75
Luxembourg ECOC 1995	1,100,000	24,400,000	22.18
Manchester Pillar Events 2005	550,000	1,500,000	2.72
East Midlands Festivals 2005	250,000	1,500,000	6.00
Innsbruck Events 2003	140,000	1,480,000	10.57
Chester Festivals 2004	19,000	650,000	34.21
Average cost per visit			13.30

Source: Palmer-Rae, 2004; city reports.

Table 6.4	Budgets of Major Festivals in Amsterdam, 2001				
Festival	**2001 budget €**	**Visitors**	**Performances**	**Cost per visitor €**	**Cost per performance €**
Holland festival	3,013,122	90,900	79	33	38,141
IDFA	1,642,729	90,000	402	18	4,086
Crossing border festival	882,352	11,000	120	80	7,353
Cinekid	800,905	32,340	478	25	1,676
Theatre festival	603,299	7,000	30	86	20,110
World wide video festival	579,905	40,000	78	14	7,435
Uitmarkt	484,162	600,000	350	1	1,383
Roots festival	461,643	35,000	50	13	9,233
Julidans	359,366	9,235	27	39	13,310
Canal festival	356,000	45,000	70	8	5,086
International theatre school	343,093	8,000	85	43	4,036
Over het IJ festival	319,004	22,500	27	14	11,815
Total	9,845,580	990,975	1,796	10	5,482

In the Dutch city of Amsterdam, there are about 60 significant annual events. The 12 most important events are represented by the Amsterdam Festivals Group, providing a total of 1700 performances attracting over one million people a year (Table 6.4) (van Eeden & Elshout, 2002). These festivals are also becoming more focused on attracting visitors – some looking for more international visitors, others concentrating more on the local market. This is because many of the festivals have reached their growth limits within the capacity of local audiences.

The total cost of these 12 festivals was almost €10 million for an audience approaching one million visitors. Not all of this funding is contributed by the City of Amsterdam, however, because there is also considerable funding by central government and commercial sponsors for major events. Table 6.4 shows that these events vary greatly in terms of cost, depending mainly on the facilities used. Festivals in Amsterdam that involve performances indoors will usually cost more to stage than open-air events and will usually attract lower visitor numbers, due to restricted capacities.

| Table 6.5 | Breakdown of Cost per Visit for Festivals in Amsterdam, Excluding the Uitmarkt |

	Central Govt. subsidy	City of Amsterdam	Other subsidies	Arts councils	Sponsors	Own revenue	Other	Total
Cost per visit	€ 6.76	€ 3.67	€ 2.61	€ 3.37	€ 2.96	€ 3.89	€0.68	€ 23.94

Over 60% of the total visitors came to one single event, the Uitmarkt, which is a free outdoor festival held to mark the launch of the Amsterdam cultural season. If the Uitmarkt is excluded, the average cost per visit rises from €10 to €24 euro (Table 6.5). It is clear that Amsterdam benefits from considerable central government funding for its festival programme to maintain its position as the cultural capital of the Netherlands, with strong competition from the city of Rotterdam, which spends almost €1.5 million a year on its event programme through Rotterdam Festivals. The 43 events subsidised by Rotterdam Festivals in 2005 attracted a total of 1.5 million visits at a subsidy cost of around €1 per visit. This is considerably lower than the € 3.67 per visit invested by Amsterdam (Table 6.5), although the large number of open-air events in Rotterdam, particularly in the summer, needs to be taken into account.

The €10 million cost of the annual festival programme in Amsterdam seems relatively inexpensive in comparison with ECOC, although direct comparisons between recurrent events, such as an annual programme of festivals, and one-off events, such as ECOC, are unhelpful. The €50 million cost of an average ECOC in recent years covers approximately 500 projects, with 6000 performances in a city compared with the 1700 performances a year staged by Amsterdam Festivals. Many cities utilise significant elements of their existing annual cultural programmes to include in the ECOC programmes thematic packaged events to reduce the additional cost of staging new large-scale events.

The City of Manchester in the UK makes a considerable regular investment in events through its 'Pillar' events

Table 6.6	Manchester Pillar Event Programme 2005		
		Manchester city council	
	Total costs £	Subsidy £	%
Manchester pride	565,000	20,000	3.5
Manchester food and drink festival	113,000	30,000	26.5
Starbucks Manchester jazz festival	119,000	30,000	25.2
Manchester 'smile' comedy festival	67,500	30,000	44.4
D. Percussion	127,000	30,000	23.6
Garden of delights	276,000	50,000	18.1
Manchester poetry festival	51,000	15,000	29.4
Total	1,042,500	205,000	19.7

programme (Jura Consultants, 2006). The subsidies given by the city to these seven key events amounted to £205,000 (€300,000) in 2005 (Table 6.6), although the total cost of these events was over £1 million (€1.45 million).

Manchester made a substantial addition to its regular events programme in 2007 with the launch of the Manchester International Festival (see also Chapter 9 for more information on the impact of this event), which cost £9 million (€10 million) to stage, of which the City contributed £2.3 million. As a result of the success of the first edition, the City also decided to provide a further £1 million a year for the years 2008–2010. This additional programme will effectively increase the City of Manchester's investment in major cultural programming from just over £200,000 to £2.35 million per year.

Melbourne also makes considerable investments in cultural events through the city projects of its Arts & Culture Division. In 2004/05 $AUS 500,000 was granted to the Melbourne Festival, $AUS 100,000 to the Melbourne Film Festival, $AUS 250,000 to the Comedy Festival and $AUS 150,000 to the Fringe Festival. This is a total investment of $AUS 1 million (€600,000) in major events for the city. As in the case of Amsterdam, however, the funding given by the city is supplemented by grants from the regional Government of Victoria and the national government.

In its effort to develop itself as a global arts city, Singapore has increased its spending on the arts significantly in recent years. In 2005, from a total cultural budget SG$300 million, some SG$45 million (€22 million) was allocated to 'nurturing the arts', including festival and event funding. By 2007 the heading had changed to 'Nurturing Gracious and Knowledgeable People', and the budget had increased to SG$67 million (€33 million), a growth of almost 50%. This budget included organising major arts events in Singapore such as the Singapore Arts Festival, Singapore Art Show and Singapore Writers' Festival, promoting artistic excellence and developing audiences. Some SG$7 million (€3.5 million) went to the Singapore Arts Festival.

These examples illustrate that certain cities invest considerable (and increasing) sums of money in developing their events. As public expenditure comes under increasing pressure, many cities are trying to diversify their funding sources to include commercial and earned income. The following sections look at the main funding sources for events.

PUBLIC FUNDING POLICIES

As the examples discussed so far demonstrate, the public sector often has a leading role in the funding of large events and many cities are also increasingly funding smaller events as well. As the number of events staged grows, so cities are faced with increasing funding demands and tougher decisions about which events to fund. Many cities are therefore developing strategies for event funding which lay down guidelines for the type of events that should be funded.

For example, in the Australian State of Victoria, the principle for granting public funds to major events is as follows:

> The rationale for support for major events should be that, while an event may not be able to cover all of its costs through admission charges or sponsorship, it is worthy of support because the event generates benefits for Victorians. These benefits should not only cover economic factors but also embrace other community benefits.
>
> (Victorian Auditor General, 2007:60)

This policy illustrates the need for assessment of event outcomes, as this becomes the basis for deciding what benefits are generated for the local community (see also Chapter 9).

While decisions about major 'one-off' events may be relatively straightforward, most difficult funding decisions often relate to recurring events. The challenge for the city is that these events require funding every year, and may therefore come to represent a considerable drain on budgets. In addition, the assessment of funding applications for annual events requires a considerable administrative effort. The system of annual funding rounds also presents problems for the events themselves, as they may have little continuity from what is often the largest funding source, and long term planning, which is essential to maintain the quality of many events, becomes impossible.

In response to this problem, some cities have taken a long term view, offering multi-annual events funding. Melbourne, for example, offers 3-year funding packages to major events in order to ensure continuity and to allow them to plan ahead. The Australian Government has committed AU$3 million over the next 4 years to the Australia Council for the Arts to ensure the continuation of the successful Major Festivals Initiative (MFI).

This ongoing funding for the MFI reflects the Australian Government's commitment to support uniquely Australian performing arts productions that have the capacity to engage audiences on national and international stages.

(Kemp, 2006)

The MFI supports the commissioning, development and showcasing of new, large-scale Australian performing arts productions for Australia's major international arts festivals. These include the Adelaide Festival, Brisbane Festival, Darwin Festival, Melbourne International Arts Festival, Perth International Arts Festival, Sydney Festival and the Ten Days on the Island Festival (Tasmania) (Kemp, 2006).

However, other events may not qualify for public funding, because they do not meet the criteria set by local authorities or other public funding bodies. For example, the Belfast Multi-Annual Funding scheme has a number of eligibility criteria.

In Belfast, to qualify for consideration for Multi-Annual Funding, the organisation must have:

- a minimum of one permanent staff member;

- permanent business premises;

- an appropriate range of policies in place, e.g. Child Protection Policy;

- clearly operate as a not-for-profit organisation;

- an annual turnover of not less than £100,000 (€140,000) in 2003–2004 financial year; and

- audited accounts or other equivalent financial arrangements.

Organisations will be required to demonstrate:

- high standards of management and governance;

- sound business planning and strategic direction on at least a 3-year basis; and

- the capacity to deliver Multi-Annual Funding.

(Belfast City Council, 2004)

A number of cultural events were funded under this scheme, including the Belfast Festival at Queen's, the Cathedral Quarter Arts Festival and the Belfast Film Festival. However, the majority of organisations funded were institutions such as libraries, arts centres or museums. This is because many events were unable to meet the funding criteria if they have no permanent staff, low turnover or are lacking financial planning mechanisms.

Although a number of public bodies seem to be moving towards the provision of multi-annual funding, this trend is by no means universal. The Irish Arts Council (2003) announced that it was suspending its multi-annual funding programme:

The Multi-Annual Funding scheme, which involves 70 arts organisations, has been suspended. ... After meetings with each organisation and a number of discussions around the Council table, the Arts Council has concluded that while its commitment to the principle of support for multi-annual planning in the arts is undiminished, it is unable to make forward commitments of a multi-annual nature so long as it is uncertain of its own future funding from Government.

London: A Move Away from Public Subsidy?

London Mayor Boris Johnson plans to reduce funding for cultural events in London and steer community groups towards other sources of finance. The Mayor's marketing adviser, Dan Ritterband, told the London Assembly's budget committee that 'standardised' funding offers would be made to community groups to help them stage cultural and religious events. 'We are standardising the offer so we will know for the next year the programme we are to deliver instead of people coming randomly through the year'. He indicated that the Mayor wanted to be more 'even handed' in the way funding support was distributed and to ensure public events held in iconic sites such as Trafalgar Square were balanced by commercial events that brought in revenue.

Referring to the reign of the previous Mayor, Ken Livingstone, Ritterband said community groups had 'come to expect' the Greater London authority (GLA) to provide cash and facilities. 'People show up year in year out for handouts saying "give me the money". We seem to be handing out cash to people with varying sums depending on who has the best contact with the Mayor's office'.

Ritterband said the GLA had 'no idea' where the £130,000 (€160,000) donated to the Notting Hill Carnival to pay for stewarding actually went. 'It is inappropriate that £130,000 is given blind; we want to ensure it is not just being given to their mates and it is given to proper stewarding companies. It is murky and we want to make unmurky the dealings which are GLA-sponsored events'.

Ritterband said if groups were unable to strike sponsorship deals for their events, it would suggest that the event was not commercially viable. 'We are doing workshops for all community groups to let them know where they can get funding and other sponsorship'.
(Mulholland, 2008)

These examples underline the fact that public funding for events rarely comes without strings. As transparency and accountability are important issues in public funding, the need to account for the use of public subsidy also increases (see Chapter 5). Although a large number of event programmes are reliant on public funds, many events will seek other funding sources to increase their resource base, reduce risk and to increase flexibility.

SPONSORSHIP, GRANTS AND DONATIONS

In terms of securing resources for events, sponsorship is becoming an increasingly important part of the equation. In 2002 the global events sponsorship market was estimated at US$9.57 billion (€8.94 billion), of which US$6.41 billion (67%) was spent on sport and US$1.33 billion (14%) on festivals and the arts (Yorkshire County Council, 2005). Events are an important element of arts sponsorship as a whole. The Deloitte (2008:11) study of arts funding in Ireland indicated that around 36% of all arts giving went to festivals and events. 'We estimate that businesses in Ireland invest over €20 million in arts and cultural organisations annually, with approximately €16 million of this investment in the form of sponsorship (cash and in-kind)'.

Sponsorship is increasingly being seen as an important source of support for events. Commercial sponsorship involves businesses investing in an event in return for access to the audience or for other commercial opportunities. In general, sponsors use events to achieve corporate and communications objectives, including branding, creating public awareness, image enhancement, stimulating sales, incentivising employees, enhancing consumer involvement and demonstrating corporate responsibility. A survey of cultural sponsorship in New Zealand (Ministry for Culture and Heritage, 2008) indicated that the two most important sponsorship motivations were reaching a particular market segment and increasing brand awareness. For some companies, however, sponsorship decisions may be heavily influenced by the personal interests and connections of members of the Board of Directors or high-ranking executives, and may be viewed as a form of philanthropy or donation, or seen as part of a broader concept of corporate responsibility.

Until recently major events had enjoyed a healthy sponsorship market, as noted in the case of the UK (Balakrishnan, 2006):

The in thing at the moment is to sponsor a festival, but I think this will go out of fashion when companies realise it won't continue to have a big impact. People think that they can just brand events up, but the market is at saturation point. Festivals ... that do their own thing will survive, but one-third of festivals of this summer won't take place next year.

Due to the proliferation of events in almost every major city, there is inevitably competition for sponsorship. In the UK, the organisation Arts and Business, has developed a national approach to identify sponsors and sponsorship opportunities. The UK sponsorship database uksponsorship.com listed over 25 festivals seeking sponsorship in April 2009.

There are many examples of enlightened sponsorships by companies of events. In the UK, for example, the Habitat shopping chain sponsored the Brighton Festival because it made customers aware of Habitat's role in promoting the arts. 'More people are in Brighton at Festival time so our sponsorship was commercially effective in bringing new people into the store; it also enabled us to feel more part of the local community. Being based in London, the Head Office had not really been aware of the Festival. Brighton Festival has been a pleasant surprise, we now realise how much is involved' (Brighton and Hove, 2004).

Sponsorship of the Salzburg Festival

Helga Rabl-Stadler, President of the Salzburg Festival, is not afraid of sponsor influence in the festival programme: 'Our sponsors are far too intelligent not to know that trying to influence the content of our programme would have a boomerang effect. On the contrary, I hope our sponsors continue to influence us, in the sense that they make it possible to implement projects that we could not realise otherwise for lack of money.'

Nestle (main sponsor since 1991) has supported young people's tickets. We are able to give young people the opportunity to see top

Continued

performances for the price of a movie ticket, without straining our budget.

Audi (main sponsor since 1995) had the unique idea of inviting one Festival production every season to Ingolstadt, its business head-quarters. Thus, people who cannot come to Salzburg have the opportunity to experience the quality of the Festival performances.

Siemens (main sponsor since 1999) enables us to open the Festival to a broader audience. The Siemens Festival Nights on Kapitelplatz offer highest quality broadcasts for free and also make it possible for many people to attend a premiere for which there are too few tickets and too expensive ones for many wallets.

Uniqa (main sponsor since 2002) combines its entrepreneurial triumphs throughout the former Communist states with its support for the Festival there. Not only Uniqa, but the Salzburg Festival also is opening up a new market with joint presentations in Prague, Budapest and Warsaw.

Credit Suisse (main sponsor since 2006) is a global player bringing visitors from all over the world to us, and since Credit Suisse is also engaged in the sector of fine arts, we receive a double bounty: together, we are selecting artwork for our halls.

(Salzburg Festival, 2008)

The UK's *Guardian* newspaper has been the title sponsor of the Hay Literature Festival. In attracting this sponsorship, the organisers cite several reasons why the festival is attractive, including the uniqueness and quirkiness of the festival, the potential for branding linked to 'thought leadership', and the sharing of the festival's vision of freedom of speech and the sharing of ideas (www.hayfestival.com).

A Tougher Climate for Sponsorship?

A study of cultural organisations receiving sponsorship in New Zealand (Ministry for Culture and Heritage, 2008) indicated that dealing with sponsors might involve more work in future. Respondents saw 'a change in corporate attitudes towards sponsorship, such as corporations focussing more on concrete results.'

Comments included:

'(There is) less money available generally from sponsors, (and) greater competition for the decreasing pool of sponsorship funds.

More competition for the sponsorship dollar means that we must find greater benefits for our projects to appeal to sponsors.'

'Many sponsors are increasingly wanting commercial returns which we are unable to give them. Having to convince them of the value of intangible benefits is time-consuming and ongoing.'

'(There are) higher expectations from sponsors, more leveraging activity required by the sponsor. (We) need to always remain competitive by offering more tailor-made benefits and to service sponsors more.'

For the ECOC, sponsorship on average accounts for 10% or more of the total budget of the event (see Chapter 7). In Helsinki for example, the ECOC in 2000 was supported by a wide range of main sponsors, including: TV4 (television channel); Elisa communications (tele-operator); ICL invia (IT) and airline Finnair. There was also a wide range of official partners including Nokia, Finland Post, Sodexho, The Finnish Forest Foundation, Marja Kurki (textiles), Helsingin Energia (energy and power), Scandic (hotels), Silja Line (cruises) and Tapiola (insurance). In order to maximise the total amount of sponsorship, the ECOC team approached the international offices of potential sponsors first, on the basis that these would tend to have larger sponsorship budgets. They also played one off against the other, telling each one how much their competitors had already promised as leverage to get more money.

Raising sponsorship may not be an easy option and many events struggle to attract sponsorship due to the nature of the event itself or to the absence of a strong fund raising strategy. Nurse (2003:8) remarks in the case of the Caribbean Festival that: 'Business sponsorship is another weak area of festival management. This is so because the corporate community has had limited experience with festival and arts sponsorship and many festival organisers don't have skills in writing business and sponsorship proposals.'

Sponsors often expect a direct return of some kind for their investment in events, such as privileged access or free tickets. It is essential that events calculate the real cost of sponsorship. At the Lucerne Festival in Switzerland, for example, almost 12% of tickets are allocated to sponsors and 24% to the Friends of the Lucerne Festival (Scherer, 2006).

One common element of an event sponsorship strategy is the development of a tiered approach relating the level of sponsorship to the benefits received. Major sponsors are offered high-profile coverage with maximum benefits in return for relatively large cash investments, with more minor sponsors offered less benefits at a lower level of sponsorship. For the 2007 ECOC in Luxembourg and Greater Region, four levels of sponsorship were offered:

- Exclusive Sponsor: €600,000, optimum visibility in all forms of communication of the ECOC.

- Thematic Sponsor: €400,000, optimum visibility in one thematic area of the ECOC.

- Official Sponsor: €300,000, visibility in some forms of communication (e.g. not on posters).

- Official Supplier: €40,000, minimum of in-kind sponsorship.

Companies may also be willing to invest large sums in events in return for direct association of the event with their brand (Masterman, 2004). Companies such as Coca Cola, Guinness, Barclays and General Motors have often sponsored events that bear their names. Coca Cola sponsored the Coke Fest music events in Johannesburg and Cape Town in 2009. The Drum Rhythm Festival in the Netherlands would not have existed without tobacco sponsorship for the concept. However, there are many events that will not accept sponsorship from tobacco and other types of companies for ethical reasons.

In July 2000, a demonstration at the opening of '@ Bristol' – a £98 million (€159 million) science and art discovery centre – drew the attention of local media to sponsorship by Nestlé – a company criticised for its marketing of breast-milk substitutes. In 2002, UNICEF found itself the target of an international campaign of public health professionals for lending its good name and endorsement to McDonald's for events to mark World Children's Day. As certain events have developed approaches to risk management, the reputation risk of association with certain sponsors has emerged as an area of concern. The Charities Commission in the UK has recommended the development of clear policy in this area. Some of the main recommendations from the report *Charities and Commercial Partners* were:

■ Charities should consider establishing an ethical policy which clearly sets out the charity's values. This will form part of their wider fund raising strategy and they can use it to ensure that trustees, staff and any potential commercial partners share a common understanding of the charity's ethical values.

■ As best practice, charities should highlight their ethical policies and any commercial partnerships they have in their Annual Report and yearly accounts.

■ Against the framework of their ethical policy, charities need to carefully consider whether a proposed commercial partnership is appropriate and in the best interests of the charity.

(Charities Commission, 2002)

Most ethical sponsorship policies will be built around a list of the types of business that events will avoid. Tobacco and armaments manufacturers commonly find themselves on avoidance lists, along with other categories.

An important part of managing sponsorship is therefore to be clear about what sponsorship the city will not accept. For example, the City of Sydney policy on Corporate Sponsorship (2005:5) includes a list of types of sponsorship that the city will not entertain, including any arrangements which:

■ produce a conflict of interest;

■ restrict access to an event;

■ are not consistent with social justice;

- allow ownership and control of the sponsored project to go outside the City;

- pose a conflict with the broader policies and practices of the City; and

- pose a conflict between the objectives and mission of the City and those of the sponsor.

Clearly, finding sponsors who fit well with the cultural, social and economic objectives of the city may pose a challenge. As the Sydney report suggests, sponsors might be chosen following a public call for expressions of interest. However, this approach does not recognise the reality of how sponsorship arrangements work. An events sponsorship strategy is usually based around individual approaches to specific sponsors. The most effective approach is usually based on proposals that are specifically tailored to meet the requirements of a given organisation.

Attracting sponsors for events that are supported by public bodies may require more controls than commercial events. If the process of attracting sponsors cannot be fully transparent, then it is important to monitor the sponsorship attracted by a public authority. Sydney requires approval to be given for sponsorship deals according to the amounts of money involved (City of Sydney, 2005:9):

- Total value in excess of AU$150,000 – approval by Council.

- Between AU$20,000 and AU$150,000 – approval by the CEO.

- Under AU$20,000 – approval by relevant Unit Manager.

The sponsorship of events may be in the form of financial support or 'in kind' donations of goods or services. The Deloitte (2008) survey of arts giving in Ireland indicated that 38% of sponsorship (or almost €5 million in 2008) was donated in kind. Such donations may include a very wide range of needed supplies from computer systems, vehicles and staging to legal and financial services through food and beverages served at event VIP receptions.

The future prospects of raising sponsorship from businesses for events require careful study. In research carried out by the government of New Zealand on sponsorship trends, almost 47% of the surveyed firms were of the opinion that levels of sponsorship of events and activities would stay about the same. About 17% felt that cultural sponsorship was likely to increase; the same percentage predicted a decrease and 20% did not know. Comments included:

> 'Given the tighter economy, business will be closely examining sponsorship returns. It is still very difficult to assess sponsorship return value.'

> 'The current realignment going on in sponsorship will take some time to filter through to arts organisations who will need to pull up their socks to meet the expectations and drivers of the realignment.'

> 'Huge competition for sponsorship dollars and more focus on measurable business outcomes mean arts sponsorships will become more (difficult to) justify in business cases as opposed to goodwill or board whims.'

> 'I think there will be a greater emphasis on corporate social responsibility.'
>
> (Ministry of Culture and Heritage, 2008)

In-Kind Sponsorship

Research on cultural sponsorship in Australia (Cultural Ministers Council, 2002) indicated that 83% of organisations provide in-kind support as part of their sponsorship commitment.

Over 60% of respondents provide in-kind support in the form of services. Specific services referred include:

- professional expertise and advisory services, including legal, financial, I.T., auditing, marketing and management expertise;
- consultancy services, e.g. database and direct marketing consultancies;

Continued

- accommodation;
- advertising;
- transport;
- web hosting, dial-up accounts and internet connections;
- meeting room facilities and exhibition space; and
- infrastructure and logistical support, e.g. temporary supply of electricity, power and water.

  Forty percent of respondents provide goods as part of their sponsorships, including:
- freight and building supplies;
- promotional items and signage;
- merchandise, including items containing logos, such as caps, t-shirts and CDs;
- food and beverages; and
- office supplies and equipment.

Donations

Many cultural events actively solicit donations, which must be distinguished from sponsorship. A donation refers to a philanthropic gift that brings no commercial benefits to the giver. The motive for most donors is related to a desire to serve the 'public good', although they may receive minor benefits, such as the publication of their name on the list of donors or receipt of a newsletter. This contrasts with the basis of sponsorship contribution, which is a commercial transaction with an expected return on investment by means of marketing opportunities or other benefits, such as free or reduced-price tickets.

Donations have the advantage of being tax deductible in certain countries. In the UK, the Gift Aid scheme allows festivals and events to reclaim the tax paid on any donations made by any UK taxpayer. This scheme is actively promoted to events, for example, by the North East Tourist Board. The information provided on the scheme makes it clear that although this is an efficient means of soliciting donations, there are associated administrative costs, such as the need to keep adequate records of each donation. The scheme only applies to events that are registered as charities, which also involves administrative costs. In the United States most cultural events are treated as non-profit corporations exempt from federal income tax under section 501(c)(3) of the Internal Revenue Code. Donors may therefore deduct any donations from their own tax declaration.

Events may try to solicit larger donations by offering incentives to major donors. For arts festivals, for example, it is common to offer guaranteed seats, or access to specific areas of the festival (sometimes including backstage) to people who donate more than a certain amount. Although such incentives have a potentially high value for some events, the UK tax authorities have agreed that their value does not have to be declared as income by donors. The tax regimes in many countries impose clear restrictions on donations that are tax deductible.

Bequests and donations from 'friends' schemes may be other important sources of donation income. The Deloitte (2008) survey of private arts giving in the UK indicated that friends and membership schemes accounted for about 41% of funds donated to the arts, followed closely by major gifts (37%). Individual donations represented 14% of the total gift income.

Making the Kerrville Folk Festival Non-Profit

The Texas Folk Music Foundation (TFMF) has launched a capital fundraising campaign to buy the festival related assets of the Kerrville Folk Festival, Inc. (KFF) and take responsibility for putting on the Kerrville Folk Festival and the Wine and Music Festival. The TFMF Board believes this will assure the long-term future and success of TFMF and provide a greater level of financial security and funding options for the two Festivals run by KFF. The KFF and TFMF Boards and officers believe that the Festivals are a public interest, non-profit activity and are better suited for non-profit legal status to gain the many advantages of being formally organised as a 501(c)(3).

Continued

> The Kerrville Folk Festival, recently celebrating its 36th annual year, is the longest running event of its kind in the United States and is supported by a large and highly motivated volunteer workforce. TFMF intends that attendees, volunteers, performers and other friends will see no change to the 'Kerrville experience' at the festivals as a result of the change in organisation. As part of a non-profit organisation, the Festivals will see increased ability to seek and accept grants, donations, and other benefits not available to for-profit entities.
> (Kerrville Folk Festival, 2007)

The Kerrville appeal also suggests that there may be some scope for developing donations aimed at supporting a wider community remit for event programmes as a whole. As event programmes have outcomes that are beneficial to the community in terms of social cohesion and developing place identity, organisations with corporate responsibility remits should also view such programmes as worthy recipients of donations.

Earned income

For many events, ticket sales generate the bulk of event income. Maximising ticket income requires considerable marketing effort as well as effective yield management.

The amount that can be generated by ticket sales obviously varies considerably by event. The Spoleto Festival USA in Charleston budgeted total earned ticket income for the 2009 season at $2.9 million, which represented 47% of the total $6.2 million budget (€4.4 million). In the UK, the Edinburgh International Festival generated £2.47 million in income from ticket sales, accounting for over 30% of all income. In contrast, the New Zealand International Arts Festival in Wellington generated only 8% of total income from ticket sales in 2007.

However, the ratios between earned and unearned income cannot easily be compared from one event to another, without a detailed understanding of the nature of the event, its programme, its ticket pricing policies and the expectations of different stakeholders. A high level of earned income cannot be used as an indicator of success without careful analysis.

A report by the Australian Bureau of Statistics (2008) on 14 arts festivals in Victoria indicates that Arts Victoria awarded AU$8.6 million (€5 million) to festivals, around 31% of their total income. The total turnover for all festivals was AU$27.5 million. Earned income generated by the festivals themselves from ticket sales represented 41% of total revenue, compared to 40% from governments (31% channelled through Arts Victoria and 9% from state and local government). Income from sponsorship and donations generated 18% of total revenue.

The number of tickets sold is one variable, but equally important is the cost of selling each ticket. For the Edinburgh International Festival, for example, the costs of marketing, costs associated with the operation of sales (systems, staff) and other administration costs account for 31% of the total budget for the event. This is one reason why the selling of tickets may be contracted out to professional ticketing companies that cover the cost of ticket sales by charging a commission or service fee on each transaction. An increasing number of events are selling tickets online to reduce the costs of selling, and also using the information they gather from online sales to more strategically market their events. Purchasing tickets online is easy and fast for consumers, but it has introduced new security issues to the sale of tickets for the event programme.

Selling tickets for events by using an increasing number of commercial and experienced ticket agencies or through other types of ticket distribution networks have advantages for many event organisers. Eventful cities may coordinate such ticket selling operations for all events through contracts with one or more independent ticket agencies. However, there are sometimes problems arising from this approach. Cambridge City Council in the UK took legal action to recover money owed to it by a company contracted to sell Cambridge Folk Festival tickets on the Internet.

Following a competitive tendering process, a company was appointed by the council to sell tickets online for the 2008 festival. A total of £618,000 (€780,000) from ticket sales was not paid by the company, even though ticket sales were extremely high.

For many events, there are now an increasing number of unauthorised sales outlets for tickets, and this is becoming a major problem for event organisers and ticket purchasers. Event managers need to consider carefully the means of selling tickets for their event, taking into account the relative cost of each ticket that is sold and the impact of different approaches on the event itself and on the consumer.

For some events the sale of merchandise may also be a significant source of income. For the Paléo Festival in Nyon in Switzerland, for example, the rental of stalls and merchandising generated 7% of the festival's €13 million budget in 2007. Effective merchandising, however, requires careful planning and may not be realistic or even appropriate for certain types of events. Doyle (2004) argues that an event needs a merchandising strategy, which should include a clearly defined budget, a sourcing policy for merchandise, planning for the layout and location of merchandise to enhance visibility and accessibility to visitors, a pricing policy and a clear strategy for managing sales.

Catering and the provision of food and beverage service is often an important element of an event experience, and should be incorporated into the event operational and financial strategies. Decisions will need to be made about whether catering will be only a peripheral service and cost neutral, without major profit, or whether it is a significant part of an event's revenue generation strategy. Event organisers will also need to determine if the catering operation should be managed within the event's organisation or contracted out by tender or franchise to external specialist operators. Tenders can be offered by the city for a range of events, which is likely to attract more interest from potential suppliers.

Catering Operations for a City Event Programme

The City of Liverpool established a core calendar of major public events following the ECOC in 2008.

February	Chinese New Year 1 day
May	Hub 2 days
June	Lord Mayors Parade 1 day
June	Waterfront Celebration 2 days
August	Mathew Street Music Festival 2 days
November	Fireworks 3 locations 1 day

The City Council sought an experienced, high quality, management company to work with the event management team to identify, recruit, negotiate and manage catering and bar concessions at these events. The award of the contract to manage the catering was assessed on the following criteria:

- Experience of providing the service as detailed to other Local Authorities or to large major outdoor event and festival organisers.
- Awareness of and experience of working with high quality mobile caterers who offer healthy food options as a priority.
- Awareness of and experience of working with quality caterers who offer diversity of food options.
- The management company must have experience of and work with mobile caterers who have an effective environmental management policy with proven supporting evidence of implementation and effectiveness.
- The management company must have awareness of and evidence of providing catering and bar concessions that provide a value for money catering offer for the customers at festivals and events.
- The catering units must be of attractive and professional appearance and free of any damage.
- The management company must show a willingness to work with local Liverpool based companies in provision of catering units who will make every effort to source produce locally wherever practical.
- The management company must be able to provide evidence of awareness and compliance with all legislative requirements.

Continued

- The management company must be able to provide evidence of good practice and management at similar events, with a proven track record.
- The management company must be able to provide evidence of co operation and working with local authority enforcement officers.
- The management company must add value, creativity, innovation and ambition and will benefit from a retainer fee that will be offset by the income to be derived from the bars and catering concessions.
- The management company will derive 25% of gross income derived from said bar and catering concessions.

(City of Liverpool, 2009:15–16)

Rights sales

The sale of broadcasting rights may be an important source of income for some events. The rights to communicate the festival to the public includes broadcast via television, radio and Internet. Film rights to events can be managed by event organisers themselves, specialised agencies or by broadcasting companies, with conditions that allow editing rights, credits and payments.

The rapid growth in broadcast media means that there is now a large market for event broadcast material, either in terms of live coverage of major events or from the sale of images for later broadcasting (Yeoman, et al., 2004). The income generated from broadcast rights will tend to be highest for major music festivals, particularly those which feature high-profile pop performers. There is frequently competition between broadcasters for broadcast rights to certain events.

Broadcast Rights for Music Festivals

In the UK, major music festivals are increasingly sought after by broadcasters as a source of material for summer schedules. Channel 4 owned the rights to the Isle of Wight Festival between 2003 and 2007 and also owns the rights to the V Festival, while the BBC broadcasts Glastonbury Festival.Independent Television (ITV) owns the rights to the Latitude Festival and took over the Isle of Wight broadcasting from Channel 4 in 2008.

Isle of Wight organiser John Giddings said: 'After selling out all 50,000 of our tickets, it's great to be able to open the Isle of Wight Festival up to an even wider audience on ITV2 this summer. We've got some of the biggest names in music and to have live broadcasts across 3 days is both a real tribute to the event's success as well as something I've always wanted.'

Television coverage of an event can also help to attract major sponsors. In 2008 British Telecom (BT) was the main sponsor of the Isle of Wight Festival. The deal allowed BT to advertise the relationship with the festival as well as displayed its branding across the 250-acre site.

If cities want the events in their programmes to maximise and diversify their income sources, then they could provide support, encouragement and incentives for doing so.

FINANCIAL PLANNING AND MANAGEMENT

An effective and highly professional approach to financial planning and management is a critical success factor for event programmes. For events that are supported by public bodies, financial planning remains a fundamental criterion for support. Equally, for commercially driven events, the quality of financial planning determines profitability and survival. Without sufficient resources being available at the right time, events will cease to exist.

Financial management

Financial management is one essential and basic component of event programme planning. A budget is simply a plan expressed in monetary terms. Because all events need resources (both monetary and resources in kind), establishing the budget will often be one of the first tasks to be undertaken. Without some idea of the available or attainable resources, it is extremely difficult to give shape to the final programme, although it will first require an understanding of the potential shape of the event programme in order to derive the budget. For most events, there are different scenarios for the realisation of the programme and each requires to be budgeted so that comparisons can be made. Since the programme will influence the budget, which will then influence the final programme, there must be synergetic and collective planning between those responsible for the programme and financial plans of an event. Although this approach appears simplistic, there are many examples of the failure to coordinate closely the exercises of programme and financial strategy. These two essential elements must merge in the business plan that is created for an event.

Once a budget has been established, effective financial management needs to be applied to ensure that planned budgets are not exceeded. The final cost of for the 2004 Olympic Games in Athens was around €11 billion compared with an original budget of €4.6 billion. Most cities invest far less than this in events, but clearly there is a need to manage these resources effectively and to ensure that the city gets value from its events.

Budget Shortfall for Liverpool ECOC 2008

The Liverpool Culture Company was set up in 2003 as a wholly-owned subsidiary of the city council to run the 2008 ECOC. But prior to the event it was dogged by problems, including a series of resignations from executives with expensive pay-offs. The biggest problem however, was the discovery that the council had no agreed financial plan to cover £20 million (€25 million) worth of spending on the 2008 programme.

District Auditor Tim Watkinson commented 'I have been making recommendations to the council about improving its long term financial planning ... and of course part of that would be the budgeting and the planning in financial terms for the Capital of Culture expenditure. There was an element of funding for paying for Capital of Culture for 2008 some £20 million and the council didn't have a plan for funding that £20 million as part of it setting the budget for 2008/9.'

It had emerged that the £20 million was part of an overall budget shortfall of £62 million. The district auditor took the unusual step of using statutory powers to make recommendations and force the council to respond in public. A legal budget was finally set and the district auditor and others worked with the authority to plan their way out of the difficulties.

Asked why the council did not have a war chest to fund one of the most important events in the city's recent history, Councillor Bradley said: 'We

> have delivered the largest festival – cultural festival – ever in the history of
> European Capital of Culture because we realised how important it could
> be to drive regeneration in a city like Liverpool. We passed in March this
> year, a legal, balanced budget with the £20 million covered.'
> (Burnell, 2008)

Structures for financial management

All public authorities establish structures and procedures to ensure robust financial management of its event programmes. In cities that have a dedicated events unit, this will often be responsible for the monitoring of expenditure and investment in the event programme, often under the political control through an events committee or similar body that approves the budget and investments. Such committees are usually supported by the finance services of the public authority overseen by internal and external auditors, who check on the appropriate use of resources.

In order to keep costs under control and to ensure that resources are used correctly, it is important to have clear agreements between the public authority and the event organisers and facility developers who are responsible for the conception and delivery of the event programme. For example, in order to stage the Melbourne Winter Masterpieces programme, the state government of Victoria established a contract with Art Exhibitions Australia (AEA) for the identification, development, staging and promotion of exhibitions in 2003. Under the agreement, AEA was expected to bear the financial risk if the exhibition made a loss but was guaranteed 80% of the admission revenue. The remaining 20% was allocated to the venue manager, the National Gallery of Victoria, regardless of the profitability of the exhibition. The audit examined the 2005 Dutch Masters exhibition and declared that the AEA had completed all relevant payment requirements (Victorian Auditor General, 2007:31).

Cities should also be aware of the financial costs that event programmes can generate, even when delivered externally. The City of Melbourne has established a Marketing and Events Committee, one of the functions of which is to monitor the cost of events to the city. The Committee produced guidelines for the recovery of event-related costs from event organisers (City of Melbourne, 2006).

Among the costs relating to events identified in the guidelines are:

- preparation of traffic management plans;
- provision of traffic management infrastructure;
- reinstatement of damaged parklands;
- advertising of road closures and other event communications; and
- State Government fees and charges.

The council envisages that the cost of providing these services would be deducted from any grant provided, and that the labour of council staff should be considered as sponsorship in kind to events. The document also underlines that it is important not to waive fees and charges for council services to events, as these function as 'an event management tool to encourage event organisers to locate their events in the most appropriate locations and as a revenue stream that is ultimately returned to the ratepayers through provision of services.' It recommends that instead of waiving such fees, if the council wishes to support a particular event 'the covering of all or any of the fees and charges should be recorded as sponsorship of the event and appropriate benefits negotiated' (City of Melbourne, 2006:3–4).

The audit of cultural events carried out for Events for London by Deloitte (2006) provides a number of recommendations for the financial management of city event programmes.

- A significant number of events are delivered via partnership arrangements with other organisations. In such instances there should be a comprehensive Partnership Agreement, or formal contract with each of the partners.

- A scheme of delegation for funding decisions about events, as follows:

    □ Up to £10,000 (€12,500) approval by Line Management in accordance with delegated authority.

- □ Up to £25,000 approval by Head of Service.

- □ Up to £50,000 approval by Director.

- □ £50,000+ approved by Mayor.

- ■ The budget for each event should be approved by an appropriate delegated authority at the commencement of the project.

- ■ Regular budget monitoring should take place to ensure that the event remains on target and within budget.

- ■ A debriefing is carried out on completion of each event, at which learning points are considered and the success of the event is evaluated.

Planning tools

There are many basic planning tools that help guide events in cities. The most commonly used in developing financial plans for event programmes are budgeting and financial forecasting. Budgeting refers to the process of allocating resources to achieve the desired result of the programme, and financial forecasting is used to project the resource needs for the programme over a period of time.

Most cities already incorporate their event programme budgeting activities into established municipal budgetary procedures. In many cases the allocation of budgets will also take into account aspects of risk assessment and the impact of the event programme on wider city objectives and sustainability issues.

Budgeting for an Event Programme. Salford, UK

The proposed events programme for 2009/10 includes a number of key events:

Manchester International Festival (MIF)
Salford 10k Run and Cycling Race
Proms in the Park
Bonfire Events – Buile Hill Park and Prince's Park, Irlam
Salford Film Festival
Ice Rink 2009/2010

Continued

Name of event	Cost	SCC role: sponsorship (fixed cost)	SCC role: organiser (estimated costs)	Potential for income generation	Notes
Manchester International Festival	£110,000	Yes		No	
Salford 10k run and cycling race	£10,000	Yes		No	
Proms in the Park	£244,386		Yes	£103,500	Based on 100% of tickets sold £4,500 (funfair)
Bonfire events (Buile Park, Prince's Park)	£50,536		Yes		
Salford Film Festival		£24,000	Yes	No	
Potential reduction on police costs: under discussion			Yes		
Ice rink	£228,450		Yes	£85,000	Enhanced event could be provided at £246,450
TOTAL SPONSORSHIP (fixed costs)		£144,000			
TOTAL ORGANISER (estimated costs)			£523,372		
TOTAL COSTS	£667,372			£193,000	

A forecast was produced based on the role of Salford City Council and the potential for income generation of each event.

The total events cost for 2009 (all event costs minus projected income generated) was therefore estimated to be £474,472 (€560,000). These calculations indicate the maximum financial commitment of the local authority to the events funded in the event programme.

Financial forecasting deals with the long term financial implications of the event programme. For most cities the period of forecasting is likely to be fairly limited, given the relatively short cycles of municipal financial plans. In some cases, however, the development of major event programmes may require long term plans. The city of Den Bosch in the Netherlands produced a financial plan for the programme of events to celebrate the 500th anniversary of the death of Hieronymus Bosch. This covered the period 2009 to 2020 to allow for the development of a series of events leading up to the actual anniversary in 2016, as well as subsequent events linked to a bid for the ECOC in 2018 ('s-Gravesande & Sanders, 2008).

Planning over such a long period of time is difficult, because possible changes in the internal and external environment need to be taken into account in the plan. When dealing with complex events on a citywide or national basis, a technique called scenario planning might also be valuable. Scenario planning (or scenario thinking or scenario analysis) is a strategic planning method to create flexible long-term plans.

'Scenario planning is a process that provides the capability to think about the future' (Yeoman and McMahon-Beattie, 2004:276). Event organisers and public bodies can benefit from a tool that will enable them to prepare for the unknown by thinking broadly about the full range of plausible scenarios as well as constructing robust strategies for events regardless of how the future unfolds. Scenario planning is an instrument that guides and supports the imagination, creativity and vision necessary for mapping a range of viable strategies for the competitive success of events in a city. Scenario planning is not a vehicle for *predicting* the future; it is a method of *preparing* for the future regardless of what happens. This is achieved by having experienced individuals systematically share data and beliefs about their environmental assumptions, analyse their key challenges and create 'scenes' that describe combinations of critical events and trends. By sharpening thinking and improving the quality of decision making, events are better able to prepare for the unexpected by developing contingency.

Useful scenarios have the following characteristics: they should be reasonable to a critical mass of decision makers; internally consistent; relevant to the topic or issue of interest; recognisable from early and weak signals of change; and challenging as they contain some elements of surprise in directions where the city's vision needs to be stretched.

Scenarios for Event Programmes in Edinburgh

As part of the review of the Edinburgh Festivals conducted in 2006, a two-day workshop was developed to explore potential positive and negative scenarios for the future of the festivals. The Scenario Planning workshop participants, including major festival stakeholders, were confronted with two basic scenarios, one positive and one negative.

Negative Scenario – The Low Road

The British economy and the Scottish economy in particular enter a period of decline. Many of the spaces once used as non-traditional fringe venues are converted for residential, retail or commercial use. Local universities move to a year-round timetable and the availability of affordable bed spaces for visiting artists declines dramatically.

The newly recruited artistic leadership at the Edinburgh International Festival, the Edinburgh International Film Festival and the Edinburgh Mela move towards a more insular way of operating. Festivals are forced to produce sub-standard work as sponsorship and audience interest decreases, creating a vicious downward spiral. The closure of cultural venues leaves limited space for artists to develop and grow. The fragmentation of the Festivals' marketing message continues. Audiences, artists and media get the sense that Edinburgh has nothing new to offer. Other competitive cities develop comprehensive websites that provide information about their collective festivals and events throughout the year.

Positive Scenario – High Road

After being named the fifth most talked about city in the world, Edinburgh continues to build upon its existing foundations to become an even better place to live and visit. Transportation infrastructure continues to improve, the hotel infrastructure is maintained and, in fact, enhanced as additional high-end international hotels open up in the City Centre. The Leith/Granton waterfront development also provides the Festivals with additional cultural venues. A new entre-preneurial spirit permeates each of the Festivals as new delivery systems respond to changes in the global marketplace. Emerging and mid-level artists continue to view their participation in the Edinburgh Festival as essential to their career development. Additional non-traditional venues develop around the city, providing opportunities for artists to present site-specific works. The festivals have a joint marketing and sales strategy in place, which is carried out in close coordination with agencies including VisitScotland and the Convention and Visitors Bureau. The Festivals strike a programming deal with BBC Scotland (similar to the Proms), in which select Festival centrepiece events are broadcast nationally. By 2020, Festivals Edinburgh has created an umbrella organisation that manages collaborative enter-prises between the Festivals. Each Festival continues to maintain a degree of autonomy but many of the purely administrative areas are jointly managed. Other cities in the UK and around the world try to copy the Edinburgh Festivals model, but in the end, the authenticity of the Edinburgh experience prevails and the Festivals remain at the front of the pack (AEA Consulting, 2006).

Clearly these scenarios represent end members of a broad scale of potential developments and are designed as an aid to think about the future rather than being a prediction. Such tools can be very useful for focussing attention on the key issues surrounding a city and its cultural events. One of the recommendations of the final report was that:

'Financial control systems should be in place to help negate adverse cost variances, as well as business planning that uses options appraisals, scenario planning and financial modelling techniques' (p. 50).

REVENUE MANAGEMENT AND PRICING

Revenue management is a tool to ensure that the financial potential of an event or event programme is maximised by matching supply, demand and price. The issue of ticket sales has been mentioned as an integral component of an integrated marketing strategy for the event, which must include the critical issue of ticket pricing. Pricing has a particularly important role in revenue management for events, because often the supply is relatively fixed due, for example, to the fixed capacities of most venues. Although events, as leisure goods, may appear to have a high level of price elasticity, and because of competition and choice, price sensitivity is usually evident. With the exception of very 'high-value' events, which are most often influenced by star names, and the consumer habits of a very small number of highly committed 'aficionados' of certain category of event (opera, classical music, international theatre and dance), the wider public for events tend to be influenced significantly by ticket price. For this reason, the highest level of attendance is often achieved by events that are free to the public and where costs are met by other means (sponsorship, public subsidies, merchandising and catering, broadcast rights, etc.). It is clear from the Amsterdam Festivals analysed above (Table 6.2) that free events such as the Uitmarkt tend to attract many more visitors.

For some events, where there is limited capacity, and the programme is popular or there is a substantial dedicated audience, demand may exceed capacity. This is true of certain events such as the Glastonbury Festival in the UK, for example. Here, prices can be set high, because there is relatively little elasticity of demand. The same is true of many 'high-value' opera festivals, such as in Salzburg, Aix-en-Provence and Glyndeborne. The availability of public subsidies can also allow certain events to be staged at little or no cost to the audience, therefore arguably distorting the relationship between price and demand. In 2008, for example, the Parisian summer event Cinema en Plein Air was forced to start charging for entry after 18 years of operation as a free event. Pressure to start charging came from surrounding cinemas, which considered the free screenings at this subsidised event to be unfair competition.

If public sector funding and sponsorship become more difficult to obtain, many events may be forced to adopt a more commercial approach; event managers are turning to commercially-driven revenue management models to increase their income (Yeoman and McMahon-Beattie, 2004). This may have the effects of certain 'non-commercial' events being managed with a more acute and sophisticated approach to revenue management, defined as 'the application of information systems and pricing strategies to allocate the right type of capacity or inventory unit to the right type of customer at the right price at the right time so as to maximise yield or "revenue", (p. 204).

The application of such revenue management principles can apply to events that have a number of features, which include:

- relatively fixed capacity;
- predictable demand; and
- time-variable demand.

Events that are limited in time and space can fulfil these requirements. Capacity is limited by the number of days that the event runs, and for many events the level of demand will be largely predictable on the basis of previous or similar events. Events that are unable to meet such requirements may become more vulnerable in the future.

The revenue management system requires a number of key elements to function. These include market segmentation (see Chapter 7), an ability to forecast, pricing knowledge and an ability to manage information and reservations.

CONCLUSION

Event programmes face increasing challenges in making ends meet. Events have to search for funding from a growing range of sources in order to survive in the face of rising costs and funding uncertainty. The cost of running major event programmes can vary widely, depending on the size of the city involved, the potential audience and the objectives envisaged. For larger cities, programmes may cost tens of millions of euros; although on a per visit or per resident cost basis, the investment may seem relatively small.

For individual events, the uncertainty of funding is a major challenge, and many cities are now moving towards multi-annual funding models as a means of reducing this problem. As cities and the events which comprise their event programmes come under more pressure to justify public investment, there is a greater need for careful budgeting and financial planning as well as monitoring of outcomes and 'value for money' (see Chapter 9).

As a result, event programmes are moving towards more mixed funding models, with events being encouraged to generate their own income and find sponsorship. However, such income also has a price, and sponsors have to be managed just as carefully as other funding organisations. This creates a series of financial management tasks for the eventful city, which must ensure adequate financial decision making and management in order to secure event sustainability.

CHAPTER 7

Marketing, Communications and the Role of the Media

The measurement of audiences is one of the most widely used indicators of the success of an eventful city. Matching the content and structure of the event to visitor needs, demands and expectations is an essential skill for event managers and directors. However, there are certain artistic leaders who reject the notion of a 'market led' approach to event development and prefer instead the concept of an 'artist led' approach, which emphasises 'generating demand' rather than 'matching content to demand'. In both approaches the design and distribution of information, marketing planning and marketing communications are crucial for success. As Hall (1992:162) remarks: 'The image of a one time event has to be constructed in such a way as to make it a must-see attraction'. Therefore, by extension, the image of an eventful city should arguably be that of a 'must-visit city'.

'Marketing is a process by which individuals and groups obtain what they need and want through creating, offering and exchanging products and value with each other' (Kotler, 1994:6). This implies that the eventful city has to give its target groups what they want by engaging in a process of exchange with those groups. These exchanges need not be financial, but might involve the exchange of other resources, including time, labour, power and media exposure. Chapter 4 argues that a city has many different stakeholders who are

245

involved in creating eventfulness, and the city needs to engage all of these groups in its marketing efforts to ensure that they feel the exchange has been worthwhile.

This chapter examines the marketing, promotion and communication activities of event programmes, particularly in the context of their wider role in creating an image for a city or region. The issue of branding events is also analysed, particularly from the perspective of competing brands for events and event venues.

WHAT IS THE EVENT PRODUCT?

In looking at the marketing of events by cities, it is useful to start with a consideration of the nature of events as products. What are cities trying to sell and what aspects of the event 'product' are important from a marketing perspective?

At the most basic level, a product is a means to deliver desired 'benefits' to a customer. As Kotler (1994:429) put it, a product is 'anything that might satisfy a need'. For certain events, the needs of people to celebrate are relatively simple to understand, for example their desire to commemorate or to mark a special occasion. For others, consumer needs may not be directly related to content of the product, but are related to underlying factors such as the need to belong to a group, the need to build an identity, or the need to have fun.

Although certain events may be conceived as cultural products that are created to fulfil a cultural need of a specific audience, the benefits that audiences or other event stakeholders seek from an event often relate more to 'the experience' of an event than its cultural content. In major festival cities such as Edinburgh in August or Rio de Janeiro during Carnival, attending individual events may be motivated not only by the specific event itself, but also by a collective experience of its 'atmosphere'. In Cannes, being seen to be there (preferably by the media) is as important a motivator to attend as seeing specific films; the parties, the chance meetings, the professional camaraderie, and for some people being in the company of star performers and directors are primary reasons for attending the Cannes or Sundance (Utah) film festivals. The eventfulness of a city must take account of such needs as well as consider the quality of the programmes and other more tangible factors. One of the critical success factors for Edinburgh as an eventful city is the small city centre that concentrates people, allows the staging of events on the street and provokes a powerful sense of fun. In Cannes, one of the major challenges of the film festival is managing the images produced by the media as well as the movements of film stars and their less famous admirers (see Chapter 2).

As outlined in Chapter 1, Pine and Gilmore (1999) in their study of the 'Experience Economy' suggest that the creation of economic value relies more and more on such intangible factors, and above all in creating 'experiences'. According to them, experiences need to be more than the simple provision of services: they need to engage, involve and entertain the consumer as well. This change in the nature of the basic 'product' or 'service' requires a new approach to marketing. Experiences have to be staged, and both the producers and consumers of experiences become actors on the experience stage. Creating memorable experiences also means paying attention to the different dimensions of experience, which include educational, aesthetic, escapist and entertainment elements. The experience marketer therefore needs to be at home in each of these realms, and to understand how to combine these elements into a holistic, satisfying, total experience. Beyond the promotion of individual experiences related to single events, an integrated strategy, which incorporates an understanding of the combination and added value of experiences across different events in the city, becomes a central issue in marketing the eventful city.

Problems and challenges of event experience marketing

The advantage that events have in experience marketing terms is that an event is by definition a unique experience. Even if an event is frequently repeated, each edition will be different because of the timing, weather, mix of visitors and a host of other variables. The key is to convince the visitor that the event is indeed a unique, experience that cannot be missed, so that:

- Seeing the event LIVE is better than seeing it on TV.

- Seeing the event NOW will be better than ever before.

- Seeing the event HERE is better than seeing it anywhere else.

For the eventful city, the last statement is particularly crucial to successful development of cultural events. These days, people can visit music festivals or art exhibitions almost anywhere – so a key question is why they should come to your city to experience your event. Positioning events as unique is particularly important in persuading tourists to attend (see Chapter 8).

However, a strategy that simply focuses on the organisation of individual and unconnected unique events will be insufficient to meet the needs of different publics, or to ensure the additional impact that can be created by the overall eventfulness of the city. It may not be the city itself that is the key attraction, but the collective impact, say of the quality of the event programme itself. Prentice and Andersen (2003) argue that the loyalty demonstrated by festival audiences to cities such as Edinburgh is likely to be to the overall experience of excellence in performing arts, rather than to the city as a stage for the arts. Individual and specific experiences need to be tied into the fabric and life of the city to ensure a close relationship between events and the experience of a particular place.

Achieving links between a programme of cultural events and the daily life of the city is challenging because it implies working with a range of different stakeholders, as discussed in Chapter 4. For events relating to cultural themes it is important for all of the relevant cultural institutions in the city to be involved in the planning, organisation and execution of the events, so that they collectively enhance the feeling of eventfulness. This was one of the important aspects of the Universal Forum of Cultures event organised in

Barcelona in 2004. Although the Forum itself took place in a clearly defined precinct, the programme for the year also included many events, which took place in cultural institutions throughout the city. Even though the institutions were given the freedom to interpret the themes of the year to suit their own needs, in fact, these 'peripheral' events ended up attracting almost as many visitors as the Forum itself. It is also an advantage to the city's institutions and organisations to embark on joint marketing that is linked to a city event experience.

The coordination between the marketing of a particular event or a series of events and the marketing of the city as a whole is an essential element of a successful eventful city. The approach by a city to the development and promotion of a portfolio of events remains a critical success factor.

MARKETING STRATEGIES FOR EVENTFULNESS

Zinkhan and Pereira (1994:210) define marketing strategy as 'the effective allocation and coordination of marketing resources in order to reach the aims of the organisation in a particular market.' The marketing strategy offers the operational means of communicating to different publics the vision and the incentives to participation in events.

Strategic marketing is one element of strategic management (see Chapter 5). The marketing mission needs to correspond to the level of ambition and to the proposed positioning of both an event and the eventful city. As the following example from Barcelona indicates, the development of a successful marketing strategy for the eventful city should rest on an accurate assessment of the external and internal position of the city, evaluating the impact of external factors such as economic and social change, the strategies of competing cities and the resources and capabilities of the city itself.

Barcelona's Vision

One of the keys to the success of Barcelona has been the development of high profile events (see Chapter 2), but arguably this strategy would not have been successful without an overall marketing and communication strategy to promote these events and anchor them in the wider framework of the city's vision.

In the book *Barcelona Communicates*, Puig (2005) analyses the marketing and communication strategy of Barcelona, and demonstrates how marketing campaigns are linked to the vision and objectives of the city. He argues that the city's image is central to its marketing strategy, and this in turn is based on the values of city. In his view, 'the image as value' synthesises the vision of 'always working with the people for a city of daily comfort and a secure future'. The transmission of the image as value should be: 'Simple, Direct, Suggestive, Vital and Memorable'. In building its marketing strategy, the main elements were:

- Where we are – wanting to be in the Premier League of world cities.

- What we want – not just staying in the league, but being 'a city that counts'.

- Who we will accomplish this with – a team formed by the municipality and other stakeholders.

- How we will do it – by prioritising continual improvement of the quality of the city and prioritising strategic projects, such as the 22@ high technology quarter, the 2004 Universal Forum of Cultures or the high-speed train link.

In defining what the city wanted, and the team to accomplish this with, the main aim was to involve the inhabitants of the city. This was encapsulated in the slogan *Fem-ho bé* (Let's do it well), which used the play on words of *bé* as the Catalan word for 'good' as well as the B of Barcelona. So 'let's do it Barcelona' automatically means 'Let's do it well'.

To communicate this message effectively, it was important to get the entire city working with the same messages. This was achieved through the development of a 'Barcelona Model' for communication. The bases of the Barcelona Model of communication (not to be confused with the general 'Barcelona Model' – Amalang, 2007) were:

- Take the initiative.
- Create synergy.
- Respond to the public's interest.
- Present a new image, a new municipal deed.
- Elaborate a global discourse on a strong city.

- Have the mayor at the head of everything.
- Reach the public with clarity and directness.

The image of the city is therefore part of a general strategy to communicate better with the populace. The success of Barcelona's marketing strategy is arguably based on a few important principles:

- Less is more – concentration of sharp meanings.
- Boldness – offering important choices.
- Difference – using trends (and other cities) to learn from, not copy.
- Organisational memory – a solid basis in an era of change.
- Electoral promise.
- Image plus services – an image alone is not enough, real services need to be delivered.

The development of campaigns related to events is important, because events are turning points, moments of decision in which the future can be created. However, the vision of the future is difficult to create without reference to past events. Barcelona has often celebrated previous major events held in the city, including the Olympic Games and the World Expos (see Chapter 2).

The marketing planning process for the eventful city involves a series of strategic choices about the stakeholders to be served, the competition to be met, the types of events to be staged and the long-term goals to be achieved.

TYPES OF MARKETING STRATEGY

Eventful cities generally apply a number of generic marketing strategies; the choice and combination will depend largely on the city's objectives.

Target market strategy

Target market segmentation is an approach based on the categorisation of the potential public for events, commonly by geography (place of residents and potential visitors including both local residents and tourists), demographics (age, gender, ethnicity, education and occupation) and psychographics based on interests, beliefs and attitudes. The eventful city needs to move beyond these more traditional techniques of market segmentation, particularly if the aim is to attract new audiences or to support objectives relating to education and social cohesion. Broadening participation is central to the eventful city approach. The concern is not only to define the most 'profitable' targets in terms of ticket sales in the short-term, but also to engage in long-term audience development (see Chapter 8). Where event programmes are financed and used to support the stated cultural policy of the city, target groups are sometimes already defined by the policy, and event organisers need to reflect the wider social objectives in their strategic and marketing plans.

There is a clear relationship between the city event programme strategy and the approach to marketing. The event programme and marketing strategies must be coherent and interrelated, both corresponding to the programme vision and objectives. Expanding the audience for events often involves adapting them to meet the demands of the public, without sacrificing the quality of the experience or the values of the organisers or city authorities. Arts events in particular struggle with the dilemma of adapting a programme to ensure it is market oriented; a problem which many other types of city events, such as fireworks and popular music events, do not have.

The eventful city requires broad-based programming and marketing strategies to enable the local authority to serve the needs of all its residents. In Rotterdam, the development of events has taken into account the interests of both wide segments of the population as well as smaller 'market niches'. The staging of major summer festivals, for example, provides a very popular cultural offer of wide appeal, with freely accessible, large-scale events with a varied programme. In contrast, the city has also developed much more specific events designed to appeal to specific groups. In 2001 the ACT2001 festival was run alongside the ECOC (European Capital of Culture), in an attempt to engage young people in the cultural activity taking place that year (see Chapter 8).

There are many different ways to segment an event audience. One of the most widely used is visitor origin, because this is often one of the most easy aspects of attendance to determine (through ticket sales records, for example) but segments can also be identified on the basis of motivation, repeat visitation, age and a host of other factors.

Prentice and Andersen (2003:24) describe the segmentation of the Edinburgh International Festival audience as follows:

> *The Festival offers some partying opportunities where serious consumption is also common. Repeaters account for half of the total market. At least 2 of the 7 segments identified can unequivocally be considered serious consumers .... To them can possibly be added the Scots performing arts seekers and the gallery-goers. The Festival would seem a serious business for many tourists and the label 'culture-vultures' may not be far from the mark. If so, authenticity may be defined more as involvement than as image, or .... as a quest involving the communitas (sic) of participation.*

Tourists are a particularly attractive target market for many events, since they bring additional economic impact into the area in which the event is held. Many major events are therefore designed to attract tourists in general, and foreign tourists in particular (see Chapter 8).

For each market segment, a different approach needs to be adopted, depending on factors such as origin, motivation, distance and familiarity with the destination.

Product strategy

In classic marketing theory, products should be designed around the needs of the consumer. This approach does not always work so well for the eventful city, where many events may be created by inspired and visionary producers for whom the audience may be a secondary concern (see Chapter 2). The logic of events marketing, especially for cultural events, is therefore often the reverse of conventional models, with the product being developed first, perhaps influenced by an understanding of the market, but clearly not defined by it. Eventful cities need to be engaged in developing product strategies that include the creation of new events to enhance the experience of city residents and visitors. As stated earlier, the eventful city should encompass a strategy that includes a portfolio of events which meet the needs of different stakeholders, and which can help the city to maintain unique positioning when compared to its competitors.

In the case of Edinburgh the decision to market the city as 'eventful' stems from the strong events product that the city has. The marketing strategy is therefore determined by the availability of events at key periods of the year and the different target markets that might be attracted by these events. The events themselves, as important parts of the cultural and tourism product of the city, also have a large say in how they are used to market the city.

Competitive strategy

In received marketing wisdom, it may also seem that the needs of the city's main stakeholders – primarily its residents – should be paramount in determining the events strategy. However, cities must also maintain their competitive edge against other cities. For example, as described earlier, Manchester recently launched its International Festival to compete directly against Edinburgh, using commissioned performances as a differentiating feature.

Barcelona has a history of developing events in response to competitive pressures, which may not be fully understood by local residents who may believe there are more pressing priorities. If an event is not created in response to local demand, residents may have to be persuaded that eventfulness is a good idea. The Olympic Games or the Universal Forum of Cultures were not events that were universally supported by the residents of Barcelona; it was the city administration that decided that such events were needed, and then embarked on campaigns to garner public support, which proved successful for the Olympics but not for the Universal Forum. Although the logic of cities competing to stage major events is increasingly understood, there is still a need to 'sell' the idea to different stakeholder groups, many of whom ultimately bear the resulting costs.

However, new events designed to compete with other cities may also end up competing with the existing events at home, either in terms of audiences or resources. For example, in the case of Toronto it was argued that:

> Given the level of resources available to Toronto's tourism sector, and the time required to establish a (new) signature event, (this) cannot be a priority in the short to medium term. Instead, the primary objective should be the development of a year round calendar of major tourism events that reinforce Toronto's positioning as a leisure tourism destination, and bolster travel during gaps in the high and low travel seasons.
>
> (City of Toronto, 2003:22)

Marketing is involved in all the phases of new event development. First, the internal stakeholders of the city must be convinced that an event is worth staging, in order to ensure sufficient local support. Second, the city must be marketed as a potential location for the event, to the awarding body or event organiser, in cases when there is competition to attract the event and, finally, the event has to be marketed to the potential audience who need to be persuaded to participate.

In the case of the 2000 Sydney Olympics, Waitt (1999:1055) argues that there was a tangle of culture, politics and locality in which 'the act of bidding itself becomes a promotional act'. Many other cities have also realised the value of simply bidding for events. Manchester's bid for the 1996 Olympic Games was seen as a successful promotional activity, even though the city did not secure the nomination. The lessons learned and the promotion gained from the bidding process later helped Manchester secure the 2002 Commonwealth Games (see Chapter 2). The process of bidding is also a useful device for galvanising the various stakeholder groups in the city, and providing a platform for organising events and undertaking other marketing and development activities. This is underlined by the marketing activities of a number of candidate cities for the ECOC that have often spent considerable sums on promotion. The Polish cities of Łódź and Warsaw have both advertised their role as ECOC candidate cities on CNN, for example (Richards & Palmer, 2009).

The marketing process involves a wide range of intermediaries, not only those responsible for the 'product', but also all stakeholders (see Chapter 4). Each stakeholder may have a different role or set of tasks. National and local politicians may focus on international lobbying, the tourism sector may concern itself with marketing culture to attract visitors, the city administration may integrate the event in broader marketing and image-building strategies to attract investment, and the city's cultural organisations might concentrate on widening the market reach of their own audiences through cultural events.

USING EVENTS TO MARKET CITIES

Just as events are a tool for place making, they are also used for place marketing. In many cases, events form a major part of the city marketing strategy. In the Dutch city of 's-Hertogenbosch, city marketing is defined as

> city promotion in which public affairs (e.g. lobbying), attracting businesses and the stimulation of cultural tourism are structurally integrated. City marketing has a number of aims: strengthening the image of the city and generating tourism and investment. Central to this process is the strengthening of the local economy. The target market segments are visitors, decision makers and government.
> (Gemeente's-Hertogenbosch, 2006:1)

The marketing of cities through events involves the collaboration of stakeholders from the public, private and voluntary sectors. Very often, these interests are already represented in marketing bodies such as local and national tourism marketing organisations or cultural marketing consortia and these bodies are increasingly applying cultural events as a marketing tool. In Germany, for example, the Deutsche Zentrale für Tourismus (DZT) produced a brochure entitled *Experience Culture 1999*, which listed a wide range of cultural events, including the Goethe year, the Weimar Cultural Capital programme, historic festivals and art exhibitions, along with many other events. The British Tourist Authority has packaged a number of cities together under the banner of British Art Cities, which in addition to London (which profiles itself in the brochure as 'the cultural capital of the world') also features cities such as Glasgow, Leeds, Manchester, Bristol and Cardiff. The collaborative advantages of jointly marketing events, or even eventful cities, may outweigh the traditional strategies of competitive marketing.

The rapid increase in online booking of tickets and travel products has led to a growing number of events being marketed via ticketing websites. For example www.worldticketshop.com/festivals sells tickets online for a wide range of events, ranging from the Salzburger Festspiele and the Bayreuther Festspiele to pop festivals such as Benicassim and the Isle of Wight. The availability of tickets online increases the chances that tourists will be able to buy tickets and therefore visit the location in question.

Another potential issue in marketing is event frequency. If an event is annual, then a pattern of expectation can be created in the mind of potential visitors. For one-off events, such as the ECOC, the problem is that there is no repetition of events and therefore no opportunity to develop a pattern of expectation on the part of the audience. There are a number of ways in which this problem can be overcome. One is to organise a series of events over a number of years, to probe local and visitor markets and test the cultural event product. A number of ECOCs have adopted this strategy, such as Liverpool in the UK (2008) and Pécs in Hungary (2010).

In cases where a city lacks a critical mass of cultural and/or tourism marketing expertise (which is often the case in smaller cities) an option may be to subcontract that expertise externally. The creation of an events marketing unit might be related to the general city marketing function, or a separate organisation. The City of Almere in the Netherlands had a unique challenge in city marketing because it was founded 30 years ago on a land reclaimed from the former Zuiderzee. It therefore had a population of zero, and zero image. Almere had to build a city, create a community and craft an image from scratch. In order to do this, a private marketing company was established, which had as its mission: 'Marketing the values and the image of the town in order to turn the town of Almere into an even more popular and more attractive place for its inhabitants, entrepreneurs and visitors.' One of the core tasks of this private organisation is to create and market events that help to shape and promote the image of the city. This has become particularly important because of the way that the city was built from the outside in, leaving the city centre until last. The relative lack of image for Almere was a challenge taken up in the preparation of a bid for the ECOC in 2018.

The question of the scale of city ambition in terms of marketing event programmes requires consideration. A city may be very successful in marketing itself as eventful at a local or regional level, with a good spread of high quality smaller events that appeal to the resident population. If the city wishes to raise its external profile or attract tourists, however, the tendency may be to think in terms of large 'mega events'. Mega events take on a marketing logic of their own, since in many cases the event becomes the destination, rather than the host city itself. This is certainly true of mega events such as the Olympic Games or the World Cup, and is arguably increasingly the case with other major cultural events as well, including blockbuster exhibitions, expos and large-scale festivals. When the event is finished, the destination may be remembered and connected to the past event, but this factor is unlikely to draw visitors to the city for its own sake. Richards, Geodhart and Herrijgers (2001) found that the ECOC event was often a bigger draw and a more easily recognised 'brand name' than the host city. Using mega events to market cities may help to attract attention to a city and generate media coverage, but the city needs to ensure that it does not become overshadowed by the event, or that a single mega event doesn't detract from the normal pattern of eventfulness in the city.

PRODUCING AND DEVELOPING THE MARKETING STRATEGY

Successful eventful cities link marketing strategies for the events themselves, both individually and collectively, to the wider marketing plans of the city or region. Such marketing strategies should be developed within a well-defined framework of strategic economic, social and cultural objectives and outcomes. The strategy needs to set clear goals and objectives at every level and to demonstrate clearly how these will help the city to achieve its wider aims.

In the case of Cape Town in South Africa, for example, there is a clear statement that marketing is not only more than just promotion, but also includes the production of 'social value'.

Cape Town Marketing Vision

Cape Town and the Western Cape will increasingly be confronted by two major and related challenges as it moves into the twenty-first century. The first is the need to successfully compete in a global economy characterised by increased competition and globalisation. The second is the need to eliminate poverty and address issues of inequality and marginalisation. The challenge facing the Province as an events destination is therefore twofold: how to present events equal to the best in the world; and secondly, how to channel the potential economic and social benefits of events to as broad a range of beneficiaries as possible. The aim is that:

'By the year 2010 Cape Town and the Western Cape should be recognised as a unique, world-class events destination delivering real economic and social value to all citizens through the hosting of events.'

The eventful city needs to create frameworks within which the strategy can be supported and developed. In the case of Amsterdam, a successfully marketed eventful city, festivals and events fit into the context of the overall city marketing strategy and they help to position the city in national and international markets. In order to make sure that events can fulfil this marketing role, a structure has been created which brings together the major city marketing stakeholders.

Festivals and Events as an Element of City Marketing in Amsterdam

Amsterdam initiated a new city marketing strategy in 2003 as a result of close consultation between the local authority, stakeholders from the tourism and cultural sectors and experts in marketing and communication. This new strategy led to the creation of Amsterdam Partners, a public private partnership, including private companies, local authorities, major festivals, attractions and higher education institutions. The aim is to develop a sustainable relationship between content, policy and marketing, and a bottom up approach to collaboration.

The lead in city marketing has been shifted from the city administration to Amsterdam Partners. The city will retain the rights to the 'Amsterdam' brand, and license its use to Amsterdam Partners. Amsterdam Partners will be the brand manager on behalf of the city, determine the marketing strategy and be responsible for the development of the image of the city. Other partners (such as the Amsterdam Tourist Board) will contribute funding and also give advice on policy.

In order to remain competitive in the European economy, the city wants to develop its profile as a knowledge and business centre. As part of this strategy, it also wants to strengthen its position as a centre for events. The basic aim is to strengthen the image of Amsterdam with key target markets in terms of recognition, visits, expenditure and market position (ranking relative to other cities). The key target segments are business decision makers, logistic services, creative industries, knowledge workers, active citizens, visitors and residents.

These objectives will be pursued through projects in the areas of key development projects ('pearls'), events and integrated marketing projects. The events policy will be developed through a festivals and events manager employed by Amsterdam Partners, who will be responsible for developing a 'one stop shop' for events organisers and a policy for attracting major international events.

Although only a very small portion of the city marketing budget was originally reserved for events, Amsterdam has subsequently developed a funding stream for major events which attract overnight visitors to the city. In 2008, a total of €457,000 was awarded to five major events in the city (see Chapter 8).

BUILDING COLLABORATIVE MARKETING STRATEGIES

With limited marketing budgets it is not surprising that many cities advocate collaborative marketing as a way of maximising resources and marketing effectiveness. By pooling marketing resources, individual events and venues within a city can arguably achieve more than by going it alone. This was one of the main conclusions of the East Midlands Festivals Study in the UK (Maughan & Bianchini, 2003:24), which argued that 'cultural festivals in the East Midlands would benefit from being promoted jointly with other tourism attractions aimed at people of different ages to sustain the interests of visitors,' and that 'there should be greater regional networking by festivals'. Part of this networking should revolve around marketing as 'the festivals would also benefit from joint publicity, through different media, ranging from the internet to brochures and press and possibly even broadcasting campaigns if funds allowed'.

In Edinburgh, a study suggested that the city should consider 'the possibility of a distinctive, jointly developed festivals marketing strategy, especially addressing international marketing and press campaigns', and that 'festivals should be encouraged to extend their existing gateway website to include all the festivals; links to other city-wide or national websites should be pursued' (Graham Devlin Associates, 2001:39).

The logic for collaboration seems inescapable. Better coordination of the events calendar would help avoid events competing with each other; events could learn new marketing skills and techniques from one another and bigger marketing campaigns could be organised to achieve a higher profile for the eventful city and its constituent events. In their study of events and attractions in the North of England, Tourism Research and Marketing (2006:100–102) identified a number of ways in which different actors in the region could develop collaborative marketing activities:

1. Sharing databases
   Collaboration could be based around identified

markets (e.g. heritage, arts, festivals), using the pooled marketing resources to create awareness. This could be linked to:

- Common themes across the North of England.

- City-based theme years.

2. Attraction/event clusters
   By linking together events and fixed attractions (e.g. museums, monuments) in the region, joint marketing could be developed around event themes linked to those attractions, particularly where these are close enough to permit people to visit more than one attraction. The clustering of attractions and events also helps to achieve a 'buzz', even in rural areas. Clustering events may also be a way of developing an 'identity' for a region. Clusters of events were identified in the Yorkshire and The Humber Major Events Strategy (Yorkshire Forward, 2008) as a marketing tool. The strategy envisaged the creation of five event clusters, each based on the cultural or recreational specialities of the region concerned:

- Sheffield – sport.

- West Yorkshire – cultural diversity.

- North Yorkshire – outdoor activities.

- The coast – maritime activities.

- Leeds – business and entertainment.

3. Programming the city or region
   Regions can effectively be programmed in the same way as single events or venues, providing a varied event offer in single locations while linking together similar types of events across the region.

4. Sharing information
   Events and attractions can share information about their visitors to develop powerful marketing tools. By identifying regular visitors and their consumption

patterns, specific campaigns can be targeted to these people. Developing cultural activities may be easier if there is a network approach to the collection and dissemination of audience and tourism data.

Even where events are distant from one another in physical terms, there may still be advantages to be gained from collaboration. Although the majority of visitors to most events are likely to be local, some types of events can attract audiences from long distances, and these people may be willing to travel because of their interest in the content or theme of the event. One example is the network of Mela festivals in the UK (www.melafestival.com).

In spite of the seemingly logical basis for collaboration, one often finds that events within a particular city or region may be in competition with one another. In terms of the fight to secure resources, perhaps this is natural: every event wants to obtain a larger slice of the cake for itself. But in terms of managing a city or region, this can pose considerable problems.

The reluctance of events to collaborate often stems from a lack of identification with other events in the same region. The Edinburgh study (AEA Consulting, 2006) indicated that many of the Edinburgh Festivals do not see their field of operation as the city itself, but rather the global field of their particular specialisation. Competition for the Edinburgh Film Festival comes from other film festivals globally rather than from other events in Edinburgh. Collaboration with other events in the city may therefore not even occur to festival directors who are more concerned with their international artistic peers than their neighbours. In such a situation, some events may see attempts to develop collaboration with apparently unconnected events in the same city or region as an irrelevance.

Collective Marketing of Festivals in Rotterdam

Rotterdam Festivals was established in 1993 with a brief to market the many diverse events happening in the city. Although Rotterdam Festivals is part of the municipal structure, they do not see themselves as initiators of events, but rather they help to improve the existing product.

Continued

Rotterdam Festivals is an example of collective marketing, where an entire sector combines to market a product together. Jan Moerman, Director of Rotterdam Festivals argues that the creation of a cultural climate in the city was an important first step in festival marketing. To give the cultural profile of Rotterdam a higher profile, the cluster of museums in the city centre were rebranded as the Museum Park. Having created a cultural space, the following step was to create the Rotterdam Summer Festivals, to generate a critical mass of cultural events to give the impression that there was always something going on in the summer in Rotterdam. This initiative is still successful, as evidenced by advertisements in 2005 by low cost airline Transavia for flights from the UK to Rotterdam on the basis of summer music events.

Rotterdam Festivals works closely with other organisations in the city, particularly the tourism department. In order to create a clear division of responsibility, the tourism department deals with general event promotion, while Rotterdam Festivals deals with cultural event promotion. The important point in working with individual festivals is to make sure that Rotterdam Festivals can offer them added value. There were plans for a centralised ticketing system, for example, but this was shelved because of opposition from the festivals, who argued that this would divert energy away from more important matters. Rotterdam Festivals therefore decided to concentrate on the development of Information and Communication Technology (ICT) (databases, data analysis) and the youth market.

For example, with the collaboration of the venues, a database for opera visitors was developed in 2001, which eventually generated over 26,000 names. A collective opera guide was sent to these people – a collective product which belonged to all the venues. An initiative for young cultural visitors also worked with a database developed from the venues, and involved emails and a magazine aimed at young readers. (Rossie, 2003)

The important point in collaborative marketing is to avoid re-creating the competitive situation that already exists in the marketing of individual events in the city. Rotterdam Marketing does not see its task as creating new ideas – otherwise this leads to resistance on the part of the festivals.

Internet has increasingly provided a platform for event collaboration in cities. In the UK, the York City of Festivals portal (www.yorkfestivals.com) was established by York @ Large, the cultural partnership for the city, with the following aims:

- to make the city more eventful, building on the vibrancy and diversity of York's year-round programme of festivals;

- to look for opportunities to build on the success of existing festivals and help new festivals to develop;

- to support and advise festival and events organisers on all aspects of putting on an event, including health and safety, insurance, booking a suitable venue, marketing and PR;

- to encourage a more citywide approach to events and festivals through working with the Council and other key partners to help remove barriers to filling the city with events;

- to build community participation in festivals and other cultural events.

The portal provides marketing support to festivals as well as information for consumers about events and accommodation in York. Event organisers can download guides on how to organise an event, as well as a description of event spaces in the city.

Turisme de Barcelona

As well as event based or cultural organisations, collaboration may also be instigated by the tourism sector. The Turisme de Barcelona Consortium was founded in 1993 by Barcelona Municipal Council, the Barcelona Official Chamber of Commerce, Industry and Shipping, and the Foundation Barcelona Promoció.

Turisme de Barcelona has a specific cultural tourism programme, which basically attempts to develop packages for tour operators and individual tourists. Products currently used include the ArtTicket Barcelona and membership of Art Cities in Europe.

Continued

They also collaborated with the municipality to develop the 'Barcelona is Culture' programme, which started in 2000 and culminated with the Universal Forum of Cultures in 2004. The theme years in this programme included the Year of Music (2000) and the Gaudí Year (2002). As part of this programme, a permanent body on culture and tourism was established. The Gaudí Year had a significant visitor impact, attracting an estimated 6 million visitors to the 300 events organised during the year (although this includes many visits to existing attractions, such as the Sagrada Familia). The economic impact was estimated to be €34 million. Hotel overnights grew by 17%, use of the Tourist Bus by almost 25% and visits to Gaudí-related attractions rose by between 20% and 50%.

The growth of tourism and the development of income-generating activities have enabled Turisme de Barcelona to increase its earned income from 10% to 90% of the total budget, which was €23 million in 2007.

The Eventful Edinburgh campaign also provides an example of an integrated marketing approach for the eventful city. The aim of this campaign was to position Edinburgh internationally as an eventful city: 'Welcome to Edinburgh, Scotland's magical capital and home to Europe's most vibrant calendar of international festivals and events.' The eventful-edinburgh.com website was designed to keep visitors and locals up to date with what's happening. The site provides links to each of Edinburgh's 14 major festivals. The site provides basic information on each of these events, as well as a direct link to each of the festivals' own websites. The Eventful Edinburgh campaign was developed jointly by the Edinburgh and Lothians Tourist Board (ELTB) and Edinburgh city council. It was funded largely by the city council and VisitScotland.

Collaborative activities can also be developed in the area of public relations. Singapore has worked hard to develop an image as a cultural hub in Asia, and this push has been supported by numerous PR activities. One Australian art journalist reported on one of the 'fam trips' (familiarisation trips) as follows:

> I was one of a group of arts journalists from around the world generously hosted by the National Arts Council

and the Singapore Tourist Bureau to visit the Singapore Arts Festival for 5 days in June, to meet artists, visit galleries and theatres and learn about the structure of arts-making and promotion within Singapore and beyond. Just that conjunction of arts and tourism was pretty exciting in itself, to find the mostly young staff of both agencies speaking with enthusiasm and expertise about the arts. Singapore sees itself as the hub of South-East Asia and a major part of its pull is its building and promotion of a huge events program (sport, entertainment, art) with the Esplanade arts centre and a growing arts culture playing a key role.

(Gallasch, 2004)

An important aspect of collaborative marketing is the question of who controls communications about the eventful city and its constituent events. From a destination marketing perspective, it is important that the city maintains control of individual communications that contribute to meeting its marketing aims and have an effect on the image of the city. However, there is also an argument that individual event producers should be able to design their own communication strategies, because they are closer to their own audiences. This system may work well when individual event organisers have experience of developing their own communications campaigns and where the division of responsibilities between the event organisers and the programme organisers is clear. In the Luxembourg ECOC in 2007, such a division of labour did not always work well, particularly where event organisers were expecting more to be done by the General Coordination of the event, or where individual organisers had little marketing experience (Luxembourg & Greater Region, 2008).

IMPLEMENTING THE MARKETING STRATEGY

Once a strategic marketing direction for the eventful city has been chosen, it must be operationalised. This involves the essential process of marketing planning, which takes as its starting point the basic strategy and translates this into

Table 7.1	The Marketing Planning Process for the Eventful City		
Key questions	**Process**	**Products**	**Tasks for the eventful city**
What is our business?	Mission setting	Company mission/strategy	Selecting defining events
Where are we now?	Analysis		
	Macro	External environment	Relationship to other events and eventful cities
		Macroeconomic, social and cultural trends	
	Micro	Stakeholders	Identifying the events community
		Competitors	Identify which cities/events we are competing against
	Internal	Resources and capacities of the city Strategic options	Inventory of cultural and events resources
Where should we be?	Planning		
		Strategic decisions	How eventful do we want to be? Which events do we want to highlight/develop/win?
		Target markets	Who will our events be aimed at?
		Positioning	How do we want ourselves to be seen? What is our brand?
		Marketing objectives	What are we hoping to achieve?
How do we get there?	Implementation		
		Action plans	Setting out tasks for the different stakeholders, establishing targets
		Marketing mix	Deciding how we will communicate with our chosen audiences and attract them to our events

Table 7.1 The Marketing Planning Process for the Eventful City—*Cont'd*

Key questions	Process	Products	Tasks for the eventful city
How are we doing?	Monitoring		
		Monitoring and Feedback	Measuring the overall success of our programme of events against the targets set
		Modify plans	If targets are not being met, or if the external or international environment changes, adapting our plans to ensure continued success

a series of action plans, which can be followed and monitored. This process is illustrated in Table 7.1.

Structural marketing planning systems of this type are now being implemented in a number of cities, such as Oxford in the UK (Chappell & Harriss, 2006), Gold Coast in Australia (Gold Coast City Council, 2007) and Cape Town in South Africa (City of Cape Town, 2008). The Cape Town events marketing planning process is linked to the wider strategic goals of the city:

> The City's events calendar will be linked to key marketing and strategic focus areas and will be guided by, and aligned with, the strategic objectives of the City's Tourism, Economic Development, Arts and Culture, Sport and Recreation and Communication Departments (p. 11).

In the events plan for Cape Town, the process of 'Marketing Plan Management' is described as concerning:

> the development and supervision of the overall marketing strategy and tactics to be employed, including target customer definition, acquisition and retention; the internal and external messages and mediums; and the maintenance of positive customer or guest relations to achieve the marketing aspirations for the event project and the hosting organisation (p. 25).

BRANDING

For cities as a whole the emphasis has shifted from city marketing towards city branding, which implies a much broader process:

> *City branding implies a significant change of perspective on the whole marketing effort. Marketing is a process that can be used to accomplish various goals set by the city ...(whereas) City branding is understood as the means both for achieving competitive advantage in order to increase inward investment and tourism, but also as the means for achieving community development, reinforcing local identity and identification of the citizens with their city and activating all social forces to avoid social exclusion and unrest.*
>
> (Kavaratzis, 2008:45)

Events, with their multifaceted impacts and applications, have become an essential part of the place branding process in many cities and regions. Growing competition between cities to develop events and become eventful makes it increasingly important for cities to achieve brand distinction. Not only can events achieve clear brands, but also the combination of event brands will create either a unified, clear and distinctive brand for an eventful city or one that is ambiguous, overlapping with other city brands, or simply unbelievable. A brand is a name or symbol that truly represents a product. A brand image creates an overall impression in the minds of consumers. It includes its physical characteristics, perceived benefits, name, symbols and reputation (Keller, 1998). A brand is much more than a logo; it encapsulates how residents and visitors value the experiences they have in your city as well as their expectation that you can continue to deliver interesting and engaging experiences.

There are a number of functions of a brand:

■ A communicator (a mark of ownership or differentiation).

- An image (consumer associations with the brand).

- Value enhancer (brand equity).

- A relationship (brands have a personality which can form a relationship with the consumer).

A brand image for an eventful city is not just the result of a clever logo or slogan; it encapsulates how residents and visitors value the real experiences they have in a city as well as their expectation that the city will continue to deliver interesting and engaging experiences. A successful and sustainable brand, whether of a product or a city, is dependent on the 'reality' of the experience, and not a fictitious representation, however brilliant the graphic design may be. Experience shows that a city cannot be successfully branded as eventful, or creative, or prosperous or international if the facts prove otherwise. This creates substantial problems for certain cities that may invest in marketing and branding, but not in substance. Simply stated, a champion international eventful city must have champion, high quality events of recognised international standard. Discerning publics for events will easily distinguish between the mythology and authenticity of such claims.

Assuming that the branding can be fully justified, it then needs to be developed and widely used across all forms of communication. When developing its international brand, the city of Edinburgh was advised to emphasise the significance of its festivals, a claim that can be easily defended for those who have visited the city.

The brand should, accordingly, explicitly link the city's name with the word 'festivals' (e.g. 'Edinburgh – City of Festivals' or … 'Europe's Festival Capital') for appropriate tourist markets. Such a strap line should be used widely – on print and on (for example) signage welcoming visitors at the airport, railway stations and on roadsides.

(Graham Devlin Associates, 2001:38)

The process of developing the brand must involve all essential stakeolders who contribute to the marketing efforts of the city; the branding process is therefore often a question of stakeholder management. Wally Olins of Saffron Brand Consultants has identified a number of key steps that need to be taken to develop a successful city brand:

1. Set up a working party.

2. Identify and define critical audiences.

3. Research and consultation process.

4. Create the core ideas and visual system (positioning).

5. Coordinate messages.

6. Manage the messages.

7. Influence the influencers.

(Olins, 2008)

In addition to coordinating stakeholders to develop and support the brand, the city also has to maximise the assets it has to promote and utilise its brand value. Ultimately the brand value of a city or region will depend on both the cultural and other assets that it has, as well as the way in which these assets are deployed (OECD, 2009a). In their analysis of European city brands, Saffron Brand Consultants argue that:

> Perhaps the best way for a city to raise its brand, even when lack of awareness is the problem, is not by communications (the standard direct method of raising awareness) but in fact by increasing its attractiveness. In other words, the best way to improve your image is to keep improving your reality.
>
> (Hildreth, 2008:11)

The analysis of European city brands also indicates that developing and utilising events may be one of the ways in which cities can make the most effective use of their brand assets. Cities such as Barcelona and Liverpool seem to have done this very well:

> Barcelona is the leading example of a city that has got its leaders together and focused on what it wants to be

known for by improving its assets and exploiting what
it already had. To a lesser extent Liverpool is
successfully doing this – it's decided it wants to be
a hip city and it has a plan to achieve it. Achieving
status as European Capital of Culture in 2008 was
a big step in the process.

(Hildreth, 2008:11)

The required time-scale for such an exercise, from concept to full realisation, has taken many cities more than 5 years. The process that will have sustainable impact requires the mobilisation and motivation of large numbers of stakeholders in the public, private and civil sectors. Cities can employ the branding process as a means of creating consensus, a feeling of identity and generating attention for the core city brand. Royce (2002) suggests that to achieve such consensus, a city may need to build a 'brand platform' or blueprint that all stakeholders can adhere to. The platform should contain statements about the city's vision, mission, values and position.

As well as strengthening the overall city brand, events can also add to the 'brand equity' of the eventful city in a number of ways (Hankinson, 2004):

- Brand association, linking the city to the event image (e.g. Jazz and Heritage Festival in New Orleans, see also earlier examples for Edinburgh).

- Destination awareness (e.g. the 2007 ECOC putting Sibiu 'on the map').

- Perceived quality (e.g. the opera festival in Salzburg Austria).

- Brand loyalty – stimulating repeat visits and making people loyal to the destination (e.g. Spoleto USA).

- Destination positioning – events as attributes that distinguish the destination in the minds of consumers (e.g. Edinburgh Festival, Mardi Gras in New Orleans, Carnival in Rio).

There are notable exceptions when the brand of the event may be sustainable beyond its location, and where the destination must therefore 'live up to' the standard of the event it may be hosting. Andranovich, Burbank and Heying (2001) point out that one of the reasons why the Olympic Games is so popular is because of the high level of recognition of the Olympic 'brand'. They argue that the Olympic Rings are recognised by over 90% of the world's population, more than commercial brands such as Shell or McDonald's. The value of the brand is increased by the scarcity of the event, as it is only held once every 4 years. The combination of the Olympic and city brand is what offers specificity: the Beijing Olympics and the London Olympics are distinctive brands.

According to Jago et al., (2002) there are five factors that positively contribute to the success of an event's branding of a destination:

- sustained by community;

- good match between event and city flavour – e.g., consistent with regional attributes, history;

- positive media coverage – e.g., destination welcoming the media, international interest;

- elements of event increase interest – e.g., prize money, event capacity, iconic venue;

- exclusive positioning – i.e., has one defining identity.

In parts of the cultural sector, and especially with arts events, there is often sensitivity to overt branding, because it is often linked to commercialisation and 'selling'. However, as Colbert (2003:37) points out in the case of arts organisations, branding can have other advantages that are important for the cultural sector:

> *From the point of view of the organisation, branding allows the marketing manager to simplify communication with the target segment: the stronger and clearer the brand, the less information will be needed to make the product understood – or the easier the task of persuasion. The Guggenheim Museum and the British Museum are organisations that feature the*

*five characteristics of a strong brand…: their name is
well known, they are perceived as being of high
quality, their name is associated with salient elements
(collections, special events), their visitors are loyal
(both museums are popular tourist destinations) and
they feature identifiable tangible as well as intangible
assets (architecture, quality of curators).*

The same principles apply to an eventful city where most
of the key events are cultural.

It is not always easy to deliver consistent brand value
through event programmes. The ECOC, which is now
a brand in its own right, may have associations with
achievement and quality, or an expensive failure, depending
on the city and the organisers. The ECOC that immediately follows an acclaimed ECOC, such as Glasgow 1990 or
Lille 2004 will benefit from a strong positive brand image of
the event; the opposite is certainly true. The undisputed
success of certain ECOCs partly explains the desire of some
cities to stage such events. But clearly, a successful ECOC
builds brand value, whereas an unsuccessful one devalues
it. Such lessons are also important for the eventful city,
because the brand value of the city will be affected to some
extent by all the events in the programme, which makes it
important for the city to support its events, and for the
events to support the city and to work collaboratively to
build event brand value.

If an event programme does not have an established brand
of its own, then it may achieve a certain brand value through
association with other brands. As Lord Cultural Resources
(2009:20) argue:

*Festivals and Special Events operate along the same
principles as Iconic Landmark buildings. That is, 'big
names' and influencers are regarded as an indication of
the quality of an event and as such are more likely to
attract cultural tourists than those events (art fairs,
blockbuster exhibitions, festivals) who do not have the
right 'brand' associations.*

Branding Den Bosch

The Dutch city of 's-Hertogenbosch, better known as Den Bosch, developed a city marketing programme, which was closely linked to the events policy of the city. As a first step, the city was analysed in terms of positioning on the basis of Moss Kanter's model of economically successful cities:

- Concepts (Thinker Cities) – universities, research institutes
- Competence (Maker Cities) – industry
- Connections (Trader Cities) – communications, networks

The conclusion was that Den Bosch could not compete with neighbouring cities such as Eindhoven in terms of the first two categories, but should concentrate on profiling itself as a 'meeting city'. The development of the Meeting City concept was based on three main themes:

- Cultural and Historic City
- Modern City of Contacts and Contracts
- Lively City

Although this fairly general framework provided some guidance on how the city should position itself, a subsequent evaluation of the working of this policy indicated that there was a need for a more selective events policy linked more closely to the marketing objectives of the city. In order to achieve this, multi-annual funding was allocated to a small number of 'core events' as well as special funding for theme years and special events. Key events were given long-term funding, linked to the city marketing objectives of Den Bosch. Theme years to be held once in every 3 years were allocated a budget of €100,000 a year (€300,000 for each theme year). The long term funding allows these events to be linked to national tourism marketing campaigns as well as strengthening partnerships in the city. This also provides the opportunity for existing events in the city to be given an extra impulse every few years to allow them to reach a higher level, as well as the resources necessary to attract footloose events to the city.

After a time, however, it was also realised that the 'meeting city' brand was not particularly strong, because although the concept was flexible, it did not project a very strong image of the city in the minds of potential user groups. This was one of the reasons why Den Bosch changed course in 2006 and decided to position the city as the home of the famous medieval painter Hieronymus Bosch. By linking the city brand with a figure known all over the world for his use of fantastic imagery it was hoped that a more meaningful narrative could be created about the city, its history, identity and character. Bosch is also a good starting point for developing events, and the city is now planning a series of events and theme years around the 500th anniversary of the painter's death in 2016 ('s-Gravesande and Sanders, 2008). This shift also marks an important change in the basis of city branding, away from appeals to the objective advantages of the city towards more emotional links to prospective target groups.

POSITIONING

As indicated earlier, city events products and brands do not exist in isolation; they compete with and differentiate themselves from other competitors in the marketplace. In creating a brand, eventful cities need to position the brand relative to its (potential) competitors.

Prentice and Andersen (2003:8) explain how this works in the case of Edinburgh:

> With its established arts festivals, Edinburgh has sought to position itself for innovation for much longer than its Scotland rivals and from a creative artistic base asserting continuity back to the Scottish Enlightenment of the eighteenth century. It thereby uses its historical ambience and associations as a setting for festivals. It has sought worldwide to position itself as 'the Festival City', rather than solely as Scotland's capital, offering a unique selling point of creativity as well as heritage.

Although other Scottish and UK cities have attempted to compete with this brand image of Edinburgh, no city as yet has succeeded in establishing competitive legitimacy in the long-term. There are cities that may be able to compete in terms of the quality of the programme and even the number of events, but not in relation to many other factors that also contribute to brand image, such as history and architectural beauty.

Many cities have attempted to position themselves as festival cities, often claiming a role as the main festival venue in a specific country or region. The festival city brand must compete in a rather crowded marketplace In Canada, for example, Edmonton positions itself as 'Canada's festival capital' and states that it is 'live all year'. But Montreal, Toronto, Vancouver and Calgary also use similar eventfulness branding. Melbourne, in selling itself as an 'eventful city' (Committee for Melbourne, 2009) also states that it is 'Australia's festival capital', even though similar claims are made by Adelaide, 'The wine and festival capital of Australia' (South Australia, 2009).

Over and above national and local competition, many cities increasingly need to position themselves in global markets. The analysis of the major festivals in Edinburgh, for example, revealed that they do not see their only competition as other cultural events in the UK, but often other comparable events internationally (AEA Consultants, 2006). Edinburgh as a city clearly views itself as a global competitor, and profiles itself as 'the festival capital of the world. No other city in the world can compete with Edinburgh when it comes to being festive' (Stuck on Scotland, 2009). As stated, such claims would not be believed if there were no truths behind them. It is not the slogan itself which determines legitimacy, but the authenticity of the brand.

MARKETING MIX

Once the strategy has been designed, and an appropriate positioning and branding has been created, then a city striving to present itself as eventful must concentrate on its 'Marketing Mix'. McCarthy (1960) developed the original marketing mix, which consisted of 4 p's:

- Product: what should we offer?

- Price: how much should we charge for it?

- Promotion: how do we tell people about it?

- Place: how can people access the product?

Since this original formulation, a number of other 'p's' have been suggested for the mix, including people, physical evidence and process (Bitner and Booms, 1981). For the eventful city, the marketing mix will depend to a large extent on the events portfolio.

Product

The totality of experience and benefits offered to the various event consumers and the other event stakeholders of the city. For certain cities, the events portfolio will be to a large extent dictated by tradition or resource limits, and so the major decisions to position the city in relation to its events are therefore focused on the strategy of the marketing mix.

Price

The notion of price goes beyond the pure cost of event tickets (which is dealt with in Chapter 6). Having created a brand that offers added value for the customer, the city and its events must capitalise on their brand equity by generating an economic return. This is partly related to economic pricing, where a highly desirable event or series of events can charge high prices to visitors for the opportunity to 'be there'. On the other hand, cultural events may deliberately carry a low price tag, or be free, in order to attract particular target groups or increase access to the event. The question of pricing operates differently for cultural organisations and events. As Colbert (2003) argues, the demand for culture is largely determined by the cultural capital or cultural competence of the user, not by price. Unlike other types of goods or services, such as tourism, for example, dropping the price of a cultural good will not necessarily increase demand. This explains why many theatres have empty seats in spite of heavily subsidised prices.

This problem can be illustrated by the case of Thessaloniki, which staged the ECOC in 1997. The ECOC programme had a high percentage of free events and free food was also supplied at many events. Nevertheless, many projects were poorly attended – over a third sold less than 35% of their seats (see Chapter 2). When supply exceeds demand, lowering prices may have little impact in the cultural events market. On the other hand, some cultural services attract high demand in spite of high prices, as is the case with many leading international festivals, such as Edinburgh, Salzburg and Savonlinna (Frey, 2000; Wanhill, 2007).

Some cities are beginning to use the collective power of their events programme by bundling a range of events into a single package, which can be purchased in advance by consumers. This builds on a tradition of cultural institutions for selling season tickets for groups of concerts (such as the Robeco Summer Concerts in Amsterdam). One advantage of this system is that popular events, which have high demand and low price elasticity, can be used to generate attendance at less popular events as well, providing a degree of cross-subsidy.

Ticket pricing may be one factor of the cost of an event to consumers, but there are other elements in the pricing mix, which may include cost of transport to the event, parking, food and beverages, hotels and even child care if required.

Promotion

Promotion for the eventful city relates to the whole event programme, within which events must be individually or jointly communicated and 'sold' to the different target markets. A wide range of different promotional media is used to promote the eventful city. One of the most important of these is to use paid or 'free' media publicity (see section on 'place' below).

Events make heavy use of both paid and 'free' media promotion, and as emphasised in Chapter 4, this makes the media an important stakeholder in events. The city of Brighton in the UK organised a 'Festivals in Brighton' Media Showcase in London in 2009. This event, jointly organised by the local tourism marketing organisation and four festivals, aimed to capitalise on the potential of Brighton as a true 'City of Festivals'. Over 200 press and broadcast journalists were invited to the event, which was staged in central London to ensure the greatest possible media attendance. Following this media promotion, the city launched a 'Festivals Fever' consumer campaign to encourage visits from both the UK and overseas to visit (and preferably stay) in the city whilst major festivals are on. The city developed this programme in collaboration with each of the festivals to ensure messages about staying in the city are included in their marketing activity (Visit Brighton, 2009).

An important promotional tool is the development of an image for an event or event programme. Each of the ECOC has produced a logo and slogan that try to encapsulate the identity of the event and to project a specific image, which will appeal to the potential audience. In 2007 the ECOC for Luxembourg and Greater Region used a blue stag as its logo, following a design competition and public selection process. The blue stag was a new image designed to unite the different parts of the Greater Region. Being an unexpected selection, the blue stag generated early debate about the nature of the ECOC in Luxembourg and the Greater Region and helped to raise awareness of the programme. The logo also responded to the need for a non-verbal symbol that could unite the different parts of the Greater Region. In Luxembourg, awareness of the logo was over 40% just before the start of the ECOC. In the rest of the Greater Region, awareness of the logo was much lower. Just before the opening (November 2006) only about 13% of Greater Region residents recognised the (blue) stag, and by December 2007 this had risen to 19%. One of the main reasons for this disparity was the relatively small marketing budget, which was not sufficient to promote the event and its image effectively across four different countries (Luxembourg and Greater Region, 2008).

Messages need to be tailored to different audiences, particularly in international markets. For example, an assessment of the promotional strategies for the London 2012 Olympics argues that:

> London and the UK enjoy strong and established brand images overseas. Most of these are positive, as the record number of inbound visitors in 2005 confirms. But perceptions vary widely. Visit Britain, Visit London and others involved in overseas promotional work tailor their marketing closely to the conditions of individual territories (and to specific market segments within those territories). What works in China – for the moment, at least, playing to our traditional strengths in culture and heritage – will not work in markets which seek a more modern and contemporary message about destinations. London, of course, already enjoys widely held overseas

perceptions as a world-class city, which is culturally diverse and constantly reinventing itself.

(DCMS, 2006:16)

The discourse about the differences between London and Beijing strengthened markedly during the Beijing Olympics in 2008. Having seen the impressive levels of organisation that Beijing was able to achieve, London immediately began to position itself as a different type of city – more open, democratic and therefore, by implication, less organised. This provides an interesting example of the importance of managing expectations about events. The message, which London tried to send to the Olympic Committee was effectively 'of course we will organise a good Games', but for local stakeholders the more important message was 'we won't waste taxpayer's money on facilities that will only be used for 2 weeks, and we won't disrupt the normal flow of life in the city'.

Place (distribution)

Given the importance of conveying promotional messages to a wide range of potential audiences, the way in which information is distributed is an important component of the

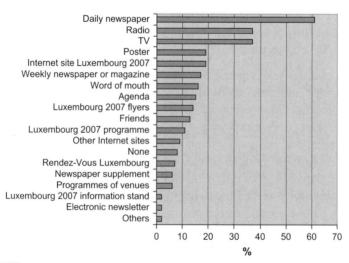

FIGURE 7.1 *Information sources used by Luxembourg visitors to ECOC events in Luxembourg in 2007.*

marketing mix. There is a bewildering array of different media that can be used, and choices must ensure that the event programme reaches all of its potential markets.

Data collected from ECOC events indicate that the use of communication channels is highly differentiated by market segment. For the ECOC in Luxembourg in 2007, the media was significantly more important as a source of information for domestic visitors (Figure 7.1). Even so, compared with Rotterdam, the internet had grown significantly as a source of information even for local residents. In both Rotterdam and Luxembourg it is clear that the printed information distributed by the event organisers is used by relatively few visitors.

For tourists, the picture is again different (Figure 7.2). Internet emerges as the single most important source of information for visitors, and information sources specifically for tourists. For Luxembourg 2007, the printed brochure was particularly important for those people travelling specifically

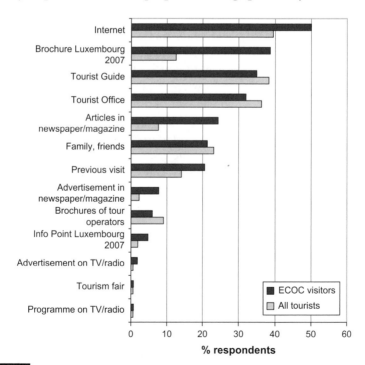

FIGURE 7.2 *Information sources used by tourists visiting ECOC events in Luxembourg in 2007, by purpose of visit.*

for ECOC events. The brochure was also more important for highly motivated 'cultural tourists' than for local residents. Most important for an event programme is to have a range of different communication channels, since each channel will be used by different publics.

The need to reach a wide range of publics places even more emphasis on collaborative marketing organisations as distribution channels for city events. For example the Amsterdam UitBuro (AUB) is a public/private partnership that provides a single ticketing service for all concerts, plays and events in Amsterdam (and also at many venues in the rest of the country). City cards are also now being used as a collaborative distribution mechanism for events. In Tallinn, Estonia, the Black Nights Film Festival offers discounts for city card holders. It is also common for major events such as the ECOC to be integrated into the city card offer.

PACKAGING

The different 'p's' of the marketing mix can often be effectively combined in the development of 'packaging'. Chapter 3 described the way in which cities are increasingly packaging cultural events by wrapping themes around them or grouping them under the banner of a festival, season or cultural year. Packaging has become an important marketing tool that has the potential to add value to events programmes. By creating critical mass, events are given greater visibility; the city is seen as having more activity and links can be made to themes of interest to potential audiences.

But how events are packaged can be an important aspect of marketing success. Effective packaging should be:

- Attractive

- Relevant

- Visible

- Distinctive

The Amsterdam Winter Adventure Programme was started in the 1990s as a means of attracting tourists to visit the city in off-peak periods and to fill empty seats at arts venues.

A full-colour brochure presenting all the major exhibitions held in the winter period has been published in two editions: Dutch/English and German/French. The brochures are made available in many hotels, museums and other cultural organisations in all the large cities in the west of the Netherlands.

In addition to the city passes described above, packaging can also be achieved through the issue of cards for specific events, as has been done for many of the ECOC. Arguably one of the successes of Lille 2004 was the range of passes offered to participants. Four different types of pass were marketed, each aimed at a different audience. Free access to a number of 2004 venues was included in all of the passes as well as free or reduced price public transport. The day pass in particular proved very successful, with almost two million being sold.

Tickets were sold via telephone and internet, as well as through a range of partner organisations. These included the Transpole website, which covers all the public transport services in the Lille conurbation, French outlets of the Carrefour supermarket chain and FNAC outlets in France, Belgium and Switzerland.

COMMUNICATIONS AND RELATIONSHIP MARKETING

As consumer markets become more fragmented and diverse, it becomes increasingly important for the marketers of eventful cities to build relationships with individual consumers in order to understand their needs better and develop ongoing sales. Many are therefore turning to a broader strategy of 'relationship marketing', which implies a consistent two-way communication with the audience.

One such strategy has been to create a 'club' to create a relationship with the audience. This has been used to good effect by ECOC host cities such as Lille (2004), which as outlined earlier recruited 17,000 ambassadors, and then maintained their interest after the event through the 'Lille 3000' campaign (www.lille3000.com), as a result of which the number of ambassadors grew still further. For the 2010

ECOC, the Hungarian city of Pécs created the Zsolnay Society (Zsolnay was the founder of the ceramic factory which is being transformed into a cultural district for the event), which has more than 1300 members. Club members receive newsletters and regular updates on progress with the event. To create contacts with the wider community, ideas are solicited through open calls. For the 'Transform your city!' project people can contribute their ideas on how they would change the outlook of the city, its image in general or a street or square in particular.

Not all such schemes work well, however. During the 2007 ECOC in Luxembourg and Greater Region, Club 2007 was established with the aim of recruiting volunteers and generating interest in the event among the local population. However, only 241 people actually joined the club out of a potential population of 11 million. This low level of participation was later attributed to a relative lack of students in Luxembourg (Luxembourg and Greater Region, 2008).

An important aspect of the communication process is the question of how the culture of a city is interpreted to the audience. For every aspect of culture, there are different and often competing interpretations that can be presented, or effectively left 'hidden'. This issue is most sensitive where the interests of minority groups in the resident population or among visitor groups are involved.

For example, the annual ROMART International Festival of Roma Culture held in the city of Subotica in Serbia aims to 'show that the Roma is an essential part of the world's culture', and pointing to their exceptional achievements as the value of being 'different'.

> Our intention is creating a backdrop for talented artists to represent vast cultural wealth of Roma community. We think that we must show the non-Roma people that there is a possibility to live together with the Roma nation. This is needed to establish better international cooperation in this topic, so that we can make a stronger ethnic and confessional tolerance.
>
> (ROMART, 2008)

Sometimes, however, the representation and interpretation of different cultures lies beyond the immediate control of the groups concerned. The culture represented through festivals and events may be more related to normative concepts of what kind of culture is 'good' for people. In Liverpool, the communications surrounding the 2008 ECOC were criticised by local residents as not giving enough information on the events being staged and being too 'posh' and highbrow for the majority of local people (Melville, et al., 2007:11).

EVENTS AND THE MEDIA

The media has already been identified as an important event programme stakeholder in Chapter 4. Cities use the media to project their desired image far and wide, and events become a means of attracting media attention to the city. Event producers increasingly see the media as a vital source of 'free' publicity that adds value to the limited marketing budgets available to the cultural sector.

Rennen (2007) argues that the emergence of place marketing has created a dynamic partnership between three essential actors in cities: the event owners, the city in which the event takes place and the media. In the case of major events, these actors have a shared interest in generating audience attention. The city wants to market itself to the media audience, the media wants to increase audience ratings and advertising revenue and the event owners want to enhance the prestige and reputation of the event. There is, to a certain extent, a shared interest in the generation of audiences which can enhance the reputation of the event and deliver economic and other benefits for the city, while the successful implementation of the event by the city guarantees large media audiences. In this way, the media becomes one of the essential partners in the city marketing process.

This is evident in the ECOC, where there seems to be a strong positive relationship between the success in generating foreign press coverage and the growth in overnight stays. The correlation between the number of foreign press cuttings generated and the change in bednights was high $(r = 0.66)$.

Table 7.2	Foreign Press Cuttings and Change in Bednights for Selected ECOCs		
City	Year	No. of foreign press cuttings	Change in bednights %
Salamanca	2002	6421	+21.6
Graz	2003	3405	+24.8
Copenhagen	1996	2400	+11.3
Stockholm	1998	1600	+9.4
Brugge	2002	1540	+9.0
Luxembourg	1995	900	−4.9
Luxembourg Region	2007	878	+ 6.0
Brussels	2000	800	+5.3
Rotterdam	2001	600	+10.6
Reykjavik	2000	522	+15.3

Source: ECOC reports.

As noted in Chapter 4, the media can affect events in different ways. The media can compete with them, it can generate audiences, or it can stop people attending through negative reviews. In the Barcelona Universal Forum of Cultures in 2004, the development of the event was marked by intense discussion in the media of the function and organisation of the event. Problems in the early days of the event helped to fuel the idea that the Forum was an over-priced waste of money, not worth visiting. In particular, the Forum took the disastrous step of banning people from bringing their own food into the event, which many people resented, particularly given the high price of catering on top of a high entry price. Public outcry was brought to a head by a local TV station sending a reporter dressed as a sandwich and filming him being refused entry to the event. In research conducted during and after the event, however, it was clear that most visitors were happy with their visit. Most of the detractors did not actually bother visiting the event to find out for themselves. In the absence of direct experience, the media took on an even more important role. The media image served to turn an important element of the local population against the Forum, which contributed to a disappointing turnout of visitors.

MARKETING EXPENDITURE

The ability to develop a marketing campaign will obviously also depend on the resources that a city has available. Although marketing budgets are usually framed in economic terms, the resources needed to market an eventful city consist not just of money, but also creative resources, and the inputs of stakeholders in time, resources in kind and influence.

Many large cities have marketing budgets running into tens of millions of euros, and other cities do a very effective job of marketing their activities with a very small level of investment. In the case of the ECOC, the budgets allocated have varied by a factor of ten from city to city. The differences are even larger on a per head of population basis, ranging from €2 per head spent by Prague in 2000 to more than €60 per head by Graz in 2003. It is clear that marketing budgets, particularly in relation to resident population, have been growing in recent years.

Table 7.3 makes it clear that there is little correlation between marketing spend and the generation of visits to the city. Money alone is not the answer – it needs to be spent effectively.

Table 7.3 Marketing Budgets of ECOCs

	Marketing budget €	Population	Total visits	Spend per visit €	Spend per head of population €
Luxembourg 1995	2,200,000	412,000	1,100,000	2.00	5
Copenhagen 1996	4,700,000	1,362,000	6,920,000	0.70	3
Thessaloniki 1997	8,168,245	1,084,000	1,500,000	5.40	8
Stockholm 1998	12,510,000	736,000			17
Helsinki 2000	6,700,000	555,000	5,400,000	1.20	12
Bologna 2000	8,198,000	380,000	2,150,000	3.80	22
Brussels 2000	3,170,000	959,000			3
Prague 2000	2,120,000	1,181,000			2
Reykjavik 2000	1,380,000	111,000	1,473,724	0.90	12
Porto 2001	9,500,000	257,800	1,246,545	7.60	37
Salamanca 2002	3,673,330	156,000	1,900,000	1.90	24
Brugge 2002	5,943,520	116,000	1,600,000	3.70	51
Graz 2003	14,139,400	226,000	2,755,271	5.10	63
Luxembourg Reg. 2007	7,500,000	480,222	3,327,678	2.20	16

Where cities gave two budget estimates, the lowest figures have been used.
Source: Adapted after Palmer/Rae, 2004.

FROM RELATIONSHIP MARKETING TO CONSUMER POWER?

Relationship marketing is being increasingly used by eventful cities to attract and retain audiences and to develop their programming. There are also signs that consumers are beginning to take some control of events. In the new online communities of Facebook, MySpace or You Tube, events can be promoted and marketed in a number of different ways. Most of the use currently being made of such sites follows established marketing practice, and is designed to draw consumer attention to events or locations. However, there are also signs that tools are emerging which facilitate consumers in directly influencing the staging of events in cities. An interesting example of this is the website www.eventful.com:

> Founded in 2004, Eventful is the leading events website which enables its community of users to discover, promote, share and create events. Eventful's community of users select from nearly 4 million events taking place in local markets throughout the world, from concerts and sports to singles events and political rallies.

People use Eventful to track and share events with their friends and community in many ways:

- Import iTunes and last.fm performer lists and keep track of which favourites are coming to town.

- Export events via feeds, calendar widgets, third-party calendar services, email alerts and much more.

- Keep track of what's happening at favourite venues and see where favourite performers are appearing.

- Weekly email event guides are completely customised based on a user's interests, with recommended events in their city.

- Add events to your personal watch list and see what events your friends and groups are watching (and going to).

- Add events to Eventful for free and promote events to the entire community.

Eventful's unique Demand service empowers users to influence where their favourite performers, candidates and other celebrities appear by creating viral grass-roots campaigns to 'Demand' them in their town. Tens of thousands of musicians, comedians and political candidates use Eventful Demand to engage with millions of their fans and supporters to find out where they are in Demand. Performers are able to use Eventful Demand to make informed decisions about where to appear and can communicate with their Demanders via highly targeted email tools. Along with MySpace, You Tube and iTunes, Eventful is an essential part of the online marketing toolkit for performers, politicians and others.

(Eventful.com, 2009)

The eventful.com website also produces a list of the top 25 'most eventful cities' in the US. It is not clear whether city administrations pay any attention to such rankings, but these sorts of measures may give useful indications of which cities are working hardest to develop their eventfulness.

CONCLUSION

The event programme marketing challenge is increasing as the experience economy grows, and a wealth of event-based experiences is available in cities around the globe. Creating distinction for city event programmes is therefore essential, and this requires careful positioning and branding. These in turn need to be based on a clear vision of what the city wishes to achieve through eventfulness, rather than creating events for the sake of having a full calendar. Once the city has developed a vision and selected a strategy, implementation requires the collaboration of a wide range of stakeholders. Not just a centralised city events unit, if one exists, but also the individual events and other stakeholders are all to some extent responsible for safeguarding and projecting the city brand through events. This is particularly true of the media, which is an essential partner for the marketing of events, but which may also do considerable damage if it becomes hostile to an event or event programme.

The brand messages need to appeal to carefully selected target groups that relate to the objectives the city wishes to achieve. The event product offered to those groups needs to be tailored in terms of the different elements of the marketing mix. The examples provided in this chapter indicate that through collaboration, cities and venues may be better able to identify and meet the needs of their target audiences. This realisation seems to be leading to a growing number of collaborative event organisations, as well as spawning a range of websites aimed at event consumers and organisers. In addition, the application of new technology is enabling cities to relate more closely to these audiences and to enter into dialogue with them. In the future, the programming of the eventful city may be a collaborative venture between the city, its cultural producers, the media and city residents, all of whom have an interest in promoting or developing eventfulness.

CHAPTER 8

Audiences and Publics of the Eventful City

The *audience* comprises those people who participate in and experience an event. The audience is one direct stakeholder group within the wider *public* of an eventful city, which includes any group with which the event programme needs to communicate, such as the media, government bodies, financial institutions, pressure groups, customers, suppliers and other stakeholders. Both audiences and publics have to be given due consideration in the development of event programmes. As the previous chapter on marketing has shown, the audiences for events can consist of many segments, and the publics for an event will be larger and more varied than the audience.

In practical terms, the difference between the audience and the public of an events programme is that the former are actual participants, while the latter are often potential participants. In order to expand the audience for events, it is important to turn potential participants into members of the audience: a process known as audience development.

This chapter considers the nature of different audiences and publics for cultural event programmes, including the different segments of the local audience as well as domestic and international tourists.

Eventful Cities

293

AUDIENCE DEVELOPMENT

Audience development refers to the process of expanding participation by turning non-attending publics into audiences. Many bodies are actively involved in audience development, trying to encourage more people to participate in events, some of which are particularly active in the cultural sector. For example, Audiences London (2009) considers audience development to be:

A planned activity to develop the range of relationships between a cultural organisation and identified audiences as an integral part of its mission. It is both a process and a philosophy. Essentially, audience development is all the activities an organisation delivers that aim to engage with audiences, visitors or participants. It covers everything that is done proactively to:

- *Retain and increase the frequency of existing audiences or visitors.*

- *Attract new audiences to existing performances, exhibitions or events.*

- *Develop audiences to experience different types of performances, exhibitions or events.*

- *Develop new types of performances, exhibitions or events to meet the needs of new audiences.*

Collaboration between different stakeholders is vital for audience development, because without this, it is difficult to understand your audience, their characteristics, opinions and needs.

This is a view echoed by a similar regional organisation in the UK, Audiences Yorkshire (2009), for whom:

The key to audience development is understanding who your audiences are. Where are they from? What do they do for a living? What are they looking for in a cultural experience? What motivates them to come to your venue?

One of the key roles of audience development agencies such as Audiences London or Audiences Yorkshire is to ensure that cultural providers have a good understanding of their audiences and publics.

Audience Development in New South Wales

Regional Arts New South Wales has been working on regional audience development projects for a number of years, including asset mapping, database development and an arts ambassador project. The work subsequently expanded into a collaborative audience research project, which is asking key questions of the arts audience: 'Did you like what you saw?', 'How often do you go to the arts?', 'How did you hear about this event?', 'Why did you come?' and 'Who are you?' The research programme was launched in response to a number of basic needs, including new ways of measuring impacts; capacity building for audience research; and building partnerships with education, tourism, economic development, local government and other stakeholders.

The project successfully addressed all of these needs, but it is perhaps in the development of local capacity that the project has the most potential. The project has included one-day forums on the social, cultural and economic impacts of arts activities, DVDs, CD-sets and annotated bibliographies of existing research on audience development.

Regional Arts New South Wales (2009)

Audience development agencies attempt to identify and reach specific groups in the wider public who are underrepresented in the audience for particular events. Children, elderly people or those on low incomes are often seen as key targets for such programmes, since such groups suffer from a number of barriers to cultural participation, and in most cases face multiple constraints on event attendance. These constraints usually relate to barriers that include the absence of time to attend, insufficient disposable income to purchase tickets and a possible lack of interest in the content of events that are offered.

Research in the UK (Ruiz, 2004) has indicated that the major constraints on participation were:

- lack of time (work and family commitments, inadequate opening hours);

- price/cost implications (particularly for those who need to travel long distances, those on low wages/living on benefits etc, taking children/family as a group);

- distance (particularly for less mobile groups, such as those without a car);

- lack of awareness; and

- perceptions of 'eligibility' (a feeling of discomfort or a sense that the event was 'not for them').

Interestingly, price alone is rarely a significant barrier to participation for those that are aware of an event and have the motivation to attend. Certain types of cultural events may be a subsidised activity in many cities, where grants are given to event organisers or arts organisations to reduce the cost paid by those attending the event. As Antwerpen Open (2005:13), the city events organisation for the Belgian city of Antwerp explained:

> Our pricing policy is consciously to keep prices very low: some performances are free, and for ticketed events we charge between 50 cents and €7. Never more than the price of a cinema ticket. It is a generous offer that is strongly appreciated (by the public).

The rationale behind such subsidies tends to focus on the educational, artistic or social role of an event, and the desire to reduce price resistance, thereby increasing the diversity of the audience. Another frequent rationale for event subsidies is the role of events as a component of economic development strategies, where economic impacts exceed the subsidies that may be provided (see Chapter 9). Those who believe that the success of an event should be judged only by market criteria often reject this rationale for public subsidies. However, there is also a view that certain events constitute an element of public service provision in the same manner as libraries, parks and sports facilities, where public subsidies are rarely questioned.

In spite of public support, it may be difficult for cities to attract new audiences to their event programmes. Cultural events often succeed in reaching those who have high levels of cultural capital (Bourdieu, 1984) and relatively high incomes. Studies of cultural participation in different areas of the world indicate that those attending cultural events tend to be highly educated, with high incomes and professional occupations.

Longitudinal research undertaken at the annual International Theatre Festival (SITF) in Sibiu, Romania underlines the strong links between education, employment and cultural event participation. The SITF calls itself:

> *the most important annual theatre and performing arts festival in Romania and the third most important in the world given its magnitude, proposes a program that brings participants from 70 countries and presents 350 events that take place in 55 venues, awaiting 60,000 spectators per day. (www.sibfest.ro).*

In spite of the large number of people attracted to the event, the audience profile is relatively homogeneous. In particular, the education level of the audience tends to be very high, with around 70% having some form of higher education. This compares with a national average of less than 13% of the Romanian working population having a tertiary education in 2002. Over time, the audience for this event has become more concentrated in the higher education groups, which seems to run counter to ideas about audience development (Table 8.1).

A similar pattern emerges for the occupational profiles of the SITF audience. In 2007, almost 60% of participants had

Table 8.1 Highest Educational Level of Visitors to the Sibiu International Theatre Festival

	2001%	2005%	2007%
Primary school	2	0	0
Secondary school	14	3	4
Further education	11	20	26
First degree	63	66	50
Postgraduate	9	10	19
Total	99	99	99

Source: ATLAS surveys (2009).

Table 8.2	Occupational Profile of Visitors to the Sibiu International Theatre Festival		
	2001%	**2005%**	**2007%**
Director or Manager	9	16	23
Professional	33	25	36
Technical professions	17	20	17
Clerical	10	23	5
Service and sales	25	12	18
Manual or crafts worker	6	4	2
Total	100	100	101

managerial or professional occupations (Table 8.2). This compares with just over 13% of the Romanian working population having such occupations in 2002.

The SITF audience is also more likely than the population at large to have an occupation linked with the cultural sector. Levels of cultural occupation were already fairly high in 2001 (31%) and 2005 (26%), but rose to 55% in 2007, when the event was part of the ECOC (European Capital of Culture) in Sibiu.

These figures confirm the strong relationship between levels of cultural capital (or cultural competence) and attendance at cultural events. It may appear obvious that those who have developed 'cultural consumption skills' either through their home background or through formal education will consume more culture (Bourdieu, 1984). The Rotterdam 2001 ECOC audience, for example, tended to be relatively frequent cultural consumers. Over 80% of the audience had visited a museum in the previous 12 months, compared with 33% of the Dutch population as a whole. This relatively high level of consumption was repeated across all cultural sectors: 54% of the participants had visited a theatre (compared with 25% for the Netherlands), 23% had been to the opera (compared with 5%) and 59% had been to a pop concert (49% for the Dutch population).

Research at the Singapore Arts Festival in 2006 indicated that the audience was dominated by professionals, who comprised 46% of attendees, compared to 30% of the Singapore population. Students represented 37% of the audience, compared with only 12% of the total population. Over a third of the festival audience had attended the event before, pointing to a core of regular festival goers (National Arts Council Singapore, 2008).

The audience for the Spoleto Festival in Charleston, South Carolina is predominantly professional, middle class, high income and white. In 2005, audience surveys showed that only 5% of the audience were Black/African American, 1 percent was Latino/Hispanic, and less than 2% were Asian. Average household incomes were high, with nearly 20% reporting total annual incomes of $250,000 (€207,000) or more. Not surprisingly, given these income levels, the age profile of the event is relatively high, with an average age of 53 (Moore School of Business, 2005).

Classical or more traditional cultural events attract an audience composed of a relatively homogeneous group of people with high incomes and education levels. The competition for the discretionary leisure time of these individuals is already intense because as high income groups, they are being chased by a wide range of cultural and leisure suppliers. With existing high levels of participation, it is unlikely that this market segment will increase its cultural participation very much. Growth in the cultural audience generally depends on two factors: the expansion of the middle class, which increases the number of highly educated people with time and money to consume culture, or reaching groups who currently have low levels of cultural consumption.

Maughan and Bianchini (2003) found that 7 of the 12 festivals surveyed in the East Midlands (UK) had developed works aimed at specific target groups (Table 8.3).

Table 8.3 Target Groups Identified by Festivals in the East Midlands

Target group	Number of festivals
Work with/for particular ethnic groups	3
Work with/for children	2
Work with/for elderly people	2
Work with/for disabled people	2
Work with asylum seekers	1
Work for a gay or lesbian audience	1

RELATIONSHIP BETWEEN PROGRAMME CONTENT AND AUDIENCES

As discussed in Chapter 3, the content of events vary considerably in terms of theme and approach, and different events will obviously appeal to different publics. In the case of the Rotterdam ECOC in 2001, for example, Richards et al. (2002) analysed the programme along two dimensions in order to examine differences in audience profile according to event type: the complexity of the content and the geographical orientation (Table 8.4).

The majority of the audience was attracted to locally-orientated events with a popular culture focus (Table 8.5). In

Table 8.4	Event Typology, Rotterdam ECOC 2001	
	Orientation	
Cultural Content	Local/national	International
Popular	6.5 million homes (Las Palmas) Between the wars (Las Palmas) Association life (Historic Museum)	WOMEX (De Doelen)
High	Strange melodies (Schouwburg), ACT2001 (various locations)	Hieronymous Bosch (Museum Boymans)

Table 8.5	Rotterdam ECOC 2001 – Event Type, Visitors and Respondents	
Scope/cultural type	**Events %**	**Visitors %**
Local/Popular	57	64
Local/High	21	8
International/High	13	21
International/Popular	9	7

terms of classical forms of cultural consumption, those events with an international focus were more popular, illustrating the more global reach of classical culture content (sometimes defined as 'high culture').

The majority of Rotterdam 2001 visitors came from the city itself or the surrounding area, with 55% being over 40 years of age. Even so, the proportion of 16 to 24 year olds in the ECOC 2001 audience was still higher than in the population of Rotterdam as a whole. Just over 13% of the population of Rotterdam was aged between 15 and 24, while over 19% of the audience were aged 16 to 24.

Similar findings emerge from the study of the festival programme in the city of Chester in the UK (Arts About Manchester, 2009). The survey of visitors to 5 festivals attracting a total audience of almost 40,000 indicated that over 50% of visitors came from outside the city, with a particularly high proportion of tourists being attracted by the Food and Drink Festival. As in most cultural audiences, there was a strong bias towards female participation, with women making up an average 64% of visitors. Male participation was highest for the Summer Music Festival (46%) and relatively low for the Chester Mystery Plays (31%). In terms of the age profile, festival visitors tended to be relatively old, with only 34% under the age of 45. The Food and Drink Festival attracted a noticeably younger audience, with over 50% under the age of 45. The festival programme did not attract large numbers of ethnic minority participants, with almost 97% of the audience being white (which reflects the ethnic balance of the city). Only one event, Something Wishful, managed to attract a significant proportion of ethnic minority participants (9.5%). Analysis of the extent to which festival audiences visit different events in the programme suggest that there is strong audience crossover between the Literature Festival, the Summer Music Festival and the Mystery Plays, which offers potential for collaborative marketing.

Identifying the appropriate audience group for event programmes in the eventful city is made more complicated by crossover and 'omnivorous' consumption patterns. Recent work on cultural consumption patterns points to the extent to which consumers mix different cultural forms. For example, Bellavance (2008:215) identifies:

three different forms of eclecticism – omnivorous, enlightened and creative/connected – that are quite distinct models of the 'mixing of genres.' The first, more opportunistic, is evidently linked to 'business opportunities.' The second strongly upholds the belief in the supremacy of the intellectual functions of culture. The third, on the contrary, could be associated with the reconfiguration of the legitimate cultural field in view of the rise of the culture industries.

Bellavance (2008:215) also emphasises the fact that 'despite everything, our individuals share one and the same belief in the value of "art and culture." ' This seems to indicate that the development of a broad events programme in a city does have the potential to unify audiences around a general cultural product, even though the audience may have very different motivations, backgrounds and modes of cultural consumption.

Research during the 2007 ECOC in Luxembourg indicated that the programme was successful at attracting a representative mix of the different nationalities living in the country. In particular, there was a high level of participation among Portuguese residents of Luxembourg, who tended to reject the regular cultural programme offered by the established arts venues. The Youth Programme offered by the ECOC in specially-converted venues was also very successful in attracting young people (Luxembourg and Greater Region, 2008).

The desire to attract new audiences, particularly among ethnic minorities and the young, can lead to a certain amount of 'cultural drift' in the events programme, as more traditional cultural forms fall out of fashion with audiences or lose pubic sector funding, and new events emerge at the cultural margins. In Barcelona, for example, attendance at 'traditional' music festivals such as Grec (the main performing arts festival) has declined, whereas 'new' cultural forms, such as world music and electronic music, have increased in popularity (Table 8.6).

Table 8.6	Attendance at Music Festivals in Barcelona 1999–2007				
	1999	**2000**	**2001**	**2002**	**2007**
Grec	319,866	165,967	150,740	169,235	129,681
Barcelona international jazz festival	19,578	12,288	12,402	27,537	45,353
Antique music festival	9,929	8,256	8,890	8,468	5,116
World music	3,900	4,936	4,635	5,622	
Barcelona guitar festival	7,177	5,606	13,806	13,034	11,853
Festival of contemporary music	4,191	3,211	3,736	5,383	4,320
Tradicionàrius (traditional music)	15,431	15,000	18,000	18,500	8,100
Sónar (electronic music)	42,620	53,628	80,251	91,014	81,467

Source: Institut de Cultura, City of Barcelona, Annual Reports

HOW CAN AUDIENCES BE REACHED?

Identifying target groups for events is one task, but reaching and convincing a specific public to attend a particular event presents significant challenges. Major barriers to participation in terms of cost and convenience may need to be removed or lowered, and perceptions of value and interest may need to be altered to convince a target group that it is worth their while to attend. People's leisure time has become more pressurised thereby requiring people to make increasingly hard choices abut the use of their time. These challenges mean that different strategies may have to be employed to reach new target groups and develop the audience for event programmes.

Programmes aimed at specific target groups

As outlined above, specific groups which are considered as under-represented in the cultural event audience are often targeted by event programmes. The young and ethnic minority groups are particularly prominent in this respect. It is often felt that particular types of events will appeal more to such target groups, and therefore extend the 'reach' of the event programme. In the case of the Prague Fringe Festival, for example, the audience evaluation report shows that 'the festival attracts a wide age-range (from under 15 to over 60), but with the 15 to 44 year old groups most well represented (83% of the total).' This is argued to be consistent with findings from similar 'fringe' events that are 'popular with young students, artists and middle-age professionals' (Hollands, 2007:7). Clearly, providing a mix of events specifically tailored to the needs of such target groups is one way to grow the audience.

Such targeted programmes were also offered during the Rotterdam ECOC in 2001. These events particularly targeted young people and ethnic minorities, who were seen as being under-represented in the traditional cultural audience of the city (Trienekens, 2004). One of the specific measures employed by Rotterdam to attract a younger cultural audience was to organise events specifically aimed at young people. ACT 2001 presented works under the subtitle: Urban Culture on Stage, which included break-dance performances and DJ sets.

These activities had success in developing the audience for culture among young people and ethnic minorities in the city. Research on the audience for the overall programme of Rotterdam 2001 showed that the proportion of 16 to 24 year olds was higher than in the population of Rotterdam as a whole. The younger visitors also came mainly from the city of Rotterdam itself, which was the key target area for the programme.

A survey of more than 150 young people attending events organised for the ACT 2001 programme indicated that the largest age group was 16 to 19 year old (33% of respondents) with only 17% being over the age of 25. These visitors were much more likely to be habitual consumers of popular culture than 'high' culture. In terms of the reasons why young people participated in cultural activities, the most important factor was feeling welcome; being affordable was certainly a factor but less important than feeling welcome (Table 8.7). Young people tended not to be attracted to events organised only for young people; they preferred events with mixed audiences.

The research also indicated the importance of particular marketing initiatives, such as the Youth Cultural Passport (CJP) in Rotterdam, a card that offers people under the age of 26 discounts for the cinema, theatres, festivals, games and

Table 8.7	Which of the Following Factors Are Important to You in Deciding to Participate in a Cultural Event? (Percent of respondents, ACT 2001)		
I will participate in an event if …	**Disagree**	**Neutral**	**Agree**
It is with people of my own age	36	51	13
It costs little money	29	43	28
My parents approve	43	37	20
It is close	30	51	19
It is not too 'difficult'	37	49	14
Girls and boys are separated	60	36	4
I feel welcome	9	29	62
It doesn't take much time	33	55	12
It is for my own group of people	40	52	8
It is during the week	31	64	5
It is at the weekend	21	64	15

travel. Over half of the respondents who indicated that they had a discount card were CJP members. However, the local Rotterdam Pass accounted for only 11% of those with a discount card.

One of the aims of the 2001 Rotterdam ECOC event was to engage the whole population of the city in the event. In common with the other major cities in the Netherlands, Rotterdam has a significant proportion of residents who are first or second generation immigrants. In particular, there are large populations of Moroccan or Turkish origin in Rotterdam. In total, about 19% of the Dutch respondents at Rotterdam 2001 events were born abroad, or had at least one parent born abroad. This is slightly higher than the proportion in the Dutch population (17%), but substantially lower than the proportion in the city of Rotterdam (55%). In particular, people from the 'ethnic minorities' (i.e. Indonesia, Surinam, Turkey, Morocco) made up only 8% of the sample, and were therefore even less well-represented than their share in the Rotterdam population (35%).

It also seemed that ethnic minorities were attracted most strongly to international/popular events, while 'white' Rotterdammers were best represented at locally-orientated events. This may represent a reaction to feelings of exclusion and a lack of contact with the 'indigenous' culture of the city.

One of the specific aims of the Rotterdam ECOC was to create unity in diversity – marked by the slogan 'Rotterdam is Many Cities'. One measure of the extent to which the ECOC succeeded in bringing different groups together is the degree of mixing between the different groups of event consumers.

However, 'mixed' audiences have tended to be attracted by offering a range of events tailored to the specific needs of different audience segments. By offering 'something for everyone', a greater range of groups can be tempted to participate in the programme, but this does not mean that the audience for individual events is mixed. Although events may be seen as a tool for social integration, very often the appearance of cosmopolitan mixing masks continuing spatial segregation of audiences (Crespi-Vallbona & Richards, 2007).

Tool Box to Attract Young People to Australia Day Event Celebrations

The tool box developed for Australia Day events focuses on young people aged 15 to 21, a group perceived to be low in involvement with cultural events in general, and Australia Day in particular. The tool box includes a profile of 'Generation Y', strategies to attract young people to become involved and some 'seeding' ideas for events. The aim is to offer pointers to ensure that events are more inclusive, attractive and relevant for young people. This tool concentrates on attracting and engaging young people in Australia Day events and celebrations because:

- Survey results confirm a general concern by all Australia Day organisers about attracting more young people.

- Young people are under-represented in terms of inclusion and parity with general population profiles.

- It is important to attract younger people to ensure continuity and sustainability of Australia Day celebrations at the local level.

- If young people engage with Australia Day activities, they are supported in developing values and respect for their country and its people, and have a sense of belonging, They may recognise the significance and enjoyment of Australia Day celebrations, and later in their lives become involved with an activity (for example in volunteering or in active involvement or membership of a Local Australia Day Committee).

- Anecdotal evidence suggests that during our lives, we all go through cycles of engagement with activities, and we prioritise differently in different stages of our life. Good experiences have impacts and may lead to our reengagement at a later stage of our life cycle.

- Using the term 'young people' rather than 'youth'. The term 'young people' avoids the negative connotations of 'deviance,' which in contemporary use (albeit not in a conscious way) is connected with the term 'youth'. It is also arguable that 'youth' carries a connotation of 'young males'.

The tool box emphasises that young people do not constitute a homogeneous group, and that they differ widely in terms of access to resources and cultural facilities, and may come from very different cultural, economic and family circumstances. It provides a set of ideas, which can act as models for event programme design.
(excerpt from the Australia Day Toolkit, www.australiaday.gov.au)

Opening up new spaces

One of the major issues in events policy for cities is the spatial location of facilities and events (see Chapter 3). In many cities most of the high-profile event activity is located in the city centre, while the other areas of the city stage many local, community-based events. There are obvious reasons for this, including the ease of access of central locations and the benefits of clustering cultural production. However, such concentrations tend to strengthen the uniformity of the events audience, since those living in or near the city centre are often the same highly educated professionals who are usually found at cultural events (Richards, 2001). There are therefore arguments for dispersing cultural facilities and events more widely across the city or region, providing more access to those who find it difficult to access the city centre.

Because events are usually much more flexible and mobile than physical facilities, they can often be useful tools in spreading cultural activities to new areas of the city. In Barcelona, for example, major festivals have tended to increase their spatial reach over the years, bringing new areas into the events calendar (see Chapter 2). One of the major successes of the Rotterdam ECOC in 2001 was the event 'Preaching in another parish', which brought people together to hear sermons from different faiths in each other's religious spaces.

In the case of the ECOC in Lille in 2004, the event was used to open 12 new cultural centres called *Maisons Folies* in the city and the surrounding region, including in neighbouring Belgium. These were new venues used by artists, associations and inhabitants as places where people could meet, create and exchange ideas in the districts. They continue to offer exhibition areas, rehearsal rooms, artists' residences and auditoriums. The Condition Publique in Roubaix is the largest Maison Folie. The centre is housed in two former market halls, which now contain performance spaces, offices, a roof garden and a glass-roofed indoor street. The centre is host to local cultural associations, an artists' residence, rehearsal spaces and a café-restaurant. In Lille, the two Maisons Folies were set up on restored industrial wasteland. The Maison Folie in the Wazemmes district of the city is a former spinning mill, to which a contemporary building has been added by the Dutch group of architects NOX, identified by its undulating metal shell. The former factory's vaulted brick basement now houses oriental baths. In the Moulins district of Lille, a former brewing and malting works was also transformed into a Maison Folie.

The Maison Folies are publicly owned cultural centres, with facilities for cultural production (studios, artists' residences) and distribution (exhibition and performance rooms). They have an important role in cultural development in the local community, and the basic idea was to bring culture to the different areas of the region. The Maison Folies were located in restored industrial or religious buildings, usually in disadvantaged areas with few cultural facilities. The National Government Cultural Office (DRAC) in the Nord-Pas-de-Calais Region helped to finance the Maisons Folies.

As well as providing a lasting legacy of the Lille 2004 event, the Maisons Folies provided a basis for spreading cultural production and consumption through the region. For example, one of the best-attended events of the 2004 programme was the Picasso exhibition held at the Piscine de Roubaix, which attracted 128,000 visitors. The Roubaix venues continued to stage events and attract substantial visitor numbers after the event as well (170,000 visitors in 2005; 219,000 in 2007).

Events can also help ease the problem of providing access to heritage, as is the case with events that mark European Heritage Days, when buildings that usually charge an entry fee are free, and buildings that are normally closed or inaccessible are opened up for an inquisitive public. Heritage Days started in Paris in 1984 and became a European event in 1991. The number of participants has been increasing steadily over the years, and in 2006 there were over 19 million visits across Europe.

There are many possibilities of using events as gateways, including private spaces. During the Brighton Festival in the UK, there is a specific programme of Open Houses, which open over the four weekends of the festival and are free to visit. The houses are the homes or studios of a wide range of artists, who have the opportunity to sell direct to a wide range of visitors, as well as offering a glimpse into the 'backstage' area of artistic production. In 2004 there were about 180 houses involved, linked through trails, which produce their own brochures. The trails can purchase publicity materials from the Brighton Festival Fringe, such as banners for the houses.

In the Catalan city of Girona, the *temps de flors* (Girona Flower Time) event opens up the courtyards of the medieval city centre with floral displays arranged by local residents and businesses. These displays invite the public into many areas that are normally closed or cut off from public view, and therefore give visitors a new perspective on the city.

How Can Festivals Support Urban Development?

In a presentation to the European Festivals Research Association, Ostrowska (2008) argued that in different Polish cities, cultural events had taken on a specific role in relation to urban space. The Polish festivals studied support processes of urban development because:

- They are visible events that focus the attention of authorities, inhabitants and media and thus can start debate on specific issues.

Continued

- Many festivals are directly connected with the theme of 'urbanity' and deal with the city as a very concrete space.
- They form part of the cultural policy of the city and help to define the identity of the place.
- They take place in cities marked with a multicultural past, that want to raise questions about their past and how it can help them to recreate their actual identity.
- The programme of these festivals is planned according to specific presentation spaces
- They all use real urban spaces, not specially designed art spaces.

One example is the Malta Festival in Poznań, which was established in 1991. This event was deliberately invented by the city authorities to animate the area around the artificial Malta Lake after it had been restored for the 1990 European Rowing Championships. For many years this area was abandoned and did not exist in the 'mental map' of Poznań inhabitants. The original concept of the festival was to rehabilitate urban spaces and to attract a wider audience, neatly summed up in the slogan: 'The art of open spaces is the art of democracy.' The festival thus became a 'theatre celebration', involving not only the performing artists, but also the thousands of spectators and co-authors. The festival had a number of positive effects for the city:

- It helped to create new public space in the city.
- Through artistic activities, the festival not only incorporated an abandoned area into the mental map of Poznań, but also changed the area of Malta Lake into a popular area for leisure.
- It made the inhabitants of Poznań more open to the new forms of art and perhaps more open in general.
- It gave the city a more artistic image.

Expanding the event audience via the media

The notions of publics and audiences have become more blurred as different means of consuming events evolve. TV programmes, DVDs, live feeds via Internet and festivals in Second Life all make it possible to expand the event audience without attracting physical visitors (see Chapter 12). The total target public for a given programme in the eventful city is likely to consist of many different groups, including both those who attend in person and those who consume events indirectly, either by watching televised performances or enjoying the festive atmosphere created by events, but without directly attending.

The Festival of World Cultures, held in Dún Laoghaire, claims to be 'Ireland's foremost intercultural event'. The festival itself features more than 150 events in 40 venues, attracting artists from 80 countries, attracting an audience of over 230,000. The festival includes music, street theatre, dance, club nights, markets, exhibitions, talks, workshops and activities for children. For the 2005 Festival, the event was also transformed into a three-part programme screened on national television. Tickets to the filming were offered free of charge.

Television and film festivals in particular are attempting to reach a wider audience through their own media and by using new forms of communication. In Berlin the main media partner of the Berlinale Festival, the media company ZDF, is responsible for the stage design, concept, script and logistics of all stage shows in the Berlinale Palast (opening, award ceremony, European Shooting Stars and daily competition screenings). The ZDF Berlinale studio is used for live in-depth coverage of the festival.

The New York Television Festival (NYTVF) was founded in 2005 as a platform for independent television. Showcasing New York City as the 'birthplace of modern television', the Festival brings together artists, executives, industry figures and fans. The Festival features the Independent Pilot Competition, panel discussions, premiere screenings and other special events 'designed to honour television as an institution and as an art form'. The Independent Pilot Competition allows producers, writers and directors to showcase their original TV pilots directly to the decision-makers of the industry.

The Wildscreen Festival held in Bristol, UK is designed to 'celebrate and promote excellence within the wildlife media industry'. It offers screenings, debates, training workshops, technical trade shows and networking opportunities. Wildscreen is a market place for buying and selling films and it is also a platform for commissioning new work. The festival culminates with the Panda Awards Ceremony - the wildlife film industry's equivalent of the Hollywood Oscars. Wildscreen attracts famous names from wildlife, conservation and environmental backgrounds, filmmakers, the media and members of the general public. In January 2007, the Wildscreen Festival toured India with a series of film screenings and workshops with some of the world's leading wildlife filmmakers.

Festivals with a valuable brand image are also increasingly being utilised by other media as a means of associating themselves with different forms of cultural practice. An interesting example is the Hay Festival (once described by Bill Clinton, former President of the United States, as 'The Woodstock of the Mind'), and which the Guardian newspaper now sponsors. As well as extensive coverage in the press, the festival is also aired through a nightly 'Hay-on-Sky' programme by the Sky Arts channel. As well as broadcasting a daily round up featuring interviews with renowned authors, artists, and politicians, the Best of Hay-on-Sky was also made available as a free download. The hour-long programme included interviews with Gordon Brown, Ian Rankin, Tony Benn and Sebastian Faulks, as well as reports from the festival.

Festivals are increasingly placing their own content online and in the media. The Bayreuth Festival has begun to show opera live online, charging virtual visitors €49 to see the festival, as well as providing free screenings in the Bayreuth public square. New York's Metropolitan Opera and Milan's Teatro alla Scala have also 'simulcasted' their performances live in cinemas. The Met is currently about to open its third season, offering live broadcasts of operas. These are offered for €49 online and about €15 euros for broadcasts in cinemas. The Met has been directly involved in broadcasts in 17 countries, as well as regular live radio broadcasts (CBC News, 2008).

Such developments underscore the increasingly close relationship between the media, events and the city (noted in Chapter 7). It is also clear that the distinction between the media and events is becoming increasingly blurred as events begin to exploit and broadcast their own content.

Festivals as Media Content

In 2007 the Australia Council and the Australian Broadcasting Commission (ABC) joined forces with UK's Channel 4 and Arts Council England to commission new British and Australian dance films and purchase existing dance films for broadcast. This initiative provides opportunities for Australian dance to find wider audiences both in Australia and the UK. It also gives established directors and choreographers and new talent an opportunity to create new work for the screen. Exploring this model for further international arts/broadcasting collaborations and utilising innovative digital platforms can open up audiences in new markets and enable skills development in areas of technical production. The performing arts are the obvious source of content but there are also opportunities to capture innovative hybrid art forms and collaborations between artists of different disciplines.

Documentary profiles of artists, particularly those that have lived and worked internationally and showcase the diversity of Australian creativity, hold real possibilities for international promotion of dance artists and their work. Festivals also provide a wealth of talent and content for broadcast. The Australia Council recently sent 42 of Australia's best indigenous artists to the 10th Festival of Pacific Arts in American Samoa. The ABC produced and screened a two-part documentary, which showcased the best of indigenous arts and enabled an exchange of cultural dialogue between artists of the Pacific.

The Australia Council supports expansion by the national broadcasters into overseas markets as a platform for advancing cultural diplomacy and opening up new and bigger audiences for the arts. The creation of commercially viable digital content for Australian and international markets will contribute to redressing the current trade deficit in digital content.

(Australia Council, 2007)

HOW CAN AUDIENCES BE MANAGED?

As we have already seen in Chapter 5, there is a need to manage audiences to ensure their enjoyment, safety and security during events. However, managing the audience at the event is just one aspect of the issue. For some events, there is also a need to manage the potential audience to ensure that the desired audience attends, or in some cases to restrict attendance.

For some very popular events there is an excess of demand over the supply of places. For ticketed events, excess demand should be dealt with during the sale of tickets. For example Glastonbury 2007 sold a large proportion of its 180,000 tickets within an hour of going on sale. For many blockbuster art exhibitions, a system of dated and timed entry tickets is used to ensure that capacity limits are not exceeded. Block-buster arts exhibitions often attract large numbers of visitors: 'once you announce a big Impressionist show, with as many Monets as you can scrounge, it's time to order the crush barriers' (Kennedy, 2007). In 2007, for example, the exhibition 'Monet's Art and its Posterity' generated over 700,000 visits in Tokyo and the 'Masterpieces of French Painting from the Met' exhibition attracted almost 700,000 visits in Berlin and almost 600,000 in Houston.

With major arts events now generating very large crowds, certain cities are faced with problems of crowd management at peak times. A few European cities have begun to develop 'demarketing' strategies, designed to keep visitors away or to divert them to less pressurised times of year. Venice introduced a Venice Card to encourage people to visit the city at off peak times and to leave their car at home. The card offered waterbus transfers from the airport and guaranteed access to major tourist attractions. However, this card was not taken up in sufficient quantities by consumers to make it worthwhile, largely because of the relatively spontaneous nature of most visits. For major events, however, one can imagine such a system working better, particularly if event admission was linked to purchasing the card. In Venice the problem of overcrowding is exacerbated by a heavy geographical concentration of attractions and the staging of many events during the peak summer tourist season.

Cultural Production in Venice: Events, Producers and Consumers

Recent research on events in Venice utilises data on events gathered through the website www.agendavenezia.org, (a product of the Venice Foundation) which documents cultural events in the city. In 2007 the website registered 1861 events in Venice Municipality, which indicates an average of 50 events per day. The events were divided into major

categories: visual arts (11.8%), music (21.3%), theatre and dance (16.3%), film reviews (19%) meetings and conferences (28.9%), traditional Venetian celebrations (0.9%), sports (1.6%) and fairs and markets (0.2%). Most of these events take place in the historic centre of the city, which adds to the event pressure on the city. The peak event periods also coincide to some extent with the main summer tourist season (90 events per day in June, for example), no doubt in an attempt to capture tourist audiences.
(Sbetti and Bertoldo, 2009)

THE ROLE OF TOURISM IN EVENT PROGRAMMES

From the perspective of the city, 'tourists' are an essential component of the audience for events. Most importantly, as people who, by definition, come from outside the city, tourists are the only participants who inject additional revenue to the city through their event expenditure. This contribution can be very significant, as studies of different events have shown (see Chapter 9). This is reflected very clearly in the policy of the City of Amsterdam (Gemeente Amsterdam, 2004), where the major aim of the events policy is attracting tourists. The original policy, developed in 2004, talked about funding major events on the basis of their ability to attract visitors, but this was later narrowed to their role in stimulating overnight tourism, largely because overnight tourists tend to spend more money. In addition, most cities seek to project their image externally, and tourists are therefore a key target segment. Outsiders also arguably add to the creativity and 'cosmopolitan' atmosphere of the city, which are viewed as assets for city development (Florida, 2002). Cultural events specifically are increasingly seen by the tourist sector as an important tool in generating tourism. For example, a report by the European Travel Commission (2005), indicated that 88% of city tourist offices in Europe are convinced that cultural events attract tourists. This seems to be supported by the empirical evidence from the ECOCs, which indicates that for the majority of events at least half the audience came from outside the city, and might therefore be regarded as 'tourists' (Table 8.8).

Surveys of visitors to the 'normal' cultural programme of a city tend to show a similarly significant proportion of tourists. In Ghent, surveys at a range of events indicated that tourists made up between 30% (classical concerts) and 80% (specialist exhibitions) of the cultural audience (Steunpunt Toerisme en Recreatie, 2003).

Many cities that might be considered as 'eventful' have witnessed significant increases in tourist numbers, which are often attributed to their successful staging of cultural events. Examples frequently cited in this book include Edinburgh, Amsterdam, Melbourne and Barcelona. Over the period 1990-2005 tourist overnights in Barcelona grew at double the average rate for other European cities. This was due at least in part to its events policy. The Olympic Games in 1992 and the Gaudí Year in 2002 in particular produced significant rises in visitor numbers, although the 2004 Universal Forum of Cultures had little effect on tourist arrivals, perhaps because of a lack of tourism promotion outside Catalunya.

The benefits of tourism for the eventful city

If well managed, tourism can contribute in many ways to the success of the eventful city.

Table 8.8 Breakdown of Visitor Types for Selected ECOC

%	Local residents	Day visitors	Domestic tourists	Foreign tourists
Luxembourg 1995 (theatres, concerts)	79	9		12
Luxembourg 1995 (Exhibitions)	34	36		31
Stockholm 1998	40	20	20	20
Rotterdam 2001	49	12	22	17
Porto 2001	30	20	26	24
Bruges 2002	50	40	10	(not measured)
Salamanca 2002	50	10	30	10
Sibiu 2007	38	1	45	16
Luxembourg Region 2007	32	21	0	47

Apart from generating larger numbers of visitors, the most important contribution of tourists is usually viewed as economic. As the impact studies in Chapter 9 show, tourists generally spend more money than local visitors, because of additional spending on food and accommodation during their stay. Although a large proportion of visitor spending will accrue direcly to the tourism sector, and particularly through hotels and restaurants, there are other ways in which tourists can benefit the city as a whole.

Cultural expenditure

Most importantly for the cultural sector, tourists can spend significant amounts of money on visits to museums, theatres and other cultural institutions. This provides a direct support to cultural organisations whose earned income is often low. It is estimated, for example, that overseas visitors account for 30% of the 12 million theatre visits in London every year (Think London, 2006).

City image

Image impacts are also an important reason for stimulating tourism. As indicated in Chapter 9, events can have a positive impact on the image of the city among both residents and visitors. In many cases, visitors actually have a more positive image of the places that they visit than residents, who may be more keenly aware of the negative aspects of the place (Richards et al., 2002).

Atmosphere

Visitors can also be an important factor in adding to the 'atmosphere' of the city. Atmosphere is extremely hard to define, but it always features highly as a motivation for city visitation and in the level of visitor satisfaction, particularly for cultural tourists (Richards, 2001). Although having too many visitors may cause problems of overcrowding and competition for facilities, not having enough visitors can detract from the atmosphere and 'cosmopolitan' feel of a city. As Ritzer (1999) has remarked in relation to centres of consumption in modern cities, people are attracted to other people, because a party in an empty house is no fun.

Self esteem

Visitors are also important for the self-esteem of a city. Although the residents of a city may feel justly proud of the place they live in, it can be a boost for local pride that people will travel especially to be in a particular city. Surveys of local residents in Catalunya indicate that the vast majority of local residents feel proud that tourists are attracted to their cultural events (Crespi-Vallbona & Richards, 2007).

Political capital

There is also a political role to attracting tourists. As consumers of the heritage and living culture of a place, tourists can form an attachment to, and empathy with, the city, which can be very important. In the Yugoslav war, for example, the shelling of Dubrovnik only stopped as a result of strong international pressure, partly due to international recognition that cultural heritage was being destroyed, which was also directly related to the role of the city as a major tourist destination. Foreigners who had visited as tourists were appalled that the city was under attack, and this helped to bring a speedy end to the bombardment (Richards, 2001). This is an extreme example, but it shows the importance of cultivating, either consciously or unconsciously, 'ambassadors' in other countries.

Stimulating people to visit a city through events is therefore more than just an economic strategy – it can also have significant practical benefits for the social, cultural and political life of the city. As suggested earlier, it is also true that attracting large numbers of visitors in certain cities may cause a number of practical problems as well, such as crowding, traffic problems and litter. In order to maximise the benefits and reduce the problems, it is important to understand the nature of tourist audiences for events.

Tourism and Events in Toronto

The Canadian city of Toronto has thought strategically about the relationship between events and tourism policy. The 1992 Strategic Plan identified three major initiatives to enhance Toronto's tourism product inventory:

- creation of a signature event or festival to support Toronto's image;

- designation (and creation, if required) of 8 to 10 recurring events as 'official';
- Toronto events, to be funded and supported by the city; and
- coordinating the structuring of an event bid team to develop a strategy for securing major one-time events.

Through Toronto Special Events (TSE), the city became a major producer of special events and festivals in Toronto. TSE identified three annual events that it defined as 'Signature Events':

- Toronto Winterfest;
- Cavalcade of Lights; and
- Celebrate Toronto Street Festival.

The vision for TSE called for generating economic impact 'by developing, producing and marketing events that are innovative and appeal to a broad and evolving audience of tourists and residents.' However, the effectiveness of TSE, and the actual tourism impact of these signature events, is not widely understood by tourism operators.

Consultants assessing the work of the TSE also questioned the need for the Tourism Division to play such a prominent role in the production and management of events. As a result, the following guiding principles were developed. Tourism events supported by the city:

- should be delivered through collaborative approaches, including but not limited to joint ventures, sponsorships and strategic alliances;
- must meet a clear tourism sector need, either across the broad sector or to a specific priority sub-sector or area;
- must be consistent with the city's Strategic Plan for the Tourism Sector;
- must be sustainable, with consideration given to the requirements for long-term dependence on city resources;
- must clearly deliver the expected benefits to the tourism sector within an agreed-upon timeframe;
- the role of media and the potential to create awareness of or interest in the city as a tourism destination to the priority and/ or developing markets for Toronto;
- event frequency – giving preference to recurring events;
- ability to secure significant private sector investment to ensure leverage of public funds; and
- fit within gaps in the Toronto event tourism calendar.

Clearly, cities need to decide what kind of approach they are going to take to events tourism and how to manage the relationship between events, tourists and residents. Stokes (2008) has identified three different frameworks for events tourism strategy making:

- The corporate, market-led framework: giving primacy to the economic effects of event tourism.

- The community, destination-led framework: more emphasis on community involvement, less emphasis on economic impact.

- A synergistic framework: a mix of corporate and community approaches which seeks to develop a balanced portfolio of events.

In terms of the strategies actually adopted by the Australian events tourism stakeholders interviewed, the 'most dominant strategy making framework was the corporate, market-led approach' (Stokes 2008:260). In most cases, event tourism strategies are determined in a top-down fashion, with limited community involvement and consultation. This is perhaps not surprising in the context of many major events which attract large numbers of tourists, since these depend far more heavily on political support than local community involvement. The strategies adopted by government also tended to be reactive rather than proactive. This is also clear from the strategy for festivals and cultural events developed by Fáilte Ireland (2007:1), the national tourist board for the Republic of Ireland:

> During the five-year period 2002 – 2006, Fáilte Ireland has supported over 400 individual festivals. This investment has largely been application driven and responsive to requests for funding. While continued support for the sector is necessary in order to sustain an attractive cultural offering for the tourist, it is now clear that a more strategic approach to Fáilte Ireland's investment is essential.

In order to maximise the range of benefits derived from tourism, it is clearly important to look at the whole range of economic, cultural and social issues involved, as well as adopting a more proactive approach to strategy development. An understanding of the tourists who visit events and the reasons why they visit is therefore crucial.

Event Tourism in Whistler, Canada

The city of Whistler is an important tourism destination, particularly for winter sports. In 2007 an Event Tourism Strategy was developed in an effort to increase tourism. This strategy evaluates the role of event tourism, explores the impact of event tourism on the Resort's stakeholders, community and its guests, and provides recommendations for Whistler to achieve its vision for events ('Whistler is an internationally recognised tourism destination – renowned for its superior quality and diverse events – making it a place to visit again and again'). Whistler has hosted a wide range of events from small local gatherings to major national and international events.

Whistler's stakeholders widely accept that it is necessary to adopt a long-term, strategic approach to event tourism, and the need for an integrated approach that considers both the needs of the guest (or 'event tourist' or 'tourist') and the community. They favour authentic, organic events that are aligned with Whistler's brand and values and which have the potential to grow and attract new and repeat visitation. Smaller, grass roots events are typically championed by locals as these events are more likely to reflect the values, community passion and products of the city, and provide a competitive edge over other destinations.

(Resort Municipality of Whistler, 2007:37)

WHO ARE THE EVENT TOURISTS?

Most importantly for our purposes, tourists are part of the event audience; they have simply travelled further to attend. Deciding who is a tourist can be notoriously difficult, however. The World Tourism Organisation (UNWTO) (2005) definition of tourism includes people who are:

travelling to and staying in places outside their usual environment for not more than one consecutive year for leisure, business and other purposes not related to the exercise of an activity remunerated from within the place visited.

In other words, almost anyone travelling 'outside their normal environment' can be considered a tourist, as long as they are not earning any money in the place they are visiting. This means that apart from being away from home, 'tourists', can be seen as temporary residents and potential event consumers. In fact, the growing mobility of people in general and event audiences in particular means that it is increasingly hard to distinguish between 'tourists' and 'locals' (Franquesa and Morrell, 2007).

Not all tourists consume events or are motivated to visit cities by events. Many of those tourists who do attend cultural events in other cities (particularly if these are free), do so as 'accidental cultural tourists' – they arrive in a city and then find out what is going on (Richards, 2002).

For the eventful city, the important point is to increase the audience that comes *because* of the event. This is particularly appropriate for cultural events that need to attract culturally motivated visitors who can be influenced to travel by the cultural events organised in the city. Research for the ATLAS Cultural Tourism Project (Richards, 2007a) has revealed much about the profile of these potential cultural consumers.

Those tourists who define their trip as 'cultural' tend to have the following profile:

- highly educated;
- professional or managerial occupations;
- high incomes; and
- occupation related to the cultural sector.

In these respects, the 'cultural tourist' does not differ much from the profile of the frequent cultural consumer in general, as discussed above. In fact, research carried out by the ATLAS Cultural Tourism Research Project shows that cultural tourists tend to be those who engage most frequently in cultural activities at home as well (Richards, 2001). The expenditure of cultural tourists also tends to be higher than the average visitor. In the UK, for example, 'high-end cultural tourists' segments spend up to 50% more than the average leisure tourist (Tourism Research and Marketing, 2006).

The general picture that emerges of the 'cultural tourist' is of a relatively well-educated professional with a high (joint) income, who travels with culture as one of the motives for being in a destination. This does not vary much from the classic picture painted of the cultural visitor. However, there are a number of important points that should be emphasised about the nature of 'cultural tourism' (Tourism Research and Marketing, 2006:12-13):

■ Not every cultural visitor is a tourist:
   Local residents make up a large proportion of visitors to many cultural attractions and events.

■ Not every tourist visiting a cultural event is culturally motivated:
   Cultural tourism data derived from the UK Tourism Survey indicate that the proportion of tourists directly motivated by culture (about 6%) is far smaller than the proportion of all tourists visiting cultural attractions during their holiday (over 50%).

■ Cultural tourists are more likely to visit static attractions than ephemeral events, largely because of the more accessible nature of attractions:
   The number of visits made by tourists to heritage attractions such as museums and monuments is far greater than tourist visits to arts performances and cultural events. Heritage attractions tend to be more accessible, both in terms of cultural content and the fact that few require prior booking. For example, the number of foreign visitors to Finland Festivals' events in 2002 was only 51,000 visitors, or 3% of the total audience (Tikkanen, 2004).

■ Not all cultural tourists fall within the upper age groups.
   In spite of the common image of cultural tourists as being predominantly drawn from the older age groups, tourists from all age ranges engage in cultural consumption.

The ATLAS surveys also point to a number of important changes in the cultural tourism market in recent years. One of the most important of these is the rise in the number of people viewing their holidays as 'cultural'. The proportion of tourists on a 'cultural holiday' increased from under 20% in 1997 to 36% in 2008 (ATLAS, 2009).

There are a number of important qualitative changes in cultural tourism demand which have taken place in recent years:

- increased number of 'cultural holidays';

- rising education, income and status levels in the market;

- shorter holiday duration, in line with the holiday market in general;

- more use of Internet for information gathering and booking;

- more visits to cultural events and festivals, apparently driven by increased supply; and

- greater interest in 'experiences' and 'creativity'.

(Richards, 2007a)

The characteristics of cultural tourists have important implications for the eventful city seeking to develop cultural tourism. Firstly, it is necessary to be fairly discerning in the choice of target market. Not all visitors are interested in culture, at least as it is often traditionally defined, and marketing which addresses itself to 'cultural tourists' will not always be positively received. It is also clear that stereotypes about the nature of the cultural tourism audience needs to be categorised in more detail, In particular, the potential of younger visitors needs to be examined and, where appropriate, developed. Finally, it is clear that events have to work harder than static attractions to reach their potential audience. There is a strong argument for developing the synergies between the marketing efforts of all events in the 'eventful city', in order to give the location a profile as a place where things happen, which can in turn lead to more visits to all individual events.

CULTURAL TOURISTS AND EVENTS

The ATLAS research on cultural tourism consumption (Richards, 2007a) provides some indications of the differences between cultural tourism related to events and cultural tourism at fixed attractions.

Of the 12,000 visitor surveys conducted by ATLAS in 2004, some 25% were conducted at cultural events and the rest at fixed cultural attractions. Of all visitors, almost 14% indicated that they were travelling specifically to visit a cultural event. As there are around 360 million international cultural tourism trips each year (OECD, 2009a), this would imply that around 50 million international tourists visit cultural events worldwide.

Not surprisingly, tourists interviewed at cultural events were much more likely to be motivated to travel by the event (Richards, 2007a). Cultural event visitors were more likely to have visited the region before, and were more likely to be domestic tourists than international tourists. Cultural events were more likely to attract those aged 20 to 30 or over 50 (in other words, they tend not to be so popular with families). This profile was produced by a relatively high proportion of retired people and students at events. The attendees were also more likely to have occupations related to culture and to come from the lower income groups.

The event visitors were less likely to be on an inclusive package, and more likely to have gathered information about the destination via Internet before arrival. Event visitors were more likely to be travelling with an organised group or with friends, and less likely to be with family or partner.

The cultural consumption of event visitors was clearly orientated more towards the 'arts' than 'heritage'. They were more likely to have visited traditional festivals, theatre, pop concerts and world music events and less likely to have visited monuments, religious sites, historic sites or heritage centres.

Further distinctions can be made between 'heritage tourists' (primarily museum and monument visitors), 'arts tourists' (attending high arts performances) and 'festival tourists' (attending festivals and other events). The festival tourists seem to be the most eclectic cultural consumers, not visiting as many attractions in total, but spreading their visits across heritage, arts and cultural events alike (Table 8.9). As specified above, festival tourists are also more important consumers of various forms of popular culture, such as pop

Table 8.9	Attractions and Events Visited During Trip by Segment (Percentage of Respondents Attending)*		
	Heritage tourists	Arts tourists	Festival tourists
Museums	100	78	29
Monuments	73	61	34
Historic sites	71	64	38
Religious sites	57	53	26
Heritage/crafts centre	23	27	21
Traditional festivals	13	0	75
Theatres	8	18	17
Cinema	6	13	17
Dance events	4	7	24
Classical music events	4	7	9
Pop concerts	3	6	19
World music events	2	4	13
Art galleries	0	100	25

*The definition of the different segments precludes heritage tourists attending art galleries and arts tourists attending festivals.

music, dance and world music (indicating that this group has a particularly high proportion of 'cultural omnivores') (Tourism Research and Marketing, 2006:33).

Although the ATLAS research gives an impression of the 'cultural tourists' visiting cultural events, it has to be recognised that many events are, and are often intended to be, primarily local affairs. In Colombia, for example, the Carnaval de Barranquilla, one of the major cultural events in the country, attracts less than 10% of its audience from outside the region. Of these tourists, over 75% stay with friends or relatives in the city, leading to a very small impact in terms of the formal tourism economy (Fundesarrollo, 2005).

As has been emphasized throughout this volume, many studies have indicated that the greatest economic impact of most events is tourist expenditure, and festivals and events are very often viewed as a means of generating tourism to a city. As discussed above, cultural events in particular are often seen as a particularly attractive option, because they can generate highly desirable cultural tourism, being high spend and high quality tourism (Richards, 2001). Events have a number of other tourism-related advantages, as the European Travel Commission (2005:44) comments:

> *Often because events are one-off and take place in a limited timeframe and because festivals offer a concentrated and often unique offering in a limited time period, they form an additional reason for cultural tourists to visit a place. They can cause a place to rise on the shortlist of places the tourist has in his or her mindset of attractive destinations. Festivals and events are both effective instruments in attracting first time visitors as well as repeat visitors.*

A key question is the extent to which people are stimulated to visit a place because a specific event is being held. Would people have come to the city without the event? Could

Table 8.10 Change in Overnight Visitors to ECOC in the Period 1995 to 2007

ECOC	Percentage change in visitor stays in ECOC year	Percentage change in visitor stays ECOC+1
Luxembourg 1995	−4.9	−4.3
Copenhagen 1996	11.3	−1.6
Thessaloniki 1997	15.3	−5.9
Stockholm 1998	9.4	−0.2
Weimar 1999	56.3	−21.9
Helsinki 2000	7.5	−1.8
Prague 2000	−6.7	5.6
Reykjavik 2000	15.3	−2.6
Bologna 2000	10.1	5.3
Brussels 2000	5.3	−1.7
Bergen 2000	1.0	1.2
Rotterdam 2001	10.6	−9.6
Salamanca 2001	21.6	−7.9
Brugge 2002	9.0	−9.6
Graz 2003	22.9	−14.0
Lille 2004	9.0	−7.0
Cork 2005	13.8	
Luxembourg Region 2007	6.0	−4.4
Sibiu 2007	8.0	−25.0
Average	11.6	−5.9

as many people have been attracted if the money were invested in other forms of development or promotion? These are key questions which are very rarely addressed in event impact research.

The research conducted on the ECOC has allowed the relative visitor impacts of a large number of cultural events to be assessed. Drawing on visitor statistics for different cities, the increase (or sometimes decrease) in visitor numbers for different events have been be compared with the years before and after the ECOC (Table 8.10).

This illustrates that visitors will not automatically be attracted, even to the largest scale events. Unless the event matches visitor motivations, it will not succeed in attracting visitors. For larger programmes, such as the ECOC, a very small number of events in the overall programme usually attract the bulk of visitor numbers. For example, the Hieronymus Bosch exhibition held in Rotterdam in 2001 attracted over 10% of the total ECOC visits and a much larger proportion of all tourists.

Using Events to Market Tourism Products

The Hard Days Night Hotel is a four-star boutique hotel in Liverpool featuring Beatles-themed artwork. The launch of the new hotel was originally planned for November 2007. However this was eventually postponed until February 2008, so the launch could fully capitalise on Liverpool's tenure as Capital of Culture.

The PR campaign started in September 2007 to create a buzz around the new hotel. The team worked closely with government agencies such as VisitBritain and Mersey Partnership to ensure journalists visiting the city as Capital of Culture were aware of Hard Days Night Hotel as a place to stay or to visit. The PR company also built relationships with key Beatles bloggers and websites by conducting special preview tours and keeping them updated regularly.

The campaign achieved over 545 pieces of press coverage with a total print circulation of more than 700 million. There was also international broadcast coverage from CNN, NBC, ABC News, Sky News and Reuters. British broadcast coverage included BBC Breakfast, BBC North West, BBC Radio 4, Granada and ITV News. Of this coverage, over 98% was positive and over 80% adhered to the key PR messages.

The Constantine exhibition staged in Trier as part of the Luxembourg and Greater Region ECOC in 2007 attracted almost 800,000 visits, or 25% of the total. The entire Rhineland-Palatinate region benefited from the Constantine the Great Exhibition in Trier. The number of visitors to the region grew to a record 7.6 million, an increase of 3.4% compared to 2006. There was also a 9.7% increase in overnight stays in the City of Trier itself in 2007, compared with 2006 (Figure 8.1).

In Trier 46% of hoteliers also reported increased business as a result of the Constantine Exhibition. Tourism figures for the surrounding Saarland region also showed a growth in tourism of around 5.2% in 2007, which indicates that the positive effects of the ECOC were also felt in that region. In spite of the increased numbers of visitors, however, most tourism businesses felt there had been relatively little impact in terms of attracting new business, particularly from cultural tourists (Figure 8.2).

The Luxembourg ECOC in 2007 also makes it clear that different types of events tend to have a greater attraction for tourists. Tourists were most likely to have visited art exhibitions, particularly painting and photography. Video art,

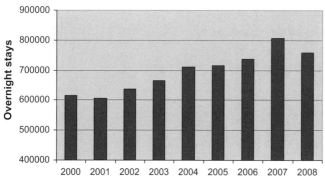

FIGURE 8.1 *Overnight stays in Trier, 2000–2008.*

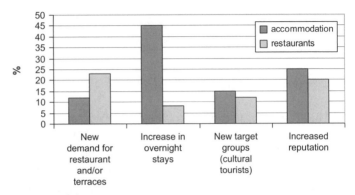

FIGURE 8.2 *How did the Constantine exhibition affect your business?*

design and architecture were also attended by a large proportion of tourists, which probably reflects the type of events being staged at the time rather than the importance of these events in the programme (Table 8.11).

Other major events and theme years have also been shown to generate significant tourism flows. For example, the 'Rembrandt 400' theme year organised in Amsterdam in 2006 was supported by an extensive international marketing programme, which helped to generate 1.7 million visits. It

Table 8.11	Type of Event Attended by Tourists in Luxembourg in 2007
Event type	**Percentage of tourists**
Painting exhibitions	64
Photography exhibitions	49
Video art, art installations	47
Design, graphics, architecture	43
Concerts (pop, rock, jazz, world music)	37
Festivals, firework displays	27
Concerts (classical music)	19
Cinema	12
Literature	12
Theatre	10
Dance, ballet	8
Opera, operetta, musical	3

Source: Luxembourg, 2007

was hailed by the organisers as 'the most successful cultural event ever held in the Netherlands', and total economic impact of the programme was estimated to be over €600 million. About 60% of the additional visits were made by foreign tourists, a fifth of whom had come to the Netherlands specifically because of the Rembrandt Year. Over two thirds of hotels in the city also indicated that the event had stimulated additional business for them. The spread of foreign tourists was greater than usual, with a large number of visitors from Spain, the UK, Italy and particularly the US, which accounted for 11% of all foreign visitors. This distribution closely matches those markets where the Netherlands Tourist Board had invested most promotional effort (Rembrandt 400, 2006).

Around 58% of hotels in Amsterdam indicated that they had received extra visitors as a result of the Rembrandt theme year. In particular, luxury (four and five star) hotels benefited from the flow of extra tourists (between 80% and 91% said they had received more visitors). This result was linked to the fact that luxury hotels were more likely to have arranged special packages related to the event. For example, two thirds of five star hotels organised special packages or activities for Rembrandt 400, compared with only 5% of those hotels with two stars or less. The most common type of package arranged by the hotels was the provision of free tickets to exhibitions or 'Rembrandt the Musical' in Theater Carré.

In contrast, the Amsterdam theme year for 2007 was 'Feel the Rhythm - Music & Dance', which placed the emphasis on local arts rather than global heritage. The familiarity of hotels with the theme year was encouraging, with 59% of hotels indicating they were familiar with the year, a figure that rose to 100% for five star hotels. However, only 11% of the hotels indicated that the year would generate extra visitors, and only 3% of the hotels had organised specific products to link with the theme year.

In the Belgian city of Brugge (Bruges) a marketing campaign was launched around the theme 'Winter in Brugge' (Brugge, 2006). The regional government developed a programme with local hotels to offer tourists a 'three nights for the price of two' deal in five price categories (€50, €75, €100,

€125 and €150 per double room including breakfast). The offer included a book of discount vouchers for concerts, exhibitions and other events. The offer was publicised via Internet with extra support from the Belgian Tourist Office in key markets. British and French tourists were targeted in particular, and specific promotions were also made using 'free' publicity generated by competitions, for which free hotel rooms were made available as prizes. The first edition of Winter in Brugge generated 1500 extra overnight stays in the period November 2006 to March 2007. The promotion worked well in France (which generated almost half the extra overnights, but less well in the UK (only 7% of the extra overnights) (Gemeente Brugge, 2006:112).

Enjoy England, the domestic marketing arm of Visit-Britain, launched 'Enjoy England Culture 08', a year-long, £250,000 (€270,000) campaign to attract tourists to cultural events. The campaign was originally designed to coincide with the ECOC in Liverpool, but was also continued in 2009 under the name 'Culture 09'. Cultural events are featured on a specific website (www.enjoyengland.com/culture) which enables consumers to search over 3000 events by region, theme and date.

Even in relatively remote areas, events can provide a substantial boost to tourism. For example, the week-long *Ceolas* music school was established on the Scottish island of South Uist in 1996 by the Gaelic Arts Agency (McLean, 2006). During the week-long programme, a wide range of events, concerts and activities are organised, and the number of people attending Ceolas events has varied between 2000 and 3500, almost as many as the total population of the island (4000). The event fills all the available beds in South Uist for a week, boosts visitor spending and helps to develop interest in local culture. The festival has increased pride in local culture among residents and raised social cohesion. In spite of the isolated location of the island, many of the participants come from abroad. The development of social events and the house *ceilidhs* have integrated the visitor into the life of the island and cleverly transformed the visitor, who may think of themselves as an outsider, into someone who is part of the life of the island – even if it is only for one week in the year.

CONCLUSIONS

Events need to develop a relationship with their audiences and publics. For the eventful city, this also means that the programme of events must be structured to appeal to those specific audiences and publics which relate to its aims. In many cases, this might be interpreted as providing 'something for everyone', but one must accept that not everyone wants to 'consume' events in the same terms. Even though audience development presents considerable challenges, it is important to target new consumers to prevent a preoccupation with offering experience primarily for the existing consumer. It is relatively easy to attract a large public with popular blockbuster exhibitions by famous artists, but each event in the programme also needs to be considered in terms of its function and contribution to building a wider public for events in the eventful city. Sometimes, events that attract few visitors generate the most attention, particularly from the media.

The core event audience tends to be composed of well-educated people with high disposable income. These tend to be the primary consumers of cultural outputs in the city. Strategies developed to foster new audiences include creating new events tailored to the needs of defined target groups, opening up new spaces in the city that may attract new publics and exploiting new media and cultural formats. It is likely that the successful eventful city will need to employ many different strategies if it wants to maintain the vibrancy in its event programme and expand its public.

Attention also needs to be paid to tourists, who are also a vital part of the event audience. Many people will travel long distances to attend specific events that meet their interests, and will spend relatively large sums of money to do so. Tourists will often contribute the bulk of the economic impact generated by events, an issue which is dealt with in the following chapter.

CHAPTER 9

Event Programme Outcomes and Impacts

As previous chapters have shown, events are increasingly designed to deliver a complex range of cultural, social and economic impacts. Events act as meeting places and as catalysts for aesthetic excellence, economic activity, regional redevelopment and tourism, while supporting education, local identity and civic pride, and stimulating diversity and social cohesion. Because of these wide-ranging expectations, evaluation needs to concentrate on results or outcomes, rather than simply reviewing the operation of the event programme itself.

Monitoring the outcomes of event programmes is increasingly important for a number of reasons:

- the demand for transparency and accountability in the application of public funding;

- the drive for value-for-money and increased quality;

- the need to evaluate what individual events contribute to the objectives of the city;

- the need to programme the eventful city effectively; and

- to support effective resource allocation.

Measuring outcomes achieved against the aims or mission of an events programme allows its effectiveness to be assessed and enables decisions to be made on the direction and management of the programme. Measuring outcomes can help a city outline the wider aims of staging events to its stakeholders, relate these aims to operational and strategic decision-making, and help gather support for event programmes in the future.

Increasingly, cities are also attempting to estimate outcomes or impacts prior to major events, in order to gather stakeholder support and finance and to make appropriate event financing decisions. Impact assessments are therefore being used as tools for lobbying, as well as for directing policy and improving events.

This chapter examines some of the main methods of assessment, including multiplier studies, the triple bottom line model, the balanced scorecard and benchmarking and the uses and abuses of impact assessment.

MEASURING IMPACTS AND OUTCOMES

Event outcomes are often thought of in terms of impacts on the community and other stakeholders. Landry et al. (1993) conceive of 'impact' as a dynamic concept, which assumes a relationship of cause and effect. Impacts can be measured by evaluating the outcomes of particular actions, policies or strategies.

Most models of impact measurement consist of four basic elements: inputs, outputs, impacts and outcomes. Inputs are the resources needed to stage an event programme – including staff time, facilities, equipment and materials. Outputs cover the services or experiences that the event programme produced, usually described in quantitative terms such as tickets sold, number of performances or visitor numbers. Impacts or outcomes are the effect of the event outputs, such as changes in image, behaviour or attitude. Outcomes are usually linked to the mission of the event or city (Figure 9.1).

As the SQW (2006b:16) report on evaluating festivals and events in the North East of England notes:

> *Outcomes can relate to an individual event or at*
> *a programme level. They include, for example, Gross*

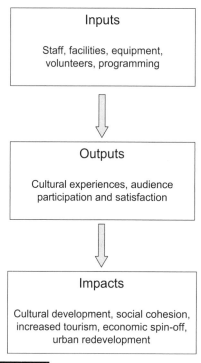

FIGURE 9.1 *Elements of impact measurement.*

Value Added generated in the cultural sector and through visitor expenditure, participation and volunteering by different groups, training opportunities, satisfaction with cultural provision, contribution to education, maintaining heritage and traditions, media coverage and value. These outcomes represent a step between the immediate outputs of events and the higher level, longer-term objectives of the strategies.

Outcomes are also the most difficult to measure. While outputs can usually be readily monitored and high level outcomes are likely to require both the use of new primary research and the application of evidence from other research sources.

Outcomes can be viewed in terms of the value they produce; not only economic value, but also cultural and social value. The inability of economic approaches to estimate the 'true value' produced by different policies and programmes helped to stimulate the idea of assessing their 'public value'. Moore's (1995) concept of public value includes the policy environment of programmes (mission and vision), the authorising environment (legitimacy and trust) and the operating environment (capacity and outcomes). Public value is not just produced by organisations or their programmes, but also by the consumer – public value is, in effect, what the public values. Applying similar arguments to the cultural sector, broadly defined, Holden (2004) argues that value can be conceived of in three ways:

- intrinsic value (subjective value of culture – intellectual, emotional, spiritual);

- instrumental value (culture for other ends – regeneration, image, social cohesion); and

- institutional value (the processes and values that organisations create when they interact with the public).

The value of culture and cultural events spans all of these elements. An event will often stimulate an intellectual or emotional reaction from the audience or participants, while at the same time generating economic activity.

Clearly, the impact measures adopted by the eventful city can be extremely varied, and should combine different aspects of 'value'. When deciding which performance measures to use for eventfulness, some basic criteria should be employed. These include:

- measurability (cities must be able to measure what they have achieved);

- consistency with organisational goals (measures must be linked to the aims of the eventful city);

- manageability (measures should relate to aspects of performance that are within the control of managers and not dependent on external factors, such as the weather);

- comparability (events should be compared year on year and against their competitors or colleagues in other cities);

- readability (all stakeholders should be able to interpret the measures); and

- capability of monitoring change (measures should be sensitive to changes taking place in the form or function of the event and its stakeholders).

For cities which are attempting to develop a coherent programme of events to produce specific outcomes, measurement needs to be made at the level of the total events programme, and not only in relation to single events. As SQW (2006b:46) argue: 'many of the outcomes of [a cultural programme] will only be apparent over time and will result from a number of events rather than just one. In other words, attempting to measure outcomes by aggregating the results of individual events could underestimate the impact of the overall programme.' Although it may be possible to estimate some impacts, such as visitor expenditure, by adding together the results of individual events, other outcomes, such as the development of cultural networks and the stimulation of cultural participation and production, will only be evident through longer-term evaluation of an entire events programme. The choice of measurement levels will also depend to a large extent on the interests of different stakeholders. Events funded by national or regional government may need to gather information about the impacts on other parts of the region or country. Where the intention is to evaluate an events programme as a whole, a careful selection will need to be made of events to analyse in order to reflect the diversity of events in the programme (Richards et al., 2002).

There may be potential conflicts of interest between individual event managers and event programme managers where evaluation is concerned. Managers and funders of event programmes generally have a greater interest in evaluation than the organisers of individual events within the programme. In many cases, evaluation is imposed from above (often by making the evaluation a condition of funding) in order to ensure that outcomes are measured. This has been the case for the ECOC (European Capital of Culture), which adopted broad evaluation procedures stipulated by the European Commission as a result of the recommendations of the Palmer Report (Palmer-Rae, 2004). Before this, very few of the ECOCs had carried out any serious evaluation.

The timing of assessment is important. Clearly, the major impacts of an event or events programme are likely to be most visible during the event itself, and this is the point at which information is fresh and most easy to gather. However, the short duration of most events often makes it difficult to gather all the information required during the event itself, and large elements of assessment are usually carried out post event. Similarly, much information will be needed prior to an event, for example an assessment of event feasibility or likely impacts, which will help potential funders make decisions about which elements of the event programme to support.

According to the Victorian Auditor General (2007), there are three major phases to the events assessment cycle:

- pre-event assessment;

- funding management; and

- post-event assessment.

Each of these phases has its own aims and objectives and is designed to produce information to support different management and decision-making tasks.

Although the different impacts and outcomes of cultural events offer the most compelling arguments for staging events, measuring and evaluating those impacts is far from easy. As Matarasso (1996a) states, 'evaluation is the process of calculating worth'. The problem is that the worth of the various outputs and impacts of events can be valued in different ways. Commercial sponsors may focus on visitor numbers that relate to their target markets, and media coverage that enhances their own image, while the education services may be more concerned with the involvement of children. This complexity leads cities to utilise a number of key indicators, several of which may concentrate on economic impact. The reason for this is twofold: if events are supported financially by public bodies, a measurement of economic benefits or returns helps to justify the investment, and economic benefits are often the easiest to measure. However, the selection of indicators should not rest solely on what is easy to measure, but should also address the wider, intangible benefits of city events.

In recent years there has been a significant movement towards the development of a broader range of indicators of success for events. The most widely-used approach is the 'triple bottom line' model, which adds social and cultural dimensions to economic impact indicators (see below). The problems in measuring the cultural, social and other less tangible impacts deter many event organisers from evaluating them, except through the qualitative use of anecdotes and stories. As Matarasso (1996a) has argued, new approaches to evaluation need to be developed which reflect the cooperative and creative nature of cultural endeavour. He suggests that there are five essential stages in evaluating cultural programmes:

- **Planning** – meet with stakeholders and identify what the project is trying to achieve (mission and objectives).

- **Performance indicators** – how you know when your objectives have been met.

- **Execution** – very often changes can be introduced at this stage as well, reflecting the need for flexible assessment models.

- **Assessment** – during the event, the management systems and processes in place to run the event could be closely monitored to record any problems emerging and improve the event experience for all involved. This is especially important for recurrent events, where constant improvement in event management needs to be supported by detailed process evaluations.

- **Reporting** – involve stakeholders and make this last phase the first step in the next edition of the programme or event.

Although this gives a useful overall framework for assessment, a wide range of quantitative and qualitative assessment tools need to be employed in order to generate the specific information required. This requires a holistic approach to measurement, which can capture the wide range of cultural, economic and social impacts of events.

The following sections consider some of the most common methods used in event impact assessment and how these can be applied to the eventful city.

Triple bottom line assessment for the eventful city

The basic concept of the triple bottom line model comes from general work on sustainability, which argues that to be sustainable, an organisation needs to consider all its potential impacts on its environment that cover Planet (environmental), People (socio-cultural) and Profits (economic) aspects of its operations. This approach has its origins in the 1992 United Nations Agenda 21 (United Nations, 1992). Elkington (1998) argues that, at its broadest, the triple bottom line refers to the entire set of values, issues and processes that organisations must address in order to minimise any harm resulting from their activities and to create economic, social and environmental value. There has been considerable work on the development of triple bottom line methodologies, but there is currently no uniform agreed approach to the model (Hede, 2008; Fredline et al., 2005).

The triple bottom line has more recently been extended to cover a number of new dimensions, including 'governance' and 'culture', which has led some authors to start talking about the 'quadruple' bottom line, which adds a fourth component of corporate governance to the environmental, social and goals of the triple bottom line.

Although the outcomes of a programme of events can only be judged effectively against its specific objectives, there are a number of key areas that often feature as quadruple bottom line indicators in any eventful city. These include economic impact in terms of job creation and income, cultural impacts such as increased participation, social goals including community cohesion and combating social exclusion and environmental aspects of events, such as the reduction of waste and noise pollution.

However, in the specific case of the eventful city, one of the important outcomes of a programme of events is increased capacity to develop eventfulness in order to meet wider goals. This is effectively an improvement in the 'orgware' (organisational software) of the city in relation to events, referring not only to the development of facilities and organisational capacity, but also to the 'learning capability' within a city that will lead to more effective growth and development of eventfulness. This adds a fifth capacity-building dimension to the model (Table 9.1), which reflects the ability of a city to organise, learn from and innovate events. This 'quintuple bottom line' model for the eventful city therefore also includes the continuing proactive development of events.

The capacity to stage events (orgware, systems, know-how, skills, timely delivery, planning and programming) adds an essentially creative aspect, which extends the ability of the city to stage more and better events, and hopefully to achieve greater impacts and improved outcomes in the future. This dimension of the quintuple bottom line model can be equated to the learning and growth perspective, which forms part of the balanced scorecard approach.

Balanced scorecard

The balanced scorecard approach is widely used in the general management sphere, but still not widely applied to events. The balanced scorecard model has been developed on the basis of management theory, including total quality management (TQM), empowerment and continuous improvement.

Kaplan and Norton (1992:72) describe the balanced scorecard as follows:

> The balanced scorecard retains traditional financial measures. But financial measures tell the story of past events, an adequate story for industrial age companies for which investments in long-term capabilities and customer relationships were not critical for success. These financial measures are inadequate, however, for guiding and evaluating the journey that information age companies must make to create future value

Table 9.1 The Quintuple Bottom Line Assessment Model for the Eventful City

Event capacity building aspects	Socio-cultural aspects	Environmental aspects	Governance	Economic aspects
Events leadership and governance	Resident attitudes towards the city	Minimising environmental footprint of events	Representation of stakeholders in decision-making bodies	Expenditure on events
Event management systems	Quality of life improvements	Appropriate use of public space	Responsiveness of governance structures to stakeholder needs	Visitor numbers
Event organisation skills and know-how	Participation level of population as a whole and of minority groups	Minimising noise pollution, litter	Independence of governance structures	Job creation
Ability to deliver planned events on time	Social inclusion	Events contribute to environmental awareness	Building creativity in events policy	Levels of media coverage
Effective event planning	Increased cultural production	Use of public transport		City image locally/nationally/globally
Effectiveness of risk management	Development of external cultural links	Event security		Development of external business links
Willingness of residents to volunteer for events	Involvement of local businesses, schools, etc.	Quality of public space		Sponsorship
Programming quality	Enjoyment of events	Event accessibility		Maximising event expenditure with local suppliers
	Feeling that events are worthwhile			Visitor spending
	Feeling that events contribute to the local community			Ticket prices, distribution
	Involvement of local cultural sector			Ticket revenue
	Awareness of events Education and training			Brand recognition

		Table 9.2 A Balanced Scorecard for the Eventful City	
Financial perspective	**Learning and growth perspective**	**Business process perspective**	**Customer perspective**
Expenditure	Human resources	Orgware	Visitor satisfaction
Visitor spending	Skill development	Quality systems	Quality of experience
Image impacts	Organisational capacity	Financial systems	Value for money
Cost per participant		Safety procedures	Intention to return
Cost per resident			

through investment in customers, suppliers, employees, processes, technology and innovation.

The balanced scorecard views an organisation from four perspectives:

- the learning and growth perspective;
- the business process perspective;
- the customer perspective; and
- the financial perspective.

The balanced scorecard examines outcomes from the perspective of different stakeholders in the organisation, city or event (Table 9.2). Various perspectives can be useful to convince different stakeholders to get involved or to continue their support. The approach attempts to answer the basic question that stakeholders often ask, namely 'What are the advantages for us?' In essence, the model focuses on the outcomes; rather than on different types of individual impacts; it views the integrated and collected mix of outcomes required by different stakeholders.

Impacts 08 – The Liverpool Model

Liverpool, the European Capital of Culture for 2008, set about creating a holistic system for monitoring the economic, social and cultural impacts of the event. The aim was 'to develop an exemplary, longitudinal "Liverpool Model" for cultural impact assessment that will measure and analyse the socio-economic and cultural impacts of

Continued

Liverpool European Capital of Culture (ECOC) 2008.' The model incorporates qualitative, quantitative, primary and secondary data collection and analysis. As a first step, a baseline study was conducted for the years 2000–2006 in order to provide a benchmark against which to measure performance in 2008 and later years (Impacts 08, 2007). This initial study included data on the economic performance of the city, tourism volume and expenditure, conference business, the number of cultural events and cultural participation.

The Impacts 08 research programme had a total budget of around £1 million (€1.25 million) to:

- Provide monitoring and longitudinal impact analysis of Liverpool ECoC cultural programmes and events, both retrospectively, to cover the impact of the bid itself, and up to 2009/10.

- Provide intelligence to guide decision-making within the Liverpool ECoC cultural programme and marketing strategy.

- Grow the evidence base for the impact of culture upon regeneration and city renaissance, to inform the UK national debate, influence funding decisions and assist regional cultural planning.

- Provide a replicable model that will add to the legacy of the Liverpool ECoC, for example informing future European Capitals of Culture and the London 2012 Olympic Games.

http://www.liverpool.ac.uk/impacts08/

Benchmarking

The benchmarking method, also adopted in Liverpool, measures performance over time or against that of comparable cities or events. This was one of the techniques used by Palmer-Rae (2004) to assess the impact of the ECOC in different cities. Benchmarking was also used by the Melbourne Commonwealth Games (2006) to compare its performance relative to the previous Games in Manchester (2002).

One extensive benchmarking exercise relating to an eventful city was carried out by the city of Edinburgh in evaluating its festival strategy (AEA Consulting, 2006). In view of the international status of Edinburgh's main festivals, the competitor festival cities that Edinburgh chose to benchmark itself against were also spread around the globe: Amsterdam,

Barcelona, Manchester, Melbourne, Montreal, Newcastle/ Gateshead, San Francisco and Singapore. The cities were compared in terms of:

- general population and other demographic data;
- quality of life data;
- innovation status;
- size and scope of cultural budgets;
- transportation infrastructure; and
- tourism data.

This study concluded that 'when viewed against the sustained development of some of the actively competitive cities over a time span of the next 5 to 7 years, Edinburgh's current enviable position as a preeminent festival city is vulnerable' (ibid:8). Although Edinburgh remains strong as an eventful city when viewed on its own, the massive investments being made by its global competitors had the potential of undermining its position as one of the world's leading festival cities. The study recommended that in order to maintain its position, Edinburgh needed to develop a long-term festival strategy, including increased funding for cultural development initiatives to ensure that world class performances continue to be attracted to the city, and for to enhance audience-building and marketing.

Although it is important to adopt a holistic approach to measuring the outcomes of the eventful city, an overall assessment of impacts depends on measuring each of the different elements described in the models. The basic measurement tools relate to each of the basic impact areas: economic, cultural, social and environmental elements, although as suggested above, the eventful city may also wish to add other indicators that relate to governance and event development capacity.

ECONOMIC IMPACTS

Measuring economic impact of events is a major priority for most cities. The growing cost of staging events increases the pressure to demonstrate positive economic impacts, which has led to a growth of economic impact studies of events. Although many of these studies have concentrated on relatively large events, such as the Olympic Games or the ECOC, smaller, local events have also been subject to studies that help evaluate direct impact on the local economy.

In general, there are three elements of economic impact, which can be estimated for events:

First, the *direct expenses*, or the costs of staging the event (wages, purchases, rental costs); second, the *indirect effects*, or expenditure by participants (accommodation, meals, transport, shopping, admission charges); and third, the *induced effects*, which are indirectly stimulated by the event, such as a general increase in the level of wages in the city. The propensity of direct expenditure to generate indirect and induced economic activity is usually referred to as the multiplier effect. The direct expenses of organising an events programme are relatively easy to measure. However, the indirect and induced elements usually account for a large proportion of the total economic impact, but are the most difficult to measure.

The Victoria Major Events Analysis (Victorian Auditor General, 2007:36–37) argues that there are two basic approaches to estimating the economic value of events:

- Cost benefit analysis (CBA):
  CBA relates the costs of staging an event to the derived economic benefits. This is particularly useful in guiding policy makers on which events should be staged or funded.

- Economic modeling involving computable general equilibrium and input-output approaches:
  Input-output (IO) models relate expansion in output in one industry to the knock-on effects in other industries in order to estimate the total expansion in production, employment and income. National and regional IO tables are used to calculate output, employment and income multipliers.

The main difference between the two methods is that cost-benefit analysis provides a picture of the net value of an event, but not its wider impact on the economy, whereas IO measures the wider economic impacts, but should not be used to decide whether an event should be staged or not. In effect, this argues for the use of both methods – CBA as a pre-event assessment to make decisions on event staging and IO analysis post-event to assess the wider economic impacts.

Examples of economic impact studies

Most economic impact studies relate to individual events, rather than the totality of event programming in a city. Although the methodologies used for measuring the impact of an entire city event programme or an individual event are essentially the same, covering all of the different types of events contained within an entire city events programme is clearly a more complex exercise. However, comprehensive analysis will offer a more accurate reflection of the effectiveness of policies and strategies to develop eventfulness.

A study of 12 festivals across the East Midlands region of the UK was made by Maughan and Bianchini (2003). They found that the festivals generated a total turnover of £1 million (€1.5 million), of which 50% was spent on artists' fees. Visitors to the festivals spent £7 million (€10.5 million) at shops and other local businesses, which in turn generated a further £4 million (€6 million) in induced spending. They also found that 33% of local businesses agreed that festivals attracted new business, and 93% believed that the festivals were beneficial in economic terms for local communities.

A study carried out in Quebec, Canada, indicated how the economic impacts of event programmes in a city can change over time. Comparing 11 events held in 1999 with the same events in 2001, this study indicated that the total visitor spending at these events had generated 13% more job creation, had stimulated 23% more income (with a total of over CA$250 million - €175 million) and 17% more tax revenue for the government. By 2004, the 21 events being studied in the city were generating a total of CA$471 million (€332 million) from almost 13 million visitors, of whom 28% came from outside the city. The 2004 revenues were estimated to have generated a total of 2226 jobs and fiscal revenues of over CA$10 million (€7 million) for the government. Between 2001 and 2004, visitors to the same 18 festivals had contributed 25% more expenditure and 40% more employment to the city (CFM Strategie, 2005). The improved results were due to the city recognising additional ways to increase impact, and taking practical steps to extend the economic and employment benefits of eventfulness.

The city of Chester in the UK carried out economic evaluation studies of its festival programme in 2004 and 2008 (The Edge Network, 2004; Arts About Manchester, 2008). The 2004 study covered 5 events, which sold a total of around 29,000 tickets, and which generated almost £700,000 (€1 million) in turnover for the organisers. When direct and indirect impacts of visitor spending in the city were added, the total estimated economic impact was calculated to be £1,477,000 (€2.1 million). This expenditure was estimated to support the equivalent of 49 full-time jobs in the city. The 2008 study covered 5 festivals attracting a total of almost 40,000 visits (estimated from surveys rather than ticket sales). The total economic impact (including multiplier effects) of these visits was estimated to be around £2 million (€2.9 million). In both studies, the greatest economic impact was generated by the Chester Miracle Plays, which are only held once every 5 years. In 2008, the Miracle Plays accounted for almost half the total impact, mainly due to the large number of tourists attracted to the event. A rise in attendance from under 10,000 in 2003 to 16,000 in 2008 helped increase the total impact of this event by over 90% between 2003 and 2008.

The 2005 Culture10 Programme, staged in the North East region of England, included 91 events that attracted funding of a total of £9.4 million (€14 million). It was estimated that these events generated a net increase of 263,000 visitors from outside the area and around £24 million (€36 million) of expenditure. This represents an increase of almost 3% in visitors to the region and the expenditure of

£24 million would represent 2.4% of the annual total visitor spending (SQW 2006:36).

Manchester supports a programme of 'pillar events' that attract over half a million visitors a year (Table 9.3). The total economic impact of these events in terms of visitor spending was estimated to be almost £50 million (€71.5 million) in 2006, compared with a local authority total subsidy of £205,000 (€293,000) (Jura Consultants, 2006).

In the Caribbean, Nurse (2003) has demonstrated that festivals have a significant economic impact. In 1998, for example, the Trinidad carnival accounted for 9.2% of arrivals and 7.6% of visitor expenditures for the year. During carnival time, hotel occupancy rates reach 95%, and departure taxes from carnival participants alone generated US$500,000 (€700,000). When value-added taxes (15%) are also considered, the government earns US$2.1 million (€2.9 million) in indirect taxes from the event. Where events are organised in the low tourist season, impacts can be even more significant. The Reggae Sunsplash event in Montego, Jamaica, raises average hotel occupancy figures by 14% during the winter season.

Table 9.3 Economic Impact of Pillar Events in Manchester, 2005

	Total costs £	Manchester city council subsidy £	Visitor spending £
Manchester Pride	565,000	20,000	7,322,831
Manchester Food and Drink Festival	113,000	30,000	23,886,035
Starbucks Manchester Jazz Festival	119,000	30,000	2,411,495
Manchester 'Smile' Comedy Festival	67,500	30,000	4,866,894
D. Percussion	127,000	30,000	3,976,324
Garden of Delights	276,000	50,000	7,114,417
Manchester Poetry Festival	51,000	15,000	309,378
Total	1,318,500	205,000	49,887,374

It is also common for economic impact to be expressed in terms of employment, since this is often an objective of event development. For example, studies show that the employment impact of the main Edinburgh festivals grew by over 70% between 1990 and 1996, and by a further 43% between 1996 and 2005 (mainly through extension of the festival programme into the winter period – see Table 9.4). It was clear that the three largest festivals in Edinburgh created the bulk of employment impact. However, the role of the other Edinburgh events in the portfolio could not be ignored, particularly in terms of the other non-economic 'bottom lines' that measure other forms of impact. For example, although the Edinburgh Film Festival attracted fewer visitors

Table 9.4	Estimates of Full Time Equivalent (FTE) Jobs Created by the Edinburgh Festivals (i.e. Direct and Indirect Employment)		
	1990	**1996**	**2005**
Edinburgh International Festival	221	575	375
Edinburgh Tattoo	626	423	452
Fringe Festival	332	883	1382
Book Festival	59	112	65
Children's Festival	0	5	5
Film Festival	14	122	42
Jazz Festival	38	107	53
Science Festival	22	24	23
Edinburgh Mela			16
Festival Cavalcade			70
TV Festival			10
International Games Festival			18
Storytelling Festival			4
Capital Christmas			196
Edinburgh's Hogmanay			439
Easter Festival			74
Ceilidh Culture			23
Children's International Theatre Festival			5
Total	**1312**	**2251**	**3252**

Source: Graham Devlin Associates, 2001; SQW/TNS, 2005.

and therefore created fewer jobs directly, it had other important impacts, such as image enhancement and attracting significant national and international media coverage for Edinburgh.

The Carnaval de Barranquilla is one of the leading cultural events in Colombia and has been declared as part of the Intangible Heritage of Humanity by UNESCO. In 2005, this 4-day event generated 13,908 million pesos (€4.37 million). This was an increase of almost 40% compared with 2003. This activity represented 0.13% of the GDP of the Atlantic region of Colombia. As in the rest of the Colombian economy, a significant proportion of the economic activity and employment generated by the Carnaval was accounted for by the informal sector. Informal labour accounted for almost two thirds of the Carnaval workforce in 2005, and there was a substantial growth in informal jobs from just over 6000 in 2001 to 9660 in 2005. Around half of those working during the Carnaval were normally unemployed (Fundesarrollo, 2005).

Temporary Public Art as Cultural Event

'The Gates, Central Park, New York City, 1979–2005', a temporary work of art by New York artists Christo and Jeanne-Claude, consisted of 7500 gates bearing hanging saffron-colored fabric panels, lining 23 miles of pedestrian paths in Central Park. The 2-week event attracted over 4 million visitors to Central Park and generated an estimated $254 million (€200 million) in economic activity in February 2004. The event not only stimulated many more visitors to Central Park (over five times the normal flow for February), but also helped to generate interest in culture across the city.

Many cultural organisations around the city experienced a surge in attendance, in particular those located along Museum Mile on the edge of Central Park. The Cooper-Hewitt National Design Museum reported a 298% increase in attendance compared to the same period in 2003. The Metropolitan Museum of Art reported a 90% rise in attendance. Cultural organisations in other parts of the city also reported similar attendance growth. In the cultural district of Long

Continued

Island City, the PS 1 Contemporary Art Center reported a 100% increase in attendance and the Noguchi Museum reported 170% more visitors. Broadway theatres experienced a 17% increase in average ticket sales per show during the first week of The Gates compared with the same period in 2003.

The event had considerable tourism impacts. More than 1.5 million tourists saw The Gates, an estimated 300,000 of whom were international visitors. Usually 13% of New York tourists are foreign visitors, but during the Gates, the international share increased to almost 20%. In 2003, Midtown Manhattan hotels reported occupancy rates of 73.6%, but in February 2004, these hotels reported average occupancy rates of 86.9% with higher room rates. During weekends of The Gates, the occupancy rates were well over 90%.

Christo and Jeanne-Claude financed the entire cost of The Gates, and did not accept any forms of sponsorship. The artists, who do not use volunteer support, provided paid employment for 1100 workers – including nearly 700 New York City residents – for the assembly, installation, maintenance, security and removal of the work of art. They also donated $3 million (€2.1 million) to the city for projects in New York parks.

www.nyc.gov/gates

Problems of measuring economic impact

Measuring the economic impact of events is frequently difficult because of the short time available for data collection at most events, and the problem of calculating the proportion of economic activity that has been generated specifically by the event. In most cases, a great deal of the total expenditure will be accounted for by money that may have been spent in the local economy anyway, for example, by visitors making a choice to attend one event rather than another in the same city, or local residents deciding to visit a local festival rather than attend the local cinema, or to purchase tickets for a performance instead of going to a restaurant that week. This means that economic impact assessment must also take into account factors such as *displacement, substitution and deadweight.* Displacement is the degree to which the outputs of the project have occurred at the expense of outputs elsewhere in the target area. Substitution arises where one activity is simply replaced by a similar one (such as recruiting a person for an event while another employee loses a job in another industry). Deadweight assesses event outputs which would have occurred anyway, whether the event had taken place or not.

Because of the widespread use of economic multipliers in economic impact studies, another problem is the calculation of induced impact that expenditure by the event organisers and visitors will have on the wider economy. The induced impact of event programmes is usually estimated by using an economic multiplier that evaluates further economic activity associated with additional local income and local supplier purchases generated by events.

A review of multiplier values used in a wide range of different event studies in the UK indicated that the mean value used was just over 1.8, although the modal (or most common value) was 1.5. In many cases, detailed multiplier studies of events or event programmes are lacking, and so values are therefore 'borrowed' from events in other cities or regions. This can then result in considerable distortion of the results, due to the wide variation in values because of differences in the structures of the different local economies. (SQW, 2006b). Multiplier figures may be adjusted after surveying local businesses to identify more precisely how much event expenditure remains in the local economy and how much is lost through 'leakage'. In the case of South Africa, for example, Saayman and Saayman (2006) found that the sales multipliers for visitor expenditure at arts festivals varied between 1.15 and 1.52, with larger towns having lower levels of leakage because of their larger economies. Using this multiplier, they estimated that the total visitor spending in 2003 was SAR33.8 million (€4.2 million), of which SAR27.6 million was retained in the local economy. After applying the sales multiplier of 1.15, this indicated a total impact of arts festivals on the local economy of SAR33.7 million.

A good illustration of the problems of estimating economic impact can be found in the estimates of the impact of the different ECOCs, which was an issue dealt with in the Palmer-Rae study (2004). A number of ECOCs have carried out economic impact assessments, but the methodology of the studies has often been very different. This can produce widely differing estimates of economic impact, even when the event is held in similar sized cities and attracts a comparable number of visitors.

If one compares Rotterdam (2001) and Salamanca (2002), for example, although the attendance in Salamanca in 2002 was slightly less than in Rotterdam, the total visitor spending was estimated to be over twice as high. Part of this difference can be explained by the fact that Salamanca is much more isolated geographically than Rotterdam, and therefore tends to attract a higher proportion of staying visitors. Most of the difference, however, can be attributed to the different assumptions made in each study.

In Salamanca, a thorough study was made of all expenditures relating to the 2002 event using IO methodology, including organisational costs and investment in infrastructure (Herrero et al., 2007). The total programme cost was estimated at almost €121 million, which when a construction sector multiplier was applied, gave a total economic impact on the Spanish economy of almost €250 million. When this was added to the estimated visitor expenditures in Salamanca (€278 million out of the total spending of €368 million) multiplied with a service sector multiplier (total €434 million), it indicated a total economic impact in Spain for the 2002 event of €682 million (Figure 9.2).

These IO model figures look very different from the CBA estimates made for the Rotterdam event by Richards et al. (2002). In Rotterdam, total visitor spending was estimated at €165 million, of which only 8% or €17 million was additional spending by people travelling specifically for the ECOC. These divergent estimates of economic impacts between these two studies were largely a result of differing assumptions and different methodologies. In Salamanca, all costs were included as economic impacts and subjected to an economic multiplier. Expenditures by residents (who comprised almost 60% of visitors) were also included, even though resident expenditures are usually considered to be a displacement of expenditures rather than an impulse to the local economy. The Salamanca study also treated the visitor

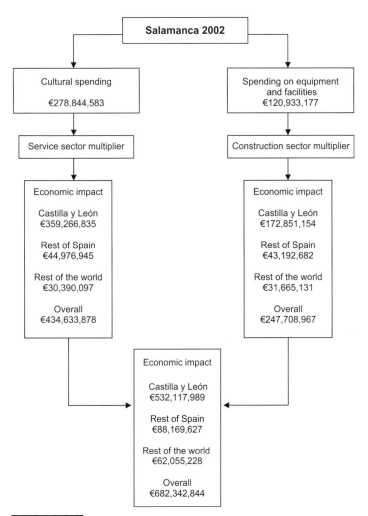

FIGURE 9.2 *Economic impact of the ECOC in Salamanca, 2002 (Herrero et al., 2007).*

expenditures and the costs incurred in staging the event as part of the total economic impact, rather than separating costs and income.

In Rotterdam, the CBA approach concentrated on those elements of visitor expenditures that could clearly be identified as directly related to the event and contributing to the local economy. Expenditures by local residents and travel expenditures by visitors were therefore excluded. The organisational and infrastructure costs of the event were treated as costs to be set against the income generated by visitors. These very different assumptions produced a visitor impact directly attributable to the event of €17 million, compared with the estimate of a total economic impact of €682 million for Salamanca.

These two studies show the considerable influence that differing assumptions can have on economic impact studies, and the problem of comparing results. If the Salamanca figures are recalculated using the same assumptions as those made in Rotterdam, then the total figure for visitor impact would be about €37.5 million, around 5% of the estimate produced by Herrero et al. (2007). However, as Table 9.5 indicates, this is still considered a relatively large economic impact compared with other ECOC.

These case studies underline the importance of relating impact studies very closely to the aim of the event. The methodology and assumptions adopted should be designed to reflect the objectives set, so that the success of the event in meeting these objectives can be assessed. One of the

Table 9.5   Visits and Visitor Expenditures to Selected ECOCs 1995–2008

	Visits (million)	Total visitor spending (€ million)	Total additional visitor spending (€ million)	Additional visitor spending directly attributable to the ECOC (€ million)
Luxembourg (1995)	1.1			14
Avignon (2000)	1.5	45		
Bologna (2000)		63		
Rotterdam (2001)	2.3	165	73	17
Porto (2001)	1.2		69	23
Salamanca (2002)	1.9	368	180	
Brugge (2002)	1.6	213	41	10
Graz (2003)	2.7		116	21
Luxembourg Region (2007)	3.3			56
Sibiu (2007)	1.0	64.5		25
Liverpool (2008)	15.0		211	

Source: Estimates based on figures from visitor surveys and city reports.

problems encountered by the ECOC, as identified in the Palmer-Rae report (2004), is that the economic impact studies (and other impact studies) were generally added as an afterthought. This makes it difficult to design and conduct research that fully reflects performance.

CULTURAL IMPACTS

In spite of the problems associated with measuring economic impact, the difficulties of estimating less tangible impacts, such as cultural and social consequences, are even more complex. There have been a number of attempts to measure cultural impacts of the ECOC, using indicators such as:

- levels of cultural participation (e.g. audience and visitor figures);

- collaboration between cultural organisations (e.g. via interviews with cultural organisations);

- levels of cultural production (e.g. number of cultural enterprises or entrepreneurs);

- changes in cultural funding (e.g. public funding, levels of sponsorship); and

- number of new creations (new plays, musical compositions, published books).

Cultural participation and collaboration

The most readily available indicators usually relate to cultural participation. Most cities regularly collect visitor numbers for cultural attractions and events, and so longitudinal comparisons can be made. These data have been collected for a number of the ECOC events, and they indicate that the ECOC has in most cases boosted cultural audiences quite significantly when compared to previous years (Table 9.6).

The increase in visitors noted at most ECOCs was not always evenly spread across all the events. In general, museum events attracted more visitors than the

Table 9.6	Increase in Cultural Visits During Selected ECOCs	
	Museum/exhibitions	**Performances**
Glasgow 1990	+40%	
Dublin 1991	+72%	+31%
Madrid 1992	+10%	+21%
Antwerp 1993	+87%	+2%
Lisbon 1994	+50%	
Luxembourg 1995	+50%	+45%
Copenhagen 1996	+13%	
Weimar 1999	+110%	
Santiago 2000	−14%	
Bologna 2000	+17%	
Luxembourg Region 2007	+14%	
Liverpool 2008	+30%	

Source: Myerscough (1996), Palmer-Rae (2004), city reports.

performing arts and particular types of museums did better than others. In Bologna, for example, the largest increases for the year 2000 were recorded at the Museo Morandi (which was established in the framework of the ECOC). In contrast, attendance at the archaeological museum fell.

One of the rationales for staging major cultural events is also the 'spin-off' effect that these have for other cultural attractions in the city. In Rotterdam in 2001, over 36% of ECOC visitors combined their trip with a visit to another permanent attraction and 49% also visited another ECOC event. In Sibiu in 2007, the proportion of multiple visits was even higher, with over 60% of visitors having attended another attraction (Table 9.7). This is related to the longer length of stay and distance travelled for the average tourist in Sibiu compared with Rotterdam. In both cities, however, it was clear that the majority of visitors combined a cultural event with a fixed cultural attraction, particularly museums and monuments.

Impact on the cultural sector

As well as stimulating more cultural consumption among residents and visitors, cultural events can also stimulate

Table 9.7	Attractions Visited in Sibiu by ECOC Visitors 2007 (Multiple Response)
Attraction	**Percentage of ECOC visitors**
Orthodox Cathedral	26.9
Bruckenthal Museum	26.9
Evangelic Church	24.9
The Lower Town	24.8
ASTRA Museum	20.0
The City Walls	19.2
Thalia Hall	14.1
National Theater Radu Stanca	13.3
Fortified Churches around Sibiu	12.2

Source: Richards and Rotariu (2007).

production in the cultural and creative sectors. As SQW (2006b) notes, cultural events will provide direct income to cultural producers, as well as act as a source of ideas, skills and opportunities. Impacts of events on the cultural sector are often measured using a narrow range of indicators, such as:

- the number of events (performances, exhibitions, etc.) that are commissioned;

- the number of artists/performers involved;

- the number of 'emerging artists' who participate; and

- the number of 'international' artists or performances.

Such measures do not take into account factors such as the impact on the audiences of the work that is seen, the positive influence of the event itself on the creative sector (such as generating new ideas or developing contacts and new collaborations), nor how such events stimulate the imagination of young people, which may have an effect on city creativity for many years. The ECOC in Glasgow (1990) was one of very few event programmes where such cultural impacts were evaluated through comprehensive interviews and surveys, which complemented the more quantitative measures used by the city. The conclusion was that the ECOC offered a dramatic engine and profound catalyst for the continuing creative and cultural development of the city (Garcia, 2005).

Glasgow also developed a unique approach to evaluating the cultural impacts of events and activities in the city, and compared these every 2 years (1990–1996), helping the city to improve its cultural performance. Unfortunately, the city stopped such measurement in 1997 when the city's strategy became preoccupied with issues connected with social impact, ignoring the importance of 'multiple' evaluation techniques, which certain political bodies find too complicated.

Festivals as Creative Breeding Grounds: The Grahamstown National Arts Festival, South Africa

The Grahamstown National Arts Festival (NAF) plays an important role in commissioning new works and exhibitions, helping to encourage South African arts. It delivers a large audience for established artists as well as offering unknown talent the opportunity for discovery. Established in 1966, the festival grew rapidly into a major arts event. In 2006 about 141,000 people attended the various events on offer from theatre to dance, music (including jazz), exhibitions, film and street theatre. As Saayman and Saayman (2006:574) note, 'For years, the NAF was the only major arts festival in South Africa where both new and existing artists had the chance to present their work, These festivals created the platform for the growth of arts in South Africa.' The NAF also stimulated the development of other arts festivals in the country. As well as delivering economic benefits, the festival acts as a breeding ground for new work. A growing trend is the emergence of 'collaborative' works that are examples of cultural synthesis. For example, the Studio Project was introduced in 1994 to create a platform for young and emerging artists from a disadvantaged background to perform at the festival.

The evaluation of the Culture10 event programme in the North East of England (SWQ, 2006a:45) posed the question whether the programme enhanced the 'quality' of cultural events in the region. The stakeholders interviewed were convinced it had 'definitely been instrumental in raising standards and profile' and that it has had a 'very strong influence in allowing partners to host events that are really of higher quality, with better recognised artists'. Working with established artists was also considered to have significant capacity-building benefits. When asked directly if Culture10's involvement enhanced the quality of cultural events in the region, the respondents scored this aspect at 7.1 on a 10-point scale. The report concluded that 'Almost unanimously, partners reported that Culture10 has increased confidence and enthusiasm in the cultural sector.'

However, in the case of the Cultural Olympiad organised for the Sydney Olympics in 2000, Garcia (2004:110) found that the cultural programme did little to bolster the cultural sector in the city:

> Local arts groups representing cultural minorities assert that the arts festivals failed to offer a vision of contemporary Australia and represent the real diversity of the city and country. Representatives from Carnivale, Sydney's multicultural arts festival, regretted the minimal funding provided during 1998 for the supposed celebration of Australia's migrant cultures. For the Carnivale Music Coordinator, 'rather than supporting new work, the festival relied on already existing initiatives and became a confusing mixture of activities without any clear focus or message.'

Garcia also found that low promotional spending meant that awareness of the event among the local population was low. This emphasises the need to link events to the local cultural sector in order to maximise cultural impacts.

Events can also act as springboards for other events. The Homeless World Cup was founded in 2001 at the Annual International Network of Street Papers Conference in Cape Town, and was staged for the first time as part of the ECOC in Graz in 2003. This event generated considerable global media coverage, and its success led to follow-up events being organised in Göteburg (2004), Edinburgh (2005), Cape Town (2006), Copenhagen (2007), Melbourne (2008) and Milan (2009). The Copenhagen event attracted over 500 players from around the world, and 4 cities vied for the honour of staging the event. The organisation of the event was initially based in Graz, but is now located in Edinburgh (which perhaps reflects the relative 'events organisation capital' of the two cities).

The Zinneke Parade in Brussels has been held every 2 years since the initial edition was launched at the ECOC in 2000, and which was managed directly by the ECOC organisers. The parade, which starts around the inner ring road of the city and then converges in the centre, views itself as a 'future urban ritual', bringing together the inhabitants of different districts to engage in participative creativity. Each group works on their own costumes and floats within the overall theme of the year, and the development of ideas and materials is devolved to a series of open workshops around the city. The 2008 edition attracted more than 2000 parade participants, boosting the creative capacity of the local community and providing support for local artists. The Zinneke Parade was one of 30 major projects stimulated by Brussels 2000 ECOC that has had a long-lasting cultural impact on the city itself.

International contacts that are offered by events can act as important drivers of cultural development. A city needs to build bridges to the outside world to enhance its economic and cultural prosperity. In the case of Graz ECOC (2003), for example, the city received 112 foreign delegations (and many more unofficial visits) from international public sector organisations and officials wanting to learn something about the city and the event. Interestingly, 31 of these delegations came from other ECOCs, particularly aspirants to the title in future years. However, there were also delegations from as far afield as Canada, China and Japan.

Events also help a city to establish itself on the international stage:

> Major events like the Commonwealth Games and Expo helped Brisbane to 'grow-up' from a country town to a city, which enjoys (and is proud of) its modern and sophisticated facilities and tourist attractions. They added that those two events had a huge impact on the local culture, generating new nightlife and providing opportunities for local people to experience other cultures.
>
> (Jago et al., 2002:133)

SOCIAL IMPACTS

In recent years there has been growing attention paid to the less tangible social impacts of cultural development. As Bayliss (2004:8) observes:

Since the late 1990s there have been signs that cultural policy has begun to turn away from narrow economic instrumentalism towards a renewed interest in the social impacts of training and participation in neighbourhood-based cultural activities…. Urban policies in general have adopted a new concern for social aspects of regeneration, marked by the reassertion of the importance of incorporating 'the community' into regeneration and the spread of a new language of social capital, community capacity and holistic approaches.

In the UK, it was Matarasso's (1996a) report on the social impact of arts participation that marked a significant change in the recognition of the social impacts of cultural programmes. The report highlighted the many different ways in which cultural participation can contribute to social development, including personal impacts (increased confidence, self-esteem, enhanced skills) and structural factors (such as better housing conditions or a more pleasant social atmosphere). Improvements in both of these areas can lead to increased social networking, employment and community involvement, which in turn lead to improved health and well-being, creating a better quality of life and civic pride.

The Palmer-Rae Report (2004) underlines the importance of the social impacts of events and devotes an entire chapter to its assessment. One of the main conclusions of the Palmer evaluation of the ECOC programmes was that social impacts are often more durable than cultural impacts because they tend to be rooted well locally and organised by committed individuals. Among the main social impacts noted by the report were:

- improved access to cultural projects and programmes;
- social programmes aimed at specific target groups;

- cultural inclusion of marginalised or excluded groups; and

- strengthening cultural and voluntary organisations.

There is a wide range of research techniques that can be applied to the assessment of social impacts, and these tend to be grouped into three broad categories:

- surveys of the perceptions of local residents of the quality of life impacts of an event;

- social impact assessments of the likely social consequences of an event; and

- techniques, such as contingency valuation, used to assign monetary values to social impacts.

The first set of techniques tends to be the most widely used. For example, Matassaro (1996b) investigated the social impact of Gaelic festivals (fèisean) in the Highlands and Islands of Scotland. He found that these festivals, in which the use of the Gaelic language plays an important role, have important impacts on personal and social development, community empowerment and identity. Surveys illustrated that over 90% of participants indicated that they had made new friends through these events and over 40% indicated an increased interest in community involvement. The social benefits of the festivals included increased confidence of participants in themselves, their communities and their culture and 87% reported feeling 'happier' after the event.

The attitudes of other stakeholders can also be used to assess social impacts. Gursoy et al. (2004) developed an instrument that utilised 12 indicators to measure the festival and special event organisers' perceptions of the impacts of festivals and special events on local communities. Their survey suggested that organisers believed that events contributed to community cohesiveness and created social incentives for the local community. The surveys also suggested that the festival and special event organisers concluded that festivals and special events created more social benefits than social costs, although a strict cost-benefit analysis was not carried out.

More complex assessments of social impacts can be made by combining different techniques to create a 'social audit'. An audit of the Belgrade Theatre in the West Midlands (UK) started by clarifying the theatre's objectives with its various stakeholders and then a structured review of how it was achieving them was undertaken through a series of questionnaires, interviews, discussion groups and data analysis (Matarasso & Pilling, 1999). The audit covered five broad themes for which indicators were developed:

- the theatre and the arts (e.g. number of performances, audience assessment);

- the theatre and the community (e.g. number of schools and community projects, audience profile);

- the theatre's partnerships (e.g. percentage of partners feeling actively involved);

- the theatre and the city (e.g. number of local trading partners); and

- the theatre's standards (e.g. staff assessment of the theatre as an employer).

The same approach could arguably be adopted at the level of the eventful city. However, as the SQW (2006a:29) report of the Culture 10 events programme in the North East of England notes, few events actually monitored their social impacts:

The main basis for assessing the social benefits is based on the attendance and participation of local residents and school children. There is little other information recorded by the events, and more would be needed to draw firm conclusions on the effectiveness of the programme in this area.

Resident Attitudes to Major Events – La Mercè in Barcelona

La Mercè is the major festival in the Catalan capital of Barcelona. In common with many other festivals, which now attract large international audiences, questions have begun to emerge about who the

Continued

festival is actually for, and to what extent the 'authenticity' of the event has been compromised by increasing scale. Recent studies (Richards, 2004; Crespi-Vallbona & Richards, 2007) indicated that local residents felt that there had been an increase in the number of events and an increased possibility to participate in La Mercè. There was also a strong feeling that the number of 'non-Catalan' elements in the programme had increased. Over 75% of the Catalan respondents indicated that La Mercè contributed towards social integration and over 60% said it had a positive effect on cross-cultural understanding. It was clear that local residents perceive that growing numbers of tourists are visiting the event every year. Over 85% agreed with the statement that 'more and more tourists visit La Mercè' and Catalan speakers were particularly likely to perceive a growth in tourism. In spite of this, there was little evidence of any negative attitudes towards tourists attending the event. Because of the strong sense of pride in the event and the opportunities, it gave to present their culture to outsiders, local residents were positive about tourism, particularly if they were directly involved in the event.

In order to maximise the social impact of events, community goals need to be built into the planning of the events with the development and implementation of a community involvement strategy.

In the Manchester Commonwealth Games, for example, the organisers stated that:

> The Commonwealth Games in Manchester will not only facilitate economic regeneration for the city but will also establish a cultural legacy from the Games. Manchester has large communities from other Commonwealth countries and the aim through the cultural programmes is to create awareness of these communities and promote understanding throughout the Commonwealth.

The cultural programme included:

■ education programmes established within schools to raise awareness and understanding of the various Commonwealth countries;

- environmental programmes, such as street dressing, during the period of the Spirit of Friendship Festival and on a long-term basis through public art commissions; and

- social and community development through cultural activities from within the Commonwealth communities which will increase mutual understanding of cultural diversity.

(Manchester 2002 Ltd, 2000).

These measures and long-term planning contributed to the high degree of local involvement in the Games, as well as the perception of the event being a success.

The Melbourne 2006 Commonwealth Games included an ambitious cultural programme, 'the biggest free cultural festival ever to be held in Australia' (Melbourne 2006, 2006:11) including 1200 performances with 2500 performers. The programme cost AU$12 million (€7.6 million) and attracted an estimated 2 million visitors. The core theme was community engagement, including a focus on indigenous culture. This was exemplified by the wide range of events offered, including the Human Momentum public art project, which involved the construction of a bamboo waterwheel of Chinese design, events for disabled people, and street theatre performances at sites around the games. The 'Art$athletes' programme also involved school-children creating artworks for the Athletes Village.

In contrast to many other large events, which tend to have a negative impact on recurrent cultural budgets (a complaint voiced about the 2012 London Olympics, for example), the organisers of the Melbourne Commonwealth Games Committee, which was responsible for the cultural programme, argued that the cultural programme added substantially to the image and local pride impacts of the Games, at a fairly small marginal cost compared to the sports programme.

Events as a means of developing sense of place

A sense of place and identity is vital to the success of events and events play a role in strengthening the identity of the places that generate them.

Events, which focus on local culture or tradition, are the most common means of achieving this, but questions of identity and sense of place can be answered by events in a number of different ways, for example by:

- building local pride;

- creative use of space; and

- integration and social cohesion.

A well-planned programme of events can help to create awareness of the local community and its identity. The Barcelona Olympic Games volunteer programme was an attempt to develop pride in the city as well as supplying labour for the games. The volunteers were seen as ambassadors who would interpret the city and its culture for participants and visitors (see Chapter 5).

Carlsen (2002) also illustrated the high degree of local pride in hosting international events in a study in Perth, Western Australia. His survey of 235 Perth residents indicated that most respondents (87%) felt a sense of community pride when Perth hosted international events.

Building Community Pride: The Goatmilk Festival in Bulgaria

The Goatmilk Festival has been held in the village of Gorna Bela Rechka in Northeast Bulgaria since 2004. The village has a population of 90 people and is located in one of the poorest regions in Bulgaria. The festival includes a combination of traditional intangible culture and new multimedia technologies, and has an accent on contemporary art forms.

The festival has considerable economic impacts, attracting investment to the village, creating local employment and developing tourism. Of the people who attended the festival, two bought new houses in the village. The local bar has expanded and takes on extra staff during the festival. Two long-term unemployed people were hired to reconstruct the building of the old school where festival events are held. The six people in the village who offer rooms for rent each earn between €40 and €60 during the festival, which is a considerable sum in rural Bulgaria.

> Alongside these important economic impacts, the festival also has a role in strengthening local identity, giving people pride in their village and creating atmosphere. In an environment dominated by economic hardship, out-migration and aging population, these are important developments.
>
> As Vulkovsky (2007:2) notes: 'most impressive is the impact of the festival at a personal level. The Festival changes the sense of the local people about their current way of life, it broadens their horizons, and it gives them opportunities to establish new friendships. It also stimulates their creativity, awakes their memories, makes them more confident and raises their self esteem.'

Creating social space

As Richards (2007b) has pointed out in the case of Barcelona, festivals can reclaim space in the city for community use. As noted in Chapter 2, major events have often been used to develop public spaces in the city. In Barcelona a number of new and recurring major events have been developed to create or regenerate public spaces, which also act as a way of helping to further integrate communities. In the inner city Raval district, festivals have become an essential element of social capital generation, aimed to promote inclusion. The events staged in the Raval are not tourist spectacles, but are clearly aimed at local people and, in particular, children. There is little sign of local resistance to the process of 'socialisation by fiesta', whereas the opposition to gentrification through property speculation (and particularly hotel construction) is clearly visible.

In Edinburgh, similar processes seem to be at work. In the report for the Edinburgh Festivals Strategy (Graham Devlin Associates, 2001:19) 'one interviewee - a senior member of Edinburgh's business community - observed that the unquantifiable benefits of the summer festivals included the fact that "they give a continental feel to the city", that they "make it an attractive place to work". He suggested that by attracting visitors to less-populated "dodgy" areas, they may even help make the city safer.' In other words, the staging of events is one way of maintaining a 'controlled edge' in areas of the city, which might otherwise be regarded as no-go areas for residents or visitors (Hannigan, 2007).

At the same time, however, events should be careful not to create new 'no-go areas' in the city. Howie (2000) described how the cordoning off of the city centre in Edinburgh for the Hogmanay (New Year) celebrations alienated many local residents. Although the event was free, residents still had to obtain tickets, which many felt to be a barrier to their free access to public space in the city centre. Since then, free access has been eliminated, and in 2008 residents were offered 10,000 passes priced at £5 (€5.50), while the remaining 90,000 tickets cost £10 per person.

Although there may be social costs as well as benefits associated with events, such impacts are rarely measured by event evaluation studies. A more holistic approach to social impact assessment should also examine problems of exclusion or displacement for the local population, the extent to which access to local facilities may be affected by events and the ways in which events may impact on the 'normal' cultural programming of the city for its residents.

URBAN REGENERATION

Cities often view large events as a means of transforming the city in physical, as well as economic, terms. This phenomenon has a long tradition, which includes the early World Expos in London (1851) and Paris (1889) and the German Garden Festivals organised in the aftermath of World War II to kick-start the regeneration of bombed cities. More recently, events such as the Barcelona Universal Forum of Cultures (2004) and the Lisbon Expo (1998) have been used to develop new areas of the city. Although the cost of regeneration may be high, the leverage obtained can be impressive. For example, the €327 million cost of the Barcelona Forum of Cultures event was balanced against attracting more than €3 billion of private investment to Barcelona in leisure and shopping facilities, hotels and housing. The creation of the Forum site also resulted in a vast public space, which was subsequently used for other events, and offered a new space for staging noisy events away from the city centre.

Glasgow 1990 was the first ECOC to specify urban regeneration objectives for the event. Now most ECOC include broad urban regeneration among its aims, such as Porto (2001), which aimed:

> To generate new cultural dynamics that would last beyond the cultural year, to increase participation in culture, to invest in cultural infrastructure and urban regeneration and promote economic development.
>
> (Palmer-Rae 2004: vol 2:202)

However, regeneration and other aims have sometimes clashed in the ECOC. The showpiece development of the Porto ECOC in 2001 was the Casa da Musica, a new concert hall designed by Rem Koolhaas. In addition, many parts of the old city were refurbished. However, as Balsas (2004:403–404) notes: 'the urban regeneration works did not benefit, but instead disturbed the fruition of the event, [and] did not secure audiences capable of portraying the image of a renovated and captivating city, as it was initially proposed.' The official assessment also revealed that the urban regeneration works in Porto cost €80 million, €16.6 million more than initially estimated, even though 14% of the works planned were not executed. However, Balsas (2004:408) concludes that '3 years after the event, the new streetscape and improved public spaces have made the city centre, to some extent, more inviting and pleasant, thus inducing new urban dynamics and liveability.'

Even where large-scale redevelopment is not a main aim of an event strategy, events can be used as a catalyst for changing the 'feel' or perception of the city and its fabric. This was arguably the case in the Brugge (Burges) ECOC (2002). Brugge in Flanders, Belgium is a historic city that has a World Heritage designation and which already attracts large numbers of visitors. However, as Boyko (2007) shows, the event still helped to develop the city. He found an interesting dynamic between the historic city and the limited number of new installations created for the event. These included Toyo Ito's Pavilion and two new modern bridges linking the medieval centre with the rest of the city.

Inevitably, there were divided opinions among local residents about the appropriateness of injecting contemporary architecture into an historic city centre. However, 'all organisers and approximately two thirds of residents believed the modern structures offered a new dynamic in the historic city. These residents felt that Brugge was more alive during the cultural year, and appearing more like a city that wanted to invest in its future.' Referring to Toyo Ito's work, one respondent stated:

> *The first time… I went to see it, I thought, 'Whoa! What happened here?' When you are going to it more times, I think it is fine. Now I can appreciate it. So it's already also the contrast between modern and historical. And it's impressive.*
>
> (Boyko, 2007:24)

Boyko identifies interesting synergies between old and new in the Brugge event. The 'old' helped to 'win' the event for the city, but the event then became a means of injecting contemporary culture into a landscape that many felt was becoming a vast 'open air museum'. The juxtaposition of old and new forced the residents to reconsider the historic image of the city.

> *For the cultural year, organisers challenged Brugge's historic identity and promoted modern elements in the form of striking new architecture and contemporary cultural events. Organisers hoped to create a meaningful dialogue with residents about how the past, present and future could be successfully integrated through modernity.*
>
> *A discussion about identity also occurred, relating to the impacts of modern elements on Brugge's image as an historic place.*
>
> (Boyko, 2007:23)

IMAGE IMPACTS

Events are increasingly recognised as a potential tool for image change by cities. In competing against other cities in global marketplaces, a positive city image is an invaluable resource. Not surprisingly, one of the major objectives of the cities hosting the ECOC was to raise the international profile of the city. Particularly in the case of cities such as Glasgow,

Rotterdam and Liverpool, which had an image based largely on their industrial past, one of the main aims of staging the ECOC was to introduce a counterbalancing 'cultural' image for the city, associated with modernity, cosmopolitanism and contemporary creation.

An Event Created Around Image – Helsinki 2000

One of Helsinki's ambitions for the ECOC in 2000 was to transform the image of the city from that of a distant, cold place into that of a vibrant cultural hub at the heart of European culture.

In the early 1990s Finland faced a serious economic crisis due to the globalising economy, the disintegration of the Soviet Union and an internal 'bank crisis'. Between 1991 and 1993 the country's GNP decreased by more than 10%. Helsinki therefore adopted more entrepreneurial development strategies, and place marketing was used as a tool for urban development. Cultural policy shifted from a Nordic model based on social and geographical equality towards a new role in constructing urban image, advancing tourism and strengthening the cultural industries.

In the early 1990s the city was encouraged to apply for ECOC status by emerging evidence of the economic impact of culture and a study by the British Consultancy Comedia in 1994, which indicated that the City of Culture was 'a vehicle for city marketing and therefore provides an opportunity to reassess the way Helsinki is marketed in every facet' (Landry and Kelly, 1994). The study argued that involvement in the ECOC bid would be a unique chance to market the city and build a positive image.

The research concluded that Helsinki had an 'image' problem. The characteristic image people had of Helsinki and Finland prior to visiting was of a dark, cold, desolated, slightly sad, empty and lonely place tinged with drunkenness. Movies by Kaurismäki or Jim Jarmuch's Night on Earth exacerbated this image. On the other hand, the image of Helsinki/Finland in the summer reflected Scandinavia in close association with Sweden's Ingmar Bergman – green countryside, lakes, water and midsummer light. However, to those few who knew the Total Balalaika Show, played by The Leningrad Cowboys (from Helsinki) and the Russian Red Army Orchestra, a lighter side of Finnish culture was revealed that contradicted their stereotypes and thus made Finland enticing, a place they wanted to know more about (Landry and Kelly, 1994).

Continued

Comedia suggested that policy-makers had to find ways of repositioning Helsinki in the eyes of foreigners. One recommendation was that Helsinki should learn from the example given by the 'Glasgow's Miles Better' campaign. Helsinki had a number of image elements that it did not want to use in its promotion. The image as a well-organised Nordic city was felt to be too boring. The close links between the city and nature clashes with the residents' perception of Helsinki as a new European metropolis.

The image finally chosen was Helsinki as a city of the future. This fitted the existing images of Helsinki as a relatively young city, and the role of the city as a centre of communications and new technology. (Heikkinen, 2000)

Measuring the actual impacts of image transformation related directly to events is very difficult. Myerscough's (1991) study of the 1990 Glasgow ECOC event briefly considered the image effects of the event. This research showed a more positive cultural image of the city developing in the run-up to the event and during the year itself. Dos Santos and da Costa (1999) examined the image impacts of the Lisbon 1998 Expo event and found that over three quarters of visitors considered that it had enhanced the international image of Lisbon and of Portugal as a whole.

The main means used by some ECOCs to establish the image impacts is visitor surveys, which usually present visitors with a preformulated list of image elements. For example, data collected by Myerscough in Luxembourg in 1995 indicated that established images of the city such as 'history and charm' (47%) were far more important images than the city being a 'cultural centre' (9%). Research conducted in Brugge (Bruges) in 2002 indicated that elements of cultural heritage such as 'like an open air museum' (47.5% of staying tourists) or 'traditional, old classic' (19.1%) dominated the visitor image of the city (WES, 2003). In the latter case, there was little evidence that Brugge had succeeded in adding a contemporary cultural element to the city image, as the ECOC had aimed to do. This was a source of conflict between the ECOC organisation and the tourism authorities, as the latter did not make use of the contemporary cultural images that were provided by the ECOC for marketing purposes. The tourism sector preferred to maintain the traditional, historic images of Brugge, perhaps believing that there were distinct advantages in reinforcing the expectations of the majority of visitors.

A study of perceptions of the Italian city of Genoa in the aftermath of its hosting of the 2004 ECOC indicated that two thirds of respondents agreed that the city had succeeded in changing its image (Demoskopea, 2005). The most frequent association with Genoa for those living outside remained that of a port city (45%), while 41% thought of Genoa primarily as a cultural city. The effects of image change were much more notable among local residents, 61% of whom linked Genoa with art and culture, compared with 34% retaining the 'old' image of a port city.

A problem with most of the image research conducted in ECOCs and other cities is that the data are rarely collected longitudinally. The regular surveys of cultural tourism in Europe by ATLAS provide one means of measuring image change over time (Richards and Wilson, 2004; Richards, 2007a).

The ECOCs held in Liverpool in 2008, Luxembourg Sibiu in 2007 and (Luxembourg and Greater Region, 2008; Richards and Rotariu, 2007) improved the international image of all three cities in the ECOC year. Liverpool had a steady rise in the strength of its cultural image, perhaps due to the strong marketing campaigns carried out prior to and during the event. However, the Romanian city of Sibiu arguably benefited more in image terms in the ECOC year, simply because before 2007 the city effectively had no image outside Romania. The element of surprise therefore helped to attract media attention to the 'new' destination, much to the dismay of some in the cultural sector in Luxembourg, who felt their Romanian partner ECOC had upstaged them in the international media in 2007. However, the surprise factor that helped Sibiu in 2007 appears not to have delivered a lasting image improvement post-ECOC for that city (Figure 9.3). Sustaining the image beyond a major event requires a comprehensive longer-term strategy; without this the 'halo effect' of a successful event can be easily eroded in a short time span (Table 9.8).

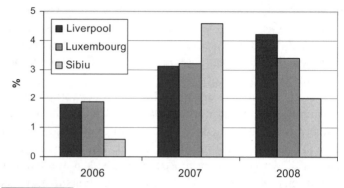

FIGURE 9.3 *Image of Liverpool, Luxembourg and Sibiu as cultural destinations in ATLAS surveys in Europe (Percentage of respondents ranking these cities among their top five cultural destinations). (Richards and Palmer, 2009).*

In spite of the problems of maintaining image impacts, the residents of Sibiu in Romania felt that the city had done a good job of projecting a new image (Table 9.8). Even two years after the event, almost all local residents felt that the ECOC in 2007 had improved the image of the city. More people agreed that the event had positive image impacts than felt that the ECOC had brought more tangible benefits, such as generating income or improving cultural facilities.

THE NEED FOR RIGOROUS MONITORING AND EVALUATION OF EVENT PROGRAMMES

Making realistic and honest assessments of event programme impacts is a challenge. It is common for the expectations of

Table 9.8	Attitudes of Local Residents in Sibiu to the Impact of the ECOC in 2007 (Percentage of Respondents)		
Do you agree that the ECOC in 2007…	**2007**	**2008**	**2009**
Improved the image of Sibiu?	98	92	97
Brought more money to Sibiu?	94	82	83
Improved cultural facilities?	89	79	80
Created more social cohesion?	67	62	62
Improved the quality of life?	53	61	51

impacts of an event to be over-stated or exaggerated in advance as a means of securing or justifying political and financial support. However, inflating the expectations of stakeholders can create problems.

For example, the original visitor projections for the Barcelona Forum in 2004 suggested that around 5 million people would visit the event during its 141-day run. Just before the event was due to open, Joan Clos, the then Mayor of Barcelona, announced that the projected visitor numbers had been increased to 7.5 million visitors, suggesting a substantial additional impact of the event. At the end, the Forum itself generated only 3.3 million visits in 2004, or 60% of the original projection and 44% of the inflated estimated projections. This helped to substantiate the claim by the event's detractors that it was a failure.

One of the problems with visitor estimates for major events is that many are unticketed, and so the figures may not be verifiable. Visitor numbers to such public events might be estimated on the basis of sample visitor counts, aerial photographs or police estimates. However, the interpretation of these data can also lead to significant differences in visitor figures. For example, the Feria de Abril in Barcelona is a major celebration of Andalucian culture, which according to the organisers, attracts around 3 million visits a year (see also Chapter 4). The media observation group Contrastant (www.contrastant.net) conducted visitor counts which indicated a maximum of just over half a million visits. Similarly, the group estimates that La Mercè, the major annual festival in Barcelona, attracts only a third of the official estimated number of visits (2.1 million in 2006). Because estimates of economic impact invariably rely on estimates of total visitor numbers and sample surveys of visitor spending, such uncertainty about visitor volumes can make economic impact assessment problematic.

Crompton (2006:67) reviewed a large number of economic impact studies for events and found that in addition to exaggerating visitation numbers, there were many 'mischievous procedures' used to calculate economic impact, such as including local residents in impact calculations, abuse of multipliers, ignoring costs borne by the local community, ignoring opportunity costs, ignoring displacement costs, and expanding the project scope. The inappropriate use of such procedures may lead to widely differing estimates of event impact, and most casual observers are unlikely to be able to tell where 'statistics' end and 'lies' begin.

The basic lesson seems to be that while exaggeration may be common, it is not helpful in the honest and professional development of an effective city events programme. Although it is important to create positive and optimistic expectations of an event, these need to be based on a realistic assessment of potential results.

CONCLUSIONS

Events have important cultural, social, economic and image impacts for the places that host them. These impacts are ultimately the reason why places want to stage events, and the stimulus for increasing numbers of events being held around the globe. In many cases, it is the economic effect of events which tends to attract much attention from stakeholders, not only because this is an important justification for the investment made in the event, but also because economic impacts are deceptively simple to measure in comparison with most other types of impact. Evaluation techniques that use multiple indicators of different types are generally most beneficial and contribute to a more integrated approach to evaluation that reflects the true benefits of events to a city.

There are signs that cities are now beginning to try and measure some of the cultural, social and image impacts of events in a more consistent way. Cities such as Liverpool and Rotterdam, Edinburgh and Antwerp have established monitoring programmes to analyse changes in their image over time, and the role that culture plays in that image. Liverpool is also undertaking extensive research on the social impacts of the 2008 ECOC. This type of monitoring might eventually allow us to better understand the ways in which cultural events can impact on many different aspects of city life, rather than simply on the additional revenue and jobs that are generated.

Measuring any kind of event impact remains a complex task. The examples provided in this chapter show how different assumptions used to measure economic impact, for example, can generate widely differing answers. Clearly, a city that seriously wants to measure the effects of its events programme needs to undertake impact measurement in a structured way. This means not just ensuring that consistent methodologies are adopted so that the results of different types of events can be compared and trends can be identified over time, but also that cities should strive to measure event programme outputs relative to the aims set. Only in this way can sensible decisions be made about future investment in the event programme.

A strategic approach to event development should be supported by studies which review what activities are effective in meeting the aims of the city, and which issues need to be addressed in order to improve results. Studies that are too narrow in scope can lead to a naïve assessment of 'success' or 'failure'. If impact studies do not draw lessons that will help contribute to development in the longer term, their value should be questioned. Public bodies that are reluctant to invest in evaluation or that wish such studies to state conclusively whether events should continue or be cut are not using such tools for developmental purposes, and inhibit the value of the studies themselves.

CHAPTER 10

Event Programme Sustainability

One of the major considerations in designing, developing and managing event programmes should be long-term sustainability. Sustainability refers to the continuation of the event programme itself, as well as ensuring that the direct and indirect impacts of events can be maintained. Since the event programmes of many cities grow in an organic, ad hoc fashion, sustainability is often an afterthought rather than an integral part of the event programme planning process.

As ephemera, events themselves may not be sustainable. For certain events, the organisation is dismantled or reduced in size soon after the event ends. This might lead to the loss of expertise that would be required in legacy planning or the planning of future events. Commitment to a long-term financial strategy is also important for sustaining eventfulness, but achieving this is often difficult. The successful eventful city needs to invest in multi-annual planning and pluri-annual financial commitments.

The growing impact that events have on their host communities (see Chapter 9) means that more attention is also being paid to ensuring the sustainability of event programmes. In Manchester, an example used earlier in this volume, the definition of a programme of 'pillar events' with guaranteed funding over a long period illustrated how a city can help to ensure event programme sustainability.

This chapter considers ways in which sustainability can be achieved given the unique context of events. In particular, attention is paid to the task of building networks to help maintain and develop the projects initiated by events. The legacy of events is considered not only from the perspective of consensus-building, but also the potential for conflict.

THE CONCEPT OF SUSTAINABILITY

The most widely-quoted definition of sustainability derives from the World Commission on Environment and Development (1987) – also known as the Brundtland Report – which views sustainable development as: 'development that meets the needs of the present without compromising the ability of future generations to meet their own needs.'

Originally, this concept was applied mainly to environmental issues, but over the years other areas of human activity have also been incorporated into an understanding of sustainability. As Bramwell, et al. (1996) pointed out, sustainability can be examined in terms of a number of different dimensions, including:

- environmental;

- economic;

- cultural;

- social; and

- political.

This multi-faceted approach to sustainability mirrors the concept of the multiple bottom line approaches (Chapter 9). However, until relatively recently, the sustainability discourse has tended to focus on environmental and economic issues; the principle of cultural sustainability has not received much attention. This is now beginning to change, as the contribution of culture to the broader approach to sustainability becomes clearer. The World Commission on Culture and Development (the 'Péres de Cuéllar Commission') published a report, *Our Creative Diversity* (WCCD, 1995) that raised issues about cultural development and related them to ideas about sustainability. Throsby (2005) has identified a number of strands of research in cultural sustainability, including interactions between culture and the environment, the concept of cultural capital as a sustainable resource and the sustainability of urban cultural heritage. The Council of Europe Report '*In From the Margins*' (1997) also makes an important contribution to the global debate on culture and sustainable development, and is a key document that takes stock of the situation in Europe.

As well as contributing to the economic sustainability of cities, culture is also an arena in which awareness of sustainability issues can be raised. Hawkes (2001) identified culture as the 'fourth pillar' of sustainability and argued that a sustainable society could be achieved most effectively by promoting cultural vitality. These arguments have also filtered into public policy (Cubeles and Baro, 2006). In the UK, the Department for Culture, Media and Sport (DCMS, 2004:1) states that:

Enjoyment of and participation in the arts is fundamental to the core of successful sustainable development, a good quality of life. The arts have always been used to engage and inform as well as entertain, and using imagination and creativity encourages attitudinal change, as well as social and environmental transformation, all of which are necessary to make truly sustainable development possible.

Events have an important role to play in sustainability policies by stimulating economic development, raising awareness of sustainability issues and creating social cohesion. The sustainability of an event programme needs to be viewed from a number of different, interlinked perspectives. For example, ensuring the financial sustainability of an event will depend on attitudes concerning the event's social sustainability (such as the support of local residents and associations) or its political sustainability (support from the local or national government). This sustainability view of events goes beyond the impact-based models of event assessment, such as the multiple bottom line or balanced scorecard approaches, because it considers not just the immediate outcomes of the event, but also the ability of the event to sustain itself and its outcomes over time.

Event sustainability was one of the key aspects considered in the evaluation of the ECOC (European Capital of Culture) (Palmer-Rae, 2004). Even though the ECOC title is only awarded for one year to each city, the expectation is that the event will generate other events and programmes, which will be sustainable and therefore generate long-term impacts for the city. This is a key argument employed by cities to justify the large investments needed to stage major events. But just how 'sustainable' are such events and their outcomes?

Successful Events Are Not Always Sustainable

Just because an event is successful in generating positive impacts for a city does not automatically mean that it is sustainable. One-off events, such as the ECOC or the Olympic Games, are rarely repeated in the same city, so ways must be found to ensure the sustainability of the outcomes of the event, rather than the event itself.

Even events which generate very positive impacts for their host city may not be sustainable in the long run. The 2003 ECOC in Graz was judged to have been extremely successful, attracting over 2.7 million visits to this small Austrian city and creating significant image impacts. However, these achievements were not sustained, arguably because a change of administration meant that less priority was given to culture at the same time that new cultural facilities created for the ECOC were in need of new events and activities to animate them. There has been considerable disillusion in the cultural sector in Graz that the success of 2003 could not be maintained and that there was less money to share among a greater number of facilities.

In Lille, there have been significant post-event problems with the financing of long-term legacy projects. The Maison Folies, cultural centres set up around the Lille region (including in neighbouring Belgium), were designed to act as community arts centres for the local population (see Chapter 8). During the ECOC in 2004 they performed well, staging a wide range of events in the fields of both popular cultural and avant garde art. Immediately after the event, however, problems began to emerge as discussions started about the long-term funding of the centres. The regional government failed to come up with promised funds, and there was a budget deficit caused

by falling income in many centres. At the same time, public expectations created by the ECOC event could not be met. 'As soon as
2004 finished, people were coming to ask us when the next festival
would be.'
(Maurice, 2005)

The examples of Graz and Lille illustrate the problems of
shifting from a short-term event perspective to a long-term
sustainability perspective. In the case of the ECOC, there is
an additional factor in that intense activity and concentrated
high levels of funding create expectations that cannot be met
in the post-event era. There is a tendency to focus on staging
the event itself to the detriment of long-term legacy planning.
One of the most important aspects of ensuring the sustainability of event programme outcomes is to change the way in
which events themselves are viewed: an event must be
conceived as a part of a dynamic, long-term process of
cultural, social and economic development.

Events as a process

The cities which have been most successful at achieving
sustainability of event impacts in the ECOC are those which
have viewed the event as part of a wider process of development and renewal. One of the best examples remains Glasgow, where the ECOC in 1990 was only one element of
a major urban redevelopment programme starting with the
'Glasgow's miles better' public confidence campaign in the
early 1980s. The city hosted the UK Garden Festival in 1988
as a lead-up to the ECOC in 1990. The legacies of the ECOC
were further enhanced through subsequent events such as
the 1999 UK City of Architecture and Design and the Charles
Rennie Mackintosh Festival in 2006. The city also renovated
its cultural infrastructure, starting with the opening of the
Burrell Collection in 1983, the Glasgow Royal Concert Hall
in 1990 and continuing with the Glasgow Museum of
Modern Art in 1996, and many other projects.

Garcia (2004:109) came to similar conclusions in her
assessment of the Sydney and Barcelona Olympics. She
describes how both cities initiated a programme of cultural

events in the years running up to the Games. Sydney held a themed festival every year, including a celebration of indigenous cultures in 1997, a focus on immigrant cultures and multiculturalism in 1998, sending touring groups abroad to bring 'Australia to the world' in 1999 and an international arts festival alongside the Games in 2000.

The need for long-term planning and a strategic approach is clear. A study for the European Commission on *The Economic Impact on Employment of Ten Festivals in Europe* concluded that:

- The social and economic feedback of a festival town is organised around an artistic coherence which exceeds the time limits of the festival. The more this coherence is planned and structured, the greater are the chances of economic development downstream, whether linked to culture or not.

- The most beneficial economic impact and employment for the community should reside in the durable establishment of the [festival]. (CEFRAC 1996: quoted in Graham Devlin Associates, 2001:17)

Success will be enhanced by a strategic approach, and so events should be closely linked to the rest of the city's cultural provision and be afforded a degree of continuity and security. However, even when an event emerges as part of a longer-term strategy, this may not in itself always be sufficient to ensure sustainability. In Rotterdam, the ECOC in 2001 arguably represented a logical step in a long process of urban and cultural redevelopment that had been going on since the World War II. During post war reconstruction, Rotterdam expanded its cultural facilities:

Which included new projects such as the extension of the Boijmans-van Beuningen Museum, a National Architecture Museum, a Museum of Natural History and a new art gallery that formed the southern edge of the museum park, which was itself improved to provide links between the various facilities. In addition, the development of the Waterstad area provided an important high-profile development, and

*new museum, cultural and entertainment uses were
located in this area.*
(McCarthy, 1998:340)

The 2001 ECOC, therefore, represented a logical extension to the development of cultural infrastructure, allowing
the existing facilities to provide the backdrop for an ambitious programme of cultural events. The theme 'Rotterdam is
many cities' was also a reference to the redevelopment
process as well as a reflection of its cultural diversity. The
2001 ECOC was relatively successful, meeting its stated
aims in terms of cultural development and attracting 2.3
million visitors. Tourism grew by 10%, the number of foreign
visitors to the city increased, and the image of the city
improved at home and abroad (Richards & Wilson, 2004).

Immediately following the ECOC, however, there was
a change of municipal government, with the socialist
administration that had conceived the 2001 event being
replaced by a centre-right coalition opposed in part to
multicultural programmes and immigration. In line with
national trends, cultural funding was cut in Rotterdam,
arguably undermining many of the gains that had been made
over the previous 25 years. As a result of these changes, the
initial plans to capitalise on the successes of the ECOC
quickly faded as key personnel were lost and funds dried up,
in contrast to Glasgow 1990, which had been the model for
Rotterdam. The original idea of creating an archive of ECOC
material evaporated and much collective experience was lost;
the intellectual capital created by the event was dissipated.
Even though the cultural sector in Rotterdam formed an
action group to campaign against the budget cuts, the culture
budget in Rotterdam nevertheless was reduced further in
2008, minimising further the possibility of sustainability.

The need to take a strategic view extends to the choice of
events to create, fund, stage and bid for. This also requires
a realistic approach in terms of competitive bidding for
events: not all bids will be won and not all events can be
financed properly. The strategic process of developing the
events programme can be an important learning exercise for
the eventful city, even where the city may not succeed in
realising its strategy completely.

Winning through losing

When a city competes for a footloose event and loses, the disappointment can cause a dissipation of the energy built up around the bid. The management of such dissipation and disappointment becomes a major issue for the continuing sustainability of events. If levels of disillusion grow too high, the basic support from stakeholders may decline and the city's ability to attract and organise successful events is weakened.

Cities should develop ways of using the experiences of both 'winning' and 'losing', both success and failure, as part of a process of acquiring experience that can further strengthen its capacity. If a city loses its bid for an event, there may be certain causes of the failure that may be difficult to overcome, such as the size or location of a city. But other factors can be addressed, such as the coherence of stakeholder networks, the visibility of public support, the organisational capacity of event programme operation and the scale and efficiency of the city's physical infrastructure, transportation or security capability.

Manchester is a city that gained intelligently from its experience of unsuccessfully competing for the Olympic Games. Manchester initially bid for the 1996 and 2000 Olympic Games, improving it's ranking from 5th to a creditable 3rd behind Sydney and Beijing. The city's Olympic aspirations were ended by an International Olympic Committee message to the UK that only London would be considered as a credible location. However:

> The 2000 Olympic bid galvanised an emergent
> network of public and private sector elites, which, for
> a short period, shared a common goal: to achieve
> regeneration through the bidding process.
> (Peck & Ward, 2002:13)

So Manchester turned its attention elsewhere and successfully bid for the 2002 Commonwealth Games, which had considerable economic, social and cultural spin-offs (see Chapter 9). Manchester's failed bid for the 2000 Olympics helped the city to reorient its vision of what it wanted to achieve. According to Andrew Stokes, managing director of

Marketing Manchester, 'The race for the Olympics was a race worth losing. The result of the failed bid was not only a drive for the Commonwealth Games, but for the large-scale development in infrastructure, facilities and accommodation a city bidding for such an event requires.' Failed bids also create a store of knowledge and skills relating to the event bidding process.

The process of being a candidate city for a major event such as the ECOC encourages a city to review or develop its strategic aims and objectives and approaches to the raising of the required resources and to further enhance stakeholder networks in the city. The process of bidding can act as a tool for rallying stakeholders in the city and instilling pride in the local population, even if the outcome of the bidding process itself is negative.

Dealing with losing also requires leadership and a carefully conceived strategy. In the German City of Weimar, the mayor was asked in an interview whether it would be 'megalomaniac' for a city with a population of 60,000 to apply for the title Cultural Capital of Europe. He replied:

> *I am not of the opinion that we are megalomaniac for a very simple reason. We have tried to lay open a policy direction that, even if Weimar did not get the title, is so forward-looking that the city plays an important part in the concert of European culture cities. If we do become a Cultural Capital, we would not have to change a lot. We might have to step on the gas a little bit - and in particular ensure that more private capital comes into the city.*
>
> (Frank & Roth, 2000:225)

The experience of some of the 'losers' of the 2008 ECOC bidding process in the UK is salutary. The 12 cities who competed for the ECOC designation cities invested significantly, some in excess of €1.5 million, in the preparation of their bids. Newcastle/Gateshead, one of the candidate cities, had prepared a very ambitious programme and, although losing the competition, decided to implement much of its planned programme in any case. The Newcastle-Gateshead Culture 10 programme delivered significant economic, cultural and social benefits to the whole North-East region, even without the ECOC title (see Chapter 9). The city also decided to place itself on the global cultural stage, hosting the World Summit of Arts and Culture in 2006. A similar, although smaller-scale continuation of a losing ECOC bid was carried out by Oxford, whose 'Evolving City' programme generated considerable social and cultural benefit (Chappell & Harriss, 2006).

Birmingham: Where Did We Go Wrong?

Birmingham was another city that failed in its bid for the UK ECOC in 2008. Local stakeholders insisted that the city would benefit from the bid, as many of the events planned for 2008 would still go ahead. Even so, many questioned the whole project and the estimated £2 million (€3 million) price tag of the bid.

Brian Woods-Scawen, chairman of the bid team, said: 'The immediate response is that we have come second again, that we are the bridesmaids once again. In many ways we have become used to finishing second, but we need to take a long and critical look at why that might be the case. We must learn the lessons of why we were not successful.' One problem seemed to be the lack of a focal point. 'I think we did begin to capture people's imaginations ... in the last few months. But we didn't have something we could point to that would generate public interest in the way the national stadium campaign did. We only had a bid document and a set of proposals and people do not necessarily get excited by such things.'

(Dale, 2003)

ENVIRONMENTAL SUSTAINABILITY

Events can have very significant impacts on the physical environment. This is increasingly being recognised by events around the world, many of which are now striving to become 'carbon neutral' or at least to minimise their impact. In fact, Manchester International Festival aspires to become a 'carbon positive festival' by 2011.

The Glastonbury Festival, which attracts 180,000 people to a farm outside a small English town, has an environmental statement which sets out the organisers' desire to limit environment impacts (Glastonbury Festival, 2009):

Glastonbury Festival recognises that running the event at Worthy Farm has a direct impact (both positive and negative) on the environment. The Festival is committed to enhancing the environment through our operations wherever possible, and minimising any negative impact.

This commitment is translated into concrete targets for:

- minimising the amount of waste;
- managing the on-site collection of waste efficiently;
- transporting sewage and waste water offsite; and
- maintaining the high level of bio-diversity at the site.

For example, in 2003, 30% of litter was moved off-site during the event, double the proportion in 2002. Over the next 5 years the Festival has set a target of increasing the amount of rubbish moved off-site during the event to 50%.

The organisers also believe that through participation in the festival, 'the public is exposed to many positive influences highlighting environmental values – and hopefully influencing subsequent behaviour.'

A Green Festival

The 2000trees Festival positions itself as 'A green festival. An ethical festival. A music festival.' Born out of the organisers' disillusionment with large, mainstream music festivals, 2000trees is an attempt to produce a less commercial, more sustainable event. The festival has explicit environmental aims, including promoting green issues and raising awareness of the threats from climate change.

- We have a comprehensive on-site recycling and composting scheme. This achieved a 78% recycling rate in 2008 (up from 66% in 2007). According to Network Recycling, the average recycling rate at festivals is only 30%.
- All food and drinks on site are served in either reusable or biodegradable (corn starch) containers.
- Where possible only locally produced, organic food and drink is sold.

Continued

- Various environmental campaigners are situated on the festival site providing information on how we can all do our bit for the environment.
- Our policy is that the vast majority (if not all our bands) are UK-based, resulting in less miles travelled to reach the festival and zero use of air transport.
- All power and lighting is produced using locally-sourced biodiesel, which is significantly better than any petro-chemical alternative; and at last year's festival ensured that we saved over 2 tonnes of carbon (in just one weekend!). That's great, but the use of solar, wind and even pedal power is more environmentally friendly and thus our long-term plan is to increase our use of renewable energy sources.

(2000trees Festival, 2009)

Environmental sustainability is seen by these festival organisers not just as a matter of doing less harm to the planet, but also as a means of achieving other goals, such as developing new target markets and attracting media attention, improving stakeholder relations and expanding organisational capacity.

Of course, there is an irony of staging a 'carbon neutral' event that is designed to attract hundreds of thousands of participants who travel by car or plane to the event destination. The eventful city requires a coordinated environmental impact plan, which looks not only at the environmental cost of staging the event, but also the wider impacts in terms of the negative effects of travel by certain means. The public sector in particular can begin to plan effectively so that low-impact travel options are prioritised. In the final analysis, however, the objective of reducing environmental impact may be outweighed by the potential economic impact resulting from increased visitors to the event. There is a need to use events as a catalyst for starting a balanced and informed debate within the eventful city that may help raise awareness of both environmental and economic consequences of events and public policies in general.

The environmental sustainability of cultural events relates not just to ecological issues, but also to the physical legacies in the form of venues, attractions or broader programmes of urban redevelopment that are linked to events. However, problems associated with physical infrastructure projects may also result in negative impacts in terms of traffic circulation and parking, pedestrian access and even negative public attitudes caused by increased budgets and delays. In Porto (ECOC 2001) and Thessaloniki (ECOC 1997) failure to complete major infrastructure projects caused problems for the staging of the events themselves, but also created major disruption to the daily life of the city. In the run-up to Liverpool ECOC 2008, building works for the new shopping complex in the city centre (one of the projects linked to the ECOC) caused the popular Mathew Street Festival to be cancelled in 2007, which attracted substantial negative media attention locally and nationally and severe criticism of the Liverpool 2008 ECOC organisation.

Physical overcrowding from festival visitors, and overcrowded event programmes also need to be avoided. One Montreal resident commented on his experience of this 'Festival City' during the summer:

> Whenever I want to feel like a HUMAN BEING I flee Montreal because it has become a nightmare in the summertime. There are no less than 10 major events ... in the downtown area, in a 45-day period, starting with the F1 extravaganza in early June all the way to the gay bash in August. The weekly fireworks display sound like Beirut under Israeli fighter jets, even if you're 5km away. Not to mention the soccer dudes honking for hours when Portugal or Italy wins the quarter final of some overseas tournament.
>
> Journalists at Le Devoir newspaper coined the 'hyper festivity' term to describe the phenomenon. My own definition is: 'crack cocaine for the masses' (Spacing Toronto, 2007).

At present it seems that environmental impacts of event programmes are still not taken very seriously and the search for environmental sustainability is more a question of individual event philosophies than strategic planning. There is an increasing need for local authorities to integrate environmental sustainability into their event policies.

CULTURAL SUSTAINABILITY

The concept of cultural sustainability revolves around the continued support and enhancement of local cultural processes and structures. Sustainability is directly linked to the processes of cultural planning (see Chapter 5) and a city's events strategies need to be embedded in such planning. Without an integrated and strategic approach, events might even damage local culture, for example, by reducing the resources of key organisations that form part of the city's regular cultural infrastructure or are a central element of the city's cultural ecology. Supporting additional events at the expense of maintaining and developing other components of the city's cultural infrastructure (that may or not be associated to the events) may create negative displacement that undermines the position of the eventful city.

In certain ECOC, finance was reduced to the city's ongoing cultural offer to fund special projects and events. Although this may seem an appealing strategy to municipal councils and private sector sponsors, the cultural impact and sustainability of ECOC have been significantly improved by strategies that strengthened existing infrastructure as well as supporting additional cultural projects (one-off and ongoing) through real increases to the city's cultural budgets. No ECOC has ever succeeded by reducing one component of cultural funding to increase another (Palmer-Rae, 2004).

In some cases, the unthinking proliferation of cultural events has led to unsustainable programmes. For example, the Palmer-Rae report (2004, vol. 2:47) indicated problems with 'cultural event fatigue' in some ECOC host cities. In Thessaloniki in 1997:

> *Many projects were poorly attended – only one fifth of ticketed events had 75% capacity or more, while over one third sold less than 35% of their seats. Even big-name events could not be sure of a high turn-out. It seems likely that the audience was simply saturated by events – in 1997 Thessaloniki was host to a cultural programme six times larger than previous years.*

In Prague 2000, there was a slightly different problem:

The cultural programme was composed mainly of events that would have taken place anyway as part of the cultural calendar; the aim being to give these projects and events an added value in 2000 and the possibility to do things that normally would not be possible. There was a strong feeling that there was no need for new projects because so much already exists in Prague. One respondent said that 'Prague is overloaded with culture' (Palmer-Rae 2004, vol. 2:177).

Just as displacement of existing events by new ones has negative consequences, a policy of only focusing on existing events and programmes, and not introducing new elements may reduce impacts. One important aspect of the cultural sustainability of events is therefore to find a constructive relationship between the existing supply of cultural events and facilities and those that are created or presented anew. New events should demonstrate that they are adding qualitatively to the total event offer within the city.

As well as ensuring a good fit between existing and new events, cities should also consider mechanisms for ensuring the long-term viability of new events. Events may be created for some specific purpose and then rapidly cease to exist as the initial rationale fades away. This has been the case, for example, with a number of events designed to combat racism. In London, the Rock Against Racism (RAR) festival was created in 1978 when the National Front Party began organising rallies against immigration and gaining support in local elections. 'By the end of 1978 RAR had organised 300 local concerts and 5 carnivals. In the run-up to the 1979 election it staged a "Militant Entertainment Tour" featuring 40 bands at 23 concerts covering more than 2000 miles on the road' (Manzoor, 2008). In the general election support for the National Front weakened and RAR was disbanded in 1981. The concept was revived for the RAR Carnival in 2008, celebrating the 30th anniversary of the original concert in London. The Dutch Racism Beat It Festival had a similar history, being launched in Amsterdam in 1993 and discontinued in 2003.

The cultural sustainability of an events programme is not only linked to the sustainability of individual events. A healthy and productive cultural climate tends to sustain a number of important events over a long period of time. Changes to the composition of a cultural programme may be necessary to adjust to changes in audiences or the needs of the city, whose aim must be to ensure the health of the overall programme through careful, and where necessary, pruning.

In Barcelona there has been much discussion over the years about the health of the Festa Major in the district of Gràcia. Many are concerned that a reduction in the number of streets being decorated for the festival represents a decline in support for the event. Other commentators point out that the number of participating streets has always fluctuated over the 170 year history of the event and that this will continue to happen in future (Pablo, 1998).

One way of ensuring the sustainability of new events, therefore, may be to learn from the experience of traditional events that survive because they play a concrete role in the maintenance of the local community and/or the local culture. The involvement of local residents is a prerequisite for this. A good example of how new events can become sustained 'traditional events' in short space of time was the Zinneke Parade in Brussels, which was first created as an original event by Brussels ECOC in 2000 (see Chapter 9). The organisers conceived it as a continuing event and the substantial success of the first parade in 2000 consolidated support for its sustainability.

As argued earlier, in the eventful city the cultural sector as a whole must be strengthened through events, thereby contributing to the sustainability of the total cultural system. As a result of the ECOC in Antwerp in 1993, for example, an improved climate has been created for cultural production, with stronger networks and more public sector support (Corijn & van Praet, 1994). The city has also continued to develop cultural events since then, with the Van Dyke Year in 1999, Mode 2001 (a fashion event) and the Rubens Year and Antwerp Book Capital in 2004. Such positive effects do require a relative level of political commitment and stability, however. In the case of Antwerp, as already mentioned, the creation of

Antwerpen Open as a central organisation to develop, stage and manage cultural events following the ECOC was a major factor in ensuring sustainability of the event programme (see Chapter 2).

Another important aspect of the cultural sustainability of events, as identified earlier in this chapter, is the infrastructure legacy. Facilities built in response to specific events, such as the Royal Festival Hall in London, the Casa da Musica in Porto or the Royal Exhibition Building in Melbourne, have given an important impulse to the cultural life of the city. New cultural spaces, which are animated with activity, can generate new energy that builds upon the success of an event. Infrastructural development is often a central element of event legacy planning.

Glasgow's Tramway

The Tramway, one of Scotland's premiere arts venues, started life as a tram shed, going on to become the Museum of Transport when the trams went out of business in the 1960s. The building later faced demolition when the Museum moved venues, but the decision to make Glasgow European City of Culture in 1990 saved the building. Funds were raised to turn it into an arts space, which went on to play host to Peter Brooks' production Mahabharata and the sculptures of Andy Goldsworthy.

The city council agreed to redevelop the Tramway and finance it as one of the long-term legacies of Glasgow's designation as European Capital of Culture, and it now has six distinct performing and exhibition areas. The huge scale of the Tramway makes it an ever-popular choice with artists and performers alike; at any one time there are several different activities going on to appeal to all audiences, from ambitious dance productions to small exhibitions of emerging artists. The adjoining Hidden Gardens provide an unexpectedly beautiful outdoor space with an ever-changing aspect. The Tramway has now become one of Glasgow's favourite landmarks.

In some cases the maintaining of event infrastructural legacies can happen in a fairly organic way. However, there are many examples of unsustainable physical structures, where new facilities suffer from poor legacy planning, are plagued by operational and financial problems and sometimes negative public opinion and lack of support. One such example is the Millennium Dome in London, which was constructed to celebrate the advent of the third Millennium in 2000. Having operated as an eclectic leisure and cultural attraction for one year, the future of the Dome became the subject of widespread speculation as the original plans to turn it into a football stadium evaporated. The debate about the failure, cost and future of the Dome raged during the next 5 years. There was a brief respite with the staging of a 'Winter Wonderland' experience in December 2003, and over Christmas 2004 part of the Dome was used to shelter the homeless. The Dome was finally taken over by a telephone company who rebranded it as 'O2' in 2005, and the music and entertainment venue finally opened in its new form in June 2007. There clearly had been an absence of realistic and strategic legacy planning. This salutary lesson has influenced the approach to the development of the London Olympics 2012, which has a comprehensive strategy for long-term legacy planning (DCMS, 2008)

The cost of maintaining the infrastructure, which is created specifically for or by events, is often left out of the calculations of economic impact. In Barcelona, the new public space created by the Barcelona Forum 2004 is reputedly the second largest public space in the world after Tiananmen Square in China. The cost of maintaining the space is estimated at €1.5 million a year and there are now significant additional costs, such as providing animation programmes. The fact that this vast public space still has no clear future programme policy or consistent use is testimony to the lack of legacy planning for the Forum.

The physical development of facilities and event programme development are two aspects of a common strategy for an eventful city. Presenting many one-off events without adequate infrastructure can be very costly on an annual basis. Alternatively, the creation of many new buildings may generate high operational costs all year round and, if they are not programmed consistently, will give rise to a city that is lacking in animation and atmosphere.

SOCIAL SUSTAINABILITY

As was noted in Chapter 9, the social impacts of events are complex to measure, and yet they can be among the most important event outcomes. According to Polèse and Stren (2000:15–16) social sustainability for a city is:

Development (and/or growth) that is compatible with the harmonious evolution of civil society, fostering an environment conducive to the compatible cohabitation of culturally and socially diverse groups while at the same time encouraging integration, with improvements in the quality of life for all segments of the population.

Social sustainability revolves around three issues: social cohesion, equity and quality of life. If events can contribute to quality of life, improving residents' sense of belonging while ensuring that all residents can have their cultural needs met in an equitable way, then they should be socially sustainable.

Cultural events can contribute to the quality of life of local communities in a number of ways:

- giving the local community a feeling of ownership;

- giving different groups in the community a platform to express their own culture;

- making sure that different groups have access to events;

- by ensuring that events contribute to a sense of place for local residents; and

- by avoiding negative social outcomes, such as fuelling property speculation, increasing homelessness or displacement.

To attain such objectives, there should be a high level of community involvement and participation in the events programme. This can be achieved in a number of ways, but examples such as the development of 'ambassador' programmes or 'supporters clubs' can achieve significant results (see Chapter 5). Other mechanisms include:

- representative boards;

- variety of programming;

- involving community groups and schools in events; and

- creating access to public space for associations and groups to organise their own events.

The creation of sustainable social impacts was one of the aims of the 2007 ECOC in Luxembourg, and young and migrant groups were targeted in particular. The youth programme was particularly successful, with a former railway shed being transformed into a dedicated youth venue. As Georges Metz, the youth programme organiser, commented:

> It was important to dedicate from the beginning one of the Rotunda (former railway sheds) to youth. (This) became THE youth place. I am very much in favour of the Carré Rotunda and of the plans for the future development of the Rotundas, to have a place where young people can meet again (after 2007) because they know that there is a cultural space for them.
> (Luxembourg and Greater Region, 2008:79)

The special provision created for young people ensured that levels of participation in ECOC events among young people were as high as older age groups. In order to ensure that the momentum created in 2007 was not lost, a special foundation was established to carry on the development of the youth programme and to continue running the highly successful TRAFFO youth festival. Funding was provided by the City of Luxembourg to ensure the long-term future of the festival, and the national government provided funding for the renovation of the Carré Rotondes youth venue.

Promoting equity by providing events to cater to the needs of different groups is one issue, but stimulating real integration and social cohesion is another. In many cases, as Richard Sennett (1999) has argued in the case of New York, developing truly integrated communities means not just promoting tolerance but also enabling people to recognise and confront difference. This is one of the strategies employed by the Brouhaha festival in Liverpool, which has been running since 1990. The theme chosen to coincide with the Liverpool ECOC in 2008 was 'Crossing Waters – Between the Devil and the Deep Blue Sea', which was designed to explore Liverpool's relationship with the sea and its key role in the slave trade, while also reflecting on the relationship between carnival and slavery.

Events have also been shown to play an important role in healing communities divided by war and ethnic strife. In the Balkans, many cultural events continued in spite of the war in former Yugoslavia, and many of these events now act as new spaces of reconciliation between previously divided communities. The Council of Europe is one organisation that explicitly recognises events that have the objective of helping to resolve or prevent conflicts in divided cities. Many powerful examples of projects exist in divided (or once-divided) cities, such as Belfast, Sarajevo, Beirut, Jerusalem and Baghdad.

Mostar: Unique Sign – Unique Location

Mostar, the capital of Herzegovina, suffered terribly during the Yugo-slav war, with over 2000 casualties in the city alone. However, Mostar only attracted world attention when the iconic Stari Most Bridge was destroyed. The bridge was a symbol of the previously peaceful multi-cultural past of the town, a UNESCO monument as well as a popular tourist attraction.

After the war, Mostar became involved in the Cultural City Network organised by Graz, the ECOC for 2003. The Unique Sign – Unique Location project was designed to create a sign for the absence of the bridge and draw attention to the problem, which was quickly forgotten after the war. The project was largely funded by the City of Graz and was adopted by the summer festival in Mostar. The project developed floating structures and platforms to exhibit the works by 32 artists from across Europe. These included Priska Riedl's 'Floating Globeballs', a construction of 100 footballs and a flotation body, resembling a football stadium; Borut Popenko's floating fried eggs; Luise Kloos' bridge of nappies suspended above the water and Dejan Grba's 'The Deceased – Floating Points', photos of dead bodies which were floated down the river.

Aufischer (2003)

POLITICAL SUSTAINABILITY

Political support is vital to most events and, in turn, events are increasingly important as political tools, although many event organisers and participants may reject the instrumentalised use of events to help achieve explicit political objectives. Nevertheless, ensuring political sustainability of the event programme is important, because without the necessary political support, event programmes and eventful city strategies are unlikely to be sustainable in the longer term.

As indicated earlier, the ECOCs of Graz (2003) and Rotterdam (2001) both suffered from a change of government shortly after the event, and in both cases this diminished the planned legacy of the event. Barcelona and Glasgow, on the other hand, are often seen as cities where events have been able to achieve a high level of sustainable outcomes from their event programmes, arguably helped by the relative political stability of these two cities, and cross-party political support, which has allowed them to plan long-term for the achievement of specific goals through events.

The need to create stable political structures to support cultural collaboration was explicitly recognised in the development of the ECOC in Luxembourg and Greater Region (2007). Because cultural collaboration across national borders within the region had been poorly developed, the ECOC was used as a lever to create a new association to support cross-border cultural development. The work of the cross-border association established in 2007 has been continued under the name *Espace culturel Grande Région*, and the Blue Stag logo of the ECOC has become a unifying symbol for cross-border cultural activities. The exchange of information between the regions is also supported through tools such as the Internet portal www.plurio.net, which provides a guide to cultural events and institutions throughout the Greater Region. The portal also includes a ticketing application that allows tickets to be purchased at participating cultural institutions in all of the regions covered by the project.

Another of the important factors in developing political sustainability is to ensure that the event programme is seen to benefit stakeholders from different parts of the political spectrum, as well as involving different levels of government. In Luxembourg 2007, the event brought together national, regional and local government interests. At a national level, the different Ministries of Culture were able to develop collaboration which furthered their aims in international cultural policy. The regional administrations were able to mobilise resources which otherwise might not have been available (for example to allow the Rhineland Palatinate to stage the successful Constantine exhibition – see Chapter 8). The City of Luxembourg, which has a resident population of only 90,000, attracts over 100,000 cross-border workers every day. However, these people go home again in the evening without having established any real ties with the city. One of the City's main aims for 2007 was therefore to include this group and to get them more involved in the cultural life of Luxembourg.

A mixed economy of political stakeholders may also be important for ensuring continuity of funding. Where an event programme becomes over-dependent on a single source of funding (very often the municipality), it becomes vulnerable to political change. In London, the election of a Conservative Mayor in 2008 spelled the end of the Rise Festival, an anti-racism event launched with trade union support in 1996. The rationale for cutting the city's grant to the event was apparently financial, according to the official press release: 'the Rise festival [which] cost £551,000 to stage last year, will not be taking place. Without a major sponsor in place it is not considered appropriate to spend such a large amount on a single music event, particularly during a recession.' However, there were suspicions that the main reason might have been politically motivated: 'By canceling Rise, (the new Mayor) is at a stroke removing all stylistic trace of his (socialist) predecessor' (Huq, 2009).

At the same time, it is also important to ensure that political sustainability is not achieved at the cost of stifling creativity and innovation in the event programme. When

certain events become part of the 'established' cultural programme of the city, there is a tendency for them to be
considered sacrosanct. Even when such events are out of
touch with the needs of the different publics of the city and in
need of innovation and renewal, there may be a tendency to
protect them at all cost. Obtaining entrenched political
support may benefit individual events, but potentially at the
cost of an aging and stale event programme.

ECONOMIC SUSTAINABILITY

Many cities will make decisions about which events to
support based largely on their anticipated or actual
economic impact. As Chapter 9 demonstrated, cultural
programmes can generate significant economic impact, but
sustaining those impacts over a longer time period may be
problematic. Longer-term economic sustainability is influenced by a combination of factors that include the condition
of the broader financial environment (increases or decreases
of disposable income for event consumers), cost factors
outside the control of event organisers and city administrations (travel costs, energy costs, security costs), competition (losing market share to other events), media criticism
(often related to the perceived quality of event programmes
and the visitor experience), the weather and most notably
the levels of continued public sector support and private
sector sponsorship. These factors are discussed more fully
in Chapter 12.

If the policy priorities of a city change, so may its
continued level of investment in events. This may include
shifts in event policy, for example, when a city or a state
prioritises the attraction of a large-scale external event
against locally generated events, a problem that was identified earlier in this chapter. In the UK, the 2012 Olympics
have been widely criticised for reducing cultural funding as
lottery money usually allocated to arts projects is diverted to
the ever-growing Olympic budget. In Liverpool, the vast
budget for the ECOC in 2008 arguably also led to reductions
in social services provision in the city (Burnell, 2008).

Alternatives to Public Sector Funds

Lille hosted the ECOC in 2004, and had attracted significant sponsorship finance amounting to 18% of the total budget. The follow-up programme called ambitiously Lille 3000 has attracted over 30% in sponsorship to ensure its sustainability.

The continuity in the organising teams of the two programmes undoubtedly helped to build constructive long-term relationships with major sponsors. In 2008, for example, the Lille 3000 budget was €9 million, of which 45% came from commercial sponsors. According to Sosnierz (2007), the sponsorship programme developed for Lille 2004 and continued under Lille 3000 has: 'generated a new form of sponsorship, a collective, event-based form of sponsorship supporting regional cultural development'. This new form of sponsorship was based on long-term partnerships, which have continued to deliver financial support for cultural events even during the economic downturn. Major companies such as Accor (hotels), SFR (mobile telephony) and retail chain Auchan have continued to commit themselves to Lille 3000 following their positive experience with Lille 2004.

THE SUSTAINABILITY BALANCING ACT

Event programmes need to achieve sustainability across many different dimensions. Cities need to achieve a balance between the needs of producing, marketing, managing and financing the event programme, which will have a deep impact on the sustainable outcomes that can be achieved. This becomes clear just by considering some of the 'dilemmas' of programming listed by Radu (2007) in Chapter 3.

Culture as art or culture as a way of life?

The creativity which supports cultural endeavours depends to a large extent on an intrinsic approach to culture, which sees cultural production as being a largely autonomous realm, free from the socialising pressures of the society in which it operates. At the same time, art is considered to reflect society and to stimulate society to think critically about itself. This implies an active engagement with everyday life, which may threaten the autonomy so prized by the cultural sector.

Consultation or active participation in decision-making?

The desire to enhance democratic involvement in the decision-making process surrounding the event programme may sometimes hinder effective design and implementation. Arguments between different stakeholder groups can often make it difficult to reach decisions quickly, causing delays and initiating a range of managerial and operational problems. In many cases, therefore, event organisers may prefer to have limited consultation with stakeholders rather than involving them directly in decision-making. However, if stakeholders feel alienated by their lack of involvement they may withdraw support.

National or international allure?

In major event programmes such as the ECOC, there is a temptation to prioritise particular events that have an international profile, assuming that these tend to guarantee media coverage, please sponsors and deliver more impressive audience figures. In 2008 the Liverpool ECOC developed a strategy that tried to balance local talent with international 'stars' to underpin their programme. The Stavanger ECOC in 2008 deliberately produced a programme with 'no Bono, no Tall Ships' (Miller, 2007). Although this may appear risky in terms of generating large audiences, it was one means of ensuring greater attention for the work of local Norwegian artists. Without a local dimension to the programme, cities risk alienating the local cultural sector and reducing support for staging future events. However, without international stars, an event might be ignored or marginalised by the media, or attract little attention from the wider public.

The community or communities?

In the past, culture has often been used as a means of forging a shared national or local culture. But the view of the 'community' as a homogenous group has increasingly been criticised for failing to recognise difference and diversity. The view of cities as containing many different communities, each with their own culture, interests and needs, has tended to promote a 'something for everyone' approach to event programming, where each community has its own festival or event. This may satisfy the immediate need to meet demands from different communities, but it may do little to build social integration or cross-cultural understanding, unless there is an equally strong and well-integrated parallel community-building process. To serve the needs of 'the broader city-wide community' as well as each of the different 'communities' of the city, events need to develop 'bonding social capital' which supports the shared interests of those living in the city, as well as 'bridging social capital' which brings communities together and which can be a source of creativity and new cultural possibilities (Richards, 2007c).

In Luxembourg, extensive research conducted before, during and after the 2007 ECOC showed that although elements of the population remained negative or ambivalent about the event throughout, the feeling among most stakeholders and the majority of the audience was that the event had used effectively the considerable investment of resources (Margue, 2008). Those who actually attended the ECOC programme were more positive than non-attenders and were turned into 'apostles' for the ECOC rather than remaining detractors (Figures 10.1 and 10.2). For the cultural sector and the politicians in particular, there was a feeling that the event had managed to create a lasting legacy not just for the City of Luxembourg, but also for the whole Greater Region. Less than half of the previous ECOCs had such overall positive results and consistent positive views among different stakeholders (Palmer-Rae, 2004).

The Luxembourg experience also demonstrates that the sustainability 'balancing' act may not satisfy, or deliver perceived benefits for, every constituent stakeholder. (Luxembourg and Greater Region, 2008). For example, in Luxembourg, museums suggested that the key success factor for the ECOC was their own deliberate policy of creating new networks outside the established centres in order to stimulate creativity and reach new audiences, rather than the ECOC event itself.

The openness of critical debate tends to be a factor in sustaining events: dealing with criticism, managing

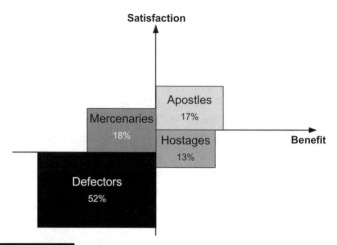

FIGURE 10.1   *TRI*M Typology Luxembourg ECOC – November 2006 (pre-event). (Margue, 2008).*

frustration and disappointment and learning from mistakes. There are many examples that illustrate the importance of using tensions within the cultural system of the city as a force for change and development. One common illustration is the emergence of most 'fringe' or 'off' festivals, which have originally provided alternatives to, or protest against, and mainstream events, but increasingly can become major events in their own right. This is most dramatically illustrated in

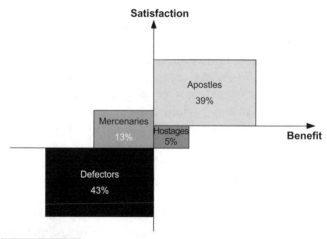

FIGURE 10.2   *TRI*M Typology Luxembourg ECOC – May 2007.*

Edinburgh, where the Fringe, originally set up as a protest to the tradition and centralised artistic control of the main International Festival, has become the largest arts festival in the world. The Edinburgh Fringe sells 1.5 million tickets a year, 900,000 of these to Edinburgh residents. In Adelaide, the Fringe Festival encompassed 543 shows in 2008 and claims to be the largest arts festival in the southern hemisphere. Fringe festivals have become unplanned arenas in which the free market holds sway and often have no strict limits on size or control on content, thereby producing a rich breeding ground for new talent, where the directors of mainstream festivals go shopping for the next hottest thing. Jon Morgan, the director of the Edinburgh Fringe notes:

> I was asked recently what a typical fringe show is, and that's a difficult question to answer. At one time it was easy: a man and his dog in a toilet doing cutting-edge poor theatre. Now, it can be anything. There's definitely a commercial element that wasn't there before and it's increasingly common for artists to appear in both fringe and curated festivals, depending on what work they're doing (Scott-Norman, 2008).

In Spain there is a long-standing tradition of organising 'alternative festivals' in order to present a different political message to the main event, often as a direct protest against local or national government. The political dimension to these events, which have sometimes been accompanied by violence, means that there have been moves to ban them in some cities. The creation of alternative events has even stretched to developing means of protesting against mainstream events themselves. In Cork in 2005, the group 'Where's me culture?' organised its own, alternative opening ceremony to protest against the perceived lack of involvement of the local cultural sector in the ECOC.

CONCLUSIONS

The eventful city needs to take account of all the different dimensions of cultural, social, environmental and economic sustainability and this requires a careful balancing act, which, in most cases, stretches beyond the responsibilities and capabilities of those organising individual events. What seems to be required is a more holistic vision of the sustainability of event programmes, which must be created at city level and managed centrally. Sustainability requires long-term planning; event issues need to be taken into account in the general planning process of the city as well as the event planning cycle. Events have lasting impacts, which will have implications for economic, cultural and social development, and legacy implications of events require careful planning.

Sustainability does not imply that all events in an eventful city must be protected and should continue. Difficult decisions may be required to reduce or stop certain events in the interests of the city's event programme overall. Events do not have an 'automatic' right of existence and need to be regularly reviewed and evaluated to determine which events best serve the aims of the city, which are failing to deliver sufficient value and which new events might better serve the future needs of the city.

In order to be sustainable in the longer term, an event programme needs to address all the different dimensions of sustainability discussed in this chapter. Economic sustainability is not sufficient if the cultural and social basis of the programme begins to be questioned, and vice versa. This is a problem which is now becoming evident for the ECOC programme as a whole. With the EU as a major stakeholder emphasising the economic and urban regeneration benefits of the programme, there is a danger that the cultural sector could become alienated from an event so that they perceive to have forgotten the original reason for its existence. Balancing the needs of all the different stakeholders in an event programme is an important skill that all cities need to develop.

CHAPTER 11

Critical Reflections: Keys to Success

A successful event is one that meets its own aims and, in doing so, benefits the city and improves the quality of life of its residents. The same principles apply to the eventful city as a whole: have the objectives of the entire city event programme been achieved and have their outcomes been of benefit to the city's economic, social and cultural prosperity? Although the broad criteria for success remain the same for all cities, the means of attaining these will vary; each city is unique and has a particular relationship to its event programme. Research has demonstrated, however, that many of those cities that might be considered as successful in their eventfulness have a number of qualities in common.

CRITICAL SUCCESS FACTORS

Our review of eventful cities has identified a number of recurring elements, which seem to be important to most city event programmes. The Palmer-Rae (2004:138) study of the ECOC (European Capital of Culture) also recognised a number of key factors, which resonate strongly with eventful cities more generally.

- **Context:** the city must develop a programme that is appropriate for the city at the time. Each city may be at a different phase of its historical, cultural, social and economic development, and this context must be taken into consideration.

- **Local involvement:** engagement and ownership by the local population need to be managed in an appropriate and effective manner.

- **Partnerships:** the development of partnerships with many different stakeholders is of primary importance, and these may include event-driven cultural institutions, local independent associations and groups, business and tourism sectors and social services/community organisations.

- **Long-term planning**: both advance planning of the event programme and legacy planning are essential.

- **Clear objectives:** clearly defined aims and objectives must be developed.

- **Strong content:** the programme should be unique and visible with a balance of different types of projects.

- **Political independence and artistic autonomy**: the event programmes should not be influenced by political interests, and the operational structure should have artistic or programming autonomy.

- **Good communication and marketing:** a clearly defined communication strategy is indispensable.

- **Sufficient funds:** a confirmed budget should be in place as early as possible in the preparation phase.

- **Strong leadership and committed team:** an independent director with international vision and leadership skills should be recruited to head a team of committed staff.

- **Political will:** the project needs political support to ensure sustainable impact.

Essentially, these factors can be grouped into a number of areas which are critical to the success of the eventful city:

- culture (content);

- place (context);

- power (leadership, political will);
- relationships (involvement, partnerships, autonomy);
- resources (funding and human resources); and
- planning (long-term vision, clear objectives).

Culture

The successful eventful city generally puts culture in its broadest sense first. Although certain events may place primary emphasis on the consumption of experiences, stimulating economic growth or improving the image of a city, the primary aim must be a wide nurturing of the broader cultural ecology of a city on which events, their producers and participants depend. It is important that a city should reflect its cultural landscape in its events programme. This means recognising a city's diversity as well as linking events clearly to place. As the AEA Consulting (2006:19) report on Edinburgh suggests:

> The city should offer a wide range and variety of year-round cultural activities and the festivals should be well-integrated into this ecology through networks, relationships and projects at local, regional and national levels. The festivals should be an integral part of their host cities' cultural life, with deep relationships with their local communities, and not have the feel of being grafted onto them.

At the same time, programming needs to be focused and innovative, not simply a narrow reflection of the local community, but a source of stimulation, provocation and critical reflection about the relationship between culture, events and the city. The issue of 'risk' is therefore important in designing the programme. A tendency towards 'safe' programming of well-known activities or productions may generate high attendance in the short term but it will not help the city to create a distinctive cultural identity that will attract attention and investment in the longer term. Planning for the eventful city is, by its very nature, a high risk if the goal is in part to be distinctive and to generate high image-impact. Being selective and making choices is a critical task when designing events, and a key to success is investment in quality rather than quantity. Consideration should be given to the size and scope of each event and to the city event programme. A common problem for ECOC and other major events is that large-scale programmes become unwieldy to manage and unreadable for audiences. Reducing the number of events may allow quality to be prioritised and resources to be targeted to the events with the most desirable outcomes.

As has been stated many times in this volume, an eventful city is not simply a city full of events, but a city that can use the events it has in a creative and sustainable way. New events should be carefully assessed before being added to the programme. Amongst the questions which should be asked are:

- What does each new event add to the cultural life of the city?

- What value (intrinsic, instrumental, institutional) will the event generate for the city and its citizens?

- What principles (diversity, social cohesion, equity) does the event support and promote?

- What will the event contribute to meeting the aims of the events policy of the city?

Flexibility is required to meet the changing needs of audiences. The rise of the 'cultural omnivore' described in Chapter 3 is a factor that may provoke greater elasticity and innovation in a city's approach to events and event marketing. Consumers of city events are increasingly comparing a wide range of different options, and interests are changing due to the influences of generational change, technology and global shifts. This will be discussed further in Chapter 12.

The 'language' used to describe events and speak to the audience in the eventful city also needs to be reconsidered. Addressing people in terms with which they can identify may be important, but also the use of new styles of branding, imagery, associations and specialised communication techniques have become critical to creating both a shared understanding of an event and encouraging publics to embrace new experiences. The principle of widening 'event inclusion' will help a city serve all of its citizens, and also stimulate creativity:

> *To nurture creativity, a city must have a generous and inclusive culture – it must have what we may term 'an attitude' It must have a nerve, it must value racial diversity, and it must have an impatient desire for new things, while valuing the old.*
>
> (Zukin, 2004:13)

However, as Crespi-Vallbona and Richards (2007) have argued, a feeling of exclusiveness is a prerequisite for creating belonging and ownership in certain events. The creation of a 'feeling of belonging' by providing certain benefits to 'insiders' is an important part of many strategies to generate resident support for events (see Chapter 7). However, the challenge for the eventful city is to balance the need for inclusion with the ability to create a feeling of exclusiveness at particular times or in particular spaces in the event programme.

Reflecting diversity is not just a question of creating events for all. This may lead to the segregation of different groups, rather than integration. Events therefore need to be approached much more in an intercultural or transcultural manner, inviting a sharing and an exchange of experience, rather than reinforcing cultural stereotypes. Interesting examples of this include the Brouhaha project in Liverpool (see Chapter 3) and the Zinneke Parade in Brussels (see Chapter 9).

Place

As the Work Foundation report on *Distinctiveness and Cities* (Lee, 2007:4) points out:

> *Cities are increasingly fighting for distinctiveness – operating with strategies designed to separate themselves from other places and develop their own individual brand. But they often follow only the first meaning of distinctiveness – the advertising – without embedding their ideas in a genuine assessment of their*

context and local place. Hiring a cutting edge architect is easy; making a statement that reflects and improves the character of the city is less so. And there is a real risk that – if they continue to ignore their local context – cities will waste a considerable amount of money for little real gain.

Sense of place is one of the key elements of distinctiveness for cities, and cultural events can be an important means of underpinning a sense of belonging and local pride. Lee (2007:21) argues that 'events are used to develop the brand of a city, get it noticed and help it stand out. But the most effective events are those that galvanise local people behind a shared vision or identity.' Events should therefore have a strong symbiotic relationship with the locations they are staged in: the event should strengthen the sense of place of that location and the location should help to distinguish the event. However, such a virtuous relationship is not automatic; it has to be carefully nurtured in the face of globalisation, commercialisation and spectacularisation.

In particular, the process of cultural globalisation (Nijman, 1999), and the increasingly rapid circulation of cultural symbols are redefining the relationship between events and place. Although location used to be important in terms of which cultural symbols were encountered, today these symbols have become largely place-independent. What makes the cultural quality of a place is now the combination of globalised and localised symbols. Place matters not so much in terms of the availability of culture, but the context in which it is consumed.

Creating sense of place is a critical success factor for many events – but how can this be achieved? There are a number of strategies which can be employed, many of which have already been examined in this volume:

■ Distinctiveness of location:
  For example, the use of rivers, canals, green spaces, unique physical features and historic or contemporary landmarks.

■ Creating an event atmosphere:
  For example, by concentrating activities in a relatively

small space or over a short period of time to create a heightened sense of animation and festivity or by organising special pathways, routes and transport networks that efficiently link event spaces and events together.

■ Developing event spaces:
For example, by creating spaces within the event where 'insiders' can meet and interact, or by transforming streets, parks and public squares into performance spaces.

■ Creating new rhythms of everyday life:
For example, finding ways of changing the pace of life in the city for a short time – slowing down hectic spaces and speeding up slow ones, such as restricting traffic circulation and introducing the short-term pedestrianisation of spaces or creating special market-places and open-air stages.

■ Creating a festival community:
For example, by developing a feeling of inclusion and building bonding and bridging social capital through special initiatives, activities and the design of intercultural gathering spaces.

The guiding principle for all such activities should be 'place making', rather than 'place marketing'. If an event is staged simply as a consumer product, it may lose its essential connection with the place and people that support it. The process of staging events should be conceived in terms of cultural and social development rather than just promotion. Concern about substance and content should be primary. Events help link intellectual capital with a specific place. One of the major challenges for all cities is the need to capitalise on the creative energy that the city generates. Cities function as nurseries for creative talent and ideas, which can then be harnessed and developed. Events can play a major role in anchoring creative talent in a particular place by showcasing talent through innovating programming, by cultivating new and appreciative audiences, and by developing a special 'atmosphere' unique to a place that cannot be found elsewhere.

Festivity is an important element in the development of creative clusters, which attract consumers not only on the basis of the creative products on offer, but also the creative atmosphere they can exude. Because the language of festivity is universal, it is also a way in which the localised 'space of places' can be linked to the global 'spaces of flows' (Castells, 1996). Even though the forms of festivity may differ from place to place, the experiences and benefits that cultural events give participants are much the same and are recognisable even to those with very different cultural backgrounds. This explains much of the recent trend towards globalisation of festive forms such as Carnival, the Mela or St. Patrick's Day parades.

Events should also be seen as time markers and time makers. Events are a means of demarcating a special time for celebration or reflection, but there are also opportunities for creating a feeling of a special time spent in a special place. Even when events have a similar content or theme, their relationship with the place in which they are staged helps to make them distinctive.

One of the means to achieve this is to ensure that events are properly rooted in a place. For example, in Luton the newly established Centre for the Carnival Arts provides a means of linking events to the city and to its local community and economy. Such 'grounded events' can provide a double linkage for a city: linking not just outwards to the global flow of culture by inviting artists and performers from different regions and cultures to come and perform, but also linking inwards into the local community, bringing the space of flows and the spaces of places together in a single event.

The events themselves should also be a means of creating trusting spaces in which performers, organisers and visitors can meet. For example, during the Bogotá theatre festival, the festival director Fanny Mikey

> opens up her home to colleagues, actors, politicians, business people with links to the cultural and theatre community and all of the friends whose help she can count on in the pursuit of her dreams. She favours the same approach during the Festival, arranging traditional

dinners and opportunities for encounters. For example, the Cabaret Big Top is a meeting place where audiences and artists can come together to the sounds of Colombian rumba music. The aim is always the same: to bring people together in a relaxed atmosphere to promote friendship and the forging of lasting relationships.

(Menza & Lapierre, 2004:69)

Meeting spaces within the eventful city can also serve the double purpose of creating internal cohesion and building bridges to the outside world. Crespi-Vallbona and Richards (2007) have argued that festivals are capable of increasing the social capital of a community, by binding the community together (bonding capital), as well as linking it to the world (bridging capital).

During the Avignon Festival, similar to many large-scale performance festivals, there is a designated meeting space for discussions, seminars and press conferences. These events focus on different aspects of the world of theatre and dance, including economic issues, legal issues, policy and artistic techniques. This space provides a focus for professionals at the event, as well as providing a platform for projecting the Festival to the outside world, as all activities are also open to the general public. This space helps to underpin the Festival's role as one of the leading events in the European festival calendar for both participants and the wider local community.

There is a need for individual events and eventful cities to be reflexive about their roles as gathering places in the modern world. Such reflection is being stimulated by the growing demands of event organisers and funders. In the case of the ECOC, the candidate cities are not only required to stage a year-long cultural programme, but are also specifically asked to examine 'the structures and capacities that it creates, as the basis for a lasting cultural development strategy for the cities concerned' (European Parliament, 2006:2). The Hungarian City of Pécs, in its application document for the 2010 designation, (City of Pécs, 2005:1) stated that:

Every applicant city must rethink what it means to be the European Capital of Culture. However, before this

*question can be answered, the cities must address two
even more important questions: how do they interpret
European urbanity, and what constitutes their own
urban character?*

Consequently Pécs examined issues such as the 'redis-
covery of urbanity' and the 'cultural turn in urban development' as key elements of their own approach. This analysis
identified the main development principles for the city and
the ECOC (ibid:22):

*The Pécs application has been compiled on the basis of
the following principles: the development projects
should be able to ensure that Pécs has cultural and
artistic spaces which are sufficient in number, size and
quality for the programmes of the European Capital of
Culture year and that promote the utilisation of the
city's economic potential and the development of the
creative industry and (cultural) tourism. They should
also ensure that the system of cultural institutions in
Pécs is made compatible with that of the European
Union so that they can fulfill international functions.
The developments should be in close connection with
the fundamental cultural tendencies of the city.
Furthermore, they should be the result of these
tendencies; should be able to revive the urban
character of individual city quarters, encouraging
talented young citizens to stay in the city; and should
have an international regional radiating impact.*

This reflexive approach was one of the impressive
elements of the application, which ultimately led to Pécs
winning the nomination.

As has been mentioned previously, learning from others is
clearly helpful for cities. But simply copying or borrowing
ideas from others does not provide distinctiveness. Unless
the form of eventfulness fits the mood and character of the
city, it may fail to take root. This is a principle understood in
Barcelona:

*When I grow up I want to be New York. Or perhaps
a mixture of London and Florence. Or maybe a bit of*

*Amsterdam and a bit of Paris. No, no. That's it. The
best of all is to be Barcelona.*

(Poster for the exhibition Barcelona(s): The futures of
the city, organised by the City of Barcelona in 1999,
quoted in Benach Rovira and Albet i Mas, 2004).

In contrast, Harcup (2000:221) describes the efforts of
Leeds to reimage itself as 'The Barcelona of the North'
through the creation of a '24 hour city' and the development
of 'carnivalesque' events. Manchester engaged a 'creative
director' to 'bring to life the creative expression of Manchester's image' (Hall, 2004). In spite of the best efforts of the
planners and the image-makers, none of these strategies
seems to end up totally convincing people that Leeds or
Manchester can be Barcelona.

One of the inherent tensions in such place-making
strategies is that successful places need to be distinctive, but
at the same time familiar to both residents and visitors.
Although familiarity can be created relatively easily through
theming (Gottdiener, 1997), this runs the risk of producing
look-alike events and event spaces as successful concepts
proliferate themselves to different cities. In fact, very few
events are exact copies of other events. In most cases, there is
some adaptation to place, giving the event a more local
flavour. For example, there are several different styles of
carnival in Brazil, with each region of the country having
different parade formats, music and competitive structures.

It is also important not to be over-protective of the event
programme. Although many cities see copying of their
concepts as a threat, in fact such copies can often add as
much to the original location of the event as to the other
places that 'borrow' the concept.

Power

The cultural arena is deeply infused with power. The very
notions of 'high' and 'popular' or 'mass' culture have
connotations of elitism and privilege that still echo today.
Even cities which are deeply committed to equity and
providing access to their citizens may still have to consider
issues of power. Who decides which events are staged or

funded? To what extent can local communities organise their own events? Who decides the programme? Should artistic freedom be absolute, or should there be political control to ensure the whole city meets its wider objectives?

As AEA Consulting (2006:21) points out, the public sector has a key role to play in such issues, because:

> *Investment by the public sector should offer a measure of confidence in each festival and to the festivals' system as a whole, to help lever other forms of support and partnership development. The public sector has a prime responsibility for supporting the development of festival infrastructure in the delivery of publicly-managed or public-private partnership projects and in the setting of priorities and offering incentives to the private sector. In addition, the public sector should take the major responsibility for ensuring longer term impacts of festivals and their sustainable benefits, based on end-user research and engagement, are monitored and understood.*

Those cities that have successfully used their power of decision-making to develop eventfulness tend to have:

- a top-down approach to establishing guidelines and structures;

- a bottom-up approach to generating ideas and enabling access to culture; and

- trusted experienced event directors to deliver programme quality, combining their own vision and knowledge with the interests of the communities they serve.

Although this volume has stressed the need for inclusion and public participation in decision-making about eventfulness, there has to be certain recognition that many events would not be staged or sustained without strong political leadership and commitment to a long-term vision. Having set out the strategic direction that the city should follow, the political leadership should trust the citizens and the event professionals to deliver. This does not necessarily imply a totally 'hands off' approach. Some degree of 'bureaucracy' is almost inevitable if a wide range of actors is to be given access to the cultural programme (Luxembourg and Greater Region, 2008). By establishing clear evaluation and selection procedures to consider ideas and proposals, all stakeholders are given a chance to claim a space in the programme. However, in the end, choices need to be made and this requires a professional skill that event organisers must possess. This is not a political or social skill, but a programming skill that balances intuition, experience and pragmatism (see Chapter 3). It is regrettable that many cities do not recognise the value of such programming skills. One of the main findings of studies of ECOCs is that the confusion between political and event programming decisions creates insurmountable dilemmas which may affect the ability of the event programme to meet its aims (Palmer-Rae, 2004).

Sustained public sector support is dependent on strong and effective event leadership being offered by the event governing structures. They need to have sufficient independence from political interests and the politically driven administrative structures of the city to enable them to make decisions in the interests of the event programme. The exercise of power is dependent on the networks within which it flows and, as discussed in Chapter 4, governance bodies must have the knowledge and skills necessary to ensure that an events programme can meet the objectives of the city. As identified earlier, the basic skills required include:

- strategic and financial management;

- marketing;

- event operations;

- legal skills;

- diplomacy;

- political experience; and

- leadership.

The growing external competition that faces cities forces them to increase their internal efficiency of operation in order to attract and retain events. In terms of event management, many cities are streamlining events procedures and setting up events offices, coordination mechanisms and one-stop shops for event organisers and other stakeholders. The city of Edinburgh is one strong example. The main aim of such strategies is to improve efficiency, impact and the quality of relationships between stakeholders in the eventful city.

Relationships

The notion of trust extends to all the relationships that the eventful city has with its stakeholders. Trust should be under-pinned by clear legal frameworks and responsibility, but the overriding concern should be to enable partners to achieve their goals and to produce sustainable outcomes, not to enforce compliance. Notions of trust also need to extend to the rela-tionship that a city has with other cities and regions. In an environment of global competition, successful cities realise that collaboration is essential: collaborative advantage may be a more appropriate strategy than competitive advantage. Strategic and tactical alliances should allow a city to derive the maximum benefit from working with, rather than against, other cities.

Hieronymus Bosch 2016: Collaboration or Coopertition?

The year 2016 is the 500th anniversary of the death of the painter Hieronymus Bosch. The event is being marked in particular in his birthplace, the Dutch city of 's-Hertogenbosch (or Den Bosch). One of the main problems that the city faces in organising the event is that it has no paintings by Bosch himself. His work is now scattered in many cities in Europe and America, but obtaining these works on loan to mount an exhibition is a major undertaking, made more complicated by the age and fragility of the artworks.

The solution to this problem has been to establish a restoration project, with the City of Den Bosch raising money to fund work on a number of pieces in return for their loan during 2016. A number of institutions around the world in cities such as Rotterdam, London, Lisbon, Berlin, Ghent, New York, Madrid and Vienna have agreed to this proposal, and Den Bosch is also helping Madrid and Vienna stage exhibitions of Bosch artworks during 2016. It is hoped that these exhibitions, rather than detracting from the main event in Den Bosch, will draw more attention from international visitors keen to see works by Bosch in his birthplace.

Similar principles apply to relationships with the media. Given that one of the most important aims of an eventful city may be to improve and strengthen its image nationally or internationally, the media is a vital partner. The ability to attract national and international press coverage is critical to the success of an events programme. Media coverage helps the eventful city both in terms of supply and demand. In terms of cultural supply, the prospect of strong media coverage will allow the city's events to secure artists who might not otherwise attend, or to engage them at a lower cost. Media coverage also stimulates demand in local, national and particularly in international markets.

Attracting media coverage is also helped by having a strong city and events brand, which can help the city stand out from the plethora of events that are available. An effective marketing and branding strategy depends, to a large extent, on positive relationships between stakeholders:

- A strong brand requires the support of stakeholders to be successful. If there is disagreement about the brand, mixed messages are likely to emerge, which will undermine the brand.

- A balance needs to be struck between the marketing and branding of individual events and that of the city. Is the city bigger than the event, or vice versa?

- Responsibilities for marketing and promotion need to be clearly defined.

- The city needs to determine the extent to which collaborative marketing of its events under a centralised umbrella is an effective strategy. This will depend on a wide range of factors, including the size and content of events in the programme, the markets to be addressed and the relationship between the tourism and cultural sectors.

Resources

As other chapters in this volume have demonstrated, the availability of resources is crucial to any events programme. This not only refers to public sector funding, but also corporate giving and sponsorship, commercial income, labour and cultural resources in general. Andersson (1999:386–387) noted that cities that have become major centres of creativity have usually benefited from rich financial resources for the arts in combination with 'relaxed control of resource use', because 'creativity is easily constrained or even destroyed by policy makers'.

Successful eventful cities tend to be those where adequate resources are available for the events programme, and where cultural events benefit from a broad resource base for culture as a whole. Resources must be sufficient to enable appropriate levels of quality, volume and breadth of festival and event activity in a city, with adequate opportunity for new development and risk-taking.

In order to attract private and 'alternative' funding sources, there is a need to stimulate entrepreneurialism within the events organisers of the city. The culture of waiting for public funding to be provided should be replaced by an understanding of the importance of the mixed economy in which events take responsibility for securing their own resources in addition to public funds.

Cities may need to think carefully about the allocation of public resources between events in the programme. As the number of events and possibly the demands on the public purse grows, there may be a temptation for public bodies to spread allocated budgets for events too thinly to avoid disappointment and difficult decisions. However, successful eventful cities are often those which target resources strategically.

Eventful cities may discover that 'less is more' when encouraging events. Many large-scale events or an overfull events programme may create resistance from local people suffering from 'event fatigue', which may suggest the need for increased event programme focus.

Resourcing strategy is broader than a consideration of finance. In particular, human resources are as critical for successful events as finance. Volunteers may supplement professional recruitment, but as Chapter 5 suggests, using volunteers may have its own costs particularly in terms of the training and supervision of volunteers. Successful eventful cities develop strategies for retaining professional talent. Although this should be applied at all levels of event organisation, there is no doubt that the retention of strong event leadership is particularly important. There is considerable mobility of event leaders and managers, but as AEA Consulting (2006:10) argued in the case of Edinburgh:

> *Visionary artistic and managerial leadership are essential, and conditions for recruitment, selection, retention and succession need to be carefully considered to attract the best talent and to offer platforms and solid operational frameworks that can support the creativity that such leadership inspires.*

Many successful eventful cities have managed to keep key event personnel involved in running events or managing culture in the city over a period of time in order to prevent a 'drain' of skills from a city (for example, as was the case in the ECOCs of Glasgow, Antwerp, Lille, Helsinki and Luxembourg, where skilled staff were retained).

In terms of the physical resources required for events, 'event infrastructure' needs to be developed and maintained. This includes high quality information, accommodation, transport and visitor services, as well as excellent venues, indoor and outdoor event spaces and other festival infrastructure to accommodate competitive programmes. There also needs to be continuous innovation of the use of space.

Innovative use of space is not just a physical issue, but also a question of timing. Events are forms of concentration – limited periods of time in limited spaces in which relationships and activities are magnified and distilled. George Hughes (1999) refers to festivals as a 'special form of time'. Cities may wish to recognise events as a tool for achieving concentration, which in turn can achieve other goals – an enhanced cultural atmosphere, an energetic or attractive city aesthetic, a forum for debate, or a moment of transformation.

Although the concentration of events may be an attractive strategy for certain eventful cities that may wish to draw the attention of a global audience, this strategy invariably places a strain on financial and human resources. As well as claims on the physical infrastructure of the city, events may present particular challenges to ensure transport and accommodation services and adequate security, high-level and efficient information and ticketing provision. Eventful cities may consider balancing the annual event programme, with periods of concentration mixed with specialised off season events to spread demand, utilise different locations in the city and vary the rhythm of the city (as well as give residents a break from 'hyperfestivity').

Although event programmes require investment by the city, events do become a valuable strategic resource. As discussed in Chapter 1 of this volume, events can add to the experiential dimension of the city in such a way that they enhance economic value as well as increase a city's overall organisational capacity. Events can create themes that the city can use to create economic value and make the city more readable, accessible and cohesive.

Growing the Cultural Economy in China

Changchun, the capital of north eastern China's Jilin province, has earmarked 29.3 billion yuan (€3 billion) for cultural investment between 2008 and 2012. The city feels that supporting and maintaining the city's cultural growth is the key to its future. According to the city development plan, added value sourced from the cultural sector is set to reach more than 6% of Changchun's entire GDP by 2012. Despite the potential profitability of the city's creative economy, quality of life remains the primary consideration. In a recent survey, Changchun was listed among the top 10 of Chinese cities in terms of local residents' satisfaction with their living environment.

In a bid to build these satisfaction levels still further, the local government has launched a series of high-profile events aimed at highlighting the cultural diversity of the city. So far these highly successful events have included a week-long festival of art and a well-supported book fair. In terms of more permanent artistic endeavours, the local government has also drawn up ambitious plans to renew the city's cultural infrastructure. This will lead to a major construction programme providing libraries, museums, exhibition halls, parks, stadiums, cinemas and cultural and sports centres throughout the city. It will also see the development of a purpose-built opera house. (http://www1.cei.gov.cn/ce/doc/cen1)

Planning

The need to secure resources and to offer a long-term perspective for events in the city requires careful planning, as explained in Chapter 5. A clear vision needs to be developed that provides a strategic context for individual events and illustrates how they should be contributing to the overall goals of the whole city. Strategic events studies have suggested that the vision needs to cover a period of at least 5 years, and perhaps longer. For Edinburgh, AEA Consulting (2006:8) suggests that 'festivals development should be considered in minimum blocks of 5 years and set within a longer-term strategic context of a city's long-term development and competitiveness'. Jago, et al. (2002:130) indicate that for the purposes of city branding, there is a 'need for longevity to be important in order for an event to become synonymous with a destination'. Their study suggested that 'for an event to have a good chance of successfully branding a destination, it needed to be tied to the same destination for 5–10 years'. However, the experience of the most successful ECOC host cities suggest that an even longer planning cycle may be needed. Respondents in Palmer-Rae (2004) indicated that for cities such as Glasgow and Rotterdam, it has sometimes taken 15–25 years of development for the image of certain cities, especially those that are fighting against negative stereotyping, to change substantially, for those changes to be sustainable, and for the impacts of events to be fully appreciated.

This implies that the eventful city should develop different planning horizons for its events programme and associated impacts:

- Long term – strategic vision for a period of 15–25 years, including large-scale infrastructure improvements.

- Medium term – 5–15 year tactical plan adapted to changes in the competitive environment and the available resources of the city.

- Short term – 3–5 year detailed plans with clear and measurable short-term gains, including regular reviews of the achievements and shortcomings of the programmes, with the aim of improving quality and feeding into medium- and longer-term planning.

The eventful city planning process needs to be integrated with other planning frameworks to ensure that synergies with other policy areas can be maximised, and to enable events to be embedded into the cultural fabric of the city. Events that are organised in an ad-hoc and temporary fashion are unlikely to be sustainable in the medium and long term. One important aspect of a successful eventful city has proved to be integration of the cultural dimension into the planning process. In the era of culture-led regeneration (Evans, 2007), those cities that have placed culture at the forefront of their development strategies, such as Edinburgh, Barcelona and Lille, have managed to combine sustained growth of events with significant long-term impacts.

For many events, planning should include attention to the spaces around cultural venues and facilities, in addition to planned activities that may take place in designated spaces. High quality public space is a vital prerequisite for the eventful city. Events should be planned in such a way that they 'invade' and 'occupy' the spaces of the city, providing opportunities for interaction with residents and visitors. As AEA Consulting (2006:20) suggests: 'Events should be "audience friendly" and "safe", but at the same time energising and continually surprising, creating a "spirit of excitement" or "buzz"'.

An essential component of the planning cycle is monitoring and evaluation. Effective monitoring requires the stakeholders to agree on the criteria, priorities and processes for monitoring, and clear guidelines need to be established for the evaluation of individual events as well as the events programme as a whole (see Chapter 9). The evaluation should incorporate economic, social, cultural and environmental factors as far as possible. It should also examine issues such as a city's creative capacity and management effectiveness. Effective monitoring should enable the eventful city to learn from its mistakes, as well as celebrate its successes, by presenting a realistic picture that can be read by all stakeholders.

Although the function of the planning process is usually to mitigate risk to ensure success, the eventful city also needs to incorporate the element of 'surprise' into its thinking. As discussed earlier in this volume, it is relatively easy to follow formulas made successful by other cities. It is more challenging to develop innovative and distinct events which can jolt residents and visitors into new ways of looking at the city. This can be done by creating a spectacular new museum, as in the case of the Guggenheim in Bilbao, or by landing a 'friendly alien' art space in the city centre, as Graz has done. In a climate of high levels of competition and economic adversity, certain cities have decided on a strategy of limiting the number of events. As indicated throughout this volume, a more targeted events programme may offer opportunities to highlight specific events or to develop very focused and specialised seasons. The possibility of 'de-establishing' events might be built into the process of planning the event programme, allowing it to shift with audience demand and the city's broader needs.

CONCLUSIONS

This chapter has indicated that the successful development of eventfulness is dependent on a wide range of factors. There is no single 'magic formula' that will make a city eventful, because the process of developing eventfulness tends to be one of careful planning and execution, involving stakeholders in decision-making, investing for the long term and, ultimately, taking risks, and doing the unexpected.

Producing a successful programme for the eventful city is a complex process, which requires the application of a broad range of skills and expertise as well as the effective orchestration of stakeholders and resources. Outstanding eventful cities tend to be those with long-term vision, which are willing to take artistic and financial risks and that have a broad base of stakeholder support. Effectively managing all the aspects of this multidimensional planning process requires continual monitoring, critical reflection and open debate.

At the start of the process, each city should define the meaning of 'success'. Does it involve attracting a large public, generating economic impacts or achieving global media coverage? Is the criterion of success the achievement of measurable social cohesion or reenforcing the identity of the city? Does success imply organising more events, fewer higher quality events or different events? Without knowing what 'success' means for the city, success is difficult to achieve and evaluate.

CHAPTER 12

The Future of the Eventful City: Global Trends and New Models of Eventfulness

Cities continuously adapt to a rapidly changing environment, and their event programmes must also adapt in response to such changes. Global challenges such as economic restructuring, the rethinking of energy resources and combating the potentially disastrous effects of climate change have launched a new debate about values and what is meant by quality of life. Discussions about culture, economic value, technology and community stimulate a broader consideration of values, public interest, public purpose and corporate practices. The notion, purpose and practice of events in cities are intensely influenced by such global trends.

This chapter considers which trends might be important for the eventful city in the future, paying particular attention to external 'mega-trends' that are likely to impact on the majority of cities. Different 'models' of event development can be used to help determine which strategies might offer successful adaptations to a changing environment. Given that most cities face similar challenges from the external environment, it is perhaps not surprising that many decide to adopt similar strategies or models for eventfulness.

435

Following successful models may reduce the risk involved in developing eventfulness to some extent. But even when a city has a proven track record for successful events, there needs to be a continued vigilance of factors that may impact negatively on the future of the event programme. Politicians are often complacent in times of relative stability and act only in the face of impending crisis, perhaps after it becomes unavoidable. Complacency about eventfulness may take various forms, including inadequate financial support, poor infrastructure, weak coordination and the absence of clear policies and strategies. Cities that aspire to be eventful need to take stock of their strengths and weaknesses and be aware of potential threats, particularly from the external environment. It was such thinking that prompted Edinburgh City Council, the Scottish Arts Council and other stakeholders in the festivals in Edinburgh to commission a report from external independent consultants to examine the potential threats to Edinburgh's events strategy and reputation as a world festival city (AEA Consulting, 2006). The findings of this study have been quoted in earlier chapters. This study also argues that there is a wide range of factors related to the internal organisation of the city itself that influence the supply and demand of events and other factors that depend largely on the external environment of the city. The external impacts may be less controllable, such as those due to

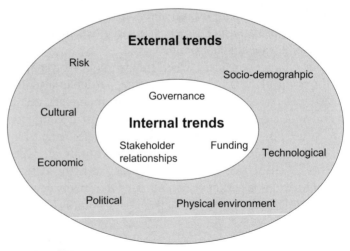

FIGURE 12.1 *External and internal trends affecting the eventful city.*

macro-economic factors, shifts in demography or growing competition from other cities and regions (see Figure 12.1).

THE EXTERNAL ENVIRONMENT OF THE EVENTFUL CITY

Environmental factors

Global warming and other environmental challenges are likely to lead to more attention being given to environmental themes in events, and growing demands for events to become environmentally sustainable and to encourage sustainability among their audiences. This is already evident in the emergence of a number of 'environmentally friendly' festivals (see Chapter 10).

Changes in climate might also have a direct impact on individual cities and their events as the weather becomes less predictable. Increased summer rainfall in some areas of Europe, for example, will involve increased costs for weatherproofing and insurance. The increased risk of extreme weather such as heat waves or flooding may need to be taken into account in risk assessments. The heavy rain and flooding in many parts of England in the summer of 2007 led to widespread cancellation of events, either through direct flood danger or because outdoor event terrains were simply too waterlogged to accommodate them.

Some events that rely directly on climate for their attractiveness may also have to reassess their strategy. In 2009, the Fifth Annual Butterflies, Dragonflies & Summertime Things Festival at Bastrop Gardens in Texas was cancelled due to an unusual heat wave and extreme drought. The Harbin International Ice and Snow Festival on the edge of Siberia is located in one of China's coldest places, where temperatures regularly drop to below $-35\,°C$. An estimated 800,000 tourists, 90% of them Chinese, visit the festival to see gigantic ice sculptures, which in 2008–2009 included a 160-m high Father Christmas. The event traditionally runs from mid-December to early February, but with global warming the ice no longer freezes well, causing problems for the sculptors, as well as safety concerns for visitors (Daily

Mail, 2008). In the future, such events may have to take place over a more limited time period, or introduce artificial cooling and ice-making. Such technology has already facilitated the first indoor Snow and Ice Sculpture Festival in Europe, staged in Brugge (Bruges), Belgium in 2007–2008. A specially built 1350 m^2 ice tent was refrigerated at a constant temperature of −5 °C (Gianola, 2008). Obviously, the use of such technology will also increase energy and water usage and raise the cost of staging such events.

The drive to reduce the carbon footprint of events might lead to certain events becoming more localised in order to reduce travel distances of targeted publics. If significant tax increases are placed on fossil fuels to reduce emissions, visitors may be reluctant to travel long distances to visit events, with the result that the audience for event programmes will become more geographically restricted.

Socio-demographic trends

Changes in population structure are likely to impact on certain events. Ageing populations in Europe and North America may increase demand for events that appeal to particular generational interests and tastes, such as performances by established and 'older' rock stars and classical music conductors and exhibitions by traditional artists. Younger audiences are increasing in regions such as Asia and Africa and some events are beginning to develop offshoots to try and tap into growing youth markets.

The fact that the global population is rapidly urbanising may also have a significant impact. Although the majority of cities that are recognised as the world's most eventful cities are now located in Europe and North America, the focus may shift towards Asia in the near future. Asia's share of the global urban population is expected to rise to 53% by 2030, and by 2015, 12 of the world's 20 largest cities will be in Asia. New eventful cities will therefore emerge, increasing the competition and pressure on existing centres of cultural event activity to retain their market share.

The development of eventfulness in Asia may well take on different forms to European or North American models.

Rapid urbanisation has put pressure on the historic core of Asian cities, which tend to have less public space than their European counterparts. Most Asian cities also have less well-developed cultural industries, and therefore less cultural infrastructure or 'orgware' to support events. A recent review by the London Development Agency (2007) for example, indicated that London has around 200 major festivals a year, compared with only 22 in Shanghai, a city over twice its size. In an attempt to better compete, there has therefore been a tendency for Asian cities to create new events which mimic traditional western cultural events to fill this perceived 'gap' in the event calendar. These events also aim to attract local visitors and more tourists from abroad, especially from countries in the Asian–Pacific Region. Many Asian cities including Shanghai, Beijing, Seoul, Taipei and Tokyo are now placing increased emphasis on developing and attracting events to compete with European and North American cities, and are investing substantially in event infrastructure, visitor services and organisational capacity. Mobile consumers will increasingly be able to decide which global cities offer the most appealing and exciting experiences.

In successful eventful cities, there is a strong relationship between the total size of the metropolitan area and the cultural core of the city. A unique festival 'atmosphere' can be generated easily in compact city centres with a clearly identifiable cultural core. However, sustaining such an atmosphere requires a critical mass of visitors, which is usually dependent on attracting a large resident population. Barcelona and Amsterdam have a larger metropolitan population to draw on, combined with a sizeable but compact cultural core. Edinburgh has the compact core, but lacks the large resident population, and is therefore dependent on tourists or on mobilising large numbers of local people for concentrated special events.

For Asian cities, this compact and identifiable historic core is often lacking (or has been decimated by redevelopment), and therefore new ways are being found to create a festival atmosphere in newly developed public spaces. Asian cities such as Shanghai and Hong Kong are building special 'cultural quarters' to create the ideal atmosphere and critical mass of spaces to generate excitement. A large number of 'shopping festivals' have been developed in cities such as Hong Kong, Singapore and Dubai in recent years, many of which have integrated events and cultural elements alongside the essential shopping activities. The Dubai Shopping Festival includes the 'Global Village', housing pavilions from around 60 countries, bringing together 'diverse customs, cultures and entertainment shows and covering a broad spectrum of activities including music, goods, dances, arts and handicrafts, theatre, costumes, and cuisine and food from different parts of the world' (Dubai Shopping Festival, 2008). In Singapore, the Noise Festival aims to give young artists a platform to showcase their works, and in order to make this work more accessible to a younger audience, the exhibition of work was held in a major shopping centre in 2008. The 'events and shopping' model may have high appeal to a certain market of consumers, where the experience and joy of shopping is of equal entertainment value to attending adjacent performing and visual events.

The impact of inward and outward migration is shifting the demography of certain cities. As noted in Chapter 1, such movements of people are reducing the cultural boundaries between places and producing and reproducing both old and new traditions in cities. Certain events have their origins in migrational movements, such as the Highland Games held in North America, the melas celebrated in Europe or the Welsh Eisteddfodau in Argentinean Patagonia. The events calendars of most major cities include celebrations of migrant cultures, such as in Baltimore, which boasts Polish, Greek, Latino, African American, Caribbean, Nigerian, Native American PowWow, Ukrainian, Irish, Korean and Russian festivals.

Such influences are likely to become more significant in the future, as levels of migration increase. The International Organisation for Migration (2008) forecasts that the number of international migrants will grow from 175 million in 2000 to 230 million in 2030, with the biggest impact on large cities. The eventful city may need to face future decisions about how to adapt events to the influences of migration flows and how different groups might be brought together to create 'intercultural' or 'transcultural' urban experiences.

Due to population shifts, it is likely that the eventful city of the future will be recreating or reinventing 'traditional' events as well as innovating new ones. In societies facing a situation of 'liquid modernity' (Bauman, 2000) with looser social bonds and less well-defined social structures, events become both a means of trying to strengthen old ties and creating new ones. Traditional events celebrate modern or even premodern notions of community, whereas many post-modern events attempt to create new forms of association and intercultural communication. As the traditional forms of social gathering wane in importance (Putnam, 2000), there may be a growing need for new moments of copresence, which many events are ideally placed to provide.

Technological trends

Information and communications technologies (ICT) are transforming the world through the radically different behaviours and expectations of current and future generations that have 'grown up digital' (Arts Council England, 2007:64).

The essence of events remains rooted in the arena of simultaneous production and consumption and the idea of 'being there' is still paramount. However, new technology is beginning to have an impact on the way in which events are produced, consumed and distributed. One notable example is the developing notion of 'online' or 'virtual' festivals. Another is the use of Websites and blogs to express views about events, such as 'Virtual Festivals' in the UK, which is attracting 2 million visitors each year who help plan, document and share information about festivals (www.virtualfestivals.com). Several hundred event organisers also use this site to connect to their audiences.

In the UK, the BBC rented a virtual tropical island where it stages online music festivals. The island in the online game Second Life held its first event in 2007 with bands including Muse, Razorlight and Gnarls Barkley. This virtual event was a mirror of BBC Radio 1's real-world, One Big Weekend event, held in Dundee, Scotland. Those attending the Second Life rock festival were able to watch and listen to live streams of the bands on stage, take part in a dance-off in the DJ tent, take a hot air balloon ride or have a virtual mud-slide. In the event, there were complaints that the level of real/virtual interaction could have been much greater, for example, by allowing real-time messaging between the two worlds. The fact that 30,000 people attended the 'live' version and only 400 experienced it in cyberspace indicates that the balance still lies heavily on the desire for 'real' experiences. However, as Web 2.0 tools become more popular, this balance could shift significantly. Since virtual events are currently much cheaper than their real counterparts, there is a possibility that virtual events may start to be used as a promotional tool for real locations. It is now possible, for example, to experience the running of the bulls in Pamplona, Spain in 3D via the Website www.sanferminencierro.com. The experience of this emblematic event has been recreated from pictures taken by those participating in the real event, using head-mounted cameras.

There are also art exhibitions being staged in Second Life. In 2009, the newBERLIN ART FESTIVAL took place in the CUBIX, a Real Life/Second Life location in newBERLIN:

> *Just as in the real Berlin, people with different individual perceptions of reality meet up in newBERLIN and exchange their ideas…. The streets of newBERLIN will be open to everyone to express his or her idea of art or its concept. The whole festival is based on a hyper social network that is internationally connected by the internet.*
>
> (Northoff & Lightfoot, 2008)

Although the new virtual events may help to strengthen rather than weaken their analogue counterparts, the new possibilities of Web 2.0 platforms might transform the ways in which events are organised and marketed. At present the distribution of event information and ticketing via Internet is still relatively new, but this is changing rapidly. Social networking sites have become an increasingly important source of information about events and ticketing on demand is beginning to make the packaging of events as simple as travel products. Over 50% of individuals in Europe now use online booking to make travel plans; two thirds do so in North America.

Websites will also become an avenue through which creative inputs are gathered for events. For example, the NOISE Festival, which labels itself as the 'Olympics of Creativity', launched a call for creative output on its Website in 2008:

NOISE, the newly launched national festival for creative talent is calling out to young creatives across the UK to submit their work to the Website www.noisefestival. com. If you're a bedroom genius aged 25 or under you have until 31st May to submit everything from music, fashion, film, design, written word and all new forms of creative expression, such as podcasts. Through the NOISE showcase and unique NOISE projects, the cross-media festival will uncover and spotlight the next generation of creative talent in the UK.

The Website attracted over 8 million hits, and in addition to the virtual elements of the event, exhibitions were staged at Urbis Manchester, Liverpool Biennial and Magma London, as well as live performances, fashion and cinema events in London.

The Virtual Festival of Aerobatic Teams

The Virtual Festival of Aerobatic Teams (VFAT) is the world's biggest virtual air show, flown using the Lock On flight simulation. VFAT is held annually in November or December and spectators can watch the virtual air show live using Internet streaming technology. The first VFAT took place in 2005 with six aerobatic teams and three solo pilots gathered on a game server. The third VFAT in 2007 featured 13 teams and 5 solo pilots, and Internet streaming technology was used to show the displays to spectators. Four thousand five hundred individual spectators viewed the VFAT 2007 live and show replays were downloaded 21,000 times during a 1 year period.

Economic trends

As the weight of economic power shifts from West to East, so one would also expect the global festival scene to shift eastwards. As outlined above, cities such as Shanghai, Singapore and Hong Kong are already investing substantially in developing their events hardware in the form of new performance facilities, museums and outdoor public spaces, which in time will become the focus of new events and festivals.

Economic competition between cities wishing to stage cultural events will become increasingly crucial as Baumol's cost disease takes effect, a phenomenon which is as applicable today as it was over 40 years ago (see Chapter 6). As the costs of event production grow, the ability to finance major events will give a vital competitive edge to particular cities.

The combination of recurrent running costs for event facilities and the staging of annual events may begin to place an increasing strain on public finances. If cities also want to compete to attract blockbuster events, such as the Universal Forum of Cultures, the World Design Capital or the ECOC (European Capital of Culture) and its counterparts (Capital of Islamic Culture, Cultural Capital of the Americas, Arab Cultural Capital), there may also be significant non-recurring expenditure devoted to infrastructure and special events. For example, the 2004 Universal Forum of Cultures in Barcelona cost €360 million, and Eindhoven proposed spending €140 million on hosting the 2012 World Design Capital.

The cost of competing for international footloose events is placing ever-higher entry costs on the global major event market. This is one of the drivers for some cities to establish their own original events – why pay the cost of bidding for an event when that money could itself be invested in a city's own self-managed events? The rising cost of events is also likely to place growing pressure on event programmes to demonstrate outputs for the community in order to justify the investment, which may lead to greater political scrutiny and regulation as well as the need to develop more professional management models.

Increasingly creative methods of financing events are also being developed to cope with the growing gap between public funding and the demand for event subsidies. The public sector finance gap may tend to place more emphasis on the Third Sector (or voluntary sector) to fund events. For example, the Tanglewood Festival in Lenox, Massachusetts began asking their 750 volunteers to donate not just their time, but also a minimum of $75 (€60) to the festival (Arts Management, 2007). These developments point to the growing importance of considering the public value of events (see Chapter 9), because the economic sustainability of many events will increasingly depend on their perceived public value.

Events are also likely to take a more significant role in the process of place making in cities in the future (Landry, 2006) and are increasingly positioned to act as a catalyst for urban regeneration and shaping public space, as well as refreshing or changing the image of cities. City-branding strategies tend to be bound up with events, and event programmes are designed to create or reinforce a particular brand. The development of the Manchester International Festival (see Chapter 9) can be placed in the context of the development of the Manchester 'original modern' brand, by underlining the creative role of the city through the commissioning of original works.

It is also important to recognise the impacts of the current global financial crisis, which may have negative consequences for events across the world. According to the latest economic forecasts, many of the world's economies are entering their most severe recessions in 50 or 60 years. The world's 'advanced' economies contracted by around 3–4% in 2009, while the growth of emerging economies is expected to slow significantly (OECD, 2009b).

The recession has been triggered by a 'crisis' in global financial markets. The consequent drop in asset values (such as stocks) is likely to feed first through to sectors that rely on asset income, such as endowments. Events that rely on corporate donations and income from interest on endowments for special programmes, operational support and long-term sustainability will most certainly be affected. Wider impacts might occur later as reassessments of wealth lead to fundamental changes in organisational and consumer behaviour. Thus, the effects ripple unpredictably outward from finance markets into the 'real economy', where their impacts may be felt for many years, including long-term unemployment and its accompanying social costs.

It is still too early to predict with any accuracy the effects of the economic downturn on events. This uncertainty is not helped by a lack of robust, objective evidence on the economic interdependencies of the events economy and the effects of previous recessions on events.

The findings of an initial report of a survey of their members and study of other relevant research by the International Federation of Arts Councils and Cultural Agencies (IFACCA) concentrate on the impact of the global financial crisis on the arts, but their conclusions are also highly relevant to the events sector:

Negative outcomes from the downturn

- Less travel/cultural tourism, particularly international tourism (with an additional effect in the US where travel tax revenues, such as motel taxes, are often put towards the arts).

- A shift to less expensive arts experiences.

- Reduction in spending on theatre tickets, particularly single ticket purchases rather than subscriptions (loyal supporters via subscription tickets likely to remain).

- Fewer art purchases by both individuals and institutions.

- Consumption of quality and major arts experiences will be stable, but smaller local arts may experience a decline in consumption (consumers will cut back on discretionary spending. This may make audiences more discriminating and risk-averse).

- Sales and private sponsorships are declining in value.

Positive outcomes from the downturn

- Local cultural tourism may increase, offsetting an expected decline in international tourism.

- People will turn to the arts in times of turmoil for the 'feel good' factor, so demand for the arts may not drop as much as in other sectors.

- A shift to the arts away from more expensive leisure pursuits.

- Innovation, creativity and flexibility in the arts sector will allow it to respond better to the downturn than other economic sectors.

- Reduction in the exchange rate softening the decline in tourism by making incoming tourism cheaper in some countries.
(IFFACA, 2009)

Financial Crisis Hurts Film Festivals

The financial crisis is hitting some US film festivals hard as local cash and in-kind sponsorship are drying up quickly. One casualty is the Jackson Hole Film Festival, which relied on local patrons more than it did national sponsors. As the market nosedived, sponsors disappeared. Having only raised a fraction of its $1.5 million (€1 million) budget in 2009, the festival was cancelled. In Europe, the impact of the downturn seems less severe. The corporate-funded Rome Film Festival has maintained a budget of €17 million. The Venice Film Festival gets 70% of its funding from the state and seems secure with a €12 million budget. In Eastern Europe, the Warsaw Film Festival has secured a multi-year agreement with the city and RWE, one of Europe's biggest energy companies.

Cultural trends

As noted in Chapter 9, events can represent critical meeting points where different cultures encounter and experience each other and exchange ideas. The growth of multicultural and intercultural events has been particularly marked in those cities with large migrant populations, but the need to provide bridges between different cultural and social groups is now paramount everywhere.

Cultural events in particular are therefore being created for the express purpose of developing cultural and social connections. The Sarajevo International Festival, organised by the International Peace Centre in Sarajevo: 'has become a symbol of freedom of creativity and a place for familiarising with diverse cultures and civilisations.' One of the ways of bringing cultures together is to create links between cultural events. The programme for the 2008 Edinburgh International Festival (EIF) was announced in Sarajevo, highlighting the participation of East West Theatre Company from Sarajevo in the EIF.

Transcultural events are also being specifically promoted by organisations established to form bridges between cultures:

> *TransCultural Exchange's mission (is) to bridge cultural, geographic, political and linguistic divides by bringing people together through the arts in order to foster a greater understanding of world cultures. At the same time, TransCultural Exchange seeks to further artistic innovation by creating large-scale, cross-discipline, global art projects and programming. In this way, TransCultural Exchange provides those in the arts with the necessary tools to become active participants in today's increasingly interdependent society. (http://www.transculturalexchange.org/index2.html)*

TransCultural Exchange's Tile Project (2004-2008) brought together artists from different countries and cultures to create site-specific artworks for different locations around the world. For 2009, 'TransCultural Exchange invites artists to work with individuals around the world to create new collaborative art works for a series of exhibitions and a catalogue entitled Here, There and Everywhere: Anticipating the Art of the Future.'

In Sweden, the organisation Intercult works on a similar basis with its aims:

> *To invigorate cultural life in Sweden with international experiences and influences, to create large-scale, ground-breaking performance art productions for the European culture scene and to link initiatives with the purpose of developing cultural competence and increasing diversity in the cultural sector.*

According to the Arts Council England (2007:60), in the UK there is also a growing transcultural audience in the UK for events that promote diversity:

> *The change is particularly pronounced among young people. Data from the 2001 census shows that the fastest growing ethnic group among the under-16s in England and Wales is 'mixed', suggesting the emergence of more complex identities, which are not easily defined by traditional forms of categorisation.*

Just as artists coming together in a single event are producing transcultural content, other events are becoming footloose and moving through different cultures on their travels. Strong examples of such an event are WOMAD (World of Music, Arts and Dance) and WOMEX (World Music Exhibition), which move between countries presenting music from different cultures, and having a different cultural reaction in each place they visit. It is likely that the footloose nature of some major events may grow, particularly as event organisers realise they can negotiate with different cities to obtain the best financial incentives for their event. Different cities often bid competitively for such events.

However, cultural mixing is not automatically accompanied by tolerance and understanding:

> *The first Sarajevo Queer Festival began on 24 September 2008. It included exhibitions, performances, public discussions and films. However, the attacks at the end of the first day left eight people injured and forced the organisers, a non-governmental organisation Udruzenje Q, to close the rest of the festival to the public and eventually cancel the whole event (www.amnesty.org).*

The problem of intolerance may become a dilemma for certain cities that wish to promote their image as tolerant diverse places, but where significant public prejudices held by certain groups of residents cannot easily be overcome. When designing event programmes, some cities have been subjected to pressure to omit sensitive subject matter and stay away from topics that may invoke anger or incite racial abuse. Controversial subjects associated with events inevitably attract attention by the local media. Negative coverage of an event programme can seriously affect the audience. A further mega-trend in certain countries unfortunately appears to be events that are influenced by an increasing preoccupation with symbolic, iconic and traditional reinforcement of national identity and self-identity. Some event organisers attempt to overcome this with programmes that help to combat ignorance and promote tolerance and internationalism.

In addition to the impacts of new technologies and changing demographics on cultural creation, production and dissemination outlined earlier, other cultural shifts are discernible that may effect the nature of event programmes. One such trend is the increasing 'blurring' of traditional boundaries between cultural sectors and disciplines (music, theatre, dance, film) and the increase of more 'interdisciplinary' production and programming. Another trend is the increasing interest in 'the spectacular' and 'the unusual', and in the importance of the entire event 'experience' that distinguishes the live event from witnessing it on television, the Internet or not at all. Allowing drinks and food into performing spaces while watching concerts and shows, offering pre- and post-event activities and parties, watching performers backstage and communicating with them using mobile phones through Twitter feeds, on Facebook and other media that promote interactivity between performers and audience are examples of new trends.

Burning Man

Burning Man is a radical week of art, exhibitionism, parades and music that culminates with the incineration of the Burning Man, where flame-throwers regularly split the night sky in Black Rock City, Nevada. It is governed by the 11 commandments of Burning Man – radical inclusion, gifting, decommodification, radical self-reliance, radical self-expression, communal effort, civic responsibility, leaving no trace, participation, immediacy and, most importantly, participation. The focus of Burning Man is therefore on cultural production, not consumption. People come to Burning Man to entertain each other, not to be entertained. It's not a consumer event – no one is catering to you, so you must provide for your own survival. Nothing is provided by the event with the exception of portable toilets, with the only items for sale being ice, coffee and lemonade, as commerce is forbidden. (www.burningman.com).

Governance and administration

Cities often need to adapt their administrative apparatus to accommodate events. As discussed in Chapter 4, not only is the creation of local or regional events units becoming more common, but also event policy is increasingly bound up in the marketing and image making of the city. This makes developing and maintaining stakeholder networks all the more crucial to the success of event programmes. Stakeholders should understand the role of events in supporting the city's other policy objectives.

The organisation of events not only impacts on the administrative structure of the city, but also can help to build the city's overall organisational capacity. By acting as a focus, events can bring stakeholders together around a specific project, and the processes of event organisation can act as a model for cooperation across different public policy areas.

In Chapter 10 it was stressed that one of the 'skills' that cities can develop from bidding for events is the persuasive presentation of its strengths and opportunities. Increasingly, cities need to compete with each other not just to attract events, but also to attract competitive funding from government or private sector investment. Bidding for events becomes a valuable learning exercise in maximizing organisational effectiveness and persuading residents to show their support for their city. Liverpool was a city that had been unsuccessful in bidding for many UK and international events, but learning from this experience, it successfully bid against 11 other cities to win the UK's nomination as European Capital of Culture 2008. In awarding the title, the judging panel stated clearly that it was the evidence of support from the people of Liverpool that had been a deciding factor. Part of the bidding process had involved a major public campaign to ensure the interest of local residents in the Liverpool 2008 idea. The internal management of the bid benefited from the city's previous successes and failures when competing against other cities.

Increasing emphasis is also being placed on the importance of involving the public in decisions about how to shape the programmes for events. In some ways this can be seen as an extension of the trend towards choice and personalisation. For example, in 2007 Bristol held public consultations on its plans to hold a Music Festival to replace the long-running Ashton Court Festival when this went bankrupt:

> *The consultation is an important feature of our efforts to encourage the public to get involved with the festival, either through raising points at the meeting or taking active participation in the events organisation.*
> (BBC Bristol, 2007)

Eventually the consultation resulted in a community group being formed to develop a new Bristol Festival, which was launched in 2008. The festival was given a more 'local feel' than the previous incarnation, in line with the wishes of people who wanted a more community-based event. Local authorities in the UK (Creative Cultures and Associates, 2007) and in North America (City of Vancouver, 2005) have carried out extensive public consultation on event policy and the use of public space. If such trends continue, then events policy is likely to reflect more local concerns in the future. Those cities which have substantial, large-scale event programmes, however, have tended to adopt a top-down approach to event planning in the belief that extensive consultation is likely to slow down the process of bidding for and winning major events. The issue is not whether or not public consultation should take place, but the manner and timescale by which the public is consulted.

Although the public sector clearly has an important role to play in creating city eventfulness, there is a tendency towards outsourcing the management of events and event programmes to independent not-for-profit or profit-making organisations. There is often pressure for local authorities to withdraw from the direct organisation of events, which is not viewed as a core service activity. For example, in New Zealand the following argument has been made:

> *Given the private interest involvement in the field of events management, the Rotorua Chamber of Commerce suggests that this activity relates to the provision of private goods and services and is an example of local authority involvement in non-core services where private interests should prevail.*
> (Rotorua Chamber of Commerce, 2007)

In some cities such opinions may lead to the creation of new private or non-governmental or public–private partnership bodies to manage events. The common ECOC model of establishing a not-for-profit organisation or a private–public partnership organisation, such as an agency with public sector oversight, may be an appropriate alternative management mechanism to direct service provision by the city itself. However, the responsibilities and authorities, skills and experience of the Board members and professional staff, as well as the relationship with the public bodies, are issues that require careful examination (Palmer-Rae, 2004).

In the future, there may be more voluntary sector involvement in events as local government in certain cities seeks to enable local communities to manage their own events. In Basingstoke in the UK, concerns about the rising costs of events and the decreasing relevance of the event programme to the needs of local people encouraged the local authority to transfer more responsibility for the event programme to local voluntary groups. By providing support in terms of event management training, information on sources of finance and streamlining event licensing procedures, cities might persuade more local bodies to organise events themselves, thereby reducing the burden on the public sector. As public sector event funding is likely to remain constrained in the future, such strategies are likely to become more widespread. As discussed in earlier chapters, a city events office, or the appropriate service department within the public authority, may develop an enhanced approach to 'arms-length' management of the event programme. This may require the development of clearly structured monitoring of events to facilitate funding decisions and to oversee events managed by other bodies.

GENERATING KNOWLEDGE ON EVENTFULNESS

The rapidly changing environment of cities creates a growing need for knowledge about the relationship between cities, their event programmes and the achievement of sustainable outcomes. At present, such knowledge is weakly developed. In particular, most existing event-related research takes place at the level of individual events, which does not necessarily add to an understanding of the eventful city. In order to understand the eventful city more fully, there are a number of areas that are worthy of more detailed research. A research agenda for the eventful city might concentrate on the totality of a city event programme, which emphasises the relationship between the city and all of the events it stages, rather than on individual events. The key questions that might be addressed include the following:

■ How does the event programme affect the eventful city?

■ How does the city affect the event programme?

■ How do stakeholders affect the eventful city?

■ How does the eventful city affect its stakeholder network?

How does the event programme affect the eventful city?

Cities become eventful in the hope of achieving a range of outcomes from the event programme. The outcomes and impacts of individual events have been researched relatively extensively, but many questions still remain about the impact of organising a coordinated event programme or series of events.

Is the impact of a city event programme greater than the sum of its individual events? The desire for eventfulness is clearly based on the assumption that there are economies of scale and scope to be gained from a city-wide event programme, but there is very little evidence available to underpin this assumption. There is a need to examine the extent to which events held in the same city help to strengthen one another, and whether having many events taking place also helps to build 'organisational capital' through retaining talent, educating sponsors, developing joint marketing and ticketing or creating more public participation and local involvement. One might expect some kind of 'event multiplier' effect to operate, but empirical evidence for this is largely lacking.

The construction of the city event programme is important. Are there particular programming strategies that offer greater benefits than others? Is it more sensible for the city to concentrate on major events which offer a large, quantitative impact in terms of visitor spending or media coverage, or can greater benefit be gained from organising more, smaller, community-based events? What should the ideal eventful programme or portfolio look like?

The impact of the event programme on the people who live in the city is also a key research area. Events often aim to develop social cohesion and bring different groups in the city together, but there is conflicting evidence about the extent to which this happens. Particularly at a time when cities are developing new strategies to promote diversity and intercultural understanding between different groups of citizens, there are important questions to be asked about the relationship between diversity, social cohesion and the event programme. Does providing a broad programme of events promote cohesion or division? Should communities be encouraged to develop their own events, or should cities try and create broad-based transcultural events to bring different cultural communities together?

How does the city affect the event programme?

In spite of the proliferation of events and the copying of event models from one place to another, it is clear that the context in which the event takes place is highly relevant. Carnivals, melas, arts festivals or summer or winter events programmes can be very different in each city they are held in. The factors that make the difference between one eventful city and another as an arena for events are clearly important to investigate further.

Do some events work better in particular cities because of their ambiance or physical layout? As suggested earlier, for example, there is evidence to suggest that cities with a small intimate city centre may find it easier to create a festive atmosphere than larger, sprawling cities, but to what extent is this true? Does the availability of event spaces in the city (both open spaces and closed venues) have an influence on the event programme?

Although tourists remain an important target audience for many cities, for most event programmes the local audience remains crucial for success. How do local audiences interact with city event programmes? Is there a cycle of expectation, interest and disappointment in certain cities with regard to event planning? How can a city maintain audience enthusiasm over the period of a long event or an entire event programme?

How do local networks within the eventful city support the event programme? Do events support one another, or do they see each other as competitors? How can cities promote the practice of collaborative advantage?

How do stakeholders affect the eventful city?

Another issue that emerges from the analysis of the eventful city is the extent to which events themselves have become important stakeholders for the city. Most analyses of event stakeholders only deal with the city as a stakeholder in events, rather than the other way round. But as events increasingly gain political and economic power, they also act as key stakeholders for the city itself. This is perhaps most clearly seen in a city like Edinburgh, where the collective power of the city's festivals has a big influence on local politics.

Another major stakeholder that merits attention is the role of media and press criticism that can influence significantly public attitudes to and attendance at events. In previous event research, the role of the media has usually been viewed most often as a distribution medium, with impact being measured in terms of the volume of coverage. The specific role of critics is usually ignored. It has become very clear during many ECOCs, such as Luxembourg, for example, that certain newspaper critics were acting as 'champions' for the event, fighting with their editors to get more coverage for the ECOC and actively cajoling people to attend specific events (Luxembourg and Greater Region, 2008). In contrast, other critics may adopt a very negative attitude towards an event or event programme. As Miller (2009:57) notes in the case of Stavanger:

> *Our marketing and communications department, already under considerable pressure, suffered personnel changes, and staff were demoralised by sporadic bursts of negativity in the media which seemed bewildering to a small team passionate about delivering its mission.*

Such criticism can also turn local residents and other stakeholders against an event. This is arguably what happened prior to the Liverpool ECOC in 2008, when coverage of the organisational disarray created a very negative impression in the city. Research on the contribution of different criticism and the attitudes of individual critics to the image of events would be very informative in uncovering the mechanisms by which event programmes are constructed and deconstructed.

How does the eventful city affect its stakeholder network?

The eventful city depends heavily on different stakeholder groups to support the event programme, but also has an influence on those groups as well. Most significantly, experience in a number of cities has shown how the development of stakeholder networks around major events or event bids can help to galvanise different groups and create a sense of purpose for the cultural sector in the city. It is clearly important to understand the dynamics of this process. Events can be a catalyst for action, but what are the keys to success in terms of getting stakeholders to support the eventful city approach? Can an eventful city programme help stakeholders work together more effectively? Are new forms of collaboration created between different sectors and interests as a result of the city event programme?

Such new knowledge about cities and their event programmes can help to support future decisions and shape new models of eventfulness.

THE FUTURE OF EVENTS IN THE CITY

As Chapter 2 explained, the event programmes of most cities have developed in an ad hoc fashion, incorporating new events as these have emerged and without any strategic view of what kind of event programme was right for the city. In the future, cities are far more likely to see event programmes as a strategic tool for achieving a wide range of civic objectives, and this requires a tool fit for the job.

The event portfolio

Getz (2007) argues that cities need to develop an event portfolio, which contains a mix of large- and small-scale festivals and events, covering a variety of different disciplines, catering to a range of audiences and producing different outcomes. This approach is now being adopted by a number of cities around the world, including Innsbruck in Austria, Gold Coast in Australia and Edinburgh in Scotland. The Edinburgh event strategy (City of Edinburgh, 2007:9–10) states:

> Our strategy is to create and deliver a balanced portfolio of major events for the next 10 years. These will achieve one or more of the following:
>
> - generate significant economic benefit for the city region;
> - help make the city lively all year round;
> - reflect the political and civic importance of Edinburgh as the capital city; and
> - reinforce the City Vision and the City Region Brand.
>
> Our events portfolio will be a mixture of established successful events, new events which we will create or commission and national/ international events which we will bring to Edinburgh. As part of the portfolio, we aim to present at least one new major event of national or international standing each year.

Just as with the construction of a financial portfolio, the selection of events for the city's portfolio should be undertaken in order to maximise the value of events to the city. As discussed in Chapter 9, the value of events should not be purely assessed in economic terms, but also in terms of cultural and social values as well.

New visions of events

Cities around the world are beginning to see events as far more than public celebrations and far more as multi-faceted vehicles for public policy. To illustrate the nature of the change, we could turn to Miralles' (1998) vision of the evolution of events as the following:

- a new link between people and place;
- a post-modern integration of tradition and contemporary culture;
- a way of thinking about the life of a city;
- a source of innovation and (re)invention;
- a means of experimenting with culture and building 'festive capital';
- a new means of pursuing social, urban and economical politics; and
- a focus for new networks across disciplinary, cultural and social boundaries.

The ability of events to deliver a wide range of outcomes for the city explains in large part why more cities have become eventful in recent decades. Not only have events increased in number and frequency, but a diverse range of event models has emerged as well. In 2002, the Holland Festival (2003) organised a symposium on *The Future of Festival Formulae*, which examined the development of different models and strategies for major cultural events. This analysis identified a number of 'festival models':

- festival as encouragement;
- festival as link;
- festival as risk-taker and debating forum;
- festival as window on the world;

- festival as international meeting place;
- festivals in big cities;
- festivals in transition; and
- festival programmers.

The symposium underlined that there are no standard models that will work in all locations at all times. Events need to be adapted to the local context, which also responds to the global flows of culture, capital and knowledge that are increasingly determining what types of events work in different locations. Major changes in the role of events have become evident from the way in which different cities have used the ECOC to achieve their objectives (see Chapter 2). In essence, a range of event models has emerged from the ECOC experience as it has grown from a narrow arts festival held in the summer to a year-round interdisciplinary event encompassing all aspects of urban life. Each city has used the ECOC to develop its own interpretation of the relationship between culture, events and the city, which in turn have become models for other cities. The main models that can be identified in the ECOC include the following:

- Summer Festival Model (Athens 1985, Florence 1986);
- All-Year Festival Model (Amsterdam 1987, Dublin 1991);
- Art City Model (Berlin 1988, Antwerp 1993);
- Urban Regeneration/Rebranding Model (Glasgow 1990, Rotterdam 2001, Lille 2004, Genoa 2004, Liverpool 2008);
- Tourism/Image Development Model (Graz 2003, Sibiu 2007);
- Regional Cultural Development Model (Luxembourg 2007, Essen 2010).

Although these 'models' grossly oversimplify such very complex events (and most cities have combined elements of these different models), they do offer a recognisable short-hand which is useful for other cities when making their choices. Events are becoming closely integrated into urban policy, with the realisation that events can impact on many different areas of urban life. As repeated throughout this volume, events provide economic benefits, stimulate redevelopment, provide animation, support social cohesion and enhance the image and quality of life of a city. What is required to maximise these benefits is a strategic view of how the different models of events can deliver value to the city and its stakeholders.

Futures Festival

One vision of how events might deliver new value to cities is provided by the Futures Festival:

> The 'Futures Festival' is a special event designed to engage people of all ages in constructive dialogue about community development issues. It is geared primarily toward youths and older adults, two population groups whose opportunities to participate in community activities are typically limited. Through murals, models, photographs, theatrical displays and other communications media, the Futures Festival brings community residents and public officials together to share their ideas about community development. All participants get the chance to answer (and learn how others answer) the all-important question: 'What would you like to see in the future of your community?' There are various ways to conduct a Futures Festival. It can be organised as a separate event or incorporated into another event, such as an annual fair, for which a strong local tradition exists. This latter approach may be more feasible in rural areas where people have greater distances to travel. Futures Festival activities can be focused on development possibilities for the entire community or the focus can be limited to the development of a particular setting, such as a local park, or to specific issues of concern. No matter how they are organised, Future Festival events provide fun, non-confrontational activities that stimulate critical reflection and constructive dialogue about the physical, social and psychological dimensions of community living and development.
>
> (Futures Festival, 2009)

New Contents

Traditionally, many events have been defined by their content – arts festivals, sports events, food festivals, opera festivals, jazz festivals and so on. Other larger-scale events such as celebrations of city anniversaries, ECOC, cultural Olympiads and seasonal events programmes have invariably been multidisciplinary and diverse in their programme content. However, there is now increasing crossover in content between traditional festivals and sectors of the 'creative industries', such as design and architecture. Such mixes are being actively promoted in certain events, such as the Doc/Fest event held in Sheffield, UK, which includes a specific theme called Crossover:

> Crossover is an international programme designed to explore the creative and the commercial challenges of developing content and services for digital media.
>
> Crossover is a unique series of creative 'laboratories' in which experienced and talented professionals from different sectors of the audio-visual industries work alongside international experts and mentors to develop ideas for innovative cross-platform programmes, products or services.

New technology will also drive new cultural content and event formats. Some music festivals have created their own social networks, such as Earthdance ('the Global Dance Festival for Peace'), which is a global simultaneous music and dance event. Earthdance had 300 locations in 60 countries participating in 2007. The Outside Lands Music Festival in San Francisco in 2008 used the Website Crowdfire.net for the audience to upload their experiences of the music to a central database, and then combined this content to produce new creative content. Twitter has also been used to coordinate real-world events, such as the 'Twestivals' held in 202 cities around the world in February 2009 (Twestival, 2009). Social networking and other new applications clearly offer potentially strong platforms for city event programmes, since the shared interest that stimulates participation in social networking is more likely to centre around event content than location.

Some events will also focus on their role as breeding grounds and platforms for new talent. For example, the Riant Theatre in New York runs the Strawberry One-Act Festival, which the New York Daily News viewed as the 'American Idol for playwrights'. The festival is a play competition in which the audience and the theatre's judges cast their votes to select the best play of the season (Riant Theatre, 2009).

Where attracting tourists is a fundamental objective of an event, cities strive to create competitive distinction in the content of their event programmes. Although there are certain financial and organisational advantages if events, for example, summer festivals, join circuits of different cities that promote similar programmes, this can lead to festivals in different places looking the same. There are advantages if cities can create a sense of uniqueness by ensuring the distinction of the experience in their location, perhaps by the way an event is staged in a particular place.

New situations, new spaces

The emergence of eventful cities around the globe may either lead to an increasing specialisation and concentration of activity in such centres or may broaden the range of cities where events are held. Those cities that already possess an advantage in terms of 'eventfulness' or 'festive capital' will likely continue to attract major, global-scale events, because they have the ability to host them. Other cities may still be in a position to create their own events or to attract footloose events. The established centres have the benefit of experience, whereas the newcomers may offer innovative approaches and the element of surprise.

Cape Town A Global Events City

Cape Town is positioning itself as a global events city. The events policy approved in October 2008 underlines Cape Town's role as the 'event capital' of South Africa and recognises the hosting of events is a significant part of the city's global competitiveness strategy. However, while the city has a good track record in the hosting of major events, the absence of a strategy has meant that the city has not been able to maximise the benefits flowing from events. The event programme has grown in an ad hoc manner and the number and complexity of events

Continued

continue to grow each year. The city is increasingly being requested to provide significant resources for the staging of events and to manage the impact on the residents of Cape Town. The new events policy establishes a framework for the approval of events and ensuring their compliance with municipal policies.

(Cape Business News, 2009)

The need to attract attention to an event often provokes the development of new and unusual event settings. As Klaic et al. (2004: 35) note: 'There is no better way for a festival to generate a sense of business NOT as usual than to stage some of its programs on unusual, unexpected spaces, on sites previously unused for performances.' By appropriating new spaces in the city, an event can take its audience on a journey from the cultural centre to the periphery, from the known to the unknown, and provoke new visions of the city and its cultural possibilities. In New York City, the Peculiar Work Project visited 12 different theatre landmarks and took audiences on walking tours of the city. The audience followed a cart, which stopped at different sites to perform scenes from productions such as 'Hair' and 'The Maids' (Arts Management, 2007).

The ECOC in Luxembourg in 2007 introduced a number of new cultural and creative spaces to the country. These included the Rotondas (old railway sheds) in Luxembourg City, the former steelworks in Esch/Belval, and the Espace Paul Wurth (situated in a former warehouse). Although the idea of reusing old industrial spaces is not new, it had never been attempted before in Luxembourg, which had always had the strategy of constructing new facilities. The reuse of industrial spaces attracted new audiences, particularly the young. The emphasis was also placed on creative, active participation rather than passive spectatorship, a strategy that proved successful and laid the basis for a new direction in cultural policy in Luxembourg.

New event spaces are also being created by certain cities through their strategies of concentrating events at particular times of year, creating a critical mass of attractiveness and crossover visits to events. The advantage of concentration is to give the city a much stronger events profile than its rivals at the peak of the festival season. However, in terms of attracting visitors, it may create capacity problems in certain cities, with the city effectively being 'full' during an event and having little opportunity for shifting this demand to other times of the year. Concentration also tends to appeal to a more specialist market than dispersal, which provides a general level of animation for the casual visitor or tourist, creating the impression of a year-round event city in which there is 'always something going on'.

The key to success in concentrating or dispersing event programmes may be in the combination of both models – developing key moments of concentrated high-quality events interspersed with a lower level of year-round activity. Barcelona offers an example of a city that uses the two models, with number of popular events throughout the year as well as a number of high quality festivals that are focused on specific periods. Clusters of events might be developed as specific 'seasons' with a relatively high level of event activity.

Cities can also use events to link themselves more closely to their surrounding regions. The Stavanger ECOC achieved this very effectively in 2008 by using the event to stage arts performances in remote rural locations, allowing the sparse rural population the opportunity to become involved in the event. For example, the Project Bandaloop dance company from the United States created a performance on the cliffs above the deep water of Gloppedalen fiord:

> *Traditional dancers, the elderly, tiny children, break-dancers, bikers and troops of mossy, bellowing trolls led the audience up the mountain road. Twilight settled, a boat slipped across the milky water as a solitary French horn player called; a singer accompanied by the sound of dripping oars sailed to find more music, and young dancers seemed to skim the lake's surface. On the cliff faces, close by, then vertiginous and distant, aerial dancers whirled and flew like crimson moths, spotlights threw shadows, and virtuosic Vivaldi swirled from a floating platform.*
> (Miller, 2009: 92)

As cities increasingly need to work together and to involve surrounding communities in their cultural lives, such 'over-spill' of events into suburbs, rural areas and neighbouring communities may become more common. This will present many new opportunities for collaboration and economies of scope and scale in events, but at the same time will increase the organisational challenge involved.

Selling the event, selling the city

Klaic et al. (2004) argue that there is a shift taking place from transactional to relational marketing, as cities and events seek to create a more long-term relationship with their publics. This requires more investment, since the marketing function now stretches far beyond the simple promotion of the event itself into the development of audience and stakeholder relationships and the development of new products related to the event and the city. To optimise the value of this relationship, Klaic et al. (2004) further make a case that events need to be increasingly strategic about the publics that they attract in order to maximise the overall value or 'profit' they can generate. The audience should not be seen in terms of numbers, but in terms of the value they can deliver to the city in economic, social and cultural terms. This in turn requires a better understanding of event publics and their motivations.

The relational approach to the development and promotion of events also links to the broader conception of marketing developed by many cities. Whereas in the past city marketing was seen in fairly narrow terms as a means of communicating with different publics, a more integrated approach is now being developed that views city marketing as one of a range of tools that aim to make the city attractive as a place to live, work, invest and visit. One example of such a strategy is South Australia's 'Brilliant Blend' brand, which was developed in 2006 and adopted by all Government agencies that market South Australia to consumers, including tourism, education, business, arts and migration. Events South Australia, the State's event coordination agency has played an important role in the Brilliant Blend programme, generating large numbers of visitors as well as incorporating events into the Brilliant Blend branding, with the Tour Down

Under cycle race recently having celebrated '10 Brilliant Years' in South Australia and the Brilliant Summer Events campaign aiming to encourage people from Sydney and Melbourne to visit Adelaide.

As discussed in Chapter 7, linking events with the media will also provide an important platform for such broad-based marketing strategies. Engaging media attention for events will continue to be a key priority for cities. Some cities have used the tactic of shock or surprise to capture media attention, such as Llanwrtyd Wells in Wales, which has attracted large numbers of visitors and media headlines with events ranging from the World Bog Snorkelling championship to the Man versus Horse race and the Real Ale Wobble.

CONCLUSIONS: THE DEVELOPMENT OF EVENTFULNESS

As argued in Chapter 1 of this volume, as models of the city have changed, so have events, event programmes and modes of eventfulness. The medieval city, with its regular cycle of religious and secular events, was succeeded by the industrial city with displays of industrial prowess, cultural achievement and military might. In the twentieth century, different models of the city came and went in response to external and internal crises: the managed city giving way to the postmodern city, quickly followed by the entrepreneurial city, the creative city and the intercultural city. This flow of changes produced a shift in the role of event programmes, from a format for display and celebration towards a tool for widespread cultural, social and economic change.

The concept of the eventful city is based on this increasingly broad and important role of event programmes. One might argue that the city is no longer simply a decor or container for events, but that the city itself has *become* an event. Cities are in some senses the major 'scapes' (Appadurai, 1990) in which flows of culture, people, resources and creativity converge to produce nodes of eventfulness. Events provide potential links between the globalised space of flows and the localised space of places (Castells, 1996), thus allowing cities to increase their economic potential while at the same time building their social and cultural fabric to create local distinctiveness. Events also provide important markers which help establish the rhythmic life of the city (Amin & Thrift, 2002). Viewing the city as an event in itself is also one means of revisioning the city, enabling new and creative solutions to be sought to the problems of modern urban life.

Of course, a city is much more than an event – it is a physical space, a community, an identity and many other things. But these things often only come alive when something happens, when there is an event. This view of the city as an event can perhaps be compared with the idea of a city as an experience. Cities provide a host of experiences for a wide range of publics and, according to the philosophy of the 'Experience Economy', (Pine & Gilmore, 1999) those providing experiences in the city need to develop engaging experiences that meet the needs of consumers – 'stage it, and they will come'. Florida (2002) suggests similar mechanisms for the creative city. He argues that the creative 'atmosphere' of cities with high levels of creativity is enough to attract the highly desirable creative class of people.

But experiences or Bohemian atmosphere are by themselves often not enough. Both consumers and producers are in search of more active forms of involvement. The concept of experiences as posited by Pine and Gilmore (1999) is relatively static and it is only in the final stages of their argument that they put forward the idea of 'transformations' as the next phase of economic value creation. Developing eventfulness, on the other hand, concentrates attention on processes of change. Change usually requires some form of catalyst, and events can help cities to make things happen and to achieve things which previously seemed impossible. Even though it usually takes a mega-event to change a whole city (such as the Olympic Games in Barcelona or the ECOC in Glasgow), small-scale events also have the potential for transformation at a local scale. Cultural events are increasingly a catalyst that can motivate the different stakeholders in a city to come together and do something that will change the city itself.

As KEA (2009) have argued, we are entering a phase in which the 'sharing economy' is becoming ever more important. In the eventful city, the concept of a sharing economy is already evident in the cooperation between stakeholders and the creation of public value through events. Eventfulness also creates far more than economic value and public value: it acts as a catalyst to develop shared experiences, shared values and shared visions about the city. By acting as a rallying point for different stakeholder groups, events can help to achieve the goals of the city in a more effective way. Given the need for cities to move faster and more efficiently in the competitive global environment, events can be used as a means of improving the 'smoothness' of internal processes in the city (for example, by optimising collaboration between stakeholders) as well as offering opportunities for external collaboration (or 'coopertition').

As cities and their publics become more complex, there is a growing need to involve event audiences in the creation of events. Event programmes almost inevitably involve a process of cocreation between events and their audiences and publics. The idea of an event programme being something which should involve cocreation between all the residents of a city and the different event programme stakeholders was a key platform of the successful bid by Umeå in Sweden for the 2014 ECOC. The bid was entitled *Curiosity and Passion – the Art of Cocreation,* and emphasised developing creativity collaboratively with its citizens and an open source approach to culture:

> *Our aim is for citizens to be far more committed to the arts and culture, because they have been active participants and cocreators. We do not want only those directly connected to the theatre, opera, gallery or library to feel a sense of ownership. We hope the people of Umeå will say of their cultural institutions that: 'This is my theatre'; or 'This is my art gallery'; or 'This museum is mine, so don't stop supporting it'.*

> *Cocreation fosters a process of commitment and mutual involvement as well as two-way communication. It is a process based on trust, and can lead to an upward spiral of inventiveness. Ultimately, it may lead to mass everyday creativity in the general population. Cocreation is at the heart of the Open*

Source software movement, where users have full access to the source code and are empowered to make their own changes and improvements to it.
(Umeå 2014, 2009:17)

The involvement of different publics in the process of developing the eventful city is important for a number of reasons. First, it democratises the process of developing cultural content and programming; second, it creates a wide base of support for the event programme; third, it increases the level of involvement of stakeholders in the event programme; fourth, it raises the level of dialogue between stakeholders; and finally, it helps to support the identity and social cohesion of the city. In moving towards a higher involvement model of eventfulness, the emphasis for the city should also shift from effect to affect – not just what is produced by the event programme, but how if affects the people who live in the city. Events are often seen as mechanisms for moving people in a physical sense, but increasingly the eventful city will need to think in terms of moving people emotionally as well.

The principle of involvement also needs to underpin event programme design, which becomes far more than a means of linking spaces in the city with cultural events, or linking events through theming. In the spirit of co-creation, programme design should begin to embrace every aspect of the ambitions of the city regarding eventfulness. Development of the programme should take into account:

- what the city wants to achieve;

- what type of city it wants to be;

- how it secures the resources it needs to develop eventfulness,

- how it differentiates itself from other cities with events; and

- how it relates to different stakeholder groups.

Addressing these issues should help the city integrate eventfulness into its cultural DNA. This genetic code should

Table 12.1	Events in the Experience Economy versus Eventfulness in the Sharing Economy

Experience Economy	Eventfulness
Experiences	Events
Static	Dynamic
Economic	People-centered
Market-driven	Collaborative
Proprietary	Sharing
Money	Meaning

incorporate the values that the city wishes to develop through eventfulness, such as:

- distinctiveness, sense of place and identity;

- improving the quality of life;

- acting in an enabling, inclusive and transparent fashion; and

- supporting the development of transcultural values.

Achieving such a transformation in how the city acts and thinks about itself requires a new frame of mind in which eventfulness is seen as a proactive tool for improving the city. As such, the event programme cannot be developed effectively simply by creating an umbrella body for events in the city or by opening a 'one stop shop' for event organisers. Rather than the city being seen as a shopkeeper, supplying the needs of others who want to organise events, it has to be viewed far more as an active event partner, an event programme coordinator and an event facilitator. Without a proactive role in events, the city gives up a great deal of the potential value of events in reaching civic goals.

The new role for cities in relation to eventfulness contrasts with the recent conceptions of events as extensions of city marketing policy or as an animation tool for civic space. The eventful city needs to go beyond the relatively narrow confines of the market-driven experience economy and city-branding mentality into a more inclusive concept based in the sharing economy. This requires a shift in the discourse about the role of events in the city, away from the idea of events as static experiences for consumption towards more collaborative and inclusive models.

Events themselves can be useful catalysts for achieving this wider dialogue about culture and events. In the case of Helsinki, Mäenpää (2005:24) argues that:

> A significant consequence of the Cultural Capital year was the emergence of a new cultural discourse in administration and decision-making. Culture expanded from its own sector into two new discourses. Outside cultural policy, culture adopted two other roles, one in social welfare and the other in business.

Also in reference to Helsinki, Harris (2005:25) poses the question of how eventfulness can be used to produce 'genuinely' creative urban culture. Her argument is that events represent an important means of appropriating urban space for creative use. Events offer one avenue for developing creativity that seems far more direct than the recipe offered by Richard Florida quoted earlier (develop a Bohemian atmosphere and the creative class will turn up). By linking the creative life of a city directly with creatives elsewhere and at the same time offering local creativity a stage and a meeting ground, events can be a direct and dynamic way of stimulating creative production and consumption.

BUILDING A PLATFORM FOR EVENTFULNESS

How can a city develop eventfulness or become more eventful? As has been stressed throughout this book, there are no easy recipes for eventfulness or standard models that can be transferred from one city to another. Eventfulness is a complex phenomenon, which requires the eventful city to multi task and think holistically. Eventfulness can be conceived of, among other things, as:

- An attitude – a stance and a vision which helps the city understand what it wants to achieve through eventfulness.

- A state of mind – a way of thinking about the city and its stakeholders.

- A catalyst – a source of renewal and new ideas.

- A space – appropriate spaces in the city that can be imbued with new meanings and possibilities.

- A time – a metronome for the life rhythms of the city as well as a wake-up call for complacent citizens and policy-makers.

- An image – cities that are perceived as being eventful also tend to be seen as more attractive.

- A risk – risk-taking is essential for a dynamic urban culture, and events are one way of facilitating creative risk in a supportive environment.

- An action – conceptions and strategies are transformed into activities and projects that can be experienced.

- A process of learning – where practice includes continual evaluation with the aim of informing further practice, and where the terminology of success and failure is replaced by the notion of process-driven knowledge acquisition and improvement.

Maximising the benefits of eventfulness therefore requires a careful process of planning and design, especially if the city wishes to develop a creative, fresh and spontaneous event programme. A city wishing to become more eventful should consider taking a few basic steps that are important in establishing a platform for eventfulness:

- **Create a vision**

    The vision for the eventful city needs to make clear what kind of city you want to live in. This can inform the mission of the city in relation to the event programme: what do we want to achieve and why? For whom?

    The event programme should become an integral part of the cultural ecology of the city, with events making an important contribution to improving the quality of life of all stakeholders. Events can take on many different roles that can contribute to this goal, including as a point of entry, a stage, a meeting space, a catalyst for cocreation, a people-magnet, a stimulus for reflection and debate and so on. In constructing their event portfolios, therefore, cities should consider the dynamic outcomes of events, rather than just trying to stage different types of events to plug holes in their calendars or to provide momentary diversions.

The outcomes to be achieved from events should also be related to the wider ambitions of the city, so that eventfulness does not become a goal in itself. The vision for the eventful city should provide a means of linking the city and its citizens with the event programme and the ideas and images that flow from those events. In this way, events should become one of the means of creating a narrative about the city, reinforcing its identity and enabling it to communicate its distinctiveness more easily to external publics.

■ **Evaluate potential**

Every city can become eventful, but the best way to develop events is to base them on the strengths of the city. Cities should not be looking just for gaps in their portfolio of events, but they should be assessing what aspects of the city and its stakeholders can best be used to generate new events or regenerate old ones. Stakeholder and network analyses are important to this process. Cities should look not only at what they already have in the city, but also which external linkages may offer the potential to develop new sources of creativity and cultural potential.

■ **Be prepared to take risks**

Risks are an essential element of a dynamic events programme. Where events are enabled to go beyond the limits of the everyday and the predictable into the realm of the unusual and the possible, then the event programme also moves from being a form of entertainment into being a positive tool for cultural and social change. This does not always sit easily with the naturally cautious nature of most public administrations, but means should be found to support artistic risk-taking without endangering prudent management. The development of independent management structures that can operate with fewer constraints and greater flexibility than many statutory and public bodies is one possible proactive management strategy.

Developing a new vision for the event programme offers an opportunity for 'conquering the context' of the city and empowering event stakeholders to do new things. Regular new impulses to the event programme inject a necessary element of unpredictability which can refresh the cultural sector and attract new audiences. As Zukin (2004) suggests, cities need to be impatient for change, and should plan to enable unpredictable change to happen.

■ Build networks

People can only cope with risk and unpredictability if support networks abound. The event programme should involve the widest possible range of stakeholders, and the aim should be to develop collaborative participation in and support for the event programme. Events can often be used as a way of galvanising stakeholders into action, sometimes through their opposition to events as well as through their support. The creative eventful city will find ways of harnessing the inevitable tensions and different points of view that will arise between stakeholders and transform this tension into a source of energy.

Maximising involvement is also a question of representation. People will only get involved if they can see their aims and aspirations embodied in the programme. The event programme should therefore develop a discourse that can combine the many different narratives that form part of the cultural ecology of the city.

■ **Develop creative spaces**

Event programmes require space. Not just physical spaces, but also symbolic and creative spaces. Events can be used as a catalyst to ensure that the city develops meeting places and mixing spaces for creative expression. Creative spaces in the city should link the established cultural institutions and other event organisations, the communal and habitual physical gathering spaces of the city with the more ephemeral creative spaces. These synergies offer a stimulus and new impulses that will impact on the entire cultural offer of a city.

The role of events as meeting spaces is both a means to develop creativity, and of providing platforms for the confrontation of difference, which can then be transformed into a source of social creativity (Sennett, 1999).

■ **Stimulate involvement**

Developing eventfulness is a collective endeavour. The different stakeholders in the eventful city work together to cocreate event programmes, but the various publics and audiences for events also become cocreators of events.

The public authorities may stimulate the vision that leads the cocreation of eventfulness, by enabling wider participation and collaboration in event design and programming. The city may assume a primary role of resource facilitator for event programmes, ensuring that sufficient resources (financial, human and physical) are coordinated from different sources to sustain the programme. The strategy of pluri-annual funding programmes for events is an essential element, and imaginative oversight can ensure that new events will emerge while other events are reduced or curtailed.

Resource allocation systems need to have clarity and transparency and be based on a well-articulated strategy.

Particularly in cases where the city or a devolved agency acts as a gatekeeper for resources, there is a need to inform all stakeholders of resource strategies and funding priorities sufficiently far ahead of decisions being made, which can prevent the need for crisis management. The city should develop mechanisms to manage the disappointment that often arises from negative funding decisions and to find ways to encourage continued event cocreation at grass-roots level.

Stimulating involvement is basically a question of enabling others to meet their own aims through eventfulness. Cities cannot run or fund all their events alone, so others need to be empowered to develop and organise events. This requires working closely with a range of partners from the commercial and voluntary sectors, all of whom will have different aims and objectives and different needs in terms of support. A flexible approach to partnership is therefore essential.

■ **Provide support and guidance to ensure that events contribute to the wider aims of the city**

Setting a vision for the eventful city offers general guidance on the direction of the event programme. But there may also be a need for more hands-on management to ensure that the events in the city's programme are contributing actively to achieving the overall goals of the city. There needs to be a clear link between the vision for eventfulness, the objectives of the event programme and the management and monitoring strategies for city events.

Many cities have developed strong 'one stop shop' or 'single door' strategies for events management in order to streamline event organisation procedures, and also to provide the city with a better overview of the scale and consequences of event activity. However, the city should also ensure that the event 'door' opens both ways, creating an active dialogue with event stakeholders. The development of a limited number of standardised procedures may also be appropriate, particularly if this facilitates constructive assessment of the event programme and its use of resources.

By becoming proactive in the event programme, the city can act on identified weaknesses and take steps to ensure that programme outputs contribute in a positive way to the wider goals of the city. As cities increasingly seek to develop and integrate 'live, work, invest and play' strategies to attract people and resources, it is important to ensure that the event programme as a whole makes the city a more livable and attractive place. Events should therefore form one part of a broader and multi level planning process for the city, in which the aims and outcomes of events are linked directly to the strategic goals of the city.

■ **Invest in people and retain talent**

Creation, development and management of the event programme require a mix of talented people with the necessary skills and experience. Cities should develop systems to nurture and retain talent – event directors, artistic managers and other key-personnel by helping to establish long-term development perspectives, security and responsive support.

Too much political interference in the event programme should be avoided – experienced event professionals and other specialists should be trusted to lead wherever possible. Political oversight should be maintained at a strategic level, but should not be allowed to impinge on the day-to-day running of the event programme.

■ **Monitor outputs and outcomes**

An event programme delivers different types of value for the city and its citizens: intrinsic, instrumental and institutional value. The amount and type of value generated by the programme should be continuously monitored, and the information used to assess and develop events. Monitoring should be built into the event programming process, so that it becomes a natural part of the organisation of events, rather than an afterthought.

Monitoring also needs to be designed sensitively so that it is perceived as helpful and constructive rather than burdensome or punitive.

For the monitoring process to be useful to the city and the event community, it is important to define what types of outputs and outcomes are desired, and what constitutes 'success' for the event programme.

■ **Learning from eventfulness**

Eventfulness is an important tool for the city to learn about itself; how people interact, how systems function and the linkages between culture, economy and society. The event programme should be implemented in such a way that each event is a learning moment for the city, with the lessons learned being applied to future event organisation and management. The city needs to draw lessons from its approach to eventfulness, including the disseminating knowledge to all event stakeholders so that the 'organisational capital' of the city can be increased.

To maintain eventfulness, a city needs to develop its skills of reflection and enquiry, 'learning how to learn' so that the event programme becomes a city-wide learning lab. The concept of continuous learning in the city is important because it places priority on evaluating, adapting and learning from change. That remains a critical key to the successful realisation of the principles of the eventful city.

Eventfulness as a system

Once a city has developed a platform for eventfulness, it needs to approach the development of the event programme in a holistic manner, paying as much attention to process and the outcomes of events as it does to staging them (Figure 12.2).

Seeing the eventful city as a system with key inputs and outputs allows us to understand more about the dynamic nature of event programmes and their impacts on the cities

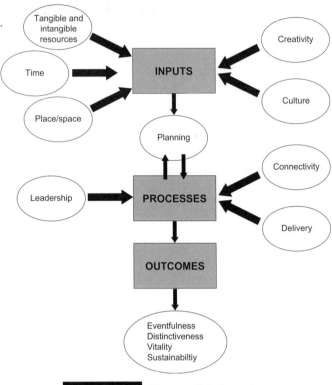

FIGURE 12.2 *The eventful city system.*

that stage them. Eventfulness is no longer just a form of civic animation, but it is increasingly a process that helps cities to attain their goals and become more dynamic and livable places.

References

Trees Festival. (2009). www.twothousandtreesfestival.co.uk/ Accessed 16.01.07.

Adelaide review. (2006). *Getting Brett's best*. www.adelaidereview. com.au/archives.php?subaction=showfull&;id=1134095440& archive=1138320065&start_from=&ucat=3&. Accessed 13.10.09.

AEA Consulting. (2006). *Thundering hooves: Maintaining the global competitive edge of Edinburgh's festivals*. Full Report. London: AEA Consulting.

Ajuntament de Barcelona. (1999). *Pla Estratègic del Sector Cultural de Barcelona*. Barcelona: Institut de Cultura.

Allen, J., O'Toole, W., & McDonnell, I. (2005). *Festival and special event management* (3rd ed.). Brisbane: Wiley.

Allen, M. S. (2005). Leadership – Key to the brand of place. In *Paper presented at the Spirit in Business – Forum 2004-Great Leaders Good Leaders*.

Amelang, J. (2007). Comparing cities: a Barcelona Model? *Urban History, 34*, 173–189.

Amin, A., & Thrift, N. (2002). *Cities: Reimagining the urban*. Cambridge: Polity.

Amsterdamse Kunstraad. (2003). *Niet het aantal telt - maar de toegevoegde waarde. Advies ten behoeve van een festivalbeleid*. Amsterdam: Amsterdamse Kunstraad.

Andersson, A. E. (1999). The creative metropolis. In L. Nyström (Ed.), *City and culture: Cultural processes and urban sustainability* (pp. 382–387). Stockholm: Swedish Urban Environment Council.

Andranovich, G., Burbank, M. J., & Heying, C. H. (2001). Olympic cities: lessons learned from mega-event politics. *Journal of Urban Affairs, 23*, 113–131.

Antwerpen Open. (2005). *Jaarverslag*. Antwerp: Anterwerpen Open.

Appadurai, A. (1990). Disjuncture and difference in the global culture economy. *Theory, Culture, and Society, 7*, 295–310.

Armour, J. (2006). *Festivals more than justify city investments.* www.ottawafestivals.ca/press/festivals-more-than-justify-city-investments/. Accessed 13.10.09.

Arts About Manchester. (2009). *Chester Festivals 2008: Visitor and economic impact assessment.* Chester: City of Chester.

Arts Council England. (2006). *Introducing the cultural leadership programme.* London: Arts Council England.

Arts Council England. (2007). *Taking part in the arts: Survey findings from the first 12 months.* London: Arts Council.

Arts management. (2007). *Arts Management no. 251.* ArtsManagementNews.com.

artsmanager.org. (2007). *Strategic planning in the arts: A practical guide.* www.artsmanager.org/strategic/primer/assets/SPP_chapter3.pdf. Accessed 27.04.07.

Asia Travel Tips. (2006). www.asiatraveltips.com/travelnews03/269Roadshow.shtml

Ashworth, G. J., & Voogd, H. (1990). *Selling the city: Marketing approaches in public sector urban planning.* London: Belhaven Press.

ATLAS. (2009). *ATLAS cultural tourism research project.* www.tram-research.com/atlas. Accessed 05.05.09.

Audiences London. (2009). *Our philosophy.* www.audienceslondon.org/?lid=63. Accessed 13.03.09.

Audiences Yorkshire. (2009). www.audiencesyorkshire.org.uk. Accessed 13.03.09.

Auditor General of Queensland. (2000). *Governance and risk management self-assessment program.* www.cmc.qld.gov.au/asp/index.asp?pgid=10869&;cid=5511&id=635. Accessed 15.08.09.

Aufischer, A. (2003). *Mostar: Unique sign – Unique location.* Graz: Cultural City Network.

Australia Council. (2007). ABC and SBS: Towards a digital future. *Australia Council submission to the ABC and SBS Review.* Surry Hills, NSW: Australia Council.

Australian Bureau of Statistics. (2008). *Arts and culture in Victoria.* www.arts.vic.gov.au/content/Public/Research_and_Resources/Cultural_Data/A_Statistical_Overview.aspx. Accessed 27.05.09.

Australian Sport Commission. (2000). *Volunteer Management Program: Managing event volunteers.* www.skillsactive.org.nz/files/Managing%20Event%20Volunteers.pdf. Accessed 13.10.09.

Balakrishnan, A. (2006). How the Summer rock festivals became one big branded beer tent. *The Guardian*. Monday 28 August 2006. www.guardian.co.uk/media/2006/aug/28/advertising. festivals. Accessed 16.09.09.

Balsas, C. J. L. (2004). City centre regeneration in the context of the 2001 European capital of culture in Porto, Portugal. *Local Economy, 19*, 396–410.

Basingstoke City Council. (2008). *Events review. Report to Economic & Community Development Overview Committee*. www.basingstoke.gov.uk. Accessed 13.10.08.

Baumol, W. J., & Bowen, W. G. (1966). *Performing arts: The economic dilemma*. New York: The Twentieth Century Fund.

Bauman, S. (2000). *Liquid modernity*. London: Polity Press.

Bayliss, D. (2004). Denmark's creative potential: the role of culture within Danish urban development strategies. *International Journal of Cultural Policy, 10*, 5–28.

BBC Bristol. (2007). *Public consultation planned for new festival*. www.bbc.co.uk/bristol/content/articles/2007/10/22/bristolfestival_consultation_feature.shtml. Accessed 13.10.09.

BBC Liverpool. (2005). *Brouhaha Festival*. www.bbc.co.uk/liverpool/content/articles/2005/07/06/brouhaha_festival_feature.shtml. Accessed 12.04.09.

BBC News. (2004). *Shouting men of Finland perform ice breaker*. news.bbc.co.uk/2/hi/europe/3454567.stm. Accessed 05.10.09.

Bedford Borough Council. (2007). Community and culture policy review and development committee. *Report by the Events and Marketing Manager, 22nd February 2007*. www.portal.bedford.gov.uk/internet/your%20council/committee%20information/2006.2007/community%20and%20culture%20/2007%2002%2022%20/Item%2010%20River%20Festival%202008.pdf. Accessed 03.03.09.

Bellavance, G. (2008). Where's high? Who's low? What's new? Classification and stratification inside cultural "Repertoires". *Poetics, 36*, 189–216.

Belfast City Council. (2004). Development Committee: Special meeting of development (arts) sub-committee, Wednesday, 13 October, 2004. www.belfastcity.gov.uk/minutesdirectory/2004/1104/ar13104s.doc. Accessed 22.05.07.

Benach Rovira, N., & Albet i Mas, A. (2004). Barcelona 1979–2004, entre el modelo y el espectáculo. In C. Minca (Ed.), *Lo spettacolo della città/The Spectacle of the City*. Padova: CEDAM.

Bennis, W. (1989). *On becoming a leader*. California: Addison-Wesley.

Bennis, W., & Nanus, B. (1985). *Leaders: The strategies for taking charge*. New York: HarperCollins.

Benito, L. (1997). Les festivals en crise. *Espaces, 146,* 54–59.

Bianchini, F. (1990). Urban renaissance? The arts and the urban regeneration process. In S. MacGregor, & B. Pimlott (Eds.), *Tackling the inner cities* (pp. 215–250). Oxford: Clarendon.

Bitner, J., & Booms, B. (1981). Marketing strategies and organizational structures for service firms. In J. Donnelly, & W. George (Eds.), *Marketing of services* (pp. 47–51). Chicago: American Marketing Association.

Bloomfield, J., & Bianchini, F. (2003). *Planning for the cosmopolitan city.* Leicester: COMEDIA and International Cultural planning and Policy Unit (ICPPU) De Montfort University.

Body-Gendrot, S. (2003). Cities, security and visitors: Managing mega-events in France. In L. Hoffman, S. S. Fainstein, & D. R. Judd (Eds.), *Cities and visitors: Regulating people, markets and city space* (pp. 37–52). Oxford: Blackwell.

Bowdin, G., Allen, J., O'Toole, W., Harris, R., & McDonnell, I. (2006). *Events management* (2nd ed.). Oxford: Elsevier.

Boyle, M., & Hughes, C. G. (1995). The politics of urban entrepreneurialism in Glasgow. *Geoforum, 25,* 453–470.

Boyko, C. T. (2008a). Breathing new life into old places through culture: A case of bad breath? In G. Richards, & J. Wilson (Eds.), *Changing places – The spatial challenge of creativity* (pp. 19–31). Arnhem: ATLAS.

Boyko, C. T. (2008b). Are You Being Served? The Impacts of a Tourist Hallmark Event on the Place Meanings of Residents. *Event Management, 11,* 161–177.

Bramwell, W., Henry, I., Jackson, G., Goytia Prat, A., Richards, G., & van der Straaten, J. (1996). *Sustainable tourism management: Principles and practice.* Tilburg: Tilburg University Press.

Bramwell, B., & Rawding, L. (1996). Tourism marketing images of industrial cities. *Annals of Tourism Research, 23*(1), 201–226.

BREAD & butter. (2007). www.breadandbutter.com/. Accessed 15.09.07.

Brettell, D. (2001). The Sydney volunteers. *Olympic Review, 42,* 37–43.

Bridge, G., & Watson, S. (2001). Retext(ur)ing the city. *City, 5*(3), 350–362.

Brighton and Hove. (2004). *The economic and cultural impact of Brighton Festival upon Brighton and Hove.* Brighton and Hove Council.

Burnell, P. (2008). *Culture capital to 'basket case'?* www.news.bbc.co.uk/2/hi/programmes/file_on_4/7420315.stm. Accessed 15.04.09.

Burns, J. P. A., Hatch, J. H., & Mules, T. J. (1986). *The Adelaide Grand Prix: The impact of a special event*. Adelaide: The Centre for South Australian Economic Studies.

Cachet, E. A., Kroes Willems, M., & Richards, G. (2003). *Culturele Identiteit van Nederlandse Gemeenten*. Rotterdam: ERBS.

Cambridge City Council. (2009). *Folk festival online ticket sales*. www.cambridge.gov.uk/ccm/content/news-releases/2009/folk-festival-online-ticket-sales.en. Accessed 03.03.09.

Cape Business News. (19 March 2009). *Cape Town: A global events city*. www.cbn.co.za/dailynews/3595.html. Accessed 17.08.09.

Carlsen, J. (2002). A Study of the Community and tourism benefits of the 'Best on Earth in Perth' events campaign in Western Australia. In *Events and Place Making Conference Proceedings* (pp. 85–110). Sydney: Australian Centre for Event Management.

Casale, E. (2004). China's new cultural revolution. *The Platform: Four One*. www.aeaconsulting.com/site/platformv4i1a.html. Accessed 17.01.07.

Castells, M. (1996). *The Rise of the network society*. Oxford: Blackwell.

Cattacin, S. (1994). Stadtentwicklungspolitik zwischen Demokratie und Komplexität. Zur politischen Organisation der Stadtentwicklung: Florenz, Wien und Zürich im Vergleich. Frankfurt: Campus.

Caust, J. (2004). A festival in disarray: The 2002 Adelaide festival: A Debacle or Another model of arts organization and leadership? *Journal of Arts Management, Law, and Society, Summer 2004*, 103.

CBC News. (2008). *High price to pay to see famed Bayreuth Festival online*. www.cbc.ca/technology/story/2008/07/02/bayreuth-online.html. Accessed 13.03.09.

CEFRAC. (1996). *The Economic impact on employment of ten festivals in Europe*. Brussels: European Commission.

CFM Strategie. (2005). *Évaluation des retombées économiques des événements membres du RÉMI*. www.remi.qc.ca/htmfr/activites8.html. Accessed 11.06.07.

Chappell, T., & Harriss, L. (2006). *Evolving city: An independent evaluation*. Oxford: City of Oxford.

Charities Commission. (2002). *Charities and commercial partners*. www.charity-commission.gov.uk/publications/rs2.asp. Accessed 21.05.09.

City of Cape Town. (2001). *Major events marketing strategy. Draft strategy for discussion and comment*. Cape Town: Joint Marketing Initiative.

City of Cape Town. (October 2008). *City of Cape Town Events Policy.* www.capetown.gov.za/en/Policies/Documents/CoCT%20Events%20Policy%2029%20October%202008.pdf. Accessed 09.03.09.

City of Coventry. (2006). *Coventry – the official guide.* Available from. www.coventry.gov.uk/ccm/navigation/council–; government-and-democracy/council/council-publications/coventry-s-official-guide/;jsessionid=apAfEDwctV14.

City of Edinburgh. (2007). *Inspiring events strategy.* www.edinburgh.gov.uk/./City./Events/Events./inspiring_events_strategy.pdf. Accessed 23.09.09.

City of Edinburgh Economic Development Department. (2008). *The City of Edinburgh Key Sectors III – An update on business perspectives from Edinburgh's key sectors.* Edinburgh: City of Edinburgh.

City of Genova. (2003). *Cultural capital of Europe 2004 press kit.* Genova: Genova 2004.

City of Liverpool. (2009). *Catering services for culture team events quotation document.* www.liverpool.gov.uk/Images/tcm21-145303.doc. Accessed 03.03.09.

City of Melbourne. (2006). Agenda Item 5.2, 8 August 2006/07 Event Programmes. *Marketing and events committee report.* Melbourne: Melbourne Division of Marketing, Tourism & Major Events.

City of Pécs. (2005). *Borderless City: European Capital of Culture Pécs 2010.* www.en.pecs2010.hu/p/pecs/the_borderless_city. Accessed 13.10.10.

City of Toronto. (2003). *Five year tourism action plan.* Toronto: City of Toronto, Tourism Division.

City of Sydney. (2005). *Corporate Sponsorship: Resolution of Council: 21 November 2005.* www.cityofsydney.nsw.gov.au/Council/documents/policies/CorporateSponsorshipPolicy.pdf. Accessed 03.03.09.

City of Vancouver. (2005). *Standing Committee on Planning and Environment.* City of Vancouver: Plaza of nations land use study.

City of Wellington. (2006). *Cultural wellbeing strategy: Shaping Wellington's unique identity.* Wellington City Council.

City University. (2006). That Time of Year Again: Community Festivals and the Challenge of Sustainability. In: *Celebrating Enterprise Festival Futures Seminar Series.* City University. 29 September 2006.

City University. (25 January 2007). Culture and commerce: Making the marriage work. In *Celebrating Enterprise festival futures seminar series.* London: Bethnal Green.

Clapés, A. (2002). Voluntaris '92. Deu anys después. In M. de Moragas, & M. Botella (Eds.), *Barcelona: l' herència dels jocs, 1992–2002* (pp. 145–163). Barcelona: Planeta.

Cocks, A. S. (2007). *Venice Biennale proposes becoming a selling show again.* Art Newspaper. 24 May 2007. www.theartnewspaper.com/article01.asp?id=644. Accessed 24.08.07.

Colbert, F. (2003). Entrepreneurship and leadership in marketing the arts. *International Journal of Arts Management, 6*(1), 30–39.

Cole, S. T., & Illum, S. F. (2006). Examining the mediating role of festival visitors' satisfaction in the relationship between service quality and behavioral intentions. *Journal of Vacation Marketing, 12*(2), 160–173.

Committee for Melbourne. (2009). www.melbourne.org.au/media-centre/extraordinary-facts-about-melbourne. Accessed 10.03.09.

Compendium of Cultural policies. (2009). www.culturalpolicies. net/web/index.php. Accessed 15.09.09.

Cork. (2005). is a date reference.

Corijn, E., & van Praet, S. (1994). *Antwerp 93 in the context of European Cultural Capitals: Art policy as politics.* Brussels: Vrije Universiteit Brussel.

Council of Europe. (1997). *In from the Margins – A contribution to the debate on culture and development in Europe.* Strasbourg: Council of Europe.

Council of Europe. (2009). *Intercultural cities: governance and policies for diverse communities.* www.coe.int/t/dg4/cultureheritage/Policies/Cities/default_en.asp. Accessed 09.06.09.

Creative Cultures and Associates. (2007). Coventry cultural and events strategies consultation draft – June 2007.

Crespi-Vallbona, M., & Richards, G. (2007). The meaning of cultural festivals: stakeholder perspectives. *International Journal of Cultural Policy, 27*, 103–122.

Crompton, J. (2006). Economic impact studies: instruments for political shenanigans? *Journal of Travel Research, 45*, 67–82.

Cruces, F. (1998) Les festes a Madrid (1977–1993) In Forum Barcelona Tradició (Ed.) Festa i Ciutat – volum 1. Collecio L'Agulla no 24, 23–50.

Cubeles, X., & Baro, F. (2006). *Culture and sustainability.* Barcelona: Generalitat de Catalunya.

Cultural Ministers Council. (2002). *The strategic direction in corporate sponsorships: practical implications for the arts.* www.arts.gov.au/__data/assets/pdf_file/0018/21960/The_Strategic_Direction_in_Corporate_Sponsorships_-_Implications_for_the_Arts.pdf. Accessed 27.05.09.

Daily Mail. (2008). Snow wonder: The amazing giant ice sculptures at China's coolest Christmas festival. *Daily Mail.* 24th December. www.dailymail.co.uk/news/article-1101189/Snow-wonder-The-amazing-giant-ice-sculptures-Chinas-coolest-Christmas-festival.html. Accessed 17.04.09.

Dale, P. (2003). Birmingham: where did we go wrong? *Birmingham Post.* 5 June, 2003.

Darmawan, D. B., Boitano, J., & Liang, Y. (2005). *The programmatic interests and financing modalities of festivals in East Asia.* www.efa-aef.eu/newpublic/?p=home&;q=efrp. Accessed 24.10.08.

Davies, P., & Russell, M-T. H. (2001). *Comparative analysis of time-limited cultural development projects, including festivals and other Capital of Culture Projects.* Research Report – Newcastle-Gateshead Initiative. Newcastle: University of Newcastle.

DCMS. (2004). DCMS Sustainable development strategy: *arts.* www.culture.gov.uk/images/publications/SDSARTS.pdf. Accessed 11.04.09.

DCMS. (2006). *Welcome legacy: Tourism strategy for the 2012 Games – A consultation.* London: Department for Culture, Media and Sport.

DCMS. (2008). *Before, during and after: making the most of the London 2012 Games.* London: Department for Culture, Media and Sport.

DEAF. (2008). www.deaf07.nl. Accessed 27.01.08.

Deffner, A. M., & Labrianidis, L. (2005). Planning culture and time in a mega-event: Thessaloniki as the European City of Culture in 1997. *International Planning Studies, 10*(3–4), 241–264.

Deloitte. (March 2006). *Final internal audit Report. Events for London.* London: Deloitte. www.london.gov.uk/assembly/audit_panel_mtgs/2006/apr25/item06e.pdf. Accessed 03.03.09.

Deloitte. (2008). *Business to arts: Private investment in arts and culture survey report.* Dublin: Deloitte & Toche.

Demoskopea. (2005). *Percezione della città.* www.genova-2004.it/default.asp?id=2010&;lingua=ITA. Accessed 11.04.09.

Digaetano, A., & Klemanski, J. S. (1999). *Power and City Governance: Comparative perspectives on urban development.* University Of Minnesota Press.

Dobney, C. (2008). How was your Sydney Festival? www.blogs.smh.com.au/entertainment/archives/the_green_room/017099.html. Accessed 18.05.09.

Dobson, P., & Starkey, K. (2004). *Strategic management: Issues and cases* (2nd ed.). Oxford: Blackwell.

Dodd, D., & van Hemel, A. (1999). *Planning cultural tourism in Europe: A presentation of theories and practice*. Amsterdam: Boekmanstichting.

Dos Santos, M. L. L., & Da Costa, A. F. (1999). *Impactos Culturais da Expo '98*. Lisbon: Observatorio das Actividades Culturais.

Doyle, S. A. (2004). Merchandising and retail. In I. Yeoman, M. Robertson, J. Ali-Knight, S. Drummond, & U. McMahon-Beattie (Eds.), *Festival and events management: An international arts and cultural perspective* (pp. 158–170). Oxford: Butterworth-Heinemann.

Dubai shopping festival. (2008). www.dsfoffer.com. Accessed 17.04.09.

Elkington, J. (1998). *Cannibals with forks: The triple bottom line of 21st century business*. New Society Publishers.

European Commission. (2009). Discussion paper 2: Improving the visibility and communication of the title. In: *Paper tabled at the ECOC strategic meeting*. Brussels. 4 May 2009.

European Parliament. (2006). Decision no 1622/2006/ec of the European Parliament and of the Council of 24 October 2006 establishing a Community action for the European Capital of Culture event for the years 2007 to 2019. *Official Journal of the European Union, L 304*, 1–6, 3 November.

European Travel Commission. (2005). *City tourism and culture: The European experience*. Brussels: European Travel Commission.

Evans, G. (2001). *Cultural planning: An urban renaissance?* London: Routledge.

Evans, G. (2003). Hard-branding the cultural city – From Prado to Prada. *International Journal of Urban and Regional Research, 27*(2), 417–440.

Evans, G. (2007). Creative spaces, tourism and the city. In G. Richards, & J. Wilson (Eds.), *Tourism, creativity and development* (pp. 57–72). London: Routledge.

Eventful.com. (2009). www.eventful.com. Accessed 11.03.09.

EventScotland. (2006). *Annual Review 2005 – 2006*. Edinburgh: EventScotland.

EventScotland. (2007). *International events programme*. Edinburgh: EventScotland.

Fáilte Ireland. (2007). *Supporting festivals and cultural events to enhance the tourism product*. Dublin: Fáilte Ireland.

Federal Foreign Office. (2008). www.auswaertiges-amt.de/diplo/en/Aussenpolitik/Kulturpolitik/Kulturprogramme.html. Accessed 27.01.08.

Festes de Sant Roc. (2009). www.festes.org/articles.php?id=531. Accessed 09.06.09.

Florida, R. L. (2002). *The rise of the creative class, and how it's transforming work, leisure, community and everyday life.* New York: Basic Books.

Frank, S., & Roth, S. (1998). Festivalisierung und Partizipation: Entscheidungs- und Aushandlungsprozesse in der Europäischen Kulturstadt Weimar. In: *Paper presented at the 29th Kongress of the Deutschen Gesellschaft für Soziologie.* Freiburg i.Br.

Frank, S., & Roth, S. (2000). Festivalization and the media: Weimar, Culture City of Europe 1999. *International Journal of Cultural Policy, 6*(2), 219–241.

Franquesa, J. B., & Morell, M. (2007). Transversal indicators and qualitative observatories of heritage tourism. In G. Richards (Ed.), *Cultural tourism: global and local perspectives* (pp. 169–194). Binghampton: Haworth Press.

Fredline, E., & Faulkner, B. (1998). Resident reactions to a major tourist event: the Gold Coast Indy Car Race. *Festival Management and Event Tourism, 5,* 185–205.

Fredline, L., Raybould, M., Jago, L., Deery, M. (2005). Triple bottom line event evaluation: A proposed framework for holistic event evaluation. In J. Allen (Ed.), *Proceedings of International Event Research Conference 'The Impact of Events',* Sydney 2005, 2–15.

Freeman, R. E. (1984). *Strategic management: A stakeholder approach.* Boston: Pitman.

Frey, B. S. (2000). *The rise and fall of festivals: Reflections on the Salzburg Festival.* Institute for Empirical Research in Economics, University of Zurich. Working Paper No. 48.

Fundesarrollo. (2005). *Carnaval Baranquilla 2005: Impacto económico local.* Baranquilla: Fundesarrollo.

Futures Festival. (2009). Futures festival. www.cdtoolbox.net/community_planning/000156.html. Accessed 10.06.09.

Gale, T. (2009). Urban beaches, virtual worlds and 'the end of tourism'. *Mobilities, 4,* 119–138.

Gallasch, K. (2004). Singapore arts festival. *Real Time, 62.* www.realtimearts.net/article/62/7546. Accessed 11.03.09.

García, E. (1999). *La Feria de Abril de Catalunya. MA Thesis in Public Management and Administration.* University of Barcelona.

García, B. (2004). Urban Regeneration, arts programming and major events: Glasgow 1990, Sydney 2000 and Barcelona 2004. *International Journal of Cultural Policy, 10,* 103–118.

Garcia, B. (2005). De-constructing the City of Culture: the long term legacies of Glasgow 1990. *Urban Studies, 42,* 1–28.

Gemeente Amsterdam. (2004). *raadsvoordracht: Instemming met de Notitie Verdelingsvoorstel publiektrekkende evenementen. Gemeenteblad afd, 1, nr. 193, 1.* Amsterdam, 18 maart 2004.

Gemeente 's-Hertogenbosch. (2006). Nota Citymarketing 's-Hertogenbosch. Raadsvoorstel. 06.0381, 15 August 2006.

Getz, D. (1997). *Event management & event tourism* (1st ed.). Cognizant Communication Corp.

Getz, D. (2005). *Event management & event tourism* (2nd ed.). Cognizant Communication Corp.

Getz, D. (2007). *Event studies: Theory, research and policy for planned events*. London: Butterworth-Heinneman.

Gianola, D. (2008). Snow and ice sculpture festival in Bruges. *VRMAG*, 29. www.vrmag.org/issue29/SNOW_AND_ICE_SCULPTURE_FESTIVAL_IN_BRUGES.html. Accessed 14.10.09.

GLA. (2001). *Culture and the cultural programme 2001/2002.* Report Number: 4, Date: 18th April 2001. Report to: Mayor's Advisory Cabinet. London: GLA.

Glastonbury Festival. (2009). *Environmental statement*. www.glastonburyfestivals.co.uk. Accessed 14.04.09.

Goffman, E. (1971). Relations in public: *Microstudies of the public order* New York: Van Nostrand Reinhold.

Goldblatt, J. J. (1990). *Special events: The art and science of celebration*. New York: Van Nostrand Reinhold.

Gold Coast City Council. (2007). Gold Coast City events strategy 2007–2009. *Gold Coast City Council.*

González, G. (2004). *Nuevo festival de música electrónica en Colonia*. www.dw-world.de/dw/article/0, 1294796,00.html. Accessed 13.10.09.

Gospodini, A. (2001). Urban design, urban space morphology, urban tourism: an emerging new paradigm concerning their relationship. *European Planning Studies, 9*, 925–934.

Gottdiener, M. (1997). *The theming of America: Dreams, visions, and commercial spaces*. Boulder, CO: Westview Press.

Gotham, K. F. (2002). Marketing Mardi Gras: commodification, spectacle and the political economy of tourism in New Orleans. *Urban Studies, 39*, 1735–1756.

Graham Devlin Associates. (2001). *Festivals and the city: The Edinburgh Festivals strategy*. Edinburgh: City of Edinburgh.

Grauman, B. (2008). *Arts Festivals brace for cost cuts as recession hits budgets*. www.bloomberg.com/apps/news?pid=20601088&;refer=muse&sid=aMIHKppEkSCU. Accessed 27.05.09.

Greenwald, G. (2007). *What "truly motivates" George W. Bush?* www.salon.com/opinion/greenwald/2007/06/20/bush_motives/. Accessed 15.09.09.

Grundy, K. W. (1994). The politics of South Africa's national arts festival: small engagements in the bigger campaign. *African Affairs, 93*, 387–409.

Gursoy, D., Kim, K., & Uysal, M. (2004). Perceived impacts of festivals and special events by organizers: an extension and validation. *Tourism Management, 25*, 171–181.

Hall, C. M. (1992). *Hallmark tourist events*. London: Bellhaven Press.

Hallet, B. & Lawson, V. Passion aplenty, now for substance. *Sydney Morning Herald*. January 29, 2008. www.smh.com.au. Acessed 18.05.09.

Hankinson, G. (2004). Relational brand networks: towards a conceptual model of place brands. *Journal of Vacation Marketing, 10*(2), 109–120.

Hannigan, J. (1998). Fantasy city: *Pleasure and profit in the postmodern metropolis* London: Routledge.

Hannigan, J. (2003). Symposium on branding, the entertainment economy and urban place building. Introduction. *International Journal of Urban and Regional Research, 27*, 352–360.

Hannigan, J. (2007). From fantasy city to creative city. In G. Richards, & J. Wilson (Eds.), *Tourism, creativity and development* (pp. 48–56). London: Routledge.

Hansen, K., Di Stefano, E., Klaic, D., Bollo, A., & Bachella, U. (2003). *Festivals: challenges of growth, distinction, support base and internationalization*. Tartu: heade motete linn. efaextra.efa-aef.org/efadoc/11/festivalbook%20Tartu.pdf.

Harcup, Tony (2000). 'Re-imaging a post-industrial city: the Leeds St Valentine's Fair as a civic spectacle. *City, 4*, 215–231.

Hargreaves, J. (2000). *Freedom for Catalonia? : Catalan nationalism, Spanish identity and the Barcelona Olympic Games*. Cambridge: Cambridge University Press.

Harris, H. (2005). Post-festival: changing cultural events in urban space. In S. Silvanto (Ed.), *Helsinki – A Festival City. The development, actors and audiences of urban festival culture* (pp. 25). Helsinki: City of Helsinki Cultural Office.

Harvey, D. (1989). *The condition of Postmodernity*. Oxford: Basil Blackwell.

Häussermann, H., & Colomb, C. (2003). The New Berlin: Marketing the city of dreams Cities and Visitors: In L. Hoffman, S. S. Fainstein, & D. R. Judd (Eds.), *Regulating people, markets and city space* (pp. 200–218) Oxford: Blackwell.

Häussermann, H., & Seibel, W. (1993). *Festivaliserung der Stadpolitik – Stadtentwicklung durch grosse Projekte.* Opladen: Westdeutscher Verlag.

Hawkes, J. (2001). *The fourth pillar of sustainability: Culture's essential role in public planning.* Altona, Victoria: Common Ground Publishing.

Hede, A.-M. (2008). Managing special events in the new era of the triple bottom line. *Event Management, 11,* 13–22.

Heikkinen, T. (2000). In from the margins: the City of Culture 2000 and image transformation of Helsinki. *International Journal of Cultural Policy, 6,* 200–218.

Henry, I. (1996). *The politics of leisure policy.* Basingstoke: Macmillan.

Herrero, L. C., Sanz, J. A., Devesa, M., Bedate, M., & del Barrio, M. J. (2007). Economic impact and social performance of cultural macrofestivals. In G. Richards (Ed.), *Cultural tourism: Global and local perspectives* (pp. 303–323). Binghampton: Hawaorth Press.

Hewett, I. (2007). *The Proms and the Promenerders.* www.telegraph.co.uk/arts/main.jhtml?xml=/arts/2007/07/12/nosplit/bmproms112.xml. Accessed 17.01.07.

Hildreth, J. (2008). The Saffron European City Brand Barometer. *Revealing which cities get the brands they deserve.* saffronconsultants.com/wp-content/uploads/Saff_CityBrandBarom.pdf. Accessed 10.03.09.

Hitters, E. (2000). The social and political construction of a Cultural Capital: Rotterdam 2001. *International Journal of Cultural Policy, 6,* 172–187.

Hitters, E. (2007). Porto and Rotterdam as European Capitals of Culture: Toward the festivalization of urban cultural policy. In G. Richards (Ed.), *Cultural tourism: Global and local perspectives* (pp. 281–301). Bonghampton: Haworth Press.

Hoggett, P. (1999). The city and the life force. In L. Nyström (Ed.), *City and Culture: City processes and urban sustainability* (pp. 388–402). Stockholm: Swedish Urban Environment Council.

Holcomb, B. (1993). Revisioning place: De- and re-constructing the image of the industrial city. In G. Kearns, & C. Philo (Eds.), *Selling places: The city as cultural capital, past and present* (pp. 133–144). Oxford: Pergamon.

Holden, J. (2004). *Capturing cultural value: How culture has become a tool of government policy.* London: Demos.

Holland Festival. (2003). *Future of Festival Formulae.* Amsterdam: Holland Festival.

Hollands, R. (2007). *Prague Fringe Festival: Audience survey report*. School of Geography, Politics and Sociology, University of Newcastle. www.praguefringe.com/2008/data/2007_fringe_festival_praha_-_survey_report.pdf. Accessed 07.07.09.

Hollway, S. (2002). Vital volunteers. *Australian Leisure Management, 30*, 58–59.

Hong Kong Government. (2006). www.info.gov.hk/gia/general/199902/01/0201077.htm. Accessed 14.10.09.

Howie, F. (2000). Establishing the common ground: tourism, ordinary places, grey-areas and environmental quality in Edinburgh, Scotland. In G. Richards, & D. Hall (Eds.), *Tourism and sustainable community development* (pp. 101–118). London: Routledge.

Hughes, G. (1999). Urban revitalization: the use of festive time strategies. *Leisure Studies, 18*, 119–135.

Huq, R. (2009). The fall of rise. *The Guardian*. Thursday 9 April 2009. www.guardian.co.uk/commentisfree/2009/apr/09/race-boris. Accessed 12.04.09.

www.ifacca.org. Accessed 13.10.09.

Impacts 08. (2007). *Benchmark indicators report 2000–2006*. Liverpool: Impacts 08.

Indymedia Liverpool. (2006). *Robin Archer conned the mug Council*. www.indymedia.org.uk/en/regions/liverpool/2006/08/346757.html. Accessed 18.08.08.

Inkei, P. (2005). *Assistance to arts and culture festivals*. D'Art Topics in Arts Policy, No. 21. Sydney: International Federation of Arts Councils and Culture Agencies. www.ifacca.org/ifacca2/en/organisation/page09_BrowseDart.asp. Accessed 13.10.09.

International Delphic Committee. (2009). *Delphic Games today*. www.idcworld.org/articles.text?id=39&;lang=en. Accessed 10.06.09.

International Organization for Migration. (2008). *Facts and figures*. www.iom.int/. Accessed 10.10.08.

Irish Arts Council. (2003). www.newsweaver.ie/artscouncil/e_article000186393.cfm?x=[[IMN.LID]],[[IMN.USER_ID]]

Istanbul 2010. (2008). www.istanbul2010.org/?p=15&;lang=eng&haberNo=130. Accessed 30.01.08.

Jago, L., Chalip, L., Brown, G., Mules, T., & Ali, S. (2002). The role of events in helping to brand a destination. In: *Events and place making conference proceedings* (pp. 111–143). Sydney: Australian Centre for Event Management.

Jamieson, K. (2004). Edinburgh: the festival gaze and its boundaries. *Space & Culture, 7*, 64–75.

Judd, D. R. (1999). Constructing the tourist bubble. In D. R. Judd, & S. S. Fainstein (Eds.), *The tourist city* (pp. 35–53). New Haven: Yale University Press.

Jura Consultants. (2006). *Economic impact assessment: The Pillar Events*. Manchester: Manchester City Council.

Jurgenson, J. (2008). Summer of Rock. Wall . online. *Street Journal, April 19th*. www.wsj.com/article/SB120855993910427809. html?mod=hps_us_inside_today. Accessed 15.09.09.

Kaplan, R. S., & Norton, D. P. (1992). The balanced scorecard: measures that drive performance. *Harvard Business Review, Jan–Feb*, 71–80.

Karlis, G. (2003). Volunteerism and multiculturalism: a linkage for future Olympics. *The Sport Journal, 6*(3), 1–16.

Kavaratzis, M. (2008). From city marketing to city branding: An interdisciplinary analysis with reference to Amsterdam, Budapest and Athens. PhD Thesis, University of Groningen. <irs.ub.rug.nl/ppn/314660232>. Accessed 10.03.09.

Kearns, G., & Philo, C. (1993). *Selling places: The city as cultural capital, past and present*. Oxford: Pergamon.

Keller, K. L. (1998). *Strategic brand management: building, measuring, and managing brand equity*. Hemel Hempstead: Prentice-Hall International.

Kemp, R. (2006). Ongoing funding for major festivals. *Press release*. Minister for the Arts and Sport, 8 May 2006. www.minister. dcita.gov.au/kemp/media/media_releases/ongoing_funding_ for_the_major_festivals_initiative. Accessed 22.05.07.

Kemp, S. (2002). The hidden workforce: volunteers' learning in the Olympics. *Journal of European Industrial Training, 26*, 109–117.

Kennedy, M. (2007). Why blockbuster shows are crowd pleasers. *Guardian Unlimited Arts Blog*. blogs.guardian.co.uk/art/ 2007/02/why_blockbuster_shows_are_crow.html. Accessed 01.10.07.

Kerrville Folk Festival. (2007). *Summer Newsletter, 2007*. www. kerrvillefolkfestival.com/tfmf_newsletter. Accessed 27.05.09.

Kirby, A. (2004). Homage to Barcelona. *Cities, 21*(3), 183–186.

Klaic, D., Bacchella, U., Bollo, A., & di Stefano, E. (2004). Festivals: Challenges of growth, distinction, support base and internationalization. Tartu: Cultural Department, City of Tartu.

Koivunen, H. (2005). *Staying Power to Finnish Cultural Exports: The Cultural Exportation Project of the Ministry of Education, the Ministry for Foreign Affairs and the Ministry of Trade and Industry*. Finland: Publications of the Ministry of Education. 2005:9.

Kotler, P. (1994). *Marketing management, analysis, planning and control.* NJ: Prentice-Hall.

Kotler, P., & Andreason, A. (1996). *Strategic marketing for nonprofit organizations.* Englewood Cliffs, NJ: Prentice-Hall.

Kozinn, A. A Calm after the storm at Spoleto? *New York Times.* May 17, 1992. query.nytimes.com/gst/fullpage.html?sec= travel&res=9E0CE1DF133BF934A25756C0A964958260.

Kunstenfestivaldesarts. (2008). www.kfda.be/temp_08/en/home/mission.html. Accessed 22.01.08.

Lai, C.-L. (2004). Art exhibitions travel the world. In M. Sheller, & J. Urry (Eds.), *Tourism mobilities: Places to play, places in play* (pp. 90–102). London: Routledge.

Lambooy, J. (2005). *Reshaping cities: Developing competence base and changing the profiles of attractiveness.* The Hague: Netherlands Institute for City Innovation Studies.

Landry, C. (2000). *The creative city: A toolkit for urban planners.* London: Earthscan.

Landry, C. (2006). *The art of city making.* London: Earthscan.

Landry, C., & Bianchini, F. (1995). *The creative city.* London: Demos.

Landry, C., Bianchini, F., Maguire, M., & Worpole, K. (1993). *The social impact of the arts: A discussion document.* Stroud: Comedia.

Landry, C., & Kelly, O. (1994). *Helsinki – A living work of art.* Helsinki: The City of Helsinki, Information Management Centre.

La, Revista (2001). *"Capital Americana de la Cultura" Escándalo en Colombia: varias ciudades rechazan comprar el premio.* www.larevista.com.mx/ed589/info1.htm. Accessed 21.08.07.

Larson, M. (2004). Managing festival stakeholders. In: *Paper presented at the 13th Nordic symposium in tourism and hospitality research 4th–7th November 2004.* Denmark: Aalborg.

Larson, M., & Wikström, E. (2001). Organising events: managing conflict and consensus in a political market square. *Event Management, 7,* 51–65.

Lash, S., & Urry, J. (1994). *Economies of signs and space.* London: Sage.

LCADT. (2007). www.lcadt.com/lcadt/. Accessed 23.08.07.

Lee, C. K., Lee, Y. K., & Wicks, B. E. (2004). Segmentation of festival motivation by nationality and satisfaction. *Tourism Management, 25,* 61–70.

Lee, N. (2007). *Distinctiveness and cities – Beyond 'Find and Replace' economic development?* London: The Work Foundation.

Lee, T. (2004). Creative shifts and directions: cultural policy in Singapore. *International Journal of Cultural Policy, 10,* 281–299.

Lee, Y. K., Lee, C. K., Lee, S. K., & Babin, B. J. (2008). Festivals capes and patrons' emotions, satisfaction, and loyalty. *Journal of Business Research, 61,* 56–64.

Legislative Council Panel on Financial Affairs. (2009). *Hong Kong Harbour Fest.* LC Paper No. CB(1)2083/03-04(05). www. legco.gov.hk/yr03-04/english/panels/fa/papers/fa0614cb1-2083-5e.pdf. Accessed 18.05.09.

Lift. (2008). *Lift New Parliament.* www.liftfest.org.uk/ newparliament/. Accessed 30.01.08.

London Development Agency. (2008). *London: A cultural audit.* London: London Development Agency.

Loney, G. (2001). *Festival Futures: Salzburg and the Ruhr.* www. nytheatre-wire.com/lt01094t.htm. Accessed 22.01.07.

Long, P. (2004). Morecambe's pretty vacant: Resort revitalisation through punk rock festivals. *Unpublished manuscript, 32.*

Long, P., & Owen, E. (2006). *The arts festival sector in Yorkshire: Economic, social and cultural benefits, benchmarks and development.* Final Report. London: Arts Council England.

Lord Cultural Resources. (2009). *Ontario Cultural and Heritage Tourism Product Research Paper.* Toronto: Queen's Printer for Ontario.

Luxembourg and Greater Region. (2008). Luxembourg and Greater Region, Cultural Capital of Europe 2007. Final report. Luxembourg: Luxembourg 2007

Lyons, C. Hollywood, the Global Village: Festivals feed a love of movies. *New York Times.* December 16, 2004. www.nytimes. com/2004/12/16/movies/16fest.html. Accessed 14.10.09.

Mäenpää, P. (2005). Festivals and the new cultural discourse in urban policy. In S. Silvanto (Ed.), *Helsinki – A Festival City. The development, actors and audiences of urban festival culture* (p. 24). Helsinki: City of Helsinki Cultural Office.

Magliocco, S. (2001). Coordinates of power and reclamation in Sardinia. *Ethnologies, 23,* 167–188.

Manchester 2000 Ltd. (2002). *Manchester Commonwealth Games.* www.gameslegacy.co.uk. Accessed 16.10.05.

Manzoor, S. The year rock found the power to unite. *The Observer.* Sunday 20 April 2008. www.guardian.co.uk/music/ 2008/apr/20/popandrock.race. Accessed 11.04.09.

Margue, C. (2008). Luxembourg and the Greater Region, European Capital of Culture 2007: Event TRI*M a tool to monitor culture events. In Paper presented at the 18th Global TRI*M Conference, Budapest, 7 March.

Masterman, G. (2004). A strategic approach for the use of sponsorship in the events industry. In I. Yeoman, M. Robertson, J. Ali-Knight, S. Drummond, & U. McMahon-Beattie (Eds.), *Festival and events management: An international arts and cultural perspective* (pp. 260–272). Oxford: Butterworth-Heinemann.

Matarasso, F. (1996a). *Defining values: Evaluating arts programmes*. London: Comedia.

Matarasso, F. (1996b). *Northern lights: The social impact of the Fèisean (Gaelic Festivals)*. Stroud: Comedia.

Matarasso, F., & Pilling, A. (1999). *The Belgrade Theatre. A first social audit 1998–1999*. Stroud: Comedia.

Maughan, C., & Bianchini, F. (2003). *Festivals and the creative region*. London: Arts Council England.

Maurice, S. (16th March 2005). Après un an de fête, Lille a la gueule de bois. *Liberation*.

Mayor of London. (2004). *Notting Hill Carnival: Strategic review*. London: Mayor of London.

Mayor of London. (2008). *Culture and place making*. www.london.gov.uk/lcsg/place-making.jsp. Accessed 09.06.09.

McCarthy, E. J. (1960). *Basic marketing: A managerial approach*. Homewood: Irwin.

McCarthy, J. (1998). Reconstruction, regeneration and re-imaging: the case of Rotterdam. *Cities, 15*, 337–344.

McLean, M. (2006). *Developing cultural and creative tourism in the Scottish Highlands. The case of Proiseact Nan Ealan*. The Gaelic Arts Agency.

McMahon-Beattie, U., & Yeoman, I. (2004). The potential for revenue management in festivals and events. In I. Yeoman, M. Robertson, J. Ali-Knight, S. Drummond, & E. McMahon-Beattie (Eds.), *Festival and events management: An international arts and culture perspective* (pp. 202–214). London: Butterworth-Heinneman.

Melbourne. (2008). *Melbourne, the world's event city*. www.vmec.com.au/. Accessed 05.10.09.

Melbourne. (2006). *Triple Bottom Line assessment of the XVIII Commonwealth Games*. Melbourne: Office of Commonwealth Games Coordination.

Melville, R., Selby, M., & Cliff, M. (2007). *Re-telling the city. Exploring narratives of Liverpool*. Liverpool: Impacts08.

Menza, C., & Lapierre, L. (2004). Fanny Mikey and the Ibero-American Theatre Festival of Bogotá. *International Journal of Arts Management*, 6(2), 66–77.

Miller, M. (2007). Stavanger 2008. In: *Presentation to the Annual conference of the University Network of the European Capitals of Culture*. Sibiu. 25 October 2007.

Miller, M. (2009). *Stavanger 2008, European Capital of Culture: Our story*. Stavanger: Stavanger 2008.

Ministry of Cultural and Heritage, New Zealand. (2008). *Sponsorship of Cultural events, organisations, and activities*. Ministry of Culture and Heritage.

Miralles, Eduard. (1998). Les festes de barri i de cuitat a Barcelona. In Forum Barcelona Tradició (ed.) Festa i Ciutat volum 1. Collecio L'Agulla no 24, pp. 54–58.

Mitchell, R. K., Agle, B. R., & Wood, D. J. (1997). Toward a theory of stakeholder identification and salience: defining the principle of who and what really counts. *Academy of Management Review*, 22, 853–886.

Mlaba, O. (2009). *Durban looks beyond the 2010 World Cup*. www.citymayors.com/economics/durban-economics.html. Accessed 09.05.09.

Moore, M. H. (1995). *Creating public value: Strategic management in government*. Cambridge Mass: Harvard University Press.

Moore School of Business. (2005). *Surveys of Spoleto Audiences*2005. mooreschool.sc.edu/export/sites/default/moore/research/presentstudy/Spoleto/spoletoreport.pdf. Accessed 13.03.09.

Morris, J. Tokyo tops list for third year, while London falls behind. *Art Newspaper*. 15 March 2007. www.theartnewspaper.com/article01.asp?id=590 Accessed 24.08.07.

Mulholland, H. (2008). Boris Johnson shakes up funding for capital's cultural events. *guardian.co.uk*. Thursday 6 November 2008. Accessed 16.09.09.

Myerscough, J. (1991). *Monitoring Glasgow*. Glasgow: Glasgow City Council.

Myerscough, J. (1996). *Luxembourg European City of Culture 1995: Report on impact*. Luxembourg: Ministry of Culture.

Nas, P. J. M., & Roymans, A. (1998). Reminiscences of the relief of Leiden: a total ritual event. *International Journal of Urban and Regional Research*, 22, 550–564.

National Arts Council Singapore. (2006). *Singapore Arts Festival 2006 audience survey*. www.nac.gov.sg/static/doc/sta/

Singapore%20Arts%20Festival%202006%20Audience%20 Survey.ppt. Accessed 13.03.09.

National Arts Council Singapore. (2008). Arts statistics 2007. www.nac.gov.sg/new/new02a.asp?id=361&;y=2008. Accessed 18.08.08.

Nijman, J. (1991). Cultural globalization and the identity of place: the reconstruction of Amsterdam. *Ecumene, 6,* 146–164.

Northoff, J., & Lightfoot, J. (2008). *Take Part at the Second Life Art Festival @ newBERLIN!* www.taggingart.org/archives/91. Accessed 17.04.09.

Nurse, K. (2003). Keeping the right balance – Embracing our heritage in The Greater Caribbean. In *Proceedings of the fifth annual Caribbean conference on sustainable tourism development*. St. Kitts and Nevis, September 9th to 12th, 2003.

OECD. (2009a). *The impact of culture on tourism.* Paris: OECD.

OECD. (2009b). *OECD Economic Outlook No. 85, June 2009.* Paris: OECD.

Olins, W. (2008). El poder de la marca. In Paper presented at the conference 'El valor de la marca y la orientación al mercado. Una nueva relación con el cliente'. Seville, 30th September 2008.

Ooi, C.-S. (2007). Creative industries and tourism in Singapore. In G. Richards, & J. Wilson (Eds.), *Tourism, creativity and development* (pp. 240–251). London: Routledge.

Ostrowska, J. (2008). How theatre festivals can support urban development? In: *EFRP workshop presentation to the EFRP workshop on urban impact of artistic festivals* (pp. 11–12) Helsinki, April.

Pablo, J. (1998). Arxiu festiu de Gràcia. In Forum Barcelona Tradició (Ed.) Festa i Ciutat volum 1. Collecio L'Agulla no. 24, 33–38.

Paddison, R. (1993). City marketing, image reconstruction and urban regeneration. *Urban Studies, 30,* 339–350.

Palmer-Rae. (2004). *European Cities and Capitals of Culture.* Brussels: Palmer-Rae Associates.

Paramon, C. C. (1997). Associacionisme étnic al Baix llobregat. *Materials del Baix llobregat 3,* 111–121.

Cork 2005 is a date reference

Pascual, J., Baltà, J., & Delgado, E. (2001). Volunteering and culture in Catalonia. *Karis, 11,* 63–77.

Peck, J., & Ward, K. (2002). *City of revolution: Restructuring Manchester.* Manchester: University of Manchester Press.

Peters, M., & Pikkemaat, B. (2005). The management of city events: the case of 'Bergsilvester' in Innsbruck, Austria. *Event Management, 9,* 147–153.

Pérez-Díaz, V. (2003). De la Guerra Civil a la Sociedad Civil: El capital social en España entre los años trienta y los años noventa del siglo XX. In R. Putnam (Ed.), *El Decline del Capital Social* (pp. 425–489). Barcelona: Galaxia Gutenberg.

Permezel, M., & Duffy, M. (2003). What about we hold another cultural festival? Negotiating cultural difference in local communities. In *State of Australian cities conference*. Parramatta. December.

Pine, J., & Gilmore, J. (1999). *The experience economy.* Boston: Harvard Business School Press.

Polèse, M., & Stren, R. E. (2000). *The social sustainability of cities.* Toronto: University of Toronto Press.

Prashad S. Festivals give Ontario a financial boost. Toronto Jazz Festival, for instance, is alive and well for 20 years. July 2nd, 2006. www.torontoalliance.ca. Accessed 17.10.08.

Prentice, R., & Andersen, V. (2003). Festival as creative destination. *Annals of Tourism Research, 30,* 7–30.

Project for Public Spaces. (2007). What makes a successful place?. www.pps.org/topics/gps/gr_place_feat. Accessed 17.01.07.

Puczkó, L., & Rátz, T. (2001). The Budapest Spring Festival – A festival for Hungarians? In G. Richards (Ed.), *Cultural attractions and European tourism* (pp. 199–214). Wallingford: CAB International.

Puig, T. (2005). We are a public image valued by the people. In Ajuntament de Barcelona. (Ed.), *Barcelona communicates* (pp. 13–41). Barcelona: ACTAR/Ajuntament de Barcelona.

Putnam, R. (2000). *Bowling alone: The collapse and revival of American community.* New York: Simon and Schuster.

Quartier des Spectacles. (2007). *Vision.* www.quartierdesspectacles.com/en/partenariat/vision/. Accessed 17.01.07.

Quinn, B. (2005). Arts festivals and the city. *Urban Studies, 42,* 927–943.

Radio Orla. (2008). *Johnson threatens cuts in funding from London's community festivals?* www.orla.fm/news/3-news/3247-lo-johnson-threatens-cuts-in-funding-from-londons-community-festivals. Accessed 13.10.09.

Radu, C. (2007). Managing Sibiu, European Capital of Culture 2007. In Presentation to the annual conference of the University Network of the European Capitals of Culture, Sibiu, 25 October 2007.

Ranshuysen, L., & Jansen, M. (2004). *De zomerfestivals van het Vierde Kwartaal: De huidige praktijk en marketingmogelijkheden*. www.lettyranshuysen.nl. Accessed 29.01.08.

Reeves, M. (2002). *Measuring the economic and social impact of the arts: A review*. London: The Arts Council.

Regional Arts New South Wales. (2009). www.regionalartsnsw. com.au/projects/aud-dev.html. Accessed 08.07.09.

Reid, S., & Arcodia, C. (2002). Understanding the role of the stakeholder in event management. In: *Events and place making conference proceedings* (pp. 479–515). Sydney: Australian Centre for Event Management.

Rembrandt 400. (2006). www.holland.com/rembrandt400/press/gb/.

Rennen, W. (2007). Place selling in a media age. PhD thesis. University of Amsterdam.

Reno-Tahoe Territory. (2006). www.travelnevada.com/story. asp?sid=43. Accessed 10.10.08.

Resort Municipality of Whistler. (2007). *Moving towards a sustainable future*. www.whistler2020.ca/whistler/site/priority. acds?instanceid=1930532&; context=1930531. Accessed 15.08.09.

Riant Theatre. (2009). *Strawberry one-act festival*. www. therianttheatre.com/strawberry.html. Accessed 05.10.09.

Richards, G. (Ed.). (1996). *Cultural tourism in Europe*. Wallingford: CAB International.

Richards, G. (Ed.). (2001). *Cultural attractions and European tourism*. Wallingford: CAB International.

Richards, G. (2004). Cultura popular, tradición y turismo en las Festes de la Mercè de Barcelona. In Joseph Font (Ed.), *Casos de turismo cultural: de la planificación estratégica a la evaluación de productos* (pp. 287–306). Barcelona: Ariel.

Richards, G. (2007a). Cultural tourism: *Global and local perspectives* Binghamton: Haworth Press.

Richards, G. (2007b). The authenticity of a traditional event – the views of residents and visitors. *Event Management, 11*, 33–44.

Richards, G. (2007c). The festivalization of society or the socialization of festivals? The case of Catalunya. In G. Richards (Ed.), *Cultural tourism: Global and local perspectives* (pp. 257–280). Binghampton: Haworth Press.

Richards, G., & Delgado, E. (2002). *Creative tourism and trusting spaces*. Barcelona: Interarts.

Richards, G., Geodhart, S., & Herrijgers, C. (2001). The cultural attraction distribution system. In G. Richards (Ed.), *Cultural Attractions and European Tourism* (pp. 71–89). Wallingford: CAB International.

Richards, G., Hitters, E., & Fernandes, C. (2002). Rotterdam and Porto: *Cultural Capitals 2001: Visitor research* Arnhem: ATLAS.

Richards, G., & Palmer, R. (2009). *European Cultural Capital Report no. 2*. Arnhem: ATLAS.

Richards, G., & Rotariu, I. (2007). *Sibiu European Capital of Culture 2007: Evaluation report*. Arnhem: ATLAS.

Richards, G., & Wilson, J. (2004). The Impact of cultural events on city image: Rotterdam Cultural Capital of Europe 2001. *Urban Studies, 41*(10), 1931–1951.

Richards, G., & Wilson, J. (2006). Developing creativity in tourist experiences: a solution to the serial reproduction of culture? *Tourism Management, 27*, 1209–1223.

Richards, G., & Wilson, J. (2007). *Tourism, creativity and development*. London: Routledge.

Riley, M. (2005). *North Sea Jazz 2005-Riley's review*. www.jazz.gr/modules.php?name=News&;file=article&sid=77.

Ritzer, G. (1999). *Enchanting a disenchanted world: Revolutionizing the means of consumption*. Pine Forge Press.

Robertson, M., & Guerrier, Y. (1998). Events as entrepreneurial displays: Seville, Barcelona and Madrid. In D. Tyler, Y. Guerrier, & M. Robertson (Eds.), *Managing tourism in cities* (pp. 215–228). Chichester: John Wiley and Sons.

ROMART. (2008). www.romartfest.com/. Accessed 11.03.09.

Rossie, J. *Collective marketing. Verslag studiereis naar Rotterdam*. 8 januari 2003. Brussels: CultuurNet Vlaanderen.

Rotorua Chamber of Commerce. (2007). *Submission to independent enquiry in to local government rates*. Rotorua: Rotorua Chamber of Commerce.

Royce, J. (2002). *Branding: from cattle ritual to company mandate*. www.cac.ca.gov/files/ami-brandfusion.pdf. Accessed 13.12.06.

Ruiz, J. (2004). *A literature review of the evidence base for culture, the arts and sport policy*. Edinburgh: Research and Economic Unit, Scottish Executive Education Department.

Saayman, M., & Saayman, A. (2006). Does the location of arts festivals matter for the economic impact? *Papers in Regional Studies, 85*, 569–584.

Sabaté I Bel, J., Frenchman, D., & Schuster, J. M. (2004). *Llocs amb esdeveniments-. Event places*. Barcelona: UPC.

Salzburg Festival. (2007). *History of the festival*. www.salzburgfestival.at/geschichte.php?lang=en&archivid=6. Accessed 22.01.07.

Salzburg Festival. (2008). *Global sponsors*. www.salzburgerfestspiele. at/dasprogramm/development3/hauptsponsoren1/. Accessed 16.09.09.

Sautter, E. T., & Leisen, B. (1999). Managing stakeholders: A tourism planning model. *Annals of Tourism Research, 26*(2), 312–328.

Savitch, H. V., & Vogel, R. K. (2000). Paths to new regionalism. *State and Local Government Review, 32*, 158–168.

Sbetti, F., & Bertoldo, M. (2009). *La produzione culturale a Venezia gli eventi, i produttori, i fruitori. Quinto Rapporto sulla produzione culturale a Venezia*. Venice: Fondazione di Venecia.

Scherer, R. (2006). *Die wirtschaftlichen Effekte von Lucerne Festival*. Schlussbericht, St. Gallen: Universität St.Gallen, Institut für öffentliche Dienstleistungen und Tourismus.

Schmeer, K. & Bethesda, M. D. *Guidelines for conducting a stakeholder analysis*. November 1999. Partnerships for Health Reform, Abt Associates Inc.

Schulze, G. (1992). *Die Erlebnisgesellschaft. Kultursoziologie der Gegenwart*. Frankfurt: Campus.

Schuster, J. M. (1995). Two urban festivals: La Mercè and First Night. *Planning Practice and Research, 10*(2), 173–187.

Scott, A. J. (2000). *The cultural economy of cities*. London: Sage.

Scott-Norman, F. Adelaide Fringe no longer oddball grunge. *The Australian*. February 15, 2008. www.news.com.au/travel/ story/0, 23483, 23218873–5012673,00.html?from=public_ rss. Accessed 15.04.09.

Scottish Arts Council. (2007). *Quality framework – Guidelines for arts organisations*. Edinburgh: SAC.

Scottish Government. (2002). Scotland's Major Events Strategy 2003–2015. *"Competing on an international stage"*. www. scotland.gov.uk/Resource/Doc/47007/0017729.pdf. Accessed 10.02.09.

Sennett, R. (1994). Flesh and Stone: *The body and the city in western civilization* London: Faber & Faber.

Sennett, R. (1999). The challenge of urban diversity. In L. Nyström (Ed.), *City and culture: Cultural processes and urban sustainability* (pp. 128–134). Stockholm: Swedish Urban Environment Council.

Seoul. (2006). *About Seoul.* www.eseoulhotels.com/. Accessed 05.10.09.

's-Gravesande, A., & Sanders, M. (2008). *Jheronimus Bosch 500. 's Hertogenbosch: Gemeente Den Bosch.*

Short, J. (1999). Urban imaginers: Boosterism and the representation of cities. In A. Jonas, & D. Wilson (Eds.), *The urban growth machine* (pp. 37–54). Albany: SUNY Press.

Silvanto, S., & Hellman, T. (2005). Helsinki – The festival city. In L. Lankinen (Ed.), *Arts and culture in Helsinki* (pp. 4–9). Helsinki: City of Helsinki.

Silvers, J.R. (2004) Global knowledge domain structure for event management. Paper presented at the 2004 Las Vegas International Hospitality and Convention Summit. www.embok. org/filemgmt_data/files/Silvers_Global_Domain_Structure.pdf Accessed 20.05.07.

Skot-Hansen, D. (1998). Holstebro i verden – verden i Holstebro. *Kulturpolitikk og – debat fra tresserne til i dag.* Århus: Klim.

Slaughter, L. (2002). Motivations of long term volunteers at events. In: *Events and place making conference proceedings* (pp. 232–252). Sydney: Australian Centre for Event Management.

Soja, E. W. (2000). Postmetropolis: *Critical studies of cities and regions* London: Wiley-Blackwell.

South Australia (2009) www.pleasetakemeto.com/australia/south-australia/state/event. Accessed March 10.03.09.

Sosnierz, A.-M. (2007). *Le mécénat culturel en Nord – Pas de Calais: pratique actuelle et perspectives.* Lille: Entreprendre en Culture.

Spacing Toronto. (2007). Comment by Pierre-E. *Paradis.* July 25, 2007 12:24 am spacing.ca/wire/?p=2122.

SQW. (2006a). *Culture10 evaluation final report.* Leeds: SQW Consultants.

SQW. (2006b). *Monitoring and evaluation framework for culture10.* Leeds: SQW Consultants.

SQW/TNS. (2005). *Edinburgh's year round festivals 2004–2005: Economic impact study.* Edinburgh: SQW Consultants.

Steunpunt Toerisme en Recreatie. (2003). *Studie van de gentse feesten: effectenmeting als beleidsinstrument.* Leuven: Steunpunt Toerisme en Recreatie.

Stokes, R. (2006). Network-based strategy making for events tourism. *European Journal of Marketing, 40,* 682–695.

Stokes, R. (2008). Tourism strategy making: insights to the events tourism domain. *Tourism Management, 29,* 252–262.

Stuck on Scotland. (2009). *How Edinburgh became the festival capital of the world.* www.stuckonscotland.co.uk/edinburgh/festivals.html. Accessed 10.03.09.

Subirós, Pep (undated). *Cultural strategies and urban renewal.* Aula Barcelona. www.aulabcn.com/catala/document_3.htm. Accessed 23.03.07.

The Edge Network. (2004). *Chester Festivals: A study for Chester City Council.* Chester: Chester City Council.

Therborn, G. (2002). Monumental Europe: the National Years. On the Iconography of European Capital Cities. Housing. *Theory and Society, 19,* 26–47.

Think London. (2006). *London: centre for leisure, entertainment and hospitality.* www.thinklondon.com/knowledge/Leisure.pdf. Accessed 14.12.06.

Throsby, D. (2005). *On the sustainability of cultural capital.* Research Paper no. 510. Macquarie University, Department of Economics.

Tikkanen, I. (2004). Music festival tourism in Finland. In: *13th Nordic symposium in tourism and hospitality research November 4–7, 2004.* Denmark: Aalborg University.

Tourism Research and Marketing. (2006). *Targeting the cultural consumer: A Pan-Northern pilot product development.* Report to the Northern Way Attractions and Events Steering Committee. London: Tourism Research and Marketing.

Trienekens, S. (2004). *Respect! Urban culture, community arts en sociale cohesie.* Rotterdam: SKVR.

Tschumi, B. (1994). *Event-Cities.* Cambridge, MA: MIT Press.

Tschumi, B. (2001). *Event-Cities 2.* Cambridge, MA: MIT Press.

Turan, K. (2002). Sundance to Sarajevo: *Film festivals and the world they made* Berkeley: University of California Press. www.ucpress.edu/books/pages/9624.php. Accessed 10.06.09.

Twestival (2009) twestival.com. (Accessed 23.09.09.).

Umeå. (2009). Curiosity and Passion – the Art of Co-Creation. *Bid for the 2014 ECOC, 2014.*

United Nations. (1997). Environment Glossary. http://unstats.un.org/unsd/environmentgl/gesform.asp?getitem=983

UNESCO. (2007). *Cultural spaces.* www.unesco.org/culture/heritage/intangible/index.shtml#Cultural spaces. Accessed 24.08.07.

UNWTO. (1995). UNWTO technical manual: collection of tourism expenditure statistics. *World Tourism Organization, 1995*, 14. pub.unwto.org/WebRoot/Store/Shops/Infoshop/Products/1034/1034-1.pdf. Accessed 26.03.09.

Urry, J. (2001). *'Globalising the Tourist Gaze'*. Department of Sociology, Lancaster University. Lancaster LA1 4YN, UK. www.comp.lancs.ac.uk/sociology/papers/Urry-Globalising-the-Tourist-Gaze.pdf. Accessed 13.10.09.

Van der Wagen, L. (2007). *Human Resource Management for Events: Managing the Event Workforce*. London: Butterworth-Heinemann.

van Eeden, P., & Elshout, P. D. (2002). *Festivals in Amsterdam: een sterkte/zwakte analyse van twaalf toonaangevende festivals*. Hilversum: Bureau Elshout & van Eeden.

van Elderen, P. L. (1997). *Suddenly One Summer: A sociological portrait of the Joensuu Festival*. Joensuu: Joensuu University Press.

van Isterdael, N. (2004). La Fiesta de la Mercè – Towards a global festival? MA Thesis. Tilburg University.

Verhoeff, R. (1994). High culture: the performing arts and its audience in the Netherlands. *Tijdschrift voor Economische en Sociale Geografie, 85*, 79–83.

Verwijnen, J. (2005). Here and nowhere. The making of the urban space. In A. Remesar (Ed.), *Art for Social Facilitation Waterfronts of Art I* (pp. 14–22). University of Barcelona.

Victorian Auditor-General. (2007). *State investment in major events*. Melbourne: Victorian Government Printer.

Visit Brighton. (2009). www.visitbrighton.com/partners/marketing-and-sales/marketing-plan. Accessed 10.03.09.

Vulkovsky, Y. (2007). Understanding the GOATMILK Festival impact on the village of Gorna Bela rechka.

Waitt. (1999). Playing games with Sydney: marketing Sydney for the 2000 Olympics. *Urban Studies, 36*, 1055–1077.

Wanhill, S. (2007). A night at the opera festival: The economics of opera. In A. Matias, P. Nijkamp, & P. Neto (Eds.), *Advances in modern tourism research: Economic perspectives* (p. 345–365). Heidelberg: Physica-Verlag.

Waterman, S. (1998). Carnivals for élites? The cultural politics of arts festivals. *Progress in Human Geography, 22*(1), 54–74.

WES. (2003). Impactonderzoek Brugge 2002, Culturele Hoofdstad van Europa. Brugge: WES.

Willems-Braun, B. (1994). Situating cultural politics: fringe festivals and the production of spaces of intersubjectivity.

Environment and Planning D: Society and Space, 12(1), 75–104.

Wilson, J. (2004). *Ciutat Project*. www.tourism-research.org/ciutat/ciutatindex.html. Accessed 18.01.08.

Wood, P., Landry, C., & Bloomfield, J. (2006). *Cultural diversity in Britain: A toolkit for cross-cultural co-operation*. York: Joseph Rowntree Foundation.

World Commission on Culture and Development. (1995). *Our creative diversity*. Paris: UNESCO.

World Commission on Environment and Development. (1987). *Our common future*. www.un-documents.net/ocf-02.htm#I. Accessed 11.04.09.

Yardimci, S. (2001). Interlocking flows: Globalisation, urbanism and culture in contemporary Istanbul. In Paper presented at the critical management conference, Manchester.

Yeoman, I., Robertson, M., Ali-Knight, J., Drummond, S., & McMahon-Beattie, E. (2004). Festival and events management: *An international arts and culture perspective*. London: Butterworth-Heinemann.

Yeoman, I., & McMahon-Beattie, U. (2004). Developing a scenario planning process using a blank piece of paper. *Tourism and Hospitality Research, 5*, 273–285.

Yorkshire Forward. (2008). *Yorkshire and the Humber major events strategy*. Leeds: Yorkshire Forward.

Yorkshire County Council. *A major events strategy for Yorkshire: Executive summary*. Yorkshire Country Council. August 2005

Zinkhan, G. M., & Pereira, A. (1994). An overview of marketing strategy and planning. *International Journal of Research in Marketing, 11*, 185–218.

Zukin, S. (1995). *The cultures of cities*. London: Blackwell.

Zukin, S. (2004). Dialogue on urban cultures: Globalization and culture in an urbanizing world. World Urban Forum, Barcelona, 13–17 September 2004. www.unhabitat.org/downloads/docs/3070_67594_K0471966%20WUF2-2.pdf. Accessed 09.06.09.

Index